UNIX for OpenVMS™ Users

Users

Third Edition

UNIX for OpenVMS™ Users
Users
Third Edition

Philip Bourne

Richard Holstein

Joseph McMullen

Digital Press
An imprint of Elsevier Science
Amsterdam • Boston • London • New York • Oxford • Paris • San Diego
San Francisco • Singapore • Sydney • Tokyo

Digital Press is an imprint of Elsevier Science.

∞ Recognizing the importance of preserving what has been written, Elsevier Science prints its books on acid-free paper whenever possible.

Library of Congress Cataloging-in-Publication Data
Bourne, Philip E.
   UNIX for Open VMS users / Philip Bourne, Richard Holstein, Joseph McMullen–3rd ed.
      p. cm.
   ISBN: 1-55558-276-1
   1. UNIX (Computer file) 2. Operating systems (Computers) 3. OpenVMS.
I. Holstein, Richard, 1950–   II. McMullen, Joseph, 1954–   III. Title.

QA76.76.O63B655 2003
005.4'229–dc21

                                                      2003043551

British Library Cataloguing-in-Publication Data
A catalogue record for this book is available from the British Library.

The publisher offers special discounts on bulk orders of this book. For information, please contact:

Manager of Special Sales
Elsevier Science
200 Wheeler Road
Burlington, MA 01803
Tel: 781-313-4700
Fax: 781-313-4882

For information on all Digital Press publications available, contact our World Wide Web home page at: http://www.digitalpress.com or http://www.bh.com/digitalpress

10 9 8 7 6 5 4 3 2 1

Printed in the United States of America

To my family: Mom, Dad, Dan, Cindy, Colleen, Tim, Randy, Annette, Leslie, Greg and Tom, and of course Barbara, Sarah and Julia.

—JM

Contents

Preface   **xiii**

    Conventions   xvii
    Preface to the Third Edition   xviii
    Acknowledgments for the Third Edition   xix
    Chapter Plates   xix

1. Introduction   **1**

    1.1   Evolution   4
    1.2   The Future   11

2. Fundamentals   **13**

    2.1   System Internals   16
    2.2   Command Structure and File Naming   27
    2.3   Device, Directory, and File Structures   32
    2.4   Special Characters   43
    2.5   Using Wildcards   46
    2.6   The Graphical User Interface   47
    2.7   Summary   48

3. Getting Started   **51**

    3.1   Terminal Characteristics   54
    3.2   User Environment   61
    3.3   Logging Out   75
    3.4   Control Key Functions   76
    3.5   Editing and Recall of Command Lines   77
    3.6   Online Help   82
    3.7   Printed Documentation   86
    3.8   Summary   86

4. Introductory File Management   **89**

     4   Introductory File Management   91
     4.1   Displaying Directory Contents: ls   100
     4.2   File Characteristics   102
     4.3   Determining the Current Directory: pwd   106
     4.4   Changing Directories: cd   107
     4.5   Creating a Directory: mkdir   108
     4.6   Deleting a Directory: rmdir and rm -r   108
     4.7   Finding a File: find   109
     4.8   Displaying a File: cat and more   110
     4.9   Paging Through a File: less   111
     4.10 Copying a File: cp   112
     4.11 Renaming a File: mv   113
     4.12 Deleting a File: rm   114
     4.13 Summary   115

5. Editing   **117**

     5.1   Line-Mode Editing: ex   122
     5.2   UNIX Screen Editor: vi   129
     5.3   UNIX Screen Editor: Emacs   136
     5.4   The Stream Editor: sed   148
     5.5   Pattern Matching and Processing: awk   151
     5.6   Summary   165

6. Communicating with Other Users   **167**

     6.1   Batch Communications: mail   170
     6.2   Comparison of OpenVMS and UNIX Mail Commands   182
     6.3   Interactive Communications: talk and write   183
     6.4   Summary   185

**7. Devices, Queues, and
Background Processing**   **189**

     7.1   Using Print Queues   192
     7.2   Submitting Print Jobs: lpr   194
     7.3   Using Tape Drives   198
     7.4   Background Processing   209
     7.5   Batch Processing   214
     7.6   Summary   215

8. File Management Revisited   219

  8.1 Advanced Directory Display Commands   222
  8.2 Advanced File Display Commands   223
  8.3 Advanced Directory Management Commands   228
  8.4 Advanced File-Management Commands   231
  8.5 Summary   249

9. Programming   251

  9.1 Compiling and Linking   257
  9.2 Simplifying Compilation: `make`   260
  9.3 Debugging Programs: `error` and `dbx`   266
  9.4 Profiling: `prof` and `gprof`   271
  9.5 Maintaining Libraries: `ar` and `ranlib`   275
  9.6 Summary   278

10. Shell Programming   283

  10.1 Executing Scripts   288
  10.2 Variables   290
  10.3 Filename Modifiers (C Shell Only)   301
  10.4 Variable Expansion   304
  10.5 Comparison Operators   306
  10.6 File Operators   310
  10.7 Mathematical Operators   315
  10.8 Flow Control   320
  10.9 Built-in Shell Commands   346
  10.10 Debugging Shell Scripts   358
  10.11 Summary   360

11. Administration   373

  11.1 Installing Software   376
  11.2 Startup Procedures   377
  11.3 System Initialization Files   379
  11.4 Managing User Accounts and Groups   385
  11.5 Backing up and Restoring Files   389
  11.6 Security   393
  11.7 Network Configuration   398
  11.8 Monitoring the Network   409
  11.9 Summary   409

12. Monitoring and Utilizing System Resources   411

    12.1   Monitoring Users and Their Processes   414
    12.2   Monitoring the System   424
    12.3   Modifying Processes   430
    12.4   Summary   434

13. Networking   437

    13.1   Communication Overview   442
    13.2   Network Communications   444
    13.3   Modem Communications   464
    13.4   Usenet: Electronic Bulletin Board   472
    13.5   Communications Between OpenVMS and UNIX   473
    13.6   Summary   473

A. Command Summaries   477

B. Editor Summaries   499

C. Important UNIX Files   509

D. A Procedure for Converting OpenVMS Mail Files to UNIX Mail Files   515

    D.1   Overview   515
    D.2   Conversion Process   516

E. Where To Look for Further Information   527

Glossary   529

Index   543

Preface

*When choosing between two evils, I always like to try the one
I've never tried before.*

—Mae West

An operating system is like an old friend. You may be in daily contact with him or only see him occasionally. Over the years a firm bond of friendship develops. You come to realize that he is not perfect, and still you feel comfortable with his idiosyncrasies. In short, you accept him for who he is.

OpenVMS, the traditional operating system used by many Digital Equipment Corporation (DEC) VAX and Alpha processors, is an old friend to many of us. However, you will likely need to learn a version of the UNIX operating system, for UNIX is the operating system of choice for most processors that use innovative hardware architectures. You may be attracted by the stability that UNIX provides as a development medium in a rapidly changing hardware market. After all, UNIX is the closest we have come to a generic operating system, suited to controlling a variety of hardwares from many vendors. Whatever your reasons for learning UNIX, if you are already familiar with OpenVMS, this may well be the book for you.

The book is intended to help you mold the interactive computing skills that you learned using OpenVMS into the skills necessary for computing in the UNIX framework. It is not meant to be a UNIX user's manual, nor is it designed to teach UNIX from first principles. The book draws upon the experience of observing professionals with varying degrees of Open-VMS expertise grapple with the concrete and philosophical issues of UNIX. This book emphasizes UNIX derived from Berkeley UNIX, or Berkeley Software Distribution (BSD), although many of the features discussed are pertinent to any version of UNIX. Both the C shell and the Korn shell, two of the most widely used command-line interfaces to

UNIX, are discussed. Thus, this text should also be useful to those migrating from OpenVMS to AIX, AT&T System V, Tru64 UNIX, HP-UX, Solaris, or any other version of UNIX.

Chapter 1 begins with a brief history of UNIX and OpenVMS. The ideas underlying the conception of each operating system differ markedly. To a casual user, these differences result in a UNIX user interface that appears to be quite different from the Digital Command Language (DCL) interpreter under OpenVMS. Chapter 1 does not discuss any of these differences in detail; the remainder of the book does that. Rather, Chapter 1 explains how these differences came about and gives some of the reasons for them. At first glance, such a discussion may appear superfluous to the central task of learning a subset of useful UNIX commands. However, an understanding of how UNIX and OpenVMS have evolved lets one begin to see the more subtle differences between the two operating systems, differences exemplified throughout this book. For example, OpenVMS is designed as a series of powerful, self-contained commands that the user issues sequentially. UNIX, on the other hand, is designed to be modular, so that users piece together two or more simple modules to form a single complex command string. Thus, effective use of UNIX requires more than learning a new command syntax; it requires a new mode of thinking. The best way to introduce this new mode of thought is to try to capture what the original UNIX developers were thinking when they laid the foundations of UNIX. Chapter 1 ends with a brief consideration of the future directions of UNIX and OpenVMS, based on emerging standards.

Before your hands touch the keyboard, you must grasp a number of ideas that will help prevent later frustration. These ideas are the subject of Chapter 2. First and foremost are the particulars of how the UNIX shell actually interprets a command, in contrast to the OpenVMS command-language interpreter. This discussion introduces the concepts of pipes, filters, and input/output redirection, features that give great power to UNIX and that you need to build the complex command strings mentioned above. Second are the UNIX concepts of the disk partition and file system, in contrast to the OpenVMS physical device and directory. These UNIX concepts are particularly important for anyone interested in UNIX system management. UNIX and OpenVMS operating system internals (data structures, input/output subsystems, and system services) are compared in only a cursory fashion.

With the formalities out of the way, you are ready to move to the terminal and begin getting acquainted with your new friend. Chapter 3 introduces the basic commands and files governing every terminal session and indicates how they differ from those of OpenVMS. You will learn how to tailor the environment to get the most from each UNIX terminal session. Chapter 3 concludes with two topics that OpenVMS users making the transition to UNIX find the most irksome: the recall and cumbersome editing of command lines and the use of online help and the UNIX document set.

At this point, you should be yearning for some serious interactive computing. Chapter 4 introduces a subset of file-management commands that you are likely to need in the first few terminal sessions. So as not to bewilder the beginner, we leave the more complex file-management commands for Chapter 8. In Chapter 4, you should begin to comprehend the power of the UNIX environment.

Chapter 5 follows with a comparison of the most commonly used UNIX and OpenVMS line and screen editors in preparation for some meaningful application development. Chapter 5 also introduces two utilities available to OpenVMS users as part of the POSIX environment that offer powerful features for pattern matching and subsequent file modification.

At this stage, you should be ready to communicate with fellow users and systems staff. Chapter 6 covers the basic features of interactive communications and batch communications via e-mail. For the reader who must communicate with users on remote computers, Chapter 13 revisits e-mail as part of a discussion of processor-to-processor communications.

Chapter 7 introduces the UNIX equivalents of queuing batch and print requests and making tape-drive requests. There are no surprises for the OpenVMS user when it comes to printing files in UNIX, but the same cannot be said of magnetic tape and batch processing. The use of magnetic tapes in UNIX is in some ways arcane, but the real surprise is UNIX's inability to handle batch processing. Chapter 7 explains that this is not a shortcoming, but a difference in philosophy. UNIX has no need for batch queues, since you can easily manage multiple tasks interactively.

By the time you get to Chapter 8, you will need more complex file-management commands. Chapter 8 builds upon the introductory discussion of file management in Chapter 4 by introducing new commands and options.

Chapter 9 discusses programming using a high-level language in the UNIX environment and provides insight into the programming tools for which UNIX is renowned, some of which are available as layered products under OpenVMS. Chapter 9 discusses tools for debugging, profiling, and maintaining large programs with examples from the C and FORTRAN languages.

In UNIX, programming is not restricted to a high-level language inasmuch as you can write programs using the user interface, or shell. Chapter 10 discusses features of shell programming and how it compares to writing OpenVMS command procedures.

Managing user and group accounts, installing software, managing networks, and other tasks are the responsibility of the system administrator. Chapter 11 discusses these and other tasks.

Effective use of any computer system requires an examination of how system resources are being consumed. Chapter 12 describes how to perform such an examination of the UNIX environment.

Finally, Chapter 13 discusses the use of UNIX in a distributed environment of UNIX or UNIX and OpenVMS processors. It considers connections both by fast dedicated networks and by slower asynchronous modems. The chapter groups network communications on the basis of trusted-host access—the UNIX equivalent to a proxy login. Chapter 13 includes a brief discussion of the Network File System (NFS).

Appendixes A and B summarize all we have learned by means of cross-reference tables that compare OpenVMS and UNIX commands and editor functions. The tables also provide the section number where you may find a detailed discussion of each command. Appendix C summarizes the various UNIX files introduced throughout the text. Appendix D is anomalous to the rest of the book, being a procedure to convert existing OpenVMS mail files to a common format used by UNIX mail handlers. Appendix E provides references to Web sites for further information.

While this book will give you basic competency in many areas of UNIX, we have included a bibliography for those who need a different perspective or a deeper understanding. Many will find the Web-based references invaluable as they sit by the keyboard wondering what to do next.

The text emphasizes the practical aspects of UNIX throughout. It is loaded with everyday examples of performing tasks, each of which is compared to its closest OpenVMS counterpart. Where no counterpart exists, that fact is noted. If you have some familiarity with the OpenVMS example presented and compare it to the UNIX example and read the explanation, you should become a competent UNIX user in a short time.

Both operating systems are so rich in their versatility and functionality that producing a concise text meant making some harsh decisions about what should be included and what should be left out. Undoubtedly, some readers will feel that certain topics have been covered in excessive detail and that others have received inadequate treatment. Nevertheless, every effort has been made to draw attention to and describe the similarities and differences between UNIX and OpenVMS that are most important to application users and developers. Any learning process is facilitated by drawing upon previous experience, and learning UNIX should be no exception.

Conventions

Throughout this book the following conventions are used:

Convention	Meaning
Form	The general form of a command.
Example	Particular example of a command defined by form.
$	A command to the OpenVMS command-language interpreter. Commands are shown in uppercase.
$	A command to the UNIX Korn shell program. Although the default prompt is the same as that for OpenVMS, we have labeled examples with the operating system for you to easily distinguish the two. Commands are shown in lowercase, unless the shell program specifically requires uppercase.
%	A command to the UNIX C shell program. Commands are shown in lowercase, unless the shell program specifically requires uppercase.
Italics	Emphasizes important terminology or features.
Code	A UNIX or OpenVMS command or file.
#	What follows to the end of the line is a comment (UNIX only).
!	What follows to the end of the line is a comment (OpenVMS only).
[argument]	Optional argument.
<CR>	A carriage return in OpenVMS and UNIX. Assumed for all commands and shown in this book only when a special meaning is implied.
<CTRL>	The control key on the terminal.
<ESC>	The escape key (F11 on many terminals).
OpenVMS	The term OpenVMS is used to refer to the OpenVMS operating system, both on VAX and Alpha processors, unless otherwise noted.

Unlike OpenVMS, UNIX interprets uppercase and lowercase characters differently.

OpenVMS   **UNIX**

```
ShOw UsErS                          % WHO

OpenVMS Interactive Users           WHO:Command not found
22-Feb-1997 11:25:34.53             % who
Total number of interactive
users = 1 UsernameProcess Name      system tty01 Feb 22 10:39
PID      Terminal SYSTEM
SYSTEM    0000001AE  TXA0:
```

The who command, found as /bin/who, provides information on each interactive user, including the login name, the terminal in use, and the time he or she logged in to the system.

Preface to the Third Edition

When we developed the second edition of this book, we both worked for Digital Equipment Corporation (DEC), the company that brought Open-VMS to the computing world. Four years later, DEC is long gone, having been bought by Compaq Computer Corporation (Compaq), which in turn was acquired by Hewlett-Packard.

Regardless of the company brand on the product, OpenVMS continues to live on with thousands of users throughout the world. Many of those OpenVMS users need to know how to do their daily tasks on UNIX or Linux systems, and that's why we revised this book again.

For this third edition, our goal has been to update the existing material. When we talk about the various flavors of UNIX, we also consider Linux. In addition, we've provided some new information about shell programming, Perl, and using the Emacs editor.

We will disappoint many who find their favorite command missing. There is simply no way to keep up with the wonderful explosion of free and open source software that clusters around UNIX. Whether it's part of one of the GNU Linux distributions or available from a Web site such as SourceForge, software written just for fun and just for the utility it can provide to others has kept the spirit and substance of the old DECUS tapes.

Whatever else the future brings, the need to mix-and-match operating systems, and the need for competence across them, will remain.

Acknowledgments for the Third Edition

Our thanks to

Our contact at Digital Press/Butterworth-Heinemann, Pam Chester;

Bill Costa of the Computing and Information Services Department of the University of New Hampshire, who provided us with thorough review comments, and also provided us with access to his own excellent Web site of UNIX and OpenVMS migration; Additional thanks to Tim for his extensive help with Perl and all of Chapter 10;

All the Linux advocates, enthusiasts, and evangelists who worked for DEC and Compaq (you know who you are!);

Special thanks to ngh, the true guru;

And of course, our families.

Richard Holstein and Joseph McMullen

April 2003

Chapter Plates

The chapter plates were drawn by Maria Ruotolo, adapted from some of the great masters:

1. Adapted from "The Thinker" by Auguste Rodin (1840–1917).

2. Adapted from "The Creation of Man" by Michelangelo Buonarroti (1475–1519).

3. Adapted from "The Lovers" by Pablo Picasso (1881–1973).

4. Adapted from "Jeune Femme Devant le Lit" by Amedeo Modigliani (1884–1920).

5. Adapted from "Three Women at the Spring" by Pablo Picasso (1881–1973).

6. Adapted from an Egyptian tomb painting—18th-Dynasty Egyptian mural.

7. Adapted from "The Suitor's Visit" by Gerard ter Borch (1677–1687).

8. Adapted from "Portrait of Dr. Gachet" by Vincent van Gogh (1853–1890).

9.   Adapted from "A Portrait of Sultan Selin II" by Ralis Haydar
       (1570–1638).

10.   Adapted from "Gare Saint-Lazare" by Edouard Monet (1832–
       1883).

11.   Adapted from "The Anatomy Lecture of Dr. Nicolaes Tulp" by
       Harmenszoon Van Rijn Rembrandt (1606–1669).

12.   Adapted from "Peasant Woman Digging" by Vincent van Gogh
       (1853–1890).

13.   Adapted from "The Last Supper" by Leonardo da Vinci (1475–
       1564).

Introduction

Introduction

> *History is philosophy teaching by examples.*
>
> *—Dionysius of Halicarnassus*

This book provides an introduction to the UNIX operating system. Most introductory UNIX texts assume no prior knowledge of interactive computing. Here, you must have a working knowledge of the OpenVMS operating system from Hewlett-Packard (HP), because this text is designed to help you make a smooth transition from OpenVMS to UNIX. This book started as a user's guide for a group of scientists who saw an increasing need for OpenVMS users to compute on processors running the UNIX operating system. Recognizing that mixed operating system environments like ours were becoming more common, we decided to expand the user's guide into the more comprehensive text presented here.

This book was developed originally in response to the increase in UNIX usage compared to OpenVMS. This book does not, however, attempt to convince the OpenVMS user that UNIX is a preferable operating system: We do not regard UNIX as a better operating system than OpenVMS, nor OpenVMS as superior to UNIX. Each has strengths and weaknesses, which we note when relevant to the comparative teaching process that the text employs throughout.

The text is intended to do more than describe how to perform a given OpenVMS command or function in UNIX. Certainly such descriptions are useful and may represent all that the occasional UNIX user requires. However, for those who intend to develop complex applications, we have tried to show some of the features that make UNIX a powerful development medium.

Unlike OpenVMS, UNIX is not a single product, but rather the evolution of an original idea and design philosophy into a number of different products, each of which has unique features. It is not possible to describe all these features, nor would it serve any purpose other than to confuse the reader. We shall concentrate on the more generic features. That said, we will look at how some versions of UNIX originated and what the original design philosophies behind them mean to today's OpenVMS user making the transition to UNIX.

1.1   Evolution

Much has been written on the subject of UNIX's evolution and the current trends toward standardization. This section gives only a synopsis and compares UNIX's evolution to the corresponding development of OpenVMS.

Ken Thompson first conceived of UNIX in 1969 at the American Telephone and Telegraph Company's (AT&T) Research Division at Bell Laboratories in Murray Hill, New Jersey, to allow him to run a program on a PDP-7 computer. The program, Space Travel, originally ran on a General Electric GE645 computer, which used an operating system called Multics. Multics was developed at the Massachusetts Institute of Technology (MIT) and was one of the first timesharing operating systems. The first version of UNIX, which was written in assembly language, incorporated many features of Multics.

The decision to rewrite UNIX in a higher-level language and, thus, to make it portable between computer systems, came in 1972, when Thompson rewrote the UNIX software in a language called B. Dennis Ritchie, also of Bell Laboratories, extensively modified B in 1973, renaming it C. Whether fortuitous or not, the decision to make UNIX portable is the main reason for the popularity of UNIX today. UNIX provides a stable development medium for a rapidly changing hardware market. Applications can often be ported directly to hardware of different types without costly redevelopment.

In 1974, the decision to license the UNIX source code to universities established a second major evolutionary pathway, the Berkeley Software Distribution (BSD). BSD Version 3.0, released in 1979, included many enhancements to the original Bell Laboratories version of UNIX, some of which we discuss in subsequent chapters. Notable were several portable language compilers that expanded the transparent operating system functionality on different types of hardware to include transparent program development tools. The development of BSD illustrates one aspect of the original design philosophy of UNIX: The system is modular; that is, it can accommodate additional functionality with relative ease.

At about the time BSD was released, the first version of UNIX appeared on VAX computers. Known as 32V, it represented a 32-bit implementation of the 16-bit Version 7 from Bell Laboratories, which was already running on a number of PDP-11 series computers.

With the relaxation of antitrust laws and its release of a line of microcomputer and minicomputer systems, AT&T found itself in a better position than previously to market UNIX aggressively. In 1983, AT&T released UNIX System V, which contained many BSD features.

In 1984, Digital Equipment Corporation (Digital or DEC) released ULTRIX, a version of UNIX derived from BSD and System V. ULTRIX gradually became available for the complete line of VAX and MIPS processors. For the personal computer market, Microsoft Corporation developed Xenix, a 16-bit microcomputer version of UNIX System V. Meanwhile, International Business Machines (IBM) had been quietly supporting several disparate versions of UNIX on different hardware platforms in response to market pressures, but without any apparent overall corporate strategy. The IBM position changed with its introduction of Advanced Interactive Executive (AIX) for the IBM RT in 1986. AIX is the standard for UNIX within IBM and can currently run on a variety of IBM processors. Other major versions of UNIX include SunOS and Solaris from Sun Microsystems, and HP-UX from Hewlett-Packard.

As corporations adopted and enhanced UNIX to create their own proprietary commercial versions, there was a grass-roots reaction to maintain the concept of "free software" for developers, particularly in educational institutions. Richard Stallman of the MIT Artificial Intelligence Lab started the GNU Project in the early 1980s. One of the primary goals of the GNU Project was to create a free operating system. This new operating system would build upon the technologies already provided in UNIX. To emphasize its uniqueness, the name GNU was chosen as an acronym for "GNU's Not UNIX." Some important early software developed by the GNU Project includes the GNU C compiler GCC and the GNU Emacs editor.

The GNU project continued its progress into the 1990s with emphasis on developing a kernel. Meanwhile, the Finnish student Linus Torvalds created Linux, his own version of a nonproprietary operating system. Torvalds made Linux available on the "net" in 1991. Very quickly, as developers downloaded and tested Linux, this new operating system gained in popularity. Before long, Linux was licensed under the GNU General Public License, ensuring that source code would be free for all to copy and change.

GNU/Linux (referred to simply as "Linux" in all subsequent references in this book) is open-source software that is available for free from Internet sites, universities, and other sources. It is also available commercially from companies such as Red Hat, Caldera, Debian, and SUSE, who package the basic Linux distribution along with their own tools and utilities.

Linux is considered a completely unique operating system that runs on a variety of processors, including Intel processors. Linux is based on UNIX, and many of its commands, shells, file systems, and utilities are almost identical to those on many standard UNIX implementations. Therefore, in this book we treat Linux as another implementation of UNIX. For further information about Linux, see the references in Appendix E.

While Linux was emerging in the 1990s, UNIX continued to make inroads into corporate "enterprise" computing. With the growth of the Internet, UNIX proved to be a reliable platform for Web servers. Not only had the technology improved, with UNIX running on faster processors, but also the importance of industry standards had made the various UNIX implementations more open.

Digital introduced its Alpha computer architecture in 1992. Boasting at that time the fastest chip in the world, the Alpha computer was the first commercial architecture to support 64-bit computing. Digital brought out support for OpenVMS on Alpha and also introduced a 64-bit UNIX for Digital computers, DEC OSF/1. Digital later renamed its UNIX product for Alpha from DEC OSF/1 to DIGITAL UNIX, and later Tru64 UNIX.

Digital earned a reputation for excellence with its OpenVMS and UNIX systems; however, like many other high-tech companies, Digital fell on hard times in the mid 1990s. A victim of the changing commercial computing marketplace, Digital was acquired by Compaq Computer Corporation (Compaq) in 1998. Compaq expanded the development of OpenVMS and Tru64 UNIX. Then, just a few years later, HP acquired Compaq. In 2002, HP planned to shift development of OpenVMS off of Alpha and onto the Intel IA-64 platform. HP also announced plans to redesign its HP-UX operating system using some of the technologies of Tru64 UNIX, while continuing to support its Alpha-based operating systems for a number of years.

The decision to write UNIX in a high-level language rather than assembly offered computer manufacturers the opportunity to use a relatively inexpensive operating system for new hardware. Development costs were lowered because manufacturers did not have to develop an operating system from scratch, but instead could purchase a license for the UNIX source code and write a C compiler (a good idea anyway, given the popularity of the language) and a small amount of assembly code to handle input/output and other hardware-specific functions.

Table 1.1 lists some companies that have adopted UNIX as an operating system to support their hardware. Some of these companies added their own tools and utilities, which themselves became de facto standards. Notable are the Network File System (NFS) and X Windows. NFS, developed by Sun Microsystems, provided transparent file access among a variety of hosts running the UNIX operating system.

Table 1.1   *Popular Versions of UNIX*

Name	Hardware Supported	Company
AIX	IBM RS/6000	IBM
IRIX	Silicon Graphics workstations	Silicon Graphics Computer Systems
Linux	Intel, PowerPC, Alpha, Sparc, etc.	
HP-UX	HP workstations	HP
Solaris	Sun workstations	Sun Microsystems
SUN-OS	Sun workstations	Sun Microsystems
Tru64 UNIX	Alpha	HP
UNICOS	Cray computers	Silicon Graphics Computer Systems

Voluntary compliance by UNIX vendors to standards and recommendations developed by various consortia have improved the "openness" of UNIX:

- X Windows, developed originally by Project Athena, a joint venture involving IBM, DEC, and MIT, provides a standard windowing interface for UNIX hosts.

- The Open Software Foundation (OSF) developed OSF/Motif as an open-system graphical user interface (GUI).

- The Common Open Software Environment (COSE) developed the Common Desktop Environment (CDE). CDE incorporates technology from the OSF/Motif and the X Windows Systems specifications. Adopted by all the major UNIX vendors, CDE gives end users a consistent GUI.

- To promote uniformity across UNIX implementations, the X/Open Group developed the Single UNIX Specification (formerly known as Spec 1170), the UNIX95 branding, and later the UNIX98 branding. Eventually, the OSF and X/Open consortia merged, resulting in the Open Group.

With so many implementations of UNIX available, one might expect the command-line interpreter to differ significantly from one implementation to another. Three command-language interpreters (called *shells* in UNIX) have become popular:

1.   The Bourne shell (sh)

2.   The C shell (csh)

3.   The Korn shell (ksh)

Another popular shell is bash (GNU Bourne-Again Shell) for the Linux system. Bash includes csh and ksh features and differs only slightly from sh[1]. Most sh scripts can run in the bash shell with no modifications. This book primarily discusses the C shell and the Korn shell.

Table 1.2 shows the comparable milestones in UNIX and OpenVMS evolution. Unlike UNIX, OpenVMS has followed a single evolutionary pathway as a result of its proprietary nature. The OpenVMS pathway is closely related to the development of VAX and Alpha hardware, the only hardware on which OpenVMS functions. Minor releases of OpenVMS generally fix bugs and provide software necessary to support new hardware. Major releases extend the range of Alpha and VAX processors that Open-VMS supports. For example, full support of VAX clustering became available with OpenVMS Version 4.0.

---

1.   For details about bash, see the bash reference page (if it is installed on your system) and the bash Web page at http://www.gnu.org/software/bash/bash.html.

Table 1.2 *OpenVMS and UNIX Genealogy*

Date[*]	OpenVMS	UNIX[†]
1969		First development for PDP-7
1970		Named UNIX
1971		First version operational at Bell Labs on PDP-11 /20, written in B
1973		Rewritten in C
1974		University licenses issued
1975		UNIX V6 Bell Labs
1978	1.0, 1.1, 1.2	UNIX V7 Bell Labs, first portable version
1979	1.3, 1.4, 1.5, 1.6	BSD 3.0; 32V Homdel, first VAX version
1980	2.0, 2.1	BSD 4.0
1981	2.2, 2.3, 2.4, 2.5	BSD 4.1
1982	3.0, 3.1, 3.2	AT&T System III
1983	3.3, 3.4, 3.5	BSD 4.2; AT&T System V; Bell Labs. V8
1984	3.6, 3.7, 4.0	AT&T System V Release 2; Microsoft Xenix; ULTRIX 1.0; X/Open founded
1985	4.1, 4.2, 4.3	POSIX standard introduced
1986	4.4, 4.5	BSD 4.3; AT&T System V Release 3; Bell Labs V9, AIX Version 1.0; first commercial release of X Windows System
1987	4.6, 4.7	
1988	5.0, 5.1	Open Software Foundation founded; HP-UX released by HP
1989	5.2, 5.3	First release of OSF/Motif
1990	5.4	AT&T System V Release 4
1992	5.5	Digital changes the name VMS to OpenVMS; Digital introduces Alpha architecture; Digital introduces first release of DEC OSF/1.
1993	6.0	COSE established; BSD 4.4
1994	6.1	Red Hat is founded; Linux V1.0 released

Table 1.2   *OpenVMS and UNIX Genealogy (continued)*

Date*	OpenVMS	UNIX†
1995	6.2	X/Open releases the UNIX95 brand
1996	7.0, 7.1	Open Group formed from the consolidation of X/Open and Open Software Foundation
1999	7.2	
1998		UNIX98 brand released; Compaq buys DEC
2000		IBM and Red Hat develop versions of Linux for all native IBM platforms; Apple Computer distributes MacOS X client, based on FreeBSD and Mach microkernel; HP releases HP-UX 11i, a 64-bit UNIX
2001	7.3	
2002		HP acquires Compaq

*   UNIX dates are approximate.
†   Only the major milestones in UNIX evolution are listed.

UNIX and OpenVMS have not evolved completely independently. New versions of OpenVMS contain enhancements first appearing in the various releases of UNIX and vice versa. This situation will likely continue, and both products will continue to converge towards common capabilities.

Operating system emulators are available for those who require computer environments possessing the functionality of both operating systems, yet do not wish to invest in two separate computing systems. Native OpenVMS systems can host what appears to be a UNIX environment and vice versa. In some instances, it is desirable to emulate specific tools and utilities rather than the complete operating system. Some software products with such capabilities are mentioned in subsequent chapters.

The nonproprietary and modular nature of UNIX illustrates that the versions available today incorporate ideas from many different programmers added over a long period of time. Although this situation has resulted in an extensive set of tools and utilities for application development, it has not produced a completely coherent design strategy. Some OpenVMS users, familiar with more stringent product management, may therefore find certain UNIX characteristics irksome. Here are a few examples:

- UNIX documentation is neither as comprehensive nor as well organized as OpenVMS documentation.

- Command names sometimes bear no resemblance to functions.

- Contributors to UNIX often devised names for their own convenience, rather than for a large community of users. Other commands owe their names to historical significance, rather than function.

- Contributors who added commands that have now become part of the standard UNIX distributions often used syntax that suited their own needs, but did not always follow a logical pattern relative to other commands.

- Some commands and utilities are complex to use, having been written for programmers by programmers.

- System security requires more diligence by both administrators and users.

- Redundant code has not been retired. For example, UNIX still supports some hardware that is no longer in use.

- Error handling is not as consistent. It can be difficult to determine what program failed or to test and trap for all possible errors.

1.2   The Future

For years, UNIX developers have worked toward solving the shortcomings described above as the operating system has gained popularity in commerce, industry, and the traditional government marketplace.

Much has happened in the world of corporate computing since the first commercial versions of UNIX and OpenVMS. The PC has become a ubiquitous tool on desktops worldwide, and Microsoft has given the world increasingly more powerful computing tools with its family of Windows operating systems. Also, the computing model has shifted from timesharing to client/server. UNIX systems continue to expand in the server market, providing the high-performance computing capability, storage, and high availability demanded there, while PCs take an increasing chunk of the client market previously held by UNIX workstations.

Faster, more powerful UNIX computers are now the foundation of a large part of the Internet. The Internet has evolved into the global platform for commerce and information distribution. This would be impossible without the foundation of *servers*, the computers that store huge databases and other files of interest. The trends in the late 1990s and early 2000s showed UNIX as the primary operating system on Internet servers.

Recognizing shifts in the industry, Digital continued to evolve Open-VMS in the 1990s, attempting to keep a share of the marketplace. In 1992, Digital renamed the product from VMS to OpenVMS,[2] stressing its compliance with various "open" standards, such as POSIX and OSF/Motif, among other specifications. Digital expanded networking options on OpenVMS to include Transmission Control Protocol/Internet Protocol (TCP/IP) and Open Systems Interconnect (OSI) specifications, in addition to its proprietary DECnet networking.

Since the late 1980s, the OpenVMS share in the marketplace has decreased. In the mid 1990s, Digital responded by recasting the image of OpenVMS from that of a specialized proprietary operating system to that of a high-end server to be used in conjunction with other operating systems including Windows. Compaq continued to improve OpenVMS in the areas of reliability, capability, and clustering. When HP acquired Compaq, it also acquired the legacy of OpenVMS.

Computer users can continue to expect faster, smaller processors that run a variety of operating systems and communicate transparently at high speeds. Users no longer have to choose between OpenVMS or UNIX (or Windows for that matter), but can have them all, with the application dictating (but more often hiding) the choice of operating system.

---

2.   Throughout this book we refer to OpenVMS regardless of the era.

2

Fundamentals

2

Fundamentals

> *The golden rule is that there are no golden rules.*
>
> —*George Bernard Shaw*

We recommend that the reader study this chapter before beginning a UNIX terminal session, for it is here that the fundamental features of the UNIX operating system are introduced and compared to those of Open-VMS. Section 2.1 provides the new UNIX user with an understanding of the basic functions of the UNIX kernel, the various UNIX utilities and tools, and the user interface, as well as of how these compare with the structure of OpenVMS.

Section 2.1.1 introduces the subject of process creation, which requires more detailed consideration. Users may run UNIX commands simultaneously as separate processes created by the shell. Understanding the interrelationships among these processes is a prerequisite to understanding how to use commands effectively. You may synchronize processes so that the output of one is used as input for the next, a procedure known as *piping* (Section 2.1.2). You may also easily redirect input and output between files and processes (Section 2.1.3).

Section 2.2 introduces the format of commands. Since many commands involve the manipulation of files, this section also discusses file and directory naming. Section 2.2.1 discusses what happens if you use an incorrect command syntax.

Section 2.3 introduces the concept of a UNIX file system and compares it to an OpenVMS physical device. This section also introduces the different types of UNIX files.

Section 2.4 introduces the concept of metacharacters, which perform special functions in command interpretation by the various shells.

Section 2.5 discusses the use of wildcards in naming files and directories, showing where there is similarity to the OpenVMS wildcard syntax.

2.1   System Internals

The internal architectures of most multiuser, multitasking, virtual memory, interactive operating systems are similar; OpenVMS and UNIX are no exceptions. Schematically, an operating system looks like a hierarchical arrangement of layers or skins, not unlike those of an onion (Figure 2.1). The system grows outward from a central core, or *kernel*.

The functions of any given layer presuppose the functions of layers closer to the core. In both OpenVMS and UNIX, the kernel directly controls the hardware. For example, the kernel handles memory management, scheduling the use of the CPU and input/output to various devices. The innermost layers surrounding the kernel comprise a set of system service routines that interact directly with the kernel. Assembly code makes direct calls to system service routines; high-level languages can also make calls to these routines to achieve the greatest possible efficiency. Calling these system service routines can be quite complex. It is the job of the next outer layer of the software comprising the tools and utilities, the hierarchy that includes high-level language compilers, to make the interface transparent to the user.

The major difference between OpenVMS and UNIX in the tools and utilities layer[1] has to do with what is included as part of the standard operating system. Both UNIX and OpenVMS provide many tools and utilities, but UNIX provides more of them as part of the standard operating system. Both OpenVMS and some implementations of UNIX require a separate software license to run tools and utilities that are standard features of other UNIX implementations. Table 2.1 lists some of the major tools and utilities available in both OpenVMS and UNIX, emphasizing those included as part of a standard distribution. Certain very common tools, such as Internet browsers, are excluded. While you will likely use such a tool, they are not a standard part of UNIX even though some manufacturers distribute them with their version of the operating system. The most commonly used UNIX tools and utilities will be introduced in following chapters.

---

1.   Throughout this book, tools and utilities are distinguished from commands on the basis of their complexity. For example, e-mail, invoked with the UNIX command `mail`, is regarded as a utility, as a number of subcommands may be issued in response to the mail prompt. Tools ease the task of application development. The UNIX debugger `dbx` is an example of a tool.

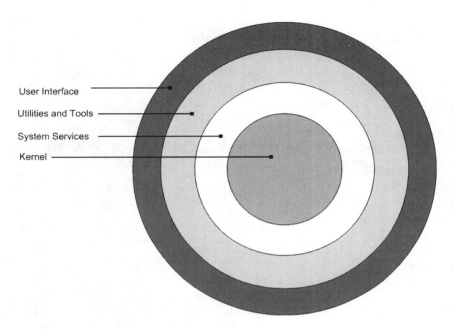

Figure 2.1
*Operating system
topology.*

User Interface

Utilities and Tools

System Services

Kernel

Both operating systems offer several editors capable of line- or screen-oriented editing. Both systems offer interactive communications and e-mail, as well as extensive networking capabilities for file transfer, remote command execution, and remote login. Many versions of UNIX include compilers, notably C and FORTRAN-77, as part of their standard distribution. Compilers written and supported by manufacturers all require separate licenses to run on an OpenVMS system. Both UNIX and OpenVMS also support the Gnu compilers from the Free Software Foundation, for which no license is required. Code written for UNIX compilers that make calls to UNIX-specific routines will generally compile and run on any type of hardware that supports UNIX. Code written with calls to OpenVMS-specific routines, such as the run-time library, is restricted to OpenVMS or requires separately purchased third-party emulation routines.

Various text-formatting tools are standard features of both systems. UNIX possesses tools for text (string) manipulation not found on Open-VMS, including a lexical analyzer useful for developing a command interpreter or compiler. Program productivity tools are also standard for many versions of UNIX.

At the outermost layer (the surface of the onion) is the user interface: the command-language interpreter, or *shell* in UNIX parlance, which surrounds all components of the operating system. The UNIX shell, like the

Digital Command Language (DCL) interpreter, is simply a program that parses commands and passes control to other programs that make up the operating system. The UNIX shells introduced in Section 1.1 differ in the functions they perform and the command syntax they accept, but all pass control to the same UNIX programs for processing, except for commands processed by the shells themselves.

Table 2.1   *Standard UNIX Tools and Utilities and Their OpenVMS Equivalents*

	OpenVMS	UNIX
Editors		
	TECO	ed, ex
	vi[†]	vi
	Emacs	Emacs
	TPU	TPU[‡]
	EDT	EDT[‡]
	EVE	
Communications		
	MAIL	mail
	REPLY	write
	PHONE	talk
	DECnet	ftp
	FTP[†]	ftp
	TELNET[†]	telnet
	r commands[†]	r commands
Compilers		
	FORTRAN*	f77
	CC*	cc
Text Processing		
	RUNOFF	troff
		nroff
	awk[†]	awk
		lex

Table 2.1   *Standard UNIX Tools and Utilities and Their OpenVMS Equivalents (continued)*

	OpenVMS	UNIX
	sed[†]	sed
	SEARCH	grep
	SORT	sort
	MERGE	merge
Program Development Tools		
	LINK	ld
	DEBUG	dbx
	LIBRARIAN	ar
	DEC MMS[‡]	make
		yacc
	DEC CMS[‡]	rcs, sccs
Miscellaneous		
		bc/dc
	DECspell[‡]	spell

[*]Available as optional products.

[†]Available as part of the POSIX layered product or TCP/IP services for OpenVMS.

[‡]Available from third parties.

Many of the features introduced in this book are independent of the shell in use. We will note features specific to the Korn and C shells. The Bourne shell predates both and is completely contained in the Korn shell; the C shell contains some incompatibilities. The shell you use will depend in part on your own tastes, in part on the default shell given to new accounts on your system, and often on the predominant preferences of experienced users you will find to help you!

2.1.1   Processes

When you begin either a UNIX or OpenVMS terminal session, the operating system establishes a unique process. A process has dynamic access to memory and CPU resources and receives a unique *process identifier* from the operating system. Whether hardware resources are available to a particular process at any time is determined (in part) by its *priority*. The kernel dynamically adjusts the priority periodically to control the sharing of resources. The part of the kernel responsible for scheduling determines the priority by means of a complex algorithm. The algorithm uses predefined variables assigned by the system, or in some cases by the system administrator, to determine the priority. Chapter 12 discusses the UNIX commands available for examining and changing the characteristics of a user's processes.

The mechanism the two operating systems use to handle command execution and multitasking[2] differ somewhat and, therefore, require further explanation. When a user begins a terminal session, the operating system starts a single *parent process*. Both DCL in OpenVMS and the various UNIX shells themselves execute certain short commands. In both operating systems, most commands either require execution of a separate binary file or begin execution of a sequence of commands held in a text file. But where OpenVMS executes such commands in the context of the process that issued the command, UNIX creates a new process for every command not executed directly by the shell. In OpenVMS terms, it's as if every command were executed using the SPAWN/WAIT command, except that process creation on a UNIX system is very fast. OpenVMS users, accustomed to process creation being a relatively expensive operation, should note that UNIX process creation is much less so.

In UNIX, this naturally leads to the creation of multiple processes, albeit *implicitly*. Both operating systems also allow you to create multiple processes *explicitly*. Such new process creation by an existing process is termed *spawning* in OpenVMS and *forking* in UNIX. The new process, which has its own unique process identifier, is called a *subprocess* in OpenVMS and a *child process* in UNIX. Forking occurs often in UNIX. Note that submitting a batch job or commencing another terminal session does not involve spawning or forking as these are not child, but parent, processes.

When UNIX creates a child process and OpenVMS creates a subprocess, the events that take place are often similar. In UNIX, it's not unusual for a single command to result in multiple child processes running simultaneously, in sequence, or as a mixture of both (a *pipeline*). When OpenVMS creates a subprocess, the parent usually remains dormant (hibernates) until the subprocess terminates, whereupon control returns to the parent. Alternatively, the OpenVMS ATTACH command gives control back to the parent process, at which time the subprocess becomes dormant. The point is that

---

2.   In this context, multitasking implies concurrent processes initiated by a single user.

only one process is active at any given time. Prior to OpenVMS V7.1, the exceptions were the OpenVMS CREATE/TERMINAL/PROCESS[/DETACH], RUN /PROCESS=image_name and SPAWN/NOWAIT commands, which ran a user-defined executable image as a process or subprocess, while the parent process was free to accept commands. With V7.1, OpenVMS introduced pipelining similar to that in UNIX. In both operating systems, a child process that creates another process becomes the parent of the new child, so a process can be both a parent and a child. Child processes can involve any valid operation. UNIX processes that are either running or stopped, but not receiving input directly from the terminal, are said to be *in the background*.

When you begin a UNIX terminal session, the login process started by the kernel provides a copy of the shell in which to work. Except for a few commands that the shell executes directly, the shell forks a child process when you issue a command to the shell. The process to execute the command takes on the characteristics of the parent and is actually a duplicate of the parent, except that it executes the instructions of the command, not the shell. The child process terminates at the end of the command, and control returns to the parent. Compare OpenVMS, where commands typically execute in the context of the original process. In both operating systems, at any time the parent or the child can fork other processes, which in turn can fork other processes, and so on. Hence, a number of parent and child processes may be running simultaneously.

<CTRL>-C can return you to the command prompt under both operating systems.[3] But a consequence of the UNIX method of command execution is that there is no concept quite like the OpenVMS CONTINUE command. Once the command terminates, the process context in which it executed disappears, and its resources, including memory and register state, return to the operating system for reuse.

We will discuss the implications of multiprocesses for multitasking in Section 7.3. The following example, although it does not illustrate UNIX multitasking, shows the UNIX analog to the OpenVMS SPAWN command and introduces the UNIX commands cat, fg, and f77.

---

3.   OpenVMS programs will occasionally trap <CTRL>-C and remain in execution. In such situations, <CTRL>-Y typically becomes the means to return to the operating system prompt. UNIX provides no such alternative.

OpenVMS	UNIX
Example:	`% f77 myfile.f`
`$ FORTRAN MYFILE.FOR`	`<CTRL>-Z`
`<CTRL>-C`	`stopped`
`$ SPAWN`	
`%DCL-S-SPAWNED, process PROCESS_1`	
`spawned`	
`%DCL-S-ATTACHED, terminal now`	
`attached to process PROCESS_1`	
`$ TYPE MYFILE.FOR`	`% cat myfile.f`
`...`	`...`
`$ ATTACH PROCESS`	`% fg`
`DCL-S-RETURNED, control returned to`	`77 myfile.f`
`process PROCESS`	
`$ CONTINUE`	

In this example, partway through a FORTRAN compilation and link (`f77`), which is itself a child process of the parent process, the user suddenly is not sure that the correct source file is being compiled. If the user issues an interrupt (`<CTRL>-C`) and then discovers that the correct file was being compiled, the compilation time already used would be wasted. Instead, the child process responsible for the compilation is suspended by typing `<CTRL>-Z` and control passes back to the parent process. The shell then creates another child process for the `cat` (catenate and print) command to run in. The `cat` command lists the contents of the source file at the terminal. The child process responsible for `cat` dies when the listing completes (or terminates with `<CTRL>-C`) and control passes back to the parent. When the user determines that the file is the correct one, the command `fg` (foreground) returns control to the child process responsible for the compilation. The command responsible for the compilation is displayed and the compilation continues.

If the `cat` command execution proved too lengthy, you could use `<CTRL>-C` to terminate the child process, but not the parent. Terminating the parent would terminate the terminal session.

All the parent and child processes in the above example use the default input/output device, namely the terminal. Input and output streams in UNIX are called standard input (`stdin`) and standard output (`stdout`). Standard error (`stderr`) also uses the terminal as its default output device. Prior to OpenVMS V7.1, redirecting input, output, and error streams away from the terminal in OpenVMS required the assignment of the logical names SYS$INPUT, SYS$OUTPUT, and SYS$ERROR to a file or alternative device (or the equivalent through the /OUTPUT qualifier). The UNIX Bourne, Korn, and C shells, and now OpenVMS V7.1, have an elegant mechanism for redirecting input, output, and error streams when running a number of tasks simultaneously (see Section 2.1.3). In the next section, we discuss a special case of redirection where the output of one command becomes input to the next.

2.1.2   Pipes

The creation of a *pipe* is a particular type of multiprocess activity synchronized by the kernel, in which the output of one command becomes input to the next command without creating any intermediate file. UNIX may synchronize two or more processes in what is termed a *pipeline*.

OpenVMS (V7.1)   **UNIX**
Form:

```
command-seq [separator -          % command1| command2| \
command-seq]                      command3
```

Example:

```
$ PIPE SHOW USERS | -             % who| sort | lpr
SORT/KEY=(POSITION:0,SIZE:12)-
SYS$INPUT SYS$PRINT
```

OpenVMS (prior to V7.1)
Example:

```
$ SHOW USERS/OUTPUT = A.TMP
$ SORT/
KEY=(POSITION:0,SIZE:12)-
A.TMP SYS$PRINT
$ DELETE A.TMP;*
```

A vertical bar (|) separates the commands forming the pipeline. In the above example, the kernel starts three child processes simultaneously. However, sort must wait for input from the processing of the who command. Likewise, lpr must await output from the sort command. (These commands are discussed and compared with their OpenVMS equivalents in

Sections 7.2 and 8.4.5.) When all output from the who command passes to sort, the child process responsible for running the who command dies. By default, sort uses the first field (delimited by a blank) as the *sort key*. The first field output by the who command is the username; hence, sort sorts records alphabetically by username. The lpr command then accepts as input the output from the sort command, and the child process responsible for sort dies. After printing the output of sort on the default printer, the child process responsible for lpr dies, and control passes back to the parent shell process. The result of the pipeline is a printed listing of all users on the system in alphabetical order.

Prior to OpenVMS V7.1, a comparable sequence of events required the creation of an intermediate file. The OpenVMS examples above show both the old and new methods to create a printed listing sorted by username. In the example from releases prior to OpenVMS V7.1, the output of the SHOW USERS command is saved in a file A.TMP. The contents of the file are then sorted on the username key, which is 12 characters long and begins in column 0, and the output passes to the default line printer. The alternate form shows a closer analog to UNIX, as the output from SHOW USERS goes directly into the SORT command.

Piping offers the opportunity to perform complex functions by creating a pipeline from a number of simple commands. Examples of piping commands appear throughout this book to emphasize the versatility they give. Effective use of piping can require a different way of thinking if you are accustomed to the sequential processing of single commands and the occasional redirection of the output of one command to a file for subsequent processing by another command. It is a useful habit always to consider how you can capture a sequence of commands in a single pipeline.

2.1.3 Input, Output, and Error Redirection

Just as the OpenVMS logical names SYS$INPUT, SYS$OUTPUT, and SYS$ERROR point to the terminal by default, so do the UNIX equivalents stdin, stdout, and stderr. However, UNIX uses a simplified method of redirecting input, output, and error messages to or from a file. UNIX does not require the equivalent of a DEFINE statement preceding the command or the /OUTPUT qualifier to perform redirection; rather, UNIX includes a redirection metacharacter as part of the command line. In this simple example, myprog <input.dat> a.lis causes the executable program myprog to read input (<) from the file input.dat and send output (>) to a.lis.

OpenVMS	UNIX

Example:

```
$ DEFINE/USER SYS$OUTPUT A.LIS
$ DEFINE/USER INPUT.DAT FOR005
$ RUN MYPROG
```

```
% myprog  <  input.dat  >
a.lis
```

Note the following:

- UNIX redirection affects only the command line in which the command appears (compare with the OpenVMS command DEFINE/ USER_MODE) .

- Error messages are not redirected in this example and appear at the terminal.

- White space between a redirection symbol and a command or file is optional.

- If the file a.lis already exists, OpenVMS creates a new version of the file with a higher version number. By default, UNIX overwrites any existing file a.lis. Overwriting a file through redirection is aptly named *clobbering*. C shell users may prevent clobbering with the shell command set noclobber, whereas Korn or Bourne shell users need the command set -o noclobber. Both warn the user that the proposed output file already exists and prevent the command from executing.

- Depending on which shell you use, there is a difference in the way one may force the shell to disregard set noclobber or set -o noclobber. While all shells will interpret ">tmp" and "> tmp" as redirecting output to the file named tmp, the C shell will interpret ">!tmp" differently from ">! tmp". In the former case, the C shell will attempt command substitution before attempting to redirect output (Section 3.5).

See Section 3.2 and Chapter 10 for more on shell commands.

Table 2.2 summarizes the characters you can use for issuing redirection commands. Let us look at some further examples of their use.

The first pair of examples shows how both C shell and Korn shell redirect standard error to a file, errfile. Error messages will be written into errfile instead of appearing on the screen.

Table 2.2 *Special Characters Used in Input, Output, and Error Redirection*

Character	Meaning
>	Redirect standard output
>!	Redirect standard output, disregarding noclobber[*]
>|	Redirect standard output, disregarding noclobber[†]
>>	Redirect and append standard output
>>!	Redirect and append standard output, suppressing error and opening a new file if output file does not exist[*]
>&	Redirect standard output and standard error[*]
>&!	Redirect standard output and standard error, disregarding noclobber[*]
>>&	Redirect and append standard output and standard error[*]
>>&!	Redirect and append standard output and standard error, suppressing error and opening a new file if output file does not exist[*]
<	Redirect standard input
<<xxx	Read input up to a line identical with xxx
|	Redirect standard output to another command
|tee	Direct standard output to both a file and standard output in parallel
|&	Redirect standard output and standard error to another command[*]

[*]Unique to the C shell.

[†]Unique to the Korn shell.

OpenVMS

Example:
```
$ DEFINE/USER SYS$ERROR A.ERR
$ DEFINE/USER SYS$OUTPUT A.OUT
$ DEFINE/USER SYS$ERROR A.ERR
```
Example:
```
$ APPEND A.ERR; A.ERR;-1
$ TYPE RUN_PROG.COM
```
Example:
```
$ RUN MYPROG
1 1 1 1 10
```

UNIX

```
% f77 myprog.f >2& errfile    # C shell
$ f77 myprog.f  2> errfile    # Korn
% f77 myprog.f >& outerr      # C shell
$ f77 myprog.f > outerr 2>&1  # Korn
% f77 myprog1.f >>& outerr    # C shell
% cat run_prog
myprog << end
1 1 1 1 10
end
```

The command `f77 myprog.f>&` outerr redirects both standard output and standard error to the file `outerr`. If `noclobber` is not set, the command overwrites any previous version of the file `outerr`. The command `f77 myprog1.f>>&` outerr has the same effect, except that it appends standard output and standard error to the file `outerr`. If the file `outerr` does not already exist, the command creates it.

The command `cat run_prog` displays a *shell script*, used here to associate data with the compiled program `myprog`. Chapter 10 discusses shell scripts and how they compare to OpenVMS DCL command procedures. Here we focus on the use of the redirection to associate data with standard input to the program `myprog`. An OpenVMS DCL command procedure reads any records following the RUN command and not preceded by a dollar sign as standard input. In a UNIX shell script, standard input is the terminal unless redirected. Here `<< end` tells UNIX to read all records from the script file and not standard input until it finds a record that begins with "end."

2.2 Command Structure and File Naming

OpenVMS is not case-sensitive in its interpretation of a command; that is, it does not distinguish between commands given in uppercase and commands given in lowercase. In UNIX, on the other hand, commands are case-sensitive, and most are lowercase. The shell will not understand commands given in the wrong case. Make sure that the caps lock key has not been depressed when beginning a UNIX terminal session.

Filenames are also case-sensitive. For example, UNIX interprets `myfile.dat` as a different file from `MYFILE.DAT`. In fact, commands *are* filenames (except for a relatively few commands built into the shells; see Chapter 8), and the shell looks for a file with the same name as the command in a search list of directories in order to execute that command. Although the case sensitivity of UNIX always causes problems to an OpenVMS user during the first few UNIX terminal sessions, it is only a temporary setback. One advantage of case sensitivity in file naming is that you can use a larger variety of files with short names. This is good news for unimaginative users who are poor typists!

Another advantage of case sensitivity is that it allows the use of uppercase filenames to represent a particular class of files. This advantage offers an alternative to the file-type convention used by OpenVMS. For example, directory pointer files to subdirectories exist in UNIX, as they do in OpenVMS. When a subdirectory is created in OpenVMS, the pointer file, which exists in the next highest level of the directory hierarchy, is automatically given a file extension of .DIR. UNIX filenames, on the other hand, do not distinguish between directory pointer files and ordinary files. When UNIX displays a default file listing, there is no way of determining which entries are files and which entries are pointers to subdirectories. One way around this situation, which appeals to some OpenVMS users, but is not standard UNIX practice, is to name all subdirectories with capital letters or beginning with a capital letter. The following example illustrates this practice with two common UNIX commands: mkdir for making subdirectories and ls for listing directory contents.[4]

OpenVMS

Example:

```
$ CREATE/DIRECTORY [.TEST]
```

Example:

```
$ DIRECTORY
DIRECTORY DUA1:[HOME]
FILE1.DAT;1    FILE2.DAT;1
FILE3.DAT;1    TEST.DIR;1
```

UNIX

```
% mkdir Test
```

```
% ls -x
Test        file1.dat
file2.dat
file3.dat
```

Note that uppercase filenames precede lowercase filenames in a UNIX alphabetical listing. UNIX typically orders filenames down a column, rather than the across a row, which is the OpenVMS style. To have the more important differences stand out in this example, we used the -x switch so that ls would order the files across the page, too. In a UNIX file listing containing lowercase file entries and an uppercase directory entry, it is immediately obvious which file is the directory file in UNIX, even though it has no file extension. It is not advisable to create a subdirectory TEST.DIR using the mkdir command for reasons that will become apparent in the following section.

Excluding directory pointer files, there is no reason why you cannot adhere to OpenVMS file-naming conventions in UNIX. Since you can legally use a period in UNIX filenames, you can use OpenVMS file extensions to indicate the particular class to which a file belongs. Most OpenVMS users feel comfortable adhering to the OpenVMS file-naming scheme in UNIX. Difficulties arise when the default file extensions used by OpenVMS disagree with UNIX file-naming conventions. For example, object files use the extension .OBJ in OpenVMS, but .o in UNIX. Likewise,

---

4.   While case-awareness is standard in Windows 95 and higher, users should note that mixed case names can cause problems for some older Windows 3.1 interoperability programs (e.g., PathWorks).

FORTRAN source code uses the extension `.FOR` in OpenVMS and `.f` in UNIX. Note that `.o` and `.f` are UNIX conventions to facilitate file recognition and that UNIX commands do not assume file extensions, as do OpenVMS commands. In the second example below, the command fails because the compiler looks for a file named `myfile`, not `myfile.f`.

Table 2.3 summarizes commonly used UNIX file extensions.

OpenVMS	UNIX
Example:	
`$ FOR MYFILE.FOR`	`% f77 myfile.f`
Example:	
`$ FOR MYFILE`	`% f77 myfile`
`$`	`ld:myfile: cannot open`

Table 2.3 *UNIX File Extensions*

OpenVMS	UNIX	Section	Definition
`.OLB`	`.a`	9.5	Library
`.BAS`	`.bas`		BASIC source code
`.C`	`.c`	9.1	C source code
`.FOR`	`.f`	9.1	FORTRAN source code
`.H`	`.h`	9.1	C header files
	`.l`		`lex` program
`.OBJ`	`.o`	9.1	Object code
`.PAS`	`.p`		Pascal source code
`.MAR`	`.s`	9.1	Symbolic assembly code
	`.ti`		Terminfo data
	`.y`		`yacc` program
`.EXE`	`a.out`		Executable image
`.ADA`			ADA source code
`.B32`			BLISS-32 source code
`.CLD`			Command description file
`.COB`			Cobal source code

Table 2.3   *UNIX File Extensions (continued)*

OpenVMS	UNIX	Section	Definition
.COM		10.1	Commands for the language interpreter
.DAT			Data file
.DIS			Distribution list file for MAIL
.DIR		2.2	Directory file
.EDT			Startup command file for the EDT editor
.DOC			Documentation
.HLP		3.6	Input source file for HELP libraries
.HTML	.html		Hypertext markup language (Web browsers)
.JAV	.jav		Java source code
.JOU		5.1.6 and 5.2.8	Journal file created by the EDT editor
.LIS			Listing of text
.LOG			Batch job output file
.MAI			MAIL message file
.MAR			VAX macro source code
.PLI			PL/I source code
.PS	.ps		PostScript® files
.SIXEL			Sixel graphic file
.SYS			System image
.TJL			Journal file created by the TPU and ACL editors
.TMP			Temporary file
.TPU			Command file for the TPU editor
.TXT			Text file

In UNIX, *command names may not be abbreviated*. In OpenVMS, the portion of the command name that renders it unique is sufficient. UNIX, on the other hand, requires a full specification of the command name because *the command is usually a filename*. Fortunately, UNIX command names are usually short[5]. Unfortunately, command names are not consistent, nor in some instances do the names have any obvious connection to the functions the commands perform.

Let us now consider the general format of UNIX commands.

OpenVMS	**UNIX**
Form:	
`$ COMMAND[/QUALIFIER(S)] -`	`% command [option(s)] \`
`[PARAMETER(S)]`	`[argument(s)]`
Example:	
`$ DIRECTORY/SIZE MYFILE.DAT`	`% ls -s myfile.dat`
`Directory DUA1:[HOME]`	`2 myfile.dat`
`MYFILE.DAT;1 3`	
UNIX	
`% ls file1 file2`	`# Check for the existence of two files (no size given)`
`% ls -s file1 file2`	`# List the size in kilobytes of two files`
`% ls -s -a`	`# List the size of all files, including hidden files`
`% ls -sa`	`# List the size of all files, including hidden files`
`% ls file1 ; ls -s file2`	`# Two sequential file listings`
`% ls file1 \` `file2`	`# Command continued on next line`
`% ls file.{c,o}`	`# List file.c and file.o (C shell only)`
`% ls file.[co]`	`# List file.c and file.o (C, Korn and Bourne shells)`

These examples illustrate the major features of the UNIX command format:

---

5.   Further abbreviation or command renaming is possible with the alias command (Section 3.2.2).

- Options, like OpenVMS qualifiers, modify command functions.

- UNIX options are usually single letters preceded by a dash. You may combine options and precede them with one dash, or give them separately and precede each with a dash. Some options appear as uppercase characters. Occasionally, a UNIX command will use both the uppercase and lowercase of the same letter for two different options.

- You must use spaces to delimit files in UNIX. A comma is not a valid delimiter when specifying more than one file in a UNIX command line, except when using curly brackets, which are unique to the C shell. In fact, most commands will interpret a comma as part of a filename.

- You can place multiple commands on a single line for sequential processing, provided they are separated by a semicolon. This arrangement is distinct from piping, as the output from one command is not used as input to the next. UNIX interprets the semicolon as a new line.

- OpenVMS uses a dash to signify that a command continues on the next line; UNIX uses a backslash. The backslash must be the last character of the line; otherwise, the shell interprets it differently.

2.2.1 Error Reporting

Users familiar with the comprehensive and easily interpreted error reporting features of OpenVMS DCL will likely be disappointed by the features offered by UNIX commands. Users face cryptic error messages and sometimes no evidence that a command string has failed. A simple syntax error often results in a "usage" message, a terse summary of command syntax including a list of switches and arguments.

One exception is the simple act of changing the current directory. OpenVMS permits the user to make any directory the current directory, whether it exists or not. Thus, OpenVMS does not report an error until a user issues a command that accesses the nonexistent current directory. UNIX, on the other hand, requires that a directory exist before the user can make it the current directory.

2.3 Device, Directory, and File Structures

OpenVMS uniquely defines a file in the following way:

```
NODE::DEVICE:[DIRECTORY]FILENAME.EXTENSION;
VERSION_NUMBER
```

where

NODE = the name of the host computer on which the file resides

DEVICE = the physical device on which the file resides

DIRECTORY = the name of a group of related files to which the file belongs

FILENAME = the name of the file

EXTENSION = a descriptor usually assigned to a class of files

VERSION_NUMBER = the version number of the file

Most UNIX commands use the following simple scheme to define a file:

```
/directory/file
```

where

directory = the name of a group of related files to which the file belongs

file = the name of the file

A few commands (the so-called r commands, Section 13.2.6.1) that explicitly reference files across a network use the form host:/directory/file, where host is the name of the host computer on which the file resides.

If the UNIX you are using supports NFS (Section 13.2.8), most network files you access will appear to be available locally, and you need not specify (or even know) the host.

Both OpenVMS and UNIX have similar rules for naming the components of a complete file specification. For example, UNIX file and directory names can have more than 30 characters, avoiding characters that have special meaning.

The differences between UNIX and OpenVMS file specifications include the following:

■ UNIX makes no provision for multiple versions of a file. Therefore, UNIX does not include version numbers as part of the filename. *UNIX saves only the most recent version of a file after any file manipulation.*

- There are no formal file extensions in UNIX. The period has no special syntactic meaning, as it does in OpenVMS. However, as we have already seen, the period can be incorporated into a filename to denote a class of files even though no UNIX commands assume that class of files. While UNIX programs will not assume the extension, and so you will have to specify it, some will require that a specific extension be used. In this way, you can use OpenVMS file specifications in a UNIX environment.

- In UNIX, no device specification is ever explicitly made.

To understand the implications of this last point, which may sound strange to an OpenVMS user, we must explore the UNIX file structure in some detail.

Like OpenVMS files, UNIX files reside on a physical device. For the purposes of this discussion, we assume that the device is a disk rather than a tape drive (tape drives are considered in Section 7.3). When a user accesses a file, the UNIX operating system determines which physical device the file resides on. The user never explicitly specifies this information. UNIX does this by referencing a list of mounted file systems, which maps those file systems onto physical devices *using a single directory hierarchy*. This may seem confusing. Let us begin with the physical device.

Each disk is divided into *partitions*. Partitions arose due to the inability of 16-bit pointers to address all the space on a large disk. This is not a problem for 32-bit or 64-bit versions of UNIX, so a large disk could be configured as a single partition. Nevertheless, let us assume the disk has two or more partitions. How the partition is formatted is irrelevant to most users, provided they have a mix of small and large files. A discussion of the partition format, however, may benefit those users who have a predominance of either small or large files.

Early versions of UNIX performed all file transfers on 512-byte blocks of data. As the cost of disk storage decreased, the amount of data storage increased, as did file size. For large files, 512-byte addressable blocks do not provide efficient transfer of data between memory and disk. The BSD version of UNIX introduced partitions, which allow larger block sizes, facilitating faster block-mode transfers. The BSD version allowed partitions with different block sizes to exist on the same physical disk. This scheme caused problems when a partition contained predominantly small files. Small files occupy large blocks on disk, so that a large portion of each block is wasted space. BSD solved this problem with the concept of a *fragment*, which is a fraction of a block.

Different files can occupy fragments of the same block, reducing disk space wastage. OpenVMS handles the analogous situation by controlling cluster size, which, for purposes of illustration, we will say is 10; that is, an OpenVMS file will occupy a minimum of 10 blocks. Writing to an Open-VMS file with the cluster size set to 10 causes the space occupied by the file to expand in 10-block increments.

In some versions of UNIX, the characteristics of partitions for each type of physical disk drive reside in the file /etc/disktab (disk tabulation), to which only the system administrator can write. The example below outlines a sample entry for a RZ drive found on a Tru64 UNIX system.

```
UNIX
% disklabel -r rz6
  # /dev/rdisk/dsk6a:
    type: SCSI
    disk: rzw7s
    label:
    flags:
    bytes/sector: 512
    sectors/track: 71
    tracks/cylinder: 15
    sectors/cylinder: 1065
    cylinders: 1900
    sectors/unit: 2023500
    rpm: 3600
    interleave: 1
    trackskew: 0
    cylinderskew: 0
    headswitch: 0          # milliseconds
    track-to-track seek: 0  # milliseconds
    drivedata: 0
    8 partitions:
    #   size     offset  fstype  [fsize bsize  cpg]
  a:  131072        0    unused  1024  8192   # (Cyl.    0 - 123*)
  b:  262144    131072   unused  1024  8192   # (Cyl.  123*- 369*)
  c: 2023500        0    unused  1024  8192   # (Cyl.    0 - 1899)
  d:  163840   1703936   unused  1024  8192   # (Cyl. 1599*- 1753*)
  e:   32768   1867776   unused  1024  8192   # (Cyl. 1753*- 1784*)
  f:  122956   1900544   unused  1024  8192   # (Cyl. 1784*- 1899*)
  g: 1310720    393216   unused  1024  8192   # (Cyl.  369*- 1599*)
```

We obtain the characteristics of an individual disk using the `disklabel` command. The `-r` switch tells `disklabel` to access the disk directly for information, rather than relying on information cached in the operating system; `rz6` names the disk unit.

The RZ29B can be formatted either as a single partition c, as four partitions a, b, g, and h, or as five partitions, a, b, d, e, and f. Note how those combinations are chosen: Within each, the partitions do not overlap. Other versions of UNIX partition a disk drive similarly, but use numbers to identify the partitions, instead of letters. For the RZ29B, the block size in each partition is fixed at 8,192 bytes, and the fragment size is 1,024 bytes. In older, smaller disks, fragment size may differ in different partitions to make better use of limited space. Users whose files do not consist of a mix of large and small should discuss which partitions to use with their system administrator.

A single *file system*, a hierarchical arrangement of files and directories, may be set up in each partition. Tru64 UNIX uses the file `/etc/fstab` to keep track of which file systems to mount; the `mount` command automatically references it each time the system is booted. File systems may also be mounted and dismounted as required (usually by the system administrator) in a manner analogous to mounting and dismounting an OpenVMS physical device. A user can list the mounted file systems and determine the amount of free space with the command `df` (disk free, Section 12.2.3).

This next example shows two file systems, / and /usr, mounted in the a and g partitions of an RZ29B disk. It is partitioned differently from the disk specified by `/etc/disktab` above.

UNIX

```
% df
Filesystem    512-blocks      Used    Available   Capacity  Mounted on
/dev/rz0a        263594      192966       44268       82%     /
/dev/rz0g       3440402     1025162     2071198       34%     /usr
```

The terms `rz0a` and `rz0g` indicate the a and g partitions of the physical device `rz0`. The approximate sizes of the a and g partitions are 131 and 1,720 megabytes, respectively. Note that /, known as the *root file system*, is usually mounted in the a, or 0, partition of the boot disk.

Physical device names vary in different versions of UNIX. Table 2.4 compares Tru64 UNIX and some Linux physical device names to their OpenVMS counterparts. Note that the physical device names are also the names of files (see Sections 7.1 and 7.2 for the implications of this fact in relation to printers and tape drives). UNIX supports devices as either *block* or *character* (raw), except for disk and tape drives, which can be both (again, see Section 7.3). In simple terms, a character device deals with input and output character by character, whereas a block device buffers characters and deals with them one block at a time.

A useful mechanism for discarding output is the *null device*, `/dev/null`; anything written to it is thrown away. Reading from `/dev/null` will cause an immediate end of file. For example, `cp /dev/null myfile.dat` (compare with the OpenVMS command `COPY NL: MYFILE.DAT`) creates an empty file with the name `myfile.dat`. We will see some further uses for `/dev/null` in later chapters.

Each file contained on an OpenVMS physical disk and each UNIX file contained in a file system has a unique identifier known as a *file identifier* (file ID) in OpenVMS and an *inode* in UNIX. Section 2.3.2 describes the UNIX file types and explains briefly how one of these file types uses inodes.

UNIX and OpenVMS directory structures are both hierarchical. Figure 2.2 illustrates the directory structure for a three-disk system, in which one disk contains the operating system and the other two disks contain the users' files. Note the similarity between the directory structures of Open-VMS and UNIX. Both operating systems use particular directories to contain certain types of system files. UNIX directories and related file types are as follows:

`/bin`	Frequently used system executable files, available when `/usr` is not mounted
`/sbin`	Commands essential to boot the operating system
`/dev`	Files that address devices (device special files)
`/etc`	Miscellaneous files
`/lib`	Library files
`/opt`	Optional application packages
`/tmp`	Scratch (temporary) files
`/usr/adm`	System administrative files
`/usr/bin`	Common utilities and applications
`/usr/dict`	Dictionary files

Figure 2.2
*OpenVMS and
UNIX file
organization.*

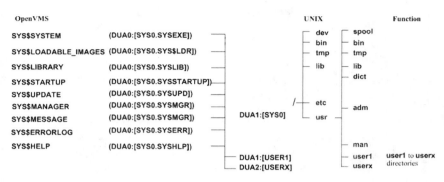

/usr/man	Manual page files (documentation)
/var/spool	Files spooled to queues
/usr/tmp	Scratch area available to all users

Table 2.4   *Examples of UNIX Physical Device–Naming Conventions*

OpenVMS	UNIX	Description
DUA0:	/dev/rz0	Disk drive (block) (Tru64 UNIX)
	/dev/rrz0	Disk drive (character) (Tru64 UNIX)
	/dev/hda	MFM or IDE disk drive (Linux)
	/dev/sda	SCSI disk drive (Linux)
OPA0:	/dev/console	System console
TTA1:	/dev/tty01	Asynchronous terminal
RTA1:	/dev/ttyp1	Remote DECnet terminal
LTA01:	/dev/ttyS1	Terminal server terminal
LCA0:	/dev/printer	Default system printer
MTA0:	/dev/mt0	Tape drive (block)
	/dev/rmt0	Tape drive (character)
	/dev/ram	Raw-mode RAM disk (Linux)
	/dev/kmem	Window into kernel memory
NL: or NLA0:	/dev/null	Wastepaper basket

Swapping and paging files vary more between UNIX vendors. On TRU64 UNIX, swapping and paging may only be done into an entire disk partition, typically the "b" partition of the boot disk. Additional swapping and paging partitions may be defined in /etc/fstab, again, into entire partitions.

The top level of the OpenVMS directory structure for a physical disk is [000000]. This directory contains all the pointers for the next level of directories. Using the example in Figure 2.2, the directory DUA0:[SYS0] has a directory pointer DUA0:[000000] SYS0.DIR;1. To locate the directory [SYS0] (or any other directory), the user must know on which device it resides or else search for it. OpenVMS circumvents this problem for system files by defining a logical name, as shown in the following example.

OpenVMS

Example:

```
$ DEFINE /SYSTEM /EXEC /TRANSLATION=(CONCEALED,TERMINAL) -
DUA0:[SYS0.] SYS$SYSROOT

$ CREATE/DIRECTORY DUA0:[SYS0.USER]

$ SET DEFAULT SYS$SYSROOT:[USER]

$ SHOW DEFAULT
SYS$SYSROOT:[USER]
```

In the above example, the system directories DUA0:[SYS0...] are made equivalent systemwide to the logical name SYS$SYSROOT with the DEFINE command. If you moved the system to a different physical disk, you would change only the definition of the logical name SYS$SYSROOT: to redefine the location of all the files it contains, provided all the file references use the logical name rather than the physical device name. In the above example, if a program references a file in SYS$SYSROOT:[USER], you need to make no changes to the program if SYS$SYSROOT: is redefined so that it points to a different physical disk. However, if the program references a file using DUA0:[SYS0.USER], then the program must be modified if a change in physical device takes place.

UNIX uses a common root not only for system files but for all files. The UNIX file hierarchy begins with / (root directory) for all files on the system irrespective of the physical device. Each file system, and each subdirectory of the root directory, has a directory pointer that can be traced back to the root directory.

UNIX

Example:

```
% ls -aF /
./              dev/            lost+found/             tp/
../             etc/                   mnt/            usr/
bin/            flp/                   sys/         vmunix*
boot*           lib/                   tmp/
```

We have introduced another feature of the ls command in order to show the directory names within the root directory. The command ls -aF / lists all files in the root directory, including two *hidden* files, "." and ".." (refer to Section 2.3.3 for a discussion of hidden files). These are directory pointers to indicate the current directory and the preceding level in the directory hierarchy, respectively,[6] corresponding to the OpenVMS syntax [ ] and [-]. The following section shows how these pointers are used.

The F (note the use of uppercase) option provides a descriptor at the end of each entry to identify the file type. The slash indicates a directory file. Although /usr is a file system (as determined in a preceding example with the df command) and the other entries are subdirectories of the root file system, the files contained therein are accessed in the same way. The asterisk indicates that the file is executable: For example, vmunix is the executable operating system kernel. The subdirectory lost+found can reside in the top-level directory of file systems and stores files for which the user reference information used by UNIX to associate that file with a particular user has been lost. The system administrator can reassign these files to the owners, if they can be identified.

2.3.1   Defining Files to the System

The explicit definition of files in a UNIX system by means of a path from the root, irrespective of the physical device, is known as *absolute file definition*. Levels down the directory pathway are delimited by a slash (compare to OpenVMS where a period is the delimiter). Any file definition that begins with a slash indicates the root is absolute. Conversely, *relative file definition* defines files not from the root, but from the current working directory. Any file definition that does not begin with a slash is a relative definition.

---

6.   In the root directory only, ".." (dot dot) is the same as "." (dot) as no higher-level directory exists. Compare to the [000000] in OpenVMS, which, as the MFD on a disk, points to itself.

OpenVMS	UNIX
Example:	
`$ DIR DUA0:[SYS0.SYSEXE]TYPE.EXE`	`% ls /bin/cat`
Example:	
`$ SET DEFAULT DUA0:[SYS0.SYSEXE]`	`% cd /bin`
Example:	
`$ DIR [-]`	`% ls ..`
Example:	
`$ DIR [-.SYSLIB]`	`% ls ../lib`
Example:	
`$ DIR SYS$LOGIN`	`% ls ~`
	`% ls ~user1`

In the first example, `ls /bin/cat` performs a directory lookup using an absolute pathname. Unlike OpenVMS, which may require a device specification, the UNIX file is defined absolutely from the root. The second example, `cd /bin`, introduces the UNIX command `cd` (change directory), which here uses an absolute pathname to change to the directory `/bin`. The third and fourth examples illustrate relative pathnames. The command `ls ..` lists the files in the directory above the current directory. The file "`..`" (dot dot) provides the pointer to the directory above.

The last example, `ls ~user1`, illustrates a feature that is not found in OpenVMS. A tilde (~) followed by the login name of a user points to that user's home directory. The ~ is an example of filename substitution and is called *globbing*. Wildcards, discussed in Section 2.5, also represent examples of globbing. Using the directory tree from Figure 2.2, `ls ~user1` lists the contents of the directory `/usr/user1`. The ~ without a login name points to the home directory of the current user and, in this instance, is equivalent to the OpenVMS logical name `SYS$LOGIN`.

It should now be evident that using OpenVMS conventions to name directories in UNIX is not useful. For example, if `user1` creates a subdirectory `temp.dir` and then creates a file in that directory called `test`, the absolute pathname to the file `test` is `/usr/user1/temp.dir /test`. The user is more likely to remember the pathname as `/usr/user1/temp/test`. To indicate which files are directories reliably and conveniently, you can use the `ls -F` command, as shown above.

2.3.2   File Types

There are three types of files in UNIX: *special files, ordinary files*, and *directory files*. UNIX treats all physical devices as if they were special files. Each device on the system has a special file associated with it. These special files reside in the directory /dev. As shown in Table 2.4, UNIX treats disks, tape drives, printers, terminals, and pseudoterminals (used for network connections) as files. Writing to a special file is a matter of course for programs when executing a command; it can also be done explicitly by the user, as later chapters will demonstrate.

Ordinary files contain ASCII characters or binary data. Copying an ordinary file to a special file will output the contents of the ordinary file on the physical device pointed to by the special file. Copying an ordinary file to another existing ordinary file overwrites the target file with the contents of the source file. OpenVMS users accustomed to working with multiple versions of the same file are likely to overwrite files inadvertently in UNIX. Sections 4.10 and 4.11 explain how to avoid losing file contents when copying or renaming files.

An ordinary file logically consists of a stream of bytes. Physically, the bytes are arranged in blocks according to the block size defined for the partition. By default, a file is not formatted. Formatting may be imposed by the user, for example, by writing fixed-length records as output to a FORTRAN program. UNIX still interprets the file as a string of bytes, but the output devices, such as terminals and printers, correctly interpret carriage returns and line feeds. Formatting is left to a user's program or the UNIX command that is interpreting the file. Thus, nearly all UNIX files have a very simple structure. There is no equivalent to the OpenVMS Record Management Service (RMS), which defines a variety of attributes for files.

We have already discussed directory files. The directory entry contains the file name and *inode number* for each file in the directory. The inode number has an associated entry in an *inode table*, which contains information on the characteristics of a file, such as the owner, the type of file access permissions, the date last modified, and the locations it occupies on disk.

2.3.3   Hidden Files

A subclass of the ordinary file is the hidden file. The names of hidden files always begin with a period, and each file has a special function. We will encounter a number of these files in chapters to come. Table 2.5 summarizes the common hidden files and their functions. Hidden files are so named because using the `ls` command without options will not list them. You must use the command `ls -a` (list all files) or `ls -A` (list all files except "." and "..") to see them. The justification for having hidden files is that if you do not see them, you are less likely to damage them!

Table 2.5 *Hidden Files*

Filename	Section	Function
.cshrc	3.2.2	Define environment (C shell)
.dt	2.6	CDE profiling directory
.exrc		Define editing environment for ex editor
.forward	6.1.4	Define a forwarding address for e-mail
.history	3.2.1	Save history list
.hushlogin	3.1	Disable some login messages
.login	3.2.1	Define environment at login time (C shell)
.logout	3.3	Define environment at logout time (C shell)
.mailrc	6.1.8	Define environment for the mail program
.netrc	13.2.6.2	Define parameters to `ftp` (file transfer program)
.profile	3.2.2	Define environment (Bourne and Korn shell)
.rhosts	13.2.3	Define private remote hosts

2.4   Special Characters

Characters that the shell interprets in a special way are known as *metacharacters*. Users should avoid using these characters in filenames as the results may be unpredictable. Metacharacters will be discussed in subsequent chapters in the context of specific functions. The tilde (~), vertical bar (|), and greater than (>) characters are examples of metacharacters that we have already encountered. Table 2.6 summarizes metacharacters and their functions in the context of the various shells. (Table 2.2 lists metacharacters associated with input/output redirection; these do not appear in Table 2.6.) The function of a metacharacter may vary depending on whether it is being interpreted by the shell or by a UNIX utility. Some of the metacharacters listed in Table 2.6 can serve as wildcards for file specifications, as discussed in the following section.

Table 2.6   *UNIX Special Characters and Their OpenVMS Equivalents*

Korn Shell Character	C Shell Character	UNIX Function	OpenVMS Equivalent
&	&	Perform command in background	
&&	&&	Boolean "and" (within expression)	.AND.
=	=	Assignment operator	=
=	==	Equal to (string)	.EQS.
!=	!=	Not equal to (string)	.NES.
==	==	Equal to (arithmetic expressions)	.EQ.
!=	!=	Not equal to (arithmetic expressions)	.NE.
<=	<=	Less than or equal to	.LE. .LES.
>=	>=	Greater than or equal to	.GE. .GES.
||	||	Boolean "or" (within expression)	.OR.
;	;	Command separator	; (V7.1 PIPE command)
\	\	Continuation of command line (quotes new line)	–
\m	\m	Literal translation of meta-character "m"	
'	'	Turn off special meaning	"
`	`	Process immediately; substitute resulting output into command	
"	"	Group characters into a single argument	"
#	#	Comment follows	!
†	!	History substitution[‡]	RECALL
†	%	Signifies a background job[‡]	

Table 2.6 *UNIX Special Characters and Their OpenVMS Equivalents (continued)*

Korn Shell Character	C Shell Character	UNIX Function	OpenVMS Equivalent
*	*	Matches any sequence of characters, including none at all	*
?	?	Matches any single character	%
$	$	Argument substitution follows	' or &
$#	$#	Argument count (C shell requires a variable name immediately following)	
$$	$$	Process ID	F$GETJPI("","PID")
$?	$status	Exit status	$STATUS
†	$<	Read one line from standard input	INQUIRE
†	@	Perform numerical calculation‡	
~	~	Home directory substitution	
[ ]	[ ]	Selective filename substitution	
( )	( )	Groups commands to run as a separate process in a subshell	
.	.	Current directory	[ ]
. .	. .	Next directory higher in hierarchy	[-]
	{ }	Filename expansion delimiters	

†Performed with a command, not metacharacters.

†May also be performed with a command, as well as with metacharacters.

‡Unique to the C shell.

2.5   **Using Wildcards**

UNIX wildcards extend those features found with OpenVMS wildcards.

```
UNIX
*              # All files (other than hidden files) in the current
                 directory and one level below
.              # Files in the current directory
.*             # All hidden files in the current directory and the
                 contents of hidden directories one level below
*.*            # All files in the current directory that contain a
                 period in the filename
*.com          # All files in the current directory that end in ".com"
?.com          # All files in the current directory that end in ".com"
                 and have one character preceding the period
name[xyz]      # Files in the current directory: namex, namey or
                 namez
name[a-z]      # All files in the current directory: namea, nameb,
                 ... namez
name[a-z4]     # All files in the current directory: namea, nameb,
                 ... namez and name4
name.{o,f}     # Files name.o and name.f in the current directory
                 (C shell only)
name.[of]      # Files name.o and name.f in the current directory
                 (C, Korn and Bourne)
```

There are no absolute rules for the use of wildcards. The output produced when using wildcards is command-dependent. For example, the command ls * produces a listing of files for both the current directory and the directory one level down the directory hierarchy. On the other hand, wc * (word count) produces output only for the files in the current directory.

As you can see, ls and wc appear to interpret the wildcard differently. The command ls . refers to all files pointed to by the "." (dot) file, that is, all files in the current directory. The command wc ., on the other hand, interprets the "." (dot) file literally, providing a word count of the pointer file itself.

In fact, neither ls nor wc actually sees an unquoted wildcard character when it processes a command. The Bourne, Korn, and C shells all perform *regular expression expansion*. In its simplest form, regular expression expansion allows OpenVMS users to use wildcards in UNIX in a familiar way.

For example, UNIX interprets `*.com` to mean any filename in the current directory ending in `.com`, even though `.com` has no meaning as a file extension. Corresponding to OpenVMS, which uses the percent sign (`%`), UNIX uses the question mark (`?`) as a wildcard for single-character replacement. Sections 5.4 and 5.5 discuss regular expressions in the context of two string manipulation commands, `sed` and `awk`. A more thorough explanation is beyond the scope of this book.

One might create a useful rule of thumb to deal with commands that give wild, unpredictable results or else produce little or no expected output: If you might be globbing, prevent it by quoting; if you're not globbing, do.

2.6 The Graphical User Interface

Depending on whether your system runs OpenVMS VAX or OpenVMS Alpha, you may well have been using either the DECwindows Motif desktop, the only supported GUI for VAX processors, or the New Desktop, Compaq's implementation of CDE on Alpha processors. If you have been using CDE, you will be happy to know that with relatively minor differences between manufacturers, CDE provides a consistent visual method for accessing applications, tools, and tasks between OpenVMS and various implementations of UNIX.

The standardization supplied by CDE means that OpenVMS users can perform some UNIX tasks without having to learn new commands and utilities. CDE provides graphical text editors, e-mail, and terminal emulators. For users new to UNIX, this means you need not master a new editor or memorize the various command options for the UNIX mail programs. The CDE File Manager provides a graphical view of directories and files with full drag-and-drop capability. File selection is a matter of mouse clicks rather than a new set of wildcards and new interpretations of special characters. You can click on the icons for various commands, rather than having to learn the character cell switches and arguments.

While many UNIX vendors support the CDE model, they have also added significant features to it in their implementations. System and network administration were traditionally rather complicated when using the command-line interface to UNIX. Several vendors have developed centralized GUIs for system and network management, reducing or removing the need to run separate scripts or utilities individually.

Similarly, there are GUIs available for Linux, including GNU Network Object Model Environment (GNOME) and K Desktop Environment

(KDE), in addition to X Windows. Depending on where you obtain the Linux distribution, you will have options as to which GUI to install.

We will not attempt in this book to teach CDE or other GUIs to those unfamiliar with them; many of the elementary modes of interaction map directly from other GUIs, such as the Microsoft Windows family of operating systems, and CDE's heritage from the X Windows System allows you to bring forward many customizations you may have used with DECwindows Motif.

2.7   Summary

The software architectures of OpenVMS and UNIX are similar. Nevertheless, the novice UNIX user must grasp several fundamental differences.

First, the novice UNIX user must learn to manage multiple processes (possibly for each window on a workstation), sometimes functioning in a cooperative fashion. In contrast, the OpenVMS user predominantly manages a single process that processes commands sequentially (discounting multiple workstation windows). Chapter 7 introduces the UNIX features for managing multiple processes, although we will encounter many examples before then.

Second, UNIX uses a different command syntax. UNIX command names, although short, cannot be abbreviated and do not always bring to mind the command's function. For example, the OpenVMS command TYPE is a more logical choice than cat for displaying a file at the terminal. Single-letter options modify the functions of UNIX commands in a manner similar to the OpenVMS command qualifiers.

Third, the novice UNIX user must learn new file and directory structures. Although bewildering at first, the elegance of the hierarchical arrangement of files and directories within the UNIX system becomes evident with use. You may address any file or directory, irrespective of the physical device, with an absolute pathname from the root or with a relative pathname from the current working directory. Numerous examples of these concepts appear in Chapter 4.

Fourth, the novice UNIX user must understand the concept of metacharacters, which have special functions when interpreted by the shell. We met several metacharacters in this chapter. Section 3.5 introduces the use of metacharacters for the recall and editing of command lines, known as *history substitution*.

Finally, many OpenVMS users will meet an old friend in the GUI CDE. Even if you have preferred the OpenVMS command-line interface, you may well find yourself more productive by taking advantage of the GUI, at least to start.

Getting Started

3

3

Getting Started

> *I was thinking that all these tables [pointing to some logarithms] might be calculated by machinery.*
>
> —*Charles Babbage*

You are now ready to begin a terminal session. This chapter explains how to tailor the interactive computing environment to suit your needs and introduces features helpful to the first-time user.

First, we discuss how to set the terminal characteristics to match a host computer environment. This process corresponds to the SET TERMINAL command in OpenVMS. Second, we provide instructions on how to customize the UNIX environment. This process corresponds to customizing the user's LOGIN.COM file in OpenVMS. Next, we discuss the important features of command-line editing and recall, which help you correct incorrect commands. Last, we discuss the UNIX online help system and printed documentation.

At first glance, defining a useful environment for interactive computing using UNIX appears complex. Fortunately, the novice user usually has to do very little (or nothing) to establish a usable environment. The system is distributed with default .profile, .login, .cshrc, and other hidden files, located in the directory /usr/skel in many versions of UNIX. The system administrator may have modified these files to reflect site-specific features. In any case, these files should have been copied to your home directory when your account was established. If these files are present, then you should already have a usable interactive environment.

Customizing the environment to suit individual needs, on the other hand, requires an understanding of the concepts introduced in Sections 3.1 and 3.2. Many readers may wish to work in the default environment until they become relatively adept at using UNIX, then reread Sections 3.1 and 3.2 in preparation for making changes to the interactive environment to better serve their needs.

At the conclusion of this chapter, you should be able to initiate a terminal session, issue commands, and log off; this is suitable preparation for the manipulation and editing of files, which we discuss in Chapters 4 and 5.

3.1   Terminal Characteristics

UNIX supports a wide range of hardware types. You may connect a terminal to each of these hardware types in a variety of ways; for example, by direct cable, modem, terminal server, network, or port selector. If your terminal is connected, but not displaying a banner message (usually identifying a particular computer) and the login prompt from the UNIX host, first check the terminal setup features. If your terminal is set up correctly, but is still not communicating with the UNIX host, see your system administrator.

If the wiring of your terminal to the host computer puts Data Terminal Ready (DTR) into operation, turn on the power to initiate a terminal session. If DTR is not in operation, initiate a terminal session by pressing <CR>.

Once the login prompt appears, UNIX performs a number of operations that determine which characteristics to assign the terminal requesting initialization. These operations illustrate a number of UNIX programs and lookup tables working cooperatively.

When you begin a terminal session, a program named /sbin/init[1] reads a lookup table residing in a file named /etc/ttys. This file contains an argument string for each physical terminal device /dev/tty and pseudoterminal device /dev/ptty (used for network connections) available on the system. OpenVMS and UNIX use different descriptors to define terminal devices. For terminals hard-wired to the computer, OpenVMS uses a four-character descriptor followed by a colon. The four characters consist of T for terminal, T or X depending on the controller type, a letter of the alphabet to designate the controller, and 0-7 (octal) to designate the device number. TTA0: and TXB7: are examples of OpenVMS descriptors. UNIX, on the other hand, uses a five-character descriptor: tty for a terminal device, 0-f (hexadecimal) for the controller ordinal, and 0-f for the line ordinal. Examples of UNIX descriptors are tty01 and ttyff. You can use

---

1.   This book uses absolute filenames for programs throughout.

the UNIX command `tty`, like the OpenVMS command `SHOW PROCESS`, to determine to which device or computer port your terminal is wired.

OpenVMS	**UNIX**
Example:	

```
$ SHOW PROCESS                              % tty
9-Nov-1997 22:59:26.84 User: TIWT           /dev/tty0f
Process ID: 8391
Node: YES1 Process name "TIWT"
Terminal    VTA116: LTA5125: (LLAT3-1)
...
```

The `/sbin/init` program passes the argument string to another program, `/usr/sbin/getty`, which looks for the argument string in the lookup table `/etc/gettydefs`. If `/usr/sbin/getty` does not find the argument, it uses default terminal settings. The settings derived from `/etc/gettydefs` include baud rate, parity, and the system banner message (equivalent to `SYS$ANNOUNCE` in OpenVMS). The table `/etc/gettydefs` also assigns a function to the `<BREAK>` key. Usually, pressing `<BREAK>` changes the baud rate of the host computer port. OpenVMS achieves the same effect more elegantly: The system administrator simply sets the terminal to `AUTOBAUD`, which automatically matches the speed of the computer port to the speed of the terminal.

When you enter your username at the login prompt, `/usr/sbin/getty` reads it and passes control to the `/usr/bin/login` program, which prompts you for your password. The `/usr/bin/login` program then checks for your username in the `/etc/passwd` file. If your username is there, it checks for the associated password. If the encrypted password entry in `/etc/passwd` agrees with the password you entered, the program grants you access to the system.

The sequence is a little different on systems that share accounts under Network Information Services (NIS) (Chapter 13). Account names and passwords are served to several systems through common files, `/var/yp/domain/passwd*`. When you log into a client system, it requests your account information from a server system in the same NIS domain. Once the account information is gathered, the rest of the login procedure is similar to the local model.

Note how this differs from OpenVMS! OpenVMS associates no process with a terminal line until it senses activity on that line. Only then does LOG-INOUT run, and it is responsible for the entire login sequence. Once you see the login prompt, you may type your username, a <RETURN>, and the password without hesitation. On UNIX, there is already a process associated with the line, and it is only responsible for beginning the login sequence. It then starts another process, passing to it the first line you type, your username. Text typed after the username may be lost unless the second process is ready to accept that text as indicated by the password: prompt.

The login program updates accounting information and searches the file /etc/group to determine to which groups a user belongs. Group names function similarly to the OpenVMS User Identification Code (UIC) for the protection of files. All files have group-level protection, which applies to users with the same group name. The difference is that an OpenVMS user always has a single UIC, whereas a UNIX user may belong to multiple groups. Group-level protection is distinct from world-level protection, which applies to all users. Refer to Section 4.2 for more information on file permissions. You can determine to which groups you belong with the groups command.

UNIX

Example:

```
% groups
system
```

The /usr/bin/login program invokes /etc/csh.login or /etc/profile, depending on your preferred shell. These are scripts for setting *environment variables*. Environment variables defined this way have effects similar to systemwide logical name assignments in OpenVMS (see Section 3.2), although any user may change or remove those defined for his or her login session. At this point a copy of the default shell, defined in /etc/passwd or var/yp/domain /passwd*, is made available to the user. The shell presents the default prompt: a pound sign (#) for the Bourne shell, a dollar sign ($) for the Korn and bash shells, and a percent sign (%) for the C shell. The shell is now ready to receive commands.

In OpenVMS, the system administrator can assign an entire range of privileges to each individual user, such as the ability to change the characteristics of the user's own or other users' processes, or the ability to change the characteristics of physical devices attached to the system. In UNIX, on the other hand, each user has the same limited set of privileges with the exception of the *superuser* (login name root). The superuser possesses all privileges, including access to all files on the system, irrespective of their assigned protection.

The on-screen messages that appear when a user logs in successfully depend on the host computer, but will likely include features familiar to OpenVMS users, such as the current time and the time when the user last logged in. If the .hushlogin file is present in the user's home directory, these messages will not appear. Note that .hushlogin is an example of a hidden file (see Section 2.3.3). The mere existence of this file suppresses the introductory messages; its contents are irrelevant.

In the following example, the user issues the cp command (see Section 4.10) to create an empty file named .hushlogin in the home directory. When the user logs out and logs in again, the system's introductory messages no longer appear.

OpenVMS

Example:

```
GOBLUE - OpenVMS V7.1
Username SYSTEM
Password:
Last interactive login on Thursday, 15-DEC-1996 10:14
Last noninteractive login on Tuesday, 13-DEC-1996 19:30
Welcome to OpenVMS V7.1
$
```

UNIX

Example:

```
HP-UX eupher B.11.22 U ia64 (ta)
login: root
password
(c)Copyright 1983-2002 Hewlett-Packard Co., All Rights Reserved.
(c)Copyright 1979, 1980, 1983, 1985-1993 The Regents of the Univ. of
California
(c)Copyright 1980, 1984, 1986 Novell, Inc.
(c)Copyright 1986-2000 Sun Microsystems, Inc.
(c)Copyright 1985, 1986, 1988 Massachusetts Institute of Technology
(c)Copyright 1989-1993  The Open Software Foundation, Inc.
(c)Copyright 1986 Digital Equipment Corp.
(c)Copyright 1990 Motorola, Inc.
(c)Copyright 1990, 1991, 1992 Cornell University
(c)Copyright 1989-1991 The University of Marylan
(c)Copyright 1988 Carnegie Mellon University
(c)Copyright 1991-2002 Mentat Inc.
(c)Copyright 1996 Morning Star Technologies, Inc.
(c)Copyright 1996 Progressive Systems,
```

Example:

```
% cp /dev/nl .hushlogin
% logout
HP-UX eupher B.11.22 U ia64 (ta)
login: root
password:
%
```

If your terminal is wired directly to the computer and is unlikely to be changed for long periods of time, the system administrator may unambiguously assign it a terminal type. This terminal descriptor resides in the file /etc/ttys, or on some systems, the file /etc/ttytype. This descriptor, for example vt100, matches an entry in the file /etc/termcap, which defines a set of characteristics for the terminal (compare with the OpenVMS command SET TERMINAL /DEVICE_TYPE=VT100). Other UNIX systems bypass this and simply specify a terminal type to /usr/sbin/getty or send one through a reference into /etc/termcap. The file /etc/termcap contains information on a large number of terminals from different manufacturers. OpenVMS, in contrast, only carries definitions for VT terminals, although you can define others. The terminal definitions in /etc/termcap are usually sufficient. The operating system has another opportunity to set terminal characteristics automatically; see above where /usr/sbin/getty is discussed. If necessary, you can change a terminal type assignment at any point during a terminal session.

In situations in which different terminals use the same computer port, for example, in the case of modem lines, port selectors, or network connections, you cannot unambiguously define the terminal type. In these situations, UNIX matches a generic terminal definition in /etc/ttys or /etc/ttytypes (e.g., dialup or network) to a generic definition in /etc/termcap. The user may then set the terminal characters, using the commands tset and stty.

OpenVMS users, presumably already using Compaq VT–compatible terminals or terminal emulators, need do very little to make their terminals respond in a satisfactory manner (see the discussion of the `setenv TERM vt100` command in the following section). For reference, we illustrate some uses of the `tset` and `stty` commands below, even though, regrettably, they are two of the more complex commands. To quote the BSD documentation on the `tset` command, "Here is a fancy example to hopelessly confuse anyone who has made it this far." Nevertheless, the documentation for `tset` does contain examples that are helpful in making terminal assignments.

UNIX
Example:
```
% stty dec
```
Example:
```
% stty crt erase ^? kill ^U
```
Example:
```
: % tset -I -Q
```
Example:
```
% tset --Q -m network:vt100
```

The `tset` command sets the input/output characteristics for a terminal session, and `stty` sets the keyboard characteristics. In the first example, `stty` sets all modes suitable for Compaq terminal users. In the second example, `stty` explicitly sets characteristics for a terminal (`crt`), rather than for a hardcopy device. The delete key backspaces over the previous character to delete it instead of echoing it and its replacement within string delimiters. The erase character (<CTRL>-H) functions like the delete key; and delete line is set to <CTRL>-U. Note that as the user types `stty crt erase` <DELETE> `kill` <CTRL>-U, the terminal echoes ^? and ^U for the <DELETE> key and <CTRL>-U, respectively.

In the third example, `tset -I -Q` suppresses terminal initialization messages (`I`) and the display of keycap definitions (`Q`). In the last example, `tset -- Q -m network:vt100` sets the terminal characteristics to a VT100 when accessing the host UNIX system via a network connection. The hyphen displays the terminal characteristics, once defined, on the terminal screen. The `m` (map) option maps the argument that follows to an entry in `/etc/ttys`, in this case a network device.

Use `stty everything` or `tset` (with no options or arguments) to review the current terminal environment, as illustrated in the following examples:

UNIX

Example:

```
% stty everything
#2 disc;speed 9600 baud; 36 rows; 94 columns
erase = ^?; werase = <undef>; kill = ^U; intr = ^C; quit = ^\
susp = ^Z; dsusp = <undef>; eof = ^D; eol = ^@; eol2 = <undef>
stop = ^S; start = ^Q; lnext = <undef>; discard = <undef>; reprint
= <undef>
status = <undef>; time = 0; min = 1
-parenb parodd cs8 cstopb hupcl cread -clocal -crtscts
-ignbrk brkint -ignpar -parmrk -inpck -istrip -inlcr -igncr icrnl
-iuclc
ixon -ixany ixoff imaxbel
isig icanon -xcase echo echoe echok -echonl -noflsh -mdmbuf -
nohang
-tostop echoctl -echoprt echoke -altwerase iexten -nokerninfo
opost -olcuc onlcr -ocrnl -onocr -onlret -ofill -ofdel tabs -
onoeot
```

Example:

```
% tset
Erase is delete
Kill is ctrl-U
Interrupt is Ctrl-C
```

The `tset` command possesses the functions of both the OpenVMS commands SET and SHOW. Used without options or arguments, `tset` displays the current terminal characteristics. With options or arguments, `tset` changes the terminal characteristics. This dual functionality is a typical feature of UNIX commands that set variables. Commands that do not set variables, yet require options or arguments, behave differently. If you give such commands without options or arguments, UNIX will likely respond with the correct syntax (a "usage" message), as shown in the example below. The two commands illustrated here, `cp` (copy) and `mv` (move or rename), are discussed in detail in Sections 4.10 and 4.11, respectively.

UNIX

Example:

```
% cp
usage: cp [-ip] f1 f2;
or: cp [-irp] f1 ... fn d2
```

```
or: cp -r [-ip] d1 d2
```
Example:
```
% mv
usage: mv [-if] f1 f2 or mv [-if] f1 ... fn d1 ('fn' is a file or
directory
```

To a novice UNIX user, the login sequence may seem complex and disconcerting. However, keep in mind that much of the sequence is *transparent* to the novice user and is included here to illustrate that UNIX has a modular structure enabling a number of programs and lookup tables to function cooperatively.

3.2   User Environment

Users have great flexibility when defining their environment. One method uses the hidden files `.login` (C shell) or `.profile` (Korn, Bourne, or bash shells) located in the parent directory. These correspond directly to the OpenVMS file LOGIN.COM. As noted above, `/etc/csh.login` (C shell) and `/etc/profile` (Korn shell) establish a set of global characteristics called *environment variables*. Users can change the default values of these variables, or add to them, during login by including the appropriate definitions in the `.profile` or `.login` file. Users can also redefine environment variables or add new ones at any time during a terminal session. Environment variables are independent of the shell; that is, they are in effect regardless of what shell is being used.

A second method for defining the user environment applies only to those commands interpreted by the shell. The hidden file `.cshrc`, located in the parent directory, governs the C shell environment; a file named by the variable ENV governs the Korn and Bourne shell environments. Entries in these files define shell variables. When the shell parses a command line, it either interprets the command (referred to as a *built-in command*) or forks a new process, which executes a separate program. By default, the new process receives the characteristics found in both `.login` and `.cshrc`, or `.profile` and ENV. Before discussing how to customize the various files, let us deal with the major environment variables and their functions.

The `printenv` command determines which environment variables have been assigned to a terminal session, either by the user or by the system. The following example shows a typical environment. By convention, environment variables appear in uppercase.

UNIX

```
% printenv

HOME=/usr/users/system              # Parent directory

SHELL=/bin/csh                      # C shell as default

TERM=network                        # Terminal type

PATH=/usr/ucb:/bin:/usr/users \     # Directories to search for
/system/bin:/usr/bin:/usr \         commands
/local:/usr/new:/etc:.

EDITOR=/usr/ucb/vi                  # Default editor

MAIL=/usr/.pool/mail/system         # Place to store mail
                                    messages

EXINIT=set ai aw ic sw=4 redraw /   # Predefine editing
wm=4|map g G|map v ~~~~             features
```

HOME serves the same function as SYS$LOGIN in OpenVMS, defining the user's home, or parent, directory. SHELL indicates the shell that is being used to process commands, corresponding to the OpenVMS command-language interpreter. TERM returns the terminal type, corresponding to the OpenVMS lexical function F$GETDVI("TT:","DEVTYP"). USER returns the user login name, corresponding to the OpenVMS lexical function F$GETJPI("pid","USERNAM"). PATH identifies the directories the system must search to resolve command requests, most closely corresponding to SYS$SYSTEM, though augmented with other directories.

When you issue a command, the shell program parses the command line and either processes it directly or passes control to a program in the first of the directories specified by PATH that contains the command. Directory paths in PATH are separated by a colon. In the example above, note the dot, which specifies the current working directory in the PATH list. You should order the PATH list so that the directories referenced most frequently appear first in the list.[2] You may add your own directories to the PATH list to search for your own specific commands. UNIX users commonly design a directory structure similar to the one used by the operating system: ~*user*/bin to store executable files, ~*user*/lib to store libraries, and so on.

---

2.   Always place the current working directory last in the PATH list to avoid a serious security risk. The reason behind this is the supposition that it is easier for an unauthorized user to place a command (e.g., ls) in a user's home directory, or that a user might do so inadvertently. In either case, a user is likely to execute the wrong command.

EDITOR specifies the default editor, in this case vi (see Section 5.2). MAIL indicates the location of e-mail messages and corresponds to the OpenVMS SET MAIL_DIRECTORY command in the MAIL utility (see Section 6.1.8). EXINIT defines the characteristics of the editing environment for the vi editor and corresponds to the definitions contained in the SYS$LOGIN:TPUINI.TPU file used to customize the OpenVMS TPU editor.

3.2.1 Customizing the .login File (C Shell)

The UNIX command setenv defines environment variables in the .login file, as shown in the following examples.

UNIX
Form:
```
% setenv NAME value        # Make Bourne shell the default
```
Example:
```
% setenv SHELL /bin/sh
% setenv TERM vt100        # Give terminal the characteristics of
                             a VT100
```

In the first example, setenv SHELL /bin/sh sets the SHELL environment variable to /bin/sh, the Bourne shell program (/bin/csh refers to the C shell program). In the second example, setenv TERM vt100 sets the terminal type to a VT100, recommended for OpenVMS users who have VT100, VT200, or VT300 series terminals or compatibles.

Some C shell variables have the same names as environment variables, but in lowercase. C shell and environment variables with the same names also have similar functions. For example, HOME and home both define the home directory. The distinction is only important when the user invokes more than one shell. If HOME is defined in the .login file as one directory, and the user then invokes the C shell with home defined in the file .cshrc as a different directory, the latter will be in effect. The set command defines shell variables. Shell variable definitions can reside in the .login file, which is meaningful if you invoke the C shell during login, or in the shell definition file .cshrc, discussed in the following section. Figure 3.1 illustrates a simple .login file for a terminal session, including examples of the setenv and set commands.

In this example, the tset and stty commands set the terminal environment (see Section 3.1). The umask command sets the default file protec-

Figure 3.1
A sample .login file.

```
stty dec new cr0
tset -I -Q umask 027
setenv EDITOR '/usr/ucb/vi'
setenv MAIL /usr/spool/mail/$USER
setenv SHELL /bin/csh
setenv EXINIT 'set ai aw ic sw=4 redraw wm=4 | map g G | map v \
~~~~'
set savehist=50
set mail=$MAIL
set prompt="! - $USER>"
biff y
```

tion, and corresponds to the OpenVMS command SET PROTECTION/ DEFAULT. The three octal digits refer to owner, group, and world access, respectively. Unlike OpenVMS, UNIX offers no system-level protection; as noted above, the superuser has access to all files at all times. In this example, a value of 0 indicates read, write, and execute access, 2 indicates read and execute access, and 7 indicates no access. Thus, 027 indicates read-write-execute access for the owner, read-execute access for the group, and no world access. We will show that the umask notation is the reverse of that used for setting individual file permissions. Sections 4.2 and 8.4.1 discusses file permissions in more detail.

A C shell variable called savehist indicates the number of command lines that you may save for your next terminal session. At the conclusion of each terminal session, the last *n* commands—in this case 50— are saved to the hidden file .history located in your home directory. At the beginning of the next terminal session, the C shell reads the file .history into the *history list*. The history list is the name given to those commands that can be recalled with the C shell history command (compare with the OpenVMS command RECALL/INPUT). The history command is discussed in Section 3.5.

The shell variable mail and the environment variable MAIL define directories to store incoming and unread mail messages[3] (compare with the folder called MAIL used by the OpenVMS MAIL utility and the MAIL_DIRECTORY setting). The command mail=$MAIL introduces our first example of *variable substitution*. The dollar sign ($) functions is a metacharacter that when placed before a variable name causes substitution for the value of that variable, in this instance a directory name.

---

3.   Many mail processing programs now define this directory with their own internal settings.

The `prompt` variable defines an alternative prompt to `%` for the C shell (compare with the OpenVMS command `SET PROMPT`). The exclamation point (`!`) is a metacharacter interpreted by the C shell as the beginning of a *history substitution* (see Section 3.5). It indicates the current command number. In the example in Section 3.5, the current command number, which precedes the username (based on the substitution of the environment variable `USER`), echoes to the screen. For example, when user `root` issues the first command of a terminal session, the prompt `1 - root>` will appear on the screen. The quotes surrounding the prompt string in the `.login` file delimit the value assigned to the variable `prompt`; without quotes, a blank is used as a delimiter. We will meet other examples of the use of the exclamation point as a metacharacter to invoke a history substitution later in Section 3.5.

The last line of the sample `.login` file contains the `biff` command (BSD only), which was named after the dog of a graduate student at the University of Berkeley. The `biff` command turns notification of incoming mail on and off. Having mail notification turned on (`biff y`) is analogous to having the dog bark whenever mail arrives. The default, `biff n`, corresponds to the OpenVMS command `SET BROADCAST = NOMAIL`; `biff y` corresponds to `SET BROADCAST = MAIL`.

3.2.2   Customizing the .cshrc File (C Shell)

The C shell environment definition file `.cshrc` usually consists of two types of commands, `set` and `alias`. As discussed above, the `set` command defines C shell variables. Table 3.1 lists variables that you might use with `set` in the `.cshrc` file. We will discuss the meaning of many of these variables in later chapters. Note, however, the variable `noclobber`. All novice UNIX users should set the variable `noclobber`. Since UNIX maintains only the current version of a file, you must take care to prevent the inadvertent overwriting, or clobbering, of files when redirecting them (see Section 2.1.3). With `noclobber` set, you cannot redirect output to an existing file. If you inadvertently redirect output to an existing file, you will receive an error message.

The command `alias` (compare with the OpenVMS construct `:==`) redefines command names to make them easier to remember, to abbreviate them, or both. You may abbreviate a command, or a commonly used sequence of commands performing a specific function, to a single user-defined command.

UNIX (C Shell)

Form:

```
% alias name wordlist
```

Example:

```
% alias DIR 'ls -l | more'
```

Example:

```
% alias DIR 'ls -l \!* | more'
```

Form:

```
% unalias name
```

Example:

```
% alias
DIR     ls -l !* | more
E       emacs
back    set back = $old; set old = $cwd; cd $back; unset\back; dirs
cd      set old = $cwd; chdir !*
cp      cp -i !*
del     rm -I
mv      mv -i !*
no      /system 1/system/scripts/number.scr
q       /usr/public/queues.scr
t1500   lpr -P laser
% unalias DIR
```

In the first example, alias DIR 'ls -l | more', the name DIR is made equal to the ls -l command piped to the more command. The command ls, with the -l option, produces an extended listing of the file specification. This command corresponds to the OpenVMS command DIRECTORY/PROTECTION/DATE/OWNER/SIZE (see Section 4.1). The more command functions like the OpenVMS command TYPE/PAGE, listing the contents of a file one screen at a time (see Sections 4.8 and 8.2.1). The single quote delimits the string you wish to redefine. You can also use double quotes.

Would the command DIR *.f list all FORTRAN source files, one screen at a time? The answer is no. The shell would parse the command line as ls -l followed by more *.f. That is, it would list all files in the directory followed by the display of the contents of all files with names that terminate in .f. To associate the argument with the first command in the pipe, you must use a history substitution. In the second example, alias DIR 'ls -l \!* | more', the backslash (\), another metacharacter, prevents the immediate parsing of the history substitution when the alias is defined. Instead, the substitution takes place when the alias is invoked. As shown previously, the exclamation point invokes a command from the history list, and the asterisk, another metacharacter, indicates the last argument of that com-

Table 3.1 *Some Shell Variables*

Korn Shell* Variable	C Shell Variable	OpenVMS Equivalent	Meaning
$1, $2, etc.	argv, or $1, $2, etc.	P1, P2, etc.	Arguments to the shell or to a shell script
†allexport			Automatically exports all variables subsequently defined
TMOUT=*n*	autologout = *n*		Sets number of minutes (C) or seconds (Korn) of idle time before an interactive shell terminates
CDPATH= *string*	cdpath = *string*		Sets alternative directory tree search for cd command
PWD	cwd	F$DIRECTORY()	Sets current working directory
†xtrace	echo	SET VERIFY	Echoes command lines and arguments
EDITOR = *string*	editmode = *string*		Sets name of editor to emulate for command-line editing
	histchars = *string*		Replaces default of ! for history substitution
HISTEDIT			Sets name of the editor used for the history file
HISTFILE= *string*		RECALL/INPUT	Names the command history file
HISTSIZE=*n*	history = *n*	RECALL	Remembers last *n* commands for recall
HOME=*string*	home = *string*	SYS$LOGIN	Sets home directory
IFS=*string*	breakchars = *string*	TPU word separator definitions	Sets internal field separators, usually space, tab, and new line

Table 3.1   *Some Shell Variables (continued)*

Korn Shell[*] Variable	C Shell Variable	OpenVMS Equivalent	Meaning
[†]ignoreeof	ignoreeof		Prevents <CTRL>-D logouts; requires use of logout (C shell) or exit (Korn, Bourne shells) command
MAILPATH= *string*	mail = *string*	SET MAIL_DIRECTORY	Sets where shell checks for mail
[†]noclobber	noclobber		Prevents unintentional overwriting during redirection
[†]noglob	noglob		Prevents expansion of filenames
	nonomatch		Prevents error status if no file match to command is found
[†]notify	notify		Sets time of notification of job completion
PATH=*string*	path = *string*	logical name defined as a search list	Sets search path to resolve command calls
PS1=*string*1 PS2=*string*2	prompt = *string*	SET PROMPT	Sets an alternative prompt to the default C shell prompt of % or Korn shell $ prompt and continuation > prompt
RANDOM			Returns a random number between 0 and 32,767
REPLY		INQUIRE	Contains text of user's response to a prompt
	savehist = *n*	RECALL/OUTPUT	Remembers last *n* commands for recall at beginning of next terminal session

Table 3.1 *Some Shell Variables (continued)*

Korn Shell* Variable	C Shell Variable	OpenVMS Equivalent	Meaning
`SHELL, or` `$0 at login`	`shell = ` *`string`*	`F$GETJPI ("",` `"CLINAME")`	Sets path to the shell program
`$?`	`status`	`$STATUS`	Displays status as command completion: 1 = error; 0 = no error
`TERM`	`term`	`F$GETDVI("TT:",` `"DEVTYPE")`	Sets terminal type
	`time = ` *`n`*		Causes any command taking longer than *n* seconds to report CPU and elapsed time
`USER`	`user`	`F$GETJPI ("",` `"USERNAME")`	Sets username
†`verbose`	`verbose`	`SET VERIFY`	Causes the words of each command to be echoed after history substitution

*   Most Korn shell variables are identical in the bash shell.
†   Available using `set -o` command

mand. Using the revised definition of `DIR` from the second example, `DIR` `*.f` now functions correctly: The argument `*.f` is passed to `ls -l`, and the long directory listing of all files ending in `.f` is piped to `more` for display.

In the last example, `alias` without options or arguments illustrates the UNIX convention regarding commands that set variables: If issued without arguments, commands that set variables return the values established with previous use of the command.

The `unalias` command, as the name suggests, removes a previously defined alias. Figure 3.2 illustrates a typical `.cshrc` file composed of `alias` and `set` commands.

If you make changes to the `.cshrc` file, you must issue the command `source` before the changes take effect for the current shell. The command `source` is built into the C shell (see Section 10.9.44). The command `source` `.cshrc` corresponds to the OpenVMS command `@SYS$LOGIN:LOGIN.COM`,

Figure 3.2
A sample .cshrc file.

```
set autologout = 30
set prompt = "cuhhmd>"
set cdpath = ( $HOME/sys /usr/sys /usr/spool )
set path = (/usr/ucb /bin $HOME/bin /usr/bin /usr/local \
/usr/new /etc .)
set notify set history = 100
set inc = /usr/include
alias pwd 'echo $cwd'
alias h history
alias pd pushd
alias pop popd
alias cd 'set old = $cwd: chdir \!*'
alias back 'set back = $old; set old = $cwd; cd $back; \
unset back; dirs'
```

which the user issues after making changes to the LOGIN.COM file to have the changes take effect immediately.

You could invoke .cshrc without the source command, but because UNIX creates a new process to execute .cshrc, the effect of the set and alias commands would be lost. See Section 2.1 for a discussion of process and command execution.

```
OpenVMS                              UNIX (C shell)
Example:
$ @SYS$LOGIN:LOGIN                   % source .cshrc
```

Note that any child process created will include the characteristics defined in the new .cshrc file, for the system executes this file by default each time it forks a new process.

3.2.3 Customizing the .profile and ENV Files (Korn Shell)

Like the C shell, the Korn shell has a four-layer structure to set up a user environment: the script /etc/profile for definitions common to all users on a system; the script $HOME/.profile for the customizations you want when you first log in; the ENV environment variable script for customizations you will want every time you create a Korn shell process or run a Korn shell script; and, finally, commands you type interactively.

While the Korn shell and the C shell share most concepts and capabilities, the syntax you use can be quite different. Here are some constructs we'll soon see in practical use, bearing in mind that we will revisit this subject in Chapter 10.

OpenVMS

Form:
```
$ SYMBOL="string"
$ SYMBOL:=string
```

Example:
```
$ FISHIN="Hook      Line Sinker"
```

UNIX (Korn Shell)

```
$ variable=string
$ variable="string string"
$ variable='string'
$ fishin=Hook      Line Sinker
$ fishin="Hook      Line Sinker"
$ fishin='Hook      Line Sinker'
$ catch="$basstypes $scrod catfish"
$ catch='$basstypes $scrod catfish'
```

Form:
```
$ SYMBOL=="string"
$ SYMBOL:==string
```

Example:
```
$ MYCATS=="Blinker Tiegy"
```

```
$ variable=string
$ export string
```

```
$ mycats=Blinker Tiegy
$ export mycats
```

Form:
```
$ SYMBOL:==command/switches
```

Example:
```
$ DSD==DIRE/PROT/SIZE/DATE
```

```
$ alias symbol="command -switches"
```

```
$ alias dsd="ls -l"
```

The Korn shell is a little finicky when it comes to variable assignments. In many situations, the shell allows all the white space you could want for readability's sake, but a variable assignment requires that the equals sign have no space surrounding it.

You can quote an entire string using single (') or double quotes (") or a single character using the backslash (\). Each type is appropriate in different situations. In the first example, we want to keep the extra white space between the first two words of the string. Without quotes, the variable `fishin` contains `Hook Line Sinker`—with a single space between each word. The two quoted versions of the Korn shell assignment are exactly equivalent, keeping the `Hook` and the `Line` well away from one another. Although confusing to read, we could also have quoted each space with a backslash. The second example shows a simple instance where the two quote types differ. The double quote allows variable substitution to take place, while the single quote prevents it. If we had earlier defined `basstypes` to be `striped albino` and `scrod` to be `cod guppies`, we would end up with `catch` containing `striped albino cod guppies catfish` with the double quotes and `$basstypes $scrod catfish` with the single quoted version.

As OpenVMS variables have scope within command procedures, Korn shell variables are normally available only within the script or shell in which they're defined. To make them available elsewhere, use the `export` command. In the third example, `Blinker` and `Tiegy` become cats everywhere.

The command `alias` redefines command names to make them easier to remember, to abbreviate them, or both. You may abbreviate a single command or combine a commonly used sequence of commands that perform a specific function into a single user-defined command. The fourth example shows a way you can simplify moving between OpenVMS and UNIX by defining a symbol useful in both. An `alias` may only be used as the first word of a command. Figure 3.3 shows a simple `.profile` file to customize the user's environment.

Figure 3.3
A sample .profile file.

```
stty dec
stty erase '^H'
tset -I -Q
set -o emacs
MAIL=/usr/spool/mail/$USER
TERM=vt100 ; export TERM
PATH=$HOME:$HOME/bin:/usr/bin:/usr/sbin:/usr/ccs/bin:/usr/bin \
 /X11:/usr/local:.
export PATH
PS1="'whoami'@'hostname -s' [\${PWD}]$ "
umask 027
biff y
```

We begin with three commands to customize the terminal environment (Section 3.1). The command `set -o emacs` tells the Korn shell that we wish to use Emacs-style editing of command lines (Section 3.5).

`MAIL` defines the default directory in which to store mail messages as they are retrieved[4] (compare with the folder called `MAIL` used by the OpenVMS `MAIL` utility and the `MAIL_DIRECTORY` setting). Here we see a variable substitution used in the definition of another variable. If $USER (Section 3.2) is defined as peter, then MAIL will equate to the string /usr/spool/mail/peter.

The TERM variable, while maintained by the shell, is not used by it. Other commands, such as vi, use TERM as a reference into /etc/termcap to determine the kind of terminal on which they are run. The semicolon shows another feature of the shell: You can put more than one command on a line. For short, closely tied commands such as these two, you can make the relationship more visually obvious. Here, export TERM says that the variable should be available once .profile has completed execution, which is necessary for vi to reference it.

PATH was described in Section 3.2. Again, we see variable substitution used in the context of the definition of another variable. If $HOME (Section 3.2) is /usr/users/suzi, then the value of PATH is /usr/users/suzi:/usr/users/suzi/bin:/usr/bin:... We have chosen to put export PATH on a separate line this time, simply for the sake of readability.

The Korn shell defines three levels of prompting and another string to help with debugging:

- PS1   The primary prompt string

- PS2   The secondary prompt string, used for continuation lines

- PS3   Prompt string for a select (Section 10.8.9) command

- PS4   A marker for traced commands (Section 10.10)

In Figure 3.3, we illustrate *command substitution*, where the output written to stdout from execution of one command becomes either part of the command to another, or part of its resultant output. Korn shell allows two different syntaxes to invoke command substitution; we use the one that encloses the command in the grave accent marks. The definition of PS1 shows two cases of command substitution and one instance of variable substitution. The whoami command (Section 12.1.1) returns the current username; hostname -s returns the name of the network host on which you are running, less the domain name (Section 13.2.1). PWD is the environment variable for the present working directory (compare to the default directory). Because the whole string is quoted, command substitution does not occur until the shell needs to evaluate PS1. The backslash further quotes the

---

4.   Many mail processing programs now define this directory with their own, internal settings.

dollar sign introducing the PWD variable to the same effect. PWD is enclosed in braces so that the following character, a square bracket, does not appear to the shell as part of the variable name. If user peter is logged in to pegasus.school.edu and is in the directory /home/nathan, then the prompt becomes peter@pegasus [/home/nathan].

One feature of the Korn shell is that it lets you include the current command number in the prompt; this becomes useful if you decide to use command-line editing (Section 3.5). For example, PS1='!$' at the 23rd command you're about to issue will prompt you with "23$".

This example of a .profile file duplicates from the C shell .login example both the umask and the biff commands. The biff command is entirely separate from any shell, and umask, while implemented as both a Korn and C shell command, is essentially the same between the two. The Korn shell adds the ability to specify file permissions in their symbolic, rather than octal, forms and to display them with the -S switch. See Sections 4.2 and 8.4.1 for a discussion of file permissions.

Many users define the ENV environment variable to point to $HOME/.kshrc. You would use ENV to define symbols that are needed for each instance of a Korn shell you created (e.g., multiple windows on a workstation). Figure 3.4 gives an example.

Figure 3.4
A sample ENV (.kshrc) file.

```
alias kermit="/usr/users/kermit/wermit"
alias zip="/usr/users/zip/zip"
alias unzip="/usr/users/zip/unzip"
```

These three alias commands allow a user to invoke some popular applications without having to remember where they are located or to put their paths into PATH.

If you change either .profile or the file to which ENV points, you will

OpenVMS	UNIX (Korn shell)
Form:	
$ @*command-file*	$. script
Example:	
$ @SYS$LOGIN:LOGIN	$. $ENV

probably want the change to take effect immediately in your current shell. Simply invoking the scripts won't work, since the shell creates a new shell in order to execute a script. You must execute the script in the context of your current shell, a task you accomplish with the dot (.) command.

3.2.4 Setting the Password

You may change your password at any time using the `passwd` command (compare with the OpenVMS command `SET PASSWORD`). On systems setup to use NIS (Section 11.7.4), the `yppasswd` command is used. Regardless, neither the old nor the new password echoes to the terminal screen.

OpenVMS	UNIX
Example:	

```
$ SET PASSWORD          % passwd        # Change local password
Old password:           Old password:
New password:           New password:
Verification:           Retype new password:

                        % yppasswd      # Change distributed password
                        Changing NIS password for user Ralph
                        Old NIS password
                        New password:
                        Retype new password:
```

For security reasons, your password should be at least six characters long. Avoid using metacharacters in naming passwords, as they may provoke an unpredictable response from the UNIX operating system. It is a good idea to use nonalphabetic characters, as well as uppercase and lowercase characters, but remember that the `/bin/login` program is case-sensitive.

3.3 Logging Out

You may end a terminal session in one of two ways, depending on whether the C shell variable `ignoreeof` or the Bourne and Korn option `-o ignoreeof` has been set. If `ignoreeof` is set, you must use the `logout` command (C shell) or the `exit` command (Bourne, bash, and Korn shells) to log out of the system. If `ignoreeof` is not set, you may use <CTRL>-D.

UNIX uses the <CTRL>-D command as the end-of-file (EOF) marker, and entering it terminates input from the terminal. Think of the shell as another program, a program that reads input from the terminal rather than a file. Just as input from a file is terminated with an EOF marker, so is input from the terminal. The C shell looks in the hidden file `.logout` in your parent directory for any user-specific functions to perform before ending the terminal session. It is common practice to place the `clear` command in this file to clear the terminal screen at the end of the session: This is useful if you don't want anyone to see all the mistakes you've been making! After performing any user-specific functions, the shell searches for the system-wide logout file `/sbin/logout` for any further commands to process. Finally, the shell passes control back to `/sbin/init`, which initiated the terminal session and now gracefully ends it.

You will not be able to log out if there are any stopped jobs in the background. Novice UNIX users often generate stopped jobs in the background inadvertently. Novice users who get "stuck" while issuing commands often try <CTRL>-Z to get back to the prompt, a common strategy in OpenVMS. In UNIX, <CTRL>-Z will return the prompt, returning control to the parent process, while leaving the child process in a stopped background state. The UNIX command `jobs` lists stopped processes in the background (compare with the OpenVMS command SHOW PROCESS /SUBPROCESSES). If these are unwanted processes you may enter `logout` (C shell), or `exit` (Korn and Bourne shells), or press <CTRL>-D again (depending on whether `ignoreeof` is set) to remove the stopped processes and end the terminal session.

You do not need to understand the features of background processing at this point. Stopped jobs and background processing, great strengths of the UNIX operating system, are discussed in Section 7.4.

3.4   **Control Key Functions**

As in OpenVMS, <CTRL> plays a special role in a UNIX terminal session. You may use the `stty` command to modify the functions associated with the control key.

Although <CTRL>-Q and <CTRL>-S stop and start terminal output on most systems, most users prefer the *hold screen* key found on many keyboards. As noted above, <CTRL>-Z will suspend a child process and return control to the parent process (compare with the OpenVMS command <CTRL>-Y, followed by CONTINUE). The <CTRL>-D command will end a terminal session if `ignoreeof` is not set (Section 3.3). The <CTRL>-L command will refresh the terminal screen (compare with the command <CTRL>-W in many OpenVMS utilities). Like the OpenVMS command <CTRL>-C, UNIX <CTRL>-C kills the current child process and returns control to the parent shell process.

3.5   **Editing and Recall of Command Lines**

We have already touched briefly on the C shell `history` command and the use of the history file present in both the C and Korn shells. We will now discuss them in more detail in reference to the recall of command lines.

OpenVMS V7.1 maintains a history list of up to the last 254 commands (formerly limited to 20). Since OpenVMS command recall is memory-based rather than file-based,[5] commands are available only during the current process and terminal session by issuing the `RECALL` command. Furthermore, buffering of commands limits the total space to a maximum of 80 48-character commands, and commands that exceed that space limit, or the 254 limit on the count, are lost. UNIX trades these restrictions for the pleasures of working with limited versions of the `vi` and `Emacs` editors. Some of the comparable commands in OpenVMS and UNIX are listed below:

OpenVMS	UNIX	
`$ RECALL/ALL`	`% history`	# Display history list (C shell and bash sshell)
`$ RECALL/ALL`	`$ history` `$ fc -l`	# Display history list (Korn shell), the command for which history is an alias
`$ <uparrow>` `or <CRTL>-B`	`$ r` `$ fc -e -`	# Execute last command (Korn shell), the command for which *r* is an alias
`$ <UPARROW>` `or <CRTL>-B`	`$ <UPARROW>` `or <CRTL>-P`	# Execute previous command (bash shell)
	`% !`*n*	# Execute history list command number *n* (C shell and bash shell)
	`$ r` *n*	# Execute history list command number *n* (Korn shell)
`$ RECALL` *string*	`% !`*string*	# Execute the last command beginning with string (C shell and bash shell)
`$ RECALL` *string*	`$ r` *string*	# Execute the last command beginning with string (Korn shell)
	`$ <ESC>->`	# Execute last command in the history (bash shell)

---

5.   While explicit saves to and restores from files are possible, an individual command may only be referenced from the copy in memory.

	`% !?`*string*`?`	# Execute the last command containing string (C shell)
`$ RECALL `*N*	`% !-`*n*	# Execute *n*th command ago (C shell)
`$ RECALL `*N*	`$ r -`*n*	# Execute *n*th command ago (Korn shell)
	`$ r` *string1=string* *2 n*	# Execute history list command number *n*, but substitute *string2* for *string1* (Korn shell)
	`$ <CRTL>-N`	# Execute next command in the history (bash shell)
	`$ <ESC>-<`	# Execute first command in the history (bash shell)
	`$ <CTRL>-R`	# Search through the history starting at current line and moving backward (bash shell)
	`$ <CTRL>-S`	# Search through the history starting at current line and moving forward (bash shell)

There are five important differences between the recall of command lines in OpenVMS and UNIX.

The command sequence numbers for the OpenVMS RECALL command and the UNIX history command are different. Command 1 in Open-VMS specifies the most recent command, whereas command 1 in UNIX specifies the oldest. Similarly, *N* in OpenVMS specifies the *n*th command issued before the current one, whereas in UNIX the *n* specifies the *n*th command issued in the history file. Both the Korn and C shells require you to specify a leading hyphen to indicate a relative, rather than an absolute, number. Once you issue a UNIX command, the number associated with it never changes (compare with the OpenVMS where commands shift numbers with every new command issued).

When you recall a command in OpenVMS, you must press <RETURN> to execute it, whereas UNIX usually executes the command immediately.

If an OpenVMS command is identical to the one that immediately precedes it, the command history is unchanged. In UNIX, all commands enter the history file.

The history command itself appears in the command list; the RECALL command never appears in an OpenVMS recall buffer.

OpenVMS keeps the command history in the virtual address space of a process, making it inaccessible to other processes currently logged in under the same account. UNIX keeps the command history in a file, giving it substance from one login session to the next and allowing commands from various processes under the same account to be interspersed and accessible to all those processes. *This can cause problems with simultaneous update, especially if the file is distributed between different systems and different operating systems.* You can use a different file for each login session if you define the Korn shell variable .sh_history either interactively or using the file referenced by the ENV variable. Base the history file name on something like your process identifier along with the host name or some other combination that is unique between the competing processes.

In Section 3.2.3, we pointed out a useful feature of the Korn shell, the ability to include the current command number in the shell prompt. The r commands above can reference those numbers if they are still visible. If they are not, or if you are using the C shell, use the history command to find the command you want to modify and reexecute.

The UNIX C shell can recall a command line based on its content other than at the beginning of the command. To explain how this works, we must introduce the concept of *word identifiers*. A word identifier is a piece of a command line delimited by blanks and recognized as a unique entity by the shell. You can break each command line down into a series of word identifiers, which you can then select as part of the current command line. The following examples show the recall of word identifiers from a previous command.

UNIX (C shell)
Form:
```
% command argument1 argument2 argument3
   0       1         2         3          # word identifier
```
Example:
```
% history
1 lpr file1 file2 file3
...
```
Example:
```
% cat !1:1
cat file1
```
Example:
```
% cat !1:*
cat file1 file2 file3
```

Example:
```
% cat !1:$
cat file3
```
Example:
```
% cat !1:2--3
cat file2 file3
```
Example:
```
% cat !1:2--3 file10
cat file2 file3 file10
```

In these examples, the first command on the history list, `lpr` (offline print; compare with the OpenVMS command PRINT), has a word identifier of 0, `file1` has a word identifier of 1, file2 of 2, and so on. You can introduce metacharacters into the history substitution to manipulate the word identifiers. Each of the above examples associates one or more of the word identifiers with a different command. The first example of word substitution, `cat !1:1`, takes word identifier 1 (`:1`) from the first command in the history list (`!1`) and uses it as an argument to the `cat` command. The second example, `cat !1:*`, uses the asterisk to recall word identifiers 1 through n, but not 0. The third example, `cat !1:$`, uses the dollar sign to recall the last word identifier. The fourth example, `cat !1:2--3`, recalls word identifiers 2 and 3. The last example, `cat !1:2--3 file10`, expands the command line with new arguments.

The recall of command lines (called *command-line editing* or *in-line editing*) in UNIX is versatile, but works quite differently from the way Open-VMS performs it. Editing command lines in UNIX may be done in two entirely separate modes in both the Korn and C shells; one mode resembles the `vi` editor, and the other resembles the Emacs editor. In OpenVMS, you can position the cursor on the command line using the arrow keys and add or delete text in a manner similar to a full-screen editor. In the Korn shell you may define either the EDITOR or VISUAL variables, and in the C shell you may define the `editmode` variable to the name of the editor you prefer, either `vi` or Emacs.[6] At the shell prompt, you begin a command as though you were in insert mode in one of these editors. Scrolling up or down through commands is actually scrolling through the history file, and the current command line is always at the bottom of the file. You can search through commands, modify characters or words, and then execute the modified line as the current command.

---

6.   Other definitions are permitted, but we will omit them for the sake of simplicity.

The C shell also includes *history substitution*, a feature that allows you to edit command lines in a manner similar to a line editor and perform string substitutions, as shown below:

UNIX (C shell)

Form:

```
% ^string1^string2^        # Substitute string2 for string1 in
                           # previous command
```

Example:

```
% cat file1
```

Example:

```
% ^cat^lpr^
lpr file1
```

Form:

```
% !n:s/string1/string2/  # Substitute string2 for string1 in
                              command line n
```

Example:

```
% history
...
7 cat file1
...
% !7:s/cat/lpr/
lpr file1
```

Form:

```
% !n:p:s/string1/string2 # Display command substitution but do
not execute
% !!                     # Execute previously displayed command
```

Example:

```
% !7:p:s/cat/lpr
lpr file1
% !!
lpr file1
```

In the first example, `^cat^lpr^` substitutes `lpr` for `cat` in the previous command using the caret as a delimiter and executes the new command. In the second example, `!7:s/cat/lpr/` also performs a substitution (`:s`), but for a specific command, number 7, in the history list. Note that the slash serves as a string delimiter; other characters not found in *string1* or *string2* may also serve as delimiters. In the last example, `!7:p:s/cat/lpr/`

previews (:p), a command substitution (:s), and then executes it with a double exclamation point (!!). *Previewing your commands prior to executing them is advisable for all novice UNIX users.* You may use !! at any time to immediately execute the previously displayed command again (compare with the OpenVMS command up-arrow followed by <CR>).

The novice should not disregard the recall and editing of command lines. You should be comfortable with this feature before moving on to Chapter 4. Spend time at the terminal until you are fluent in command-line recall and editing: Time spent now will be time saved later.

3.6   **Online Help**

The major form of UNIX online help is the *man pages*, which, as the name suggests, are online versions of sections of UNIX documentation. In reviewing man pages, OpenVMS users will likely find the UNIX documentation terse, poorly structured, and lacking in examples. Nevertheless, the man command, which displays the online documentation, will likely appear frequently in a user's history list and, therefore, requires detailed discussion.

In OpenVMS, the HELP command uses the OpenVMS Librarian Utility to review library entries for each command. Each command in the library is arranged in hierarchical order. At the top is a brief description of the command, followed by a list of qualifiers, parameters, and examples that you may review in any order by using features of the Librarian Utility. The UNIX man page, on the other hand, is simply a text file that reads from top to bottom. The general form of the man page is shown below. Not all man pages contain each category.

Table 3.2   *Format of UNIX man pages*

Section	Description
NAME	Lists the name and purpose of a command or subroutine
SYNOPSIS	Summarizes usage
DESCRIPTION	Describes usage in more detail
FILES	Lists the files related to command usage
SEE ALSO	Points to related information
DIAGNOSTICS	Describes diagnostic messages
EXAMPLES	Provides examples on using the command or program

Section	Description
BUGS	Describes known bugs or deficiencies and fixes if available
RESTRICTIONS	Describes known limitations
AUTHORS	Indicates whom to blame

To grasp a particular concept, for example the use of a command option, you may have to read the whole man page several times. Compare with the OpenVMS HELP system, where you can choose the specific topic of interest and display and redisplay the information easily.

The man pages reside in the directories /usr/man/man1 through /usr/man/man9 and other alphabetically classified directories. Tru64 UNIX uses the classification outlined below; this may differ somewhat in UNIX from different suppliers, as there are no industry standards for man pages.

/usr/man/man*N*

N	Contents
1	User commands
2	System calls (kernel access points)
3	Subroutine libraries
4	File formats
5	Miscellaneous
6	Games
7	Devices
8	System administration
9	[Use varies by manufacturer]
l	Local, site-specific pages
o	Old reference pages
p	Public reference pages

UNIX systems will sometimes subdivide these sections. For example, a section /usr/man/man1X might be devoted to commands that relate to

X11, and `/usr/man/man3c` could include C-language-specific support routines.

The directory `/usr/man/man1` contains local man-page entries defined by your system administrator, similar to an OpenVMS local help library (e.g., `HLP$LIBRARY_1`). UNIX stores the various man pages as unformatted `nroff` files, and the `man` command formats and displays them as required. Each man page has an associated section number. For example, the man page for the `cat` command resides in `/usr/man/man1/cat.1` with a section number of `1`. The `man` command searches all sections for the man page unless you request a specific section. Some man page entries appear in more than one section. In such instances, only one occurrence will be displayed, with preference given to entries appearing in alphabetically earlier directories.

UNIX

Form:

```
% man command
```

Example:

```
% man cat
...
```

Form:

```
% man -k keyword
```

Example:

```
% man -k terminal
ca (see ca(4))                            - terminal multiplexor
clear (see clear(1))                      - clear terminal screen
getty (see getty(8))                      - set terminal mode
gettytab (see gettytab(5))                - terminal
                                              configuration
                                              data base

lock (see lock(1))                        - reserve a terminal
pty (see pty(4))                          - pseudoterminal driver
script (see script(1))                    - make typescript of
                                              terminal session

stty (see stty(1))                        - set terminal options
stty, gtty (see stty(3c))                 - set and get terminal
                                              state (defunct)

tabs (see tabs(1))                        - set terminal tabs
term (see term(7))                        - conventional names
                                              for terminals

termcap (see termcap(5))                  - terminal capability
                                              data base

tgetent, tgetnum, tgetflag,               - terminal independent
                                              operation routines
tgetstr, tgoto, tputs (see termcap(3x))
tset (see tset(1))                        - terminal dependent
                                              initialization
```

```
tty (see tty(1))                                 - get terminal name
tty (see tty(4))                                 - general terminal
                                                     interface
ttynam, isatty (see ttynam(3f))                  - find name of a
                                                     terminal port
ttyname, isatty, ttyslot (see ttyname(3))  - find name of a
                                                     terminal
ttys (see ttys(5))                               - terminal
                                                     initialization data
ttytype (see ttytype(5))                         - database of terminal
                                                     types by port
vhangup (see vhangup(2))                         - virtually "hangup"
                                                     the current control
                                                     terminal
```

Form:

% man *section command*

Example:

% man 3c stty

. . .

Form:

% man -f *command*

Example:

% man -f more
more, page (see more (1))   - file perusal filter
                                                     for CRT viewing

In the first example above, man cat searches the man pages for the specific command cat. The man command will search all the man directories for a file referring to this command. The man page entry is automatically piped through the more command and displayed on the output device.

In the second example, man -k terminal illustrates a situation where the user knows something about the function of the command, but not the name of the command (compare with the OpenVMS command HELP Hints). The user knows that the command relates to the use of a terminal and, therefore, displays all terminal-related commands. The user can then select the correct command and display the specific man page. Note that the section number for each command appears in parentheses. The command man -k can also be executed as the command apropos, an alias for it.

In the third example, man 3c stty, a specific section identifier, is used to review the stty subroutine; man 1 stty would display the stty command.

In the last example, the situation is the reverse of that described above for man -k; that is, the user knows the command name, but not the function. The -f option displays the header line, providing a brief synopsis of the command's function. The alias whatis can substitute for man -f.

3.7   Printed Documentation

The printed documentation available to a UNIX user depends on the UNIX version and the distributor. Many manufacturers now make their documentation available on CD-ROM or as HTML manuals available on the World Wide Web.

3.8   Summary

Conducting your first terminal session with a new operating system can be a traumatic event. UNIX is no exception. This chapter was intended to minimize that trauma.

You should know from your system administrator which shell you are using, as that will determine the way you accomplish certain tasks. If you do not know which shell is your default shell, look at the prompt: % is the default C shell prompt, $ is the default Korn shell prompt, and # is the default Bourne shell prompt.

Once you have logged in, if the terminal does not respond as expected, C shell users should issue the command setenv TERM terminal_type, whereas Bourne or Korn shell users should use TERM=terminal_type (Sections 3.1 and 3.2.3). In all cases, terminal_type is one of the terminals described in the file /etc/termcap (use the command more /etc/termcap to display this file). Users of Compaq VT-series terminals and compatibles should find the appropriate entries, for example VT100, VT200, or VT300. If the terminal still does not respond as expected, consult your system administrator.

Next, use the ls -A command to find any files beginning with a period, then invoke cat or more to examine the files. Recall that these are hidden files and that they are important to your terminal session. Particularly important at this point are the files .login (Section 3.2.1) and .cshrc (Section 3.2.2) for C shell users, and .profile (Section 3.2.3) for Bourne, bash and Korn shell users. Reconcile the commands found in your versions of these files with those discussed here.

When the inevitable typing mistakes occur and the arrow keys do not function as they do with OpenVMS, persevere with the UNIX recall and editing of command lines (Section 3.5). Finally, spend time with the UNIX man pages (Section 3.6); you are sure to use them while experimenting with the material discussed in the following chapters.

4

Introductory File Management

4

Introductory File Management

Doublethink means the power of holding two contradictory beliefs in one's mind simultaneously, and accepting both of them.

—*George Orwell*

UNIX possesses numerous commands and utilities for the creation, modification, and display of files and directories. Table 4.1, a summary of file-management commands, was created from the headers of the man page entries for all sections of the BSD documentation (see Section 3.6). Table 4.1 divides the commands into those that display files and those that manipulate them. Since display commands do not change the contents of files, the novice user may use them in complete safety. Manipulation commands do change the contents of files, and novice users should use them with care.

Table 4.1   *Summary of File-Management Commands*

UNIX	OpenVMS Equivalent	Purpose
Display Commands: Directories		
ls (see ls(1))	DIRECTORY	Lists contents of directory
stat (see stat(1))	DIRECTORY/FULL *file*	List details about a file
Display Commands: Files		
cat (see cat(1))	TYPE	Catenates and prints to a terminal
col (see col(1))		Filters line feeds

Table 4.1   *Summary of File-Management Commands (continued)*

UNIX	OpenVMS Equivalent	Purpose
`fmt (see fmt(1))`	RUNOFF	Formats lines to specified width
`fold (see fold(1))`	SET TERMINAL /WIDTH=n /WRAP	Folds long lines for finite-width output device
`head (see head(1))`	EDIT /READ	Displays first few lines
`lpr (see lpr(1))`	PRINT	Prints to the line printer
`more, page (see more(1))`	TYPE /PAGE	File perusal filter for CRT viewing
`od (see od(1))`	DUMP	Octal, decimal, hex, ASCII dump
`pr (see pr(1))`	PRINT /HEAD	Prints file to `stdout`
	ANALYZE /OBJECT	Standard object file-dump utility
`tail (see tail(1))`	TYPE /TAIL[=n]	Displays the last part of a file

Manipulation Commands: Directories

UNIX	OpenVMS Equivalent	Purpose
`cd (see cd(1))`	SET DEFAULT	Changes working directory
`chdir (see chdir(2))`	SET DEFAULT	Changes current directory—callable routine
`dir (see dir(4))`		Explains format of directories
`getdirentries (see getdirentries(2))`		Gets directory entries in a file-system-independent format
`getwd (see getwd (3))`	F$DIRECTORY()	Gets current working directory path name
`mkdir (see mkdir(1))`	CREATE /DIRECTORY	Makes a directory
`pwd (see pwd(1))`	SHOW DEFAULT, F$DIRECTORY ()	Shows working directory name
`rmdir (see rmdir(1))`	DELETE	Removes a directory file

Table 4.1 *Summary of File-Management Commands (continued)*

UNIX	OpenVMS Equivalent	Purpose
scandir, alphasort (see scandir(3))		Scans a directory
unlink (see unlink(2))		Removes directory entry—callable routine
Manipulation Commands: Files		
ar (see ar(1))	LIBRARY	Serves as archive and library maintainer
awk (see awk(1))	EDIT /TPU, *Lexical Functions*	Functions as pattern-scanning and processing language
basename (see basename(1))	F$PARSE	Returns base filename, stripping path information
bcopy, bcmp, bzero, ifs (see bstring(3))	F$FAO, *Replacement-expression assignment*	Performs bit and byte string operations
chgrp (see chgrp(1))	SET FILE /OWNER	Changes group ownership
chmod (see chmod(1))	SET PROTECTION	Changes file permissions—command
chmod (see chmod(2))	SET PROTECTION	Changes file permissions—callable routine
cmp (see cmp(1))	DIFFERENCE	Compares two files
comm (see comm(1))	SORT, MERGE	Selects or rejects lines common to two sorted files
compress, uncompress, zcat (see compress(1))		Compresses and cate-nates uncompresses files
cp (see cp(1))	COPY	Copies
creat (see creat(2))	CREATE, OPEN	Creates a new file
cksum	CHECKSUM	Returns a checksum of a file's contents

Table 4.1   *Summary of File-Management Commands (continued)*

UNIX	OpenVMS Equivalent	Purpose
`crypt`	`ENCRYPT`	Performs encode/decode command
`crypt, setkey, encrypt (see crypt (3))`	`ENCRYPT`	Perform encryption operations—callable routine
`ctags (see ctags (1))`		Creates a tags file
`dd (see dd(1))`	`EXCHANGE`	Converts and copies a file
`diff (see diff(1))`	`DIFFERENCE`	Serves as differential file and directory comparator
`diff3 (see diff(3))`		Performs three-way differential file comparison
`expand, unexpand (see expand (1))`		Expands tabs to spaces and vice versa
`file (see file (1))`	`F$PARSE, F$FILE_ATTRIBUTES`	Determines file type
`filehdr (see filehdr(5))`		Provides file header for standard format object files
`find (see find(1))`	`DIRECTORY`	Finds files
`flock (see flock(2))`	`UNLOCK`	Applies for or removes an advisory lock on an open file
`ftp (see ftp(1))`	`COPY, EXCHANGE /NETWORK`	Serves as file transfer program
`grep, egrep, fgrep (see grep(1))`	`SEARCH, TYPE`	Searches a file for a pattern
`ident (see indent(1))`	`DIRECTORY`	Identifies files
`link (see link(2))`	`ASSIGN, DEFINE, SET FILE /ENTRY`	Makes a hard link to a file—callable routine
`ln (see ln(1))`	`ASSIGN, DEFINE, SET FILE /ENTRY`	Makes links to files
`lockf (see lockf(3))`		Sets advisory record locking on files

Table 4.1 *Summary of File-Management Commands (continued)*

UNIX	OpenVMS Equivalent	Purpose
look (see look(1))	SEARCH	Finds lines in a sorted list
lorder (see lorder(1))	LIBRARY	Finds ordering relation for an object library
merge (see merge(1))	MERGE	Performs three-way file merge
mknod (see mknod(2))	EDIT /FDL, SYS$OPEN	Makes a special file (character, block, or fifo)
mknod (see mknod(8))	EDIT /FDL	Builds a special file
mktemp (see mktemp(3))		Makes a unique file name
mv (see mv(1))	RENAME	Moves or renames files
ncheck (see ncheck(8))		Generates names from 1-numbersq
open (see open(2))	OPEN	Opens a file for reading or writing, or creates a new file
qsort (see qsort(3))	SORT	Performs a quick sort— callable routine
ranlib (see ranlib(1))	LIBRARY	Converts archives to random libraries
rcp (see rcp(1))	COPY, EXCHANGE /NETWORK	Performs remote file copy
read, readv (see read(2))	READ	Reads input
readlink (see readlink(2))	F$TRNLNM	Reads value of a symbolic link
rename (see rename(2))	SYS$RENAME	Renames a file—callable routine
rev (see rev(1))		Reverses lines of a file
rm, rmdir (see rm(1))	DELETE	Removes (unlinks) files or directories
size (see size(1))	DIRECTORY /SIZE	Returns size of an object file

Table 4.1   *Summary of File-Management Commands (continued)*

UNIX	OpenVMS Equivalent	Purpose
sort (see sort(1))	SORT	Sorts or merges files
split (see split(1))	EDIT	Splits a file into pieces
stat, lstat, fstat (see stat(2))	SHOW DEVICE /FILE, F$FILE_ATTRIBUTES, SYS$OPEN	Gets file status—callable routine
strncpy, strlen, index, rindex (see string (3))	F$EXTRACT, F$EDIT, F$ELEMENT	Performs string operations
strings (see strings (1))	ANALYZE /OBJECT	Finds the printable strings in an object or other binary file
strip (see strip(1))		Removes symbols and relocation bits
sum (see sum(1))	CHECKSUM	Sums and counts blocks in a file
swab (see swab(3))		Swaps bytes
symlink (see symlink(2))	ASSIGN, DEFINE	Makes symbolic links to a file
symorder (see symorder(1))		Rearranges name list
tar (see tar(1))	BACKUP	Archives tape
tar (see tar(5))	BACKUP	Archives tape, formats file
touch (see touch(1))		Updates date last modified of a file
touch (see touch(1))	CREATE	Creates a new (empty) file
tr (see tr(1))	F$EDIT	Translates characters
truncate, ftruncate (see truncate(2))	SYS$TRUNCATE	Truncates a file to a specified length
tsort (see tsort(1))	SORT	Performs a topological sort
umask (see umask(2))	SET PROTECTION /DEFAULT	Sets file creation mode mask

Table 4.1 *Summary of File-Management Commands (continued)*

UNIX	OpenVMS Equivalent	Purpose
uniq (see uniq(1))		Reports repeated lines in a file
utime (see utime(3))		Sets file times
utimes (see utimes(2))		Sets file times
vers (see vers(1))		Sets/displays version numbers
wc (see wc(1))		Performs a word count
what (see what(1))	LINK /MAP, ANALYZE /IMAGE	Shows what versions of object modules were used to construct a file
which (see which(1))	DIRECTORY	Locates a program file including aliases

Like a spoken language, UNIX allows successful communication using only a limited vocabulary. This chapter concentrates on commands and a few options that the novice user will likely need in the first few terminal sessions. Remaining chapters introduce additional commands and options that, although used less frequently, add richness and functionality to the language. Our focus is commands, rather than callable C language routines or utilities. The following chapters deal with important utilities in the context of application development; callable routines are beyond the scope of this book. Table 4.2 summarizes the directory and file commands discussed (see Appendix A for a more complete set of commands) and indicates where to find them in this book.

We deal here only with the traditional command-line interface for file manipulation. Most commands discussed in this chapter have equivalent forms in the CDE File Manager, briefly discussed in Section 2.6.

After reading this chapter, you should be able to perform the most common tasks involving the management of UNIX files:

- Listing the files in a directory (Section 4.1)

- Describing UNIX file characteristics (Section 4.2)

- Determining the current directory (Section 4.3)

Table 4.2   *Commonly Used File-Management Commands*

UNIX Command	OpenVMS Equivalent	Location	Purpose
ar	LIBRARY	Section 9.5	Archives files
awk	EDIT /TPU	Section 5.4	Performs pattern matching
cat	TYPE	Section 4.8	Catenates and prints to a terminal
cd	SET DEFAULT	Section 4.4	Changes working directory
chgrp	SET FILE	Section 8.4.2	Changes the group ownership
chmod	SET PROTECTION	Section 8.4.1	Changes file permissions
cmp	DIFFERENCE	Section 4.5	Compares two files and reports the first difference found
cp	COPY	Sections 4.10, 8.3.1	Creates a new copy
diff	DIFFERENCE	Section 8.4.3	Reports all differences between two files
find	DIRECTORY	Sections 4.7, 8.4.4	Locates within a directory structure
fsplit	EDIT	Section 9.2	Splits into functional parts
ftp	COPY	Section 13.2.6.2	Transfers to/from a remote node
grep	SEARCH	Section 8.4.5	Finds a string
less	TYPE /PAGE	Section 4.9	Pages through a file
head	EDIT/READ	Section 8.2.3	Gives first few lines
lorder	LIBRARY	Section 9.5	Finds ordering relationship
ln	DEFINE	Section 8.4.10	Creates a symbolic link
ls	DIRECTORY	Sections 4.1, 8.1.1	Lists contents of a directory

Table 4.2 *Commonly Used File-Management Commands (continued)*

UNIX Command	OpenVMS Equivalent	Location	Purpose
merge	MERGE	Section 8.4.6	Merges files
mkdir	CREATE /DIR	Section 4.5	Makes a directory
more	TYPE /PAGE	Sections 4.8, 8.2.1	Serves as file perusal filter for CRT
mv	RENAME	Section 4.11	Moves (or renames)
od	DUMP	Section 8.2.2	Serves as octal, decimal, hex, ASCII dump
pr	PRINT /HEAD	Section 8.2.3	Prints file
pwd	SHOW DEFAULT	Section 4.3	Shows working directory name
ranlib	LIBRARY	Section 9.5	Converts archives to random libraries
rcp	COPY, EXCHANGE /NETWORK	Section 13.2.6.1	Performs remote file copy
rm	DELETE	Section 4.12	Removes or deletes
rmdir	DELETE	Section 4.6	Removes a directory file
sort	SORT	Section 8.4.6	Sorts by key
tail	EDIT /READ	Section 8.2.3	Outputs the last part of a file
tar	BACKUP	Section 7.2.1	Archives a tape
touch	CREATE	Section 8.4.7	Updates file characteristics or creates a null file
tr	EDIT	Section 8.4.8	Translates characters
uucp		Section 13.3.5	Performs remote file copy to neighboring host
uusend		Section 13.3.5	Performs remote file copy
wc	SEARCH /STATISTICS	Section 8.4.9	Counts words

- Changing the current directory (Section 4.4)

- Creating a directory (Section 4.5)

- Deleting a directory (Section 4.6)

- Locating a file (Section 4.7)

- Displaying the contents of a file (Section 4.8)

- Paging through a file (Section 4.9)

- Copying a file (Section 4.10)

- Renaming a file (Section 4.11)

- Deleting a file (Section 4.12)

As you begin displaying and managing files, you will need to learn more about their characteristics. We will begin by learning how to list the characteristics of files in Section 4.1. We will then explain each of these characteristics in Section 4.2. An understanding of file characteristics will be especially useful in Chapter 8, when we discuss commands that change file characteristics. In Sections 4.3 through 4.11, we return to our introduction of interactive file and directory management.

As before, when we give examples of UNIX commands and compare them to their OpenVMS counterparts, we use relative and absolute pathnames to emphasize the various ways of defining files in UNIX. The examples come from everyday use. We suggest that you study the examples given here and then experiment with variations of your own.

4.1   Displaying Directory Contents: ls

The `ls` command for listing the contents of a directory was introduced in Section 2.2, and it has since been used with different options. The following examples summarize some `ls` options.

Each of the four examples above pertains to a directory that contains four files: three ordinary files, `myfile.txt` (text), `program.f` (FORTRAN program), and `.login` (hidden); and a directory file, `tmp`. The subdirectory `tmp` contains one file, `test` (text). The first and simplest example, `ls`, lists the file names in the current directory excluding the hidden file (compare with the OpenVMS DIRECTORY command). Note that here and in subsequent examples, `ls` does not display the name of the current directory. The second example, `ls -A` (list all), includes the hidden file name in the listing.

OpenVMS	UNIX
Form:	
`$ DIRECTORY[/QUALIFIER(S)] -`	`% ls [-option(s)]`
`[FILE-SPEC...]`	`[argument(s)]`

OpenVMS   **UNIX**

Form:

`$ DIRECTORY[/QUALIFIER(S)] -`
`[FILE-SPEC...]`

`% ls [-option(s)]`
`[argument(s)]`

Example:

`$ DIR`

```
DUA2:[USER1]
LOGIN.COM;1
MYFILE.TXT;1
PROGRAM.FOR;1    TMP.DIR;1
```

`% ls`
`myfile.txt  program.f  tmp`

Example:

`$ DIR`
```
DUA2:[USER1]
LOGIN.COM;1
MYFILE.TXT;1
PROGRAM.FOR;1    TMP.DIR;1
```

`% ls -A`
`.login  myfile.txt  program.f`
`tmp`

Example:

`$ DIR [...]`
```
DUA2:[USER1]
LOGIN.COM;1
MYFILE.TXT;1
LOGIN.COM;1
MYFILE.TXT;1
DUA2:[USER1.TMP]
TEST.;1
```

`% ls -R`
`myfile.txt  program.f  tmp`

`tmp:`
`test`

OpenVMS

Example:

```
$ DIR/PROTECTION/DATE/SIZE/OWNER
DUA2: [USER1]
LOGIN.COM;1        1  10-JAN-1997   08:17   [USER1]
(RWED,RWED,RE,RE)
MYFILE.TXT;1       2  24-AUG-1997 13:40    [USER1]
(RWED,RWED,RE,RE)
PROGRAM.FOR;1  1  10-JUL-1996   21:10   [USER1]
(RWED,RWED,RWED,E)
TMP.DIR;1          1   2-SEP-1996    04:10   [USER1]
(RWE,RWE,RE,RE)
```

UNIX

Example:

```
% ls -1
total 1
-rwxr-xr-x  1   user1   staff   1024   24 Aug 13:40   myfile.txt
-rwxrwx--x  1   user1   staff   512   10 Jul  1996   program.f
drwxr-xr-x  2   user1   staff    30   12 Sep 1996   tmp
```

The third example, `ls -R`, lists not only the contents of the current directory, but also all files in all subdirectories lower in the hierarchical directory tree ("recursive descent"), which in this example includes the subdirectory `tmp`. This command corresponds to the OpenVMS command `DIRECTORY [...]`. The `ls *` command (not shown) lists files in the current directory and all files one level down in the directory hierarchy. Similarly, `ls */*` lists all files in the current directory and all files both one and two levels down in the directory hierarchy. The last example, `ls -l` (long listing), gives additional information on the characteristics of the file, including file type, protection, owner, group, size, and date last modified. See Section 4.2 for a discussion of each of these file characteristics. The options illustrated here may be combined: For example, `ls -Al` displays a long listing, including the hidden files.

Unless modified by an option, `ls` displays files alphabetically. The following conditions define the sort order for an alphabetical listing:

1.   File names beginning with a period

2.   Numbers

3.   Uppercase letters

4.   Lowercase letters

The following example illustrates the order in which `ls` displays files:

UNIX
```
% ls -A
.123   .Test   .test   123   Foo   foo
```

4.2   File Characteristics

Let us take a closer look at both the `ls -l` and `stat` commands, which produce a long listing of the characteristics of a file.

In this example, `ls -l ../testfile` uses a relative pathname to display the characteristics of `testfile`, which resides one directory level above the current directory. Note that the full listing given by UNIX is more concise than the equivalent listing given by the OpenVMS `DIRECTORY/FULL` command, reflecting the simpler file structure of UNIX. First, UNIX does not display record and file attributes; as we saw in Section 2.3, files consist of a string of bytes that, for a given partition, always have the same file charac-

OpenVMS
Example:

```
$ DIRECTORY/FULL [-]TESTFILE.
Directory DUA3:[BOURNE.MASS11]
TESTFILE.;1  File ID:  (11044,9,0)
Size:  1/3
Owner:  [STAFF,DANNY]
Created:  20-FEB-1996 13:15
Revised:  20-FEB-1997 13:15 (1)
Expires:  <None specified>
Backup:  <No backup recorded>
Effective:  <None specified>
Recording:  <None specified>
File organization:  Sequential
Shelved state:  Online
File attributes:  Allocation: 3, Extend: 0, Global buffer count:
0, No version limit
Record format:  Variable length, maximum 4 bytes
Record attributes:  Carriage return carriage control
Journaling enabled:  None
File protection:  System:RWED, Owner:RWED, Group:R, World:R
Access Cntrl List:  (IDENTIFIER = %X80010003.ACCESS = READ +
WRITE + EXECUTE + DELETE + CONTROL)
(IDENTIFIER = $X80010000.ACCESS = READ + WRITE + EXECUTE)
Total of 1 file, 1/3 blocks
```

UNIX
Example:

```
% ls -l ../testfile
-rwxr--r--  1  danny  staff  1000  20 Feb 12:20  testfile
```

Example:

```
% stat mmb.txt
File: "mmb.txt"
Size: 633500        Filetype: Regular File
Device:  8,23  Inode: 77958     Links: 1
Access: Sat Sep  7 10:26:15 2002(00002.20:24:45
Modify: Tue Dec  4 23:35:43 2001(00279.06:15:17)
Change: Tue Dec  4 23:35:43 2001(00279.06:15:17)
```

teristics. Second, not all versions of UNIX support an Access Control List (ACL). Third, UNIX displays a single date, in this case, the date the file was last modified. Dates such as the last backup and file creation dates are available with additional qualifiers in some implementations of UNIX.

The third example shows the use of the stat command. Like the ls -l command, stat provides information about file permissions and revision dates. The stat command displays additional file information, including inode, number of links, and other statistics.

The first character in a UNIX file description indicates the type of file. File types described by this character include the following:

d	directory file
b	block-type special file
c	character-type special file
l	symbolic link
s	socket
–	plain file

A plain file contains any ASCII or binary information. A directory file is a pointer to a subdirectory of the current directory (compare with the OpenVMS file with the extension .DIR.). Users usually only manipulate directory files by deleting them to remove a subdirectory. The next nine characters (rwxr--r--) define the file *permissions* (see Section 8.4.1; compare with OpenVMS file protection). Each file has three levels of permission: owner, group, and world (all local and remote users), defined by the first, second, and third three-character groups, respectively. Unlike Open-VMS, UNIX has no fourth level of permission defining access to the local system administrator, who always has full access to UNIX files. Each level of permission permits three types of access: read (r), write (w), and execute (x). Unlike OpenVMS, UNIX does not distinguish between write and delete. A UNIX file to which you can write can therefore also be deleted. However, you should note that like OpenVMS, UNIX requires write access to the directory containing a file, as well as proper permission on the file itself. In the above example, the owner of testfile can read, write, and execute it, and group members and all other users can read it. As in Open-VMS, the protection assigned to a directory file determines the first level of protection for all files in that directory and limits access, regardless of the file permission assigned to the individual files. For example, if the directory file has a file permission that precludes writing by the owner, the owner cannot edit any files in that directory, even if the individual file permissions indicate otherwise.

The second entry in our example, 1, indicates the number of links the file possesses (see Section 8.4.9 for a discussion of links). As the name suggests, a *link* is a connection between files and directories or between directories. A file always has at least one link to the directory file in which it resides. For example, the file specification /tmp/test1 indicates that the file `test1` has a single link to the directory file `/tmp`. Similarly, a directory file always has at least two links, one to all the files in the directory and one to its parent directory file. For example, the directory `tmp` has two links, one to `/` (the root directory) and one to all the files it contains. Creating a further subdirectory to `tmp` would increase the link count of `tmp` by one. Section 8.4.9 discusses making additional links.

The next two entries in our example, `danny` and `staff`, indicate the owner of the file and the group to which the file belongs. You can use groups in a manner similar to the OpenVMS Access Control Entry (ACE) in an ACL. A user may belong to several groups, for example, according to a department or job function. You can assign a file's group permission to give access only to members of the appropriate group. An OpenVMS ACL may comprise multiple ACEs, but only one group can be assigned to an OpenVMS or UNIX file.

If a user belongs to multiple groups and a file can belong to only one group, to which group does a file created by that user belong? The answer can be found in the files `/etc/passwd` and `/etc/group`. The file `/etc/group` contains a numeric group identifier associated with each group name. The `/etc/passwd` file contains a single group identifier and a unique user identifier for each user regardless of the number of groups to which the user belongs. Therefore, UNIX assigns the group name associated with the user's unique group identifier to a file when the file is created. The file owner can easily change the group ownership of a file with the `chgrp` or `chown` commands (see Section 8.4.2).

The following example shows a record from the `/etc/passwd` file for user `danny` the fields within the record are separated by colons.

UNIX
Example:
```
% more /etc/passwd
...
julia:9GeD4S9Hktztl:102:49:Julia Rose,523BB:/system1/julia:\
/bin/csh
%more /etc/group
...
staff:*:49:julia,danny,fred,george
...
```

The field definitions are as follows:

julia	login name
9GeD4S9Hktztl	encrypted password
102	unique user code
49	group identifier
Julia Rose...	name and demographic information
/system1/julia	parent directory
/bin/csh	default shell

User julia has the group identifier 49, which defines the default group ownership of his files. Referring to the file /etc/group, the identifier 49 belongs to the group staff. Hence, all files created by user julia will, by default, belong to the group staff.

Do not confuse a UNIX group assignment with an OpenVMS User Identification Code (UIC). A UNIX user may belong to many groups, whereas an OpenVMS user belongs only to a single group defined by the UIC. OpenVMS achieves a UNIX-like group file access by assigning an ACE to a file. An ACE defines an identifier and a level of protection for that identifier. Users possessing that identifier have access to the file in accordance with the identifier's protection. Users who do not possess the identifier have access to the file in accordance with standard OpenVMS file protections. The OpenVMS system administrator assigns identifiers to a user; the owner of the file assigns identifiers to the file.

As we return to the ls -l command, the next entry, 1000, indicates the size of the file. UNIX file sizes appear in bytes, whereas OpenVMS file sizes appear in blocks containing 512 bytes each. Thus, an OpenVMS file of three blocks appears as a file size of 1,536 in UNIX. You can tell ls to display a file's size in kilobytes (1,024 bytes) by using the -s qualifier.

The next entry, 20 Feb 12:20, indicates the date and time the file was last modified. The last entry, testfile, gives the name of the file.

4.3   Determining the Current Directory: pwd

The command pwd, print working directory, determines the current directory (compare with the OpenVMS command SHOW DEFAULT). The C shell also offers the dirs command, which displays a hierarchical list of directories called a *directory stack*, with the present working directory at the top.

Section 8.3.2 explains how to build a directory stack and how it facilitates movement between commonly used directories.

OpenVMS	UNIX
Form:	
$ SHOW DEFAULT	% pwd
Example:	
$ SHOW DEFAULT	% pwd
DUB2:[TEST]	/test

4.4   **Changing Directories:** cd

The UNIX command cd, change directory, changes the present working directory (compare with the OpenVMS command SET DEFAULT).

OpenVMS	
Form:	**UNIX**
$ SET DEFAULT *device-name*[*directory*]	% cd [*directory*]
Example:	
$ SET DEFAULT DUA2:[USER]	% cd /user
Example:	
$ SET DEFAULT [-.USER]	% cd ../user
Example:	
$ SET DEFAULT SYS$LOGIN:	% cd
	% cd ~nathan

The first two examples above are easy to understand when compared to their OpenVMS counterparts. In the third example, cd without a directory argument changes the present working directory to the user's home directory and, therefore, provides a simple means of returning to a familiar point in the directory hierarchy. UNIX provides a feature not available in OpenVMS, the ability to set the working directory to the home directory of another user. In the last example, instead of changing to one's own home directory, the path becomes that of user nathan.

The C shell extends the use of cd through the shell variable cdpath. The variable cdpath lets you move from the present working directory to a directory defined by `cdpath` without regard to the relative or absolute pathname to that directory. See Section 8.3.2 for a discussion of `cdpath`.

4.5   Creating a Directory: `mkdir`

The UNIX command `mkdir`, as the name suggests, creates directories (compare with the OpenVMS command CREATE/DIRECTORY).

OpenVMS	UNIX
Form:	
`$ CREATE/DIRECTORY[/QUALIFIER(S)]-` `directory-spec[, ...]`	`% mkdir directory`
Example:	
`$ CREATE/DIRECTORY [.TEST]`	`% mkdir test`
Example:	
`$ CREATE/DIRECTORY [USER.TMP.TEST]`	`% mkdir /user/tmp/test`

In the first example, `mkdir test` illustrates the creation of a subdirectory, `test`, to the present working directory. In the second example, `mkdir /user/tmp/test` uses an absolute pathname to create a subdirectory `test`. Note that if the `tmp` directory did not already exist, the subdirectory `test` could not be created. Contrast with OpenVMS, where CREATE/DIRECTORY creates both the TMP subdirectory and the TEST subdirectory. In both OpenVMS and UNIX, the creation of a subdirectory requires write access to the parent directory.

A variation on the `mkdir` command is `mkdir` with the `-p` option. The `mkdir -p` command creates any intermediate directories needed if there is not yet a complete path to the bottommost directory that you are creating.

4.6   Deleting a Directory: `rmdir` and `rm -r`

UNIX offers two commands for removing a directory, `rmdir` and `rm -r` (compare with the OpenVMS command DELETE). The latter is one form of the `rm` (remove) command that is used to remove files (see Section 4.12). Like the OpenVMS command DELETE, `rmdir` removes a directory only if it contains no files. The directory must be at the lowest level of the directory hierarchy before you can delete it, since only then will it contain no directory files. The command `rm -r` (recursive delete), on the other hand, deletes everything in the directory, as well as all files and directories lower in the directory hierarchy, which can either be efficient or devastating. For a novice UNIX user, it is more likely to be devastating, so be careful! In particular, `rm -r` will delete hidden files (files whose first character is a dot), as well as ordinary files, whereas `rm` will delete only ordinary files, unless you explicitly instruct it to remove hidden files.

OpenVMS	UNIX
Form:	
`$ DELETE[/QUALIFIER(S)] \`	`% rmdir directory`
`  directory`	
Example:	
`$ DELETE[USER]TMP.DIR;1`	`% rmdir /usr/user/tmp`
Form:	
`$ DELETE/QUALIFIER(S)`	`% rm -r [option(s)] directory`
`  directory`	
Example:	
`$ DELETE [USER.TMP...]*.*;*`	`% rm -r /usr/user/tmp`
`(repeated until all files`	
`  removed)`	
`$ DELETE TMP.DIR;1`	

In the first example, `rmdir /usr/user/tmp` removes the `tmp` directory (that is, the subdirectory of `/usr/user` named `tmp`), provided it contains no files. In the second example, `rm -r /usr/user/tmp` removes the `tmp` directory, all subdirectories of `tmp`, and all files in those subdirectories.

4.7   Finding a File: `find`

The command `find` offers functions in addition to those offered by `ls -R` (see Section 4.1) for locating files in a directory hierarchy. As in OpenVMS, you can use various search criteria to locate files. In UNIX, you can also perform file manipulations on files located with the `find` command. This added functionality requires a complex syntax. The following simple example locates a file; the more complex command syntax for modifying files once they have been found is discussed in Section 8.4.4.

The command `find / -name ourfile -print` searches all files on the system from the root (`/`) downward for files with the name `ourfile`. The command then prints the path of any file found on the terminal. This

OpenVMS	UNIX
Form:	
$ *DIRECTORY*[*/QUALIFIER(S)*]	% find *pathname_list criterion* \
file_spec	*action*
Example:	
$ DIR [*...]MYFILE.	% find / -name ourfile -print
	/user1/bin/ourfile
	/user3/progs/ourfile

example illustrates the elegance of the UNIX file system: You do not need to know the physical device on which a file resides in order to find it. In OpenVMS, you might have to search each disk on the system (issue the command for each device) to find a file.

4.8   Displaying a File: cat and more

The most frequently used UNIX commands for displaying the contents of a file are cat (catenate and print) and more, also called page (which displays a file a page at a time). Together these commands provide greater functionality than the OpenVMS TYPE command. The less frequently used file display commands appear in Chapter 8. First, od (octal dump, Section 8.2.2) dumps files in a variety of formats (compare with the OpenVMS DUMP command). The head command (Section 8.2.3) displays the beginning of a file. The tail command (Section 8.2.3) displays the end of a file (compare with the OpenVMS commands TYPE/TAIL and TYPE/CONTINU-OUS/INTERVAL). Finally, the command pr (Section 8.2.3) performs simple formatting for files you wish to print.

The major difference between more and cat is that cat automatically scrolls through a file from beginning to end, whereas more pauses between each screen (24 lines or the number of lines in a window by default). The more command indicates the percentage of the file already displayed and waits for a response from the user. Striking the <CR> key will scroll the file one line; striking the space bar will scroll the file one screen.

If you use the -c option with more, the screen refreshes one line at a time instead of scrolling, facilitating reading while the screen updates. As we shall see in Section 8.2.1, during pauses in file display brought about with the more command, you can make alternative responses that provide additional functionality in the display of files.

OpenVMS	UNIX
Form:	
`$ TYPE[/QUALIFIER(S)] \`	`% cat [option(s)] file(s)`
`file-spec[,...]`	
Example:	
`$ TYPE MYFILE.DAT`	`% cat myfile.dat`
	`% cat -n ~user1/myfile.dat`
	`% cat -s /tmp/myfile.dat`
Form:	
`$ TYPE[/QUALIFIER(S)]`	`% more [option(s)] file(s)`
`file-spec[,...]`	
Example:	
`$ TYPE/PAGE MYFILE.DAT`	`% more myfile.dat`
	`% more -c file1 file2`
Example:	
`$ SET TERMINAL/PAGE=15`	`% more -15 ../../file1`
`$ TYPE/PAGE [--]FILE1.`	
`$ SET TERMINAL/NOWRAP`	`% more -f widefile`
`$ TYPE/PAGE WIDEFILE.`	`% more + 10 my_file`

The cat command has useful options, which are shown in the second and third examples above. In the second example, cat -n ~user1/ myfile.dat uses an absolute file definition to display the file myfile.dat in the home directory of user1. The -n option displays the file with line numbers. OpenVMS uses an editor to interrogate the file to achieve the same result. The command cat -s /tmp/myfile, shown in the third example, removes multiple blank lines from myfile.

4.9 Paging Through a File: less

Another command available on many UNIX systems for displaying files is less. Like the OpenVMS TYPE command and the UNIX more command, the less command displays the contents of a file. However, less is more robust than more (a little joke by its author)! The less command is considered a pager. When you view a file with less, you have a variety of options for scrolling through the file (paging) and searching for text strings. In addition to these basic functions, less offers more advanced operations. For example, you can set up filters to view compressed data or other file types. The less command also allows you to view multiple files, remembering your position in each file. You can also do a single search spanning all the files with which you are working.

UNIX

Form:

`% less [option(s)] file`

Example:

`% less -V myfile.dat`

In the example, the `less` command is entered with the -v (verbose) option, which specifies that more detailed information is to be shown on the command line.

4.10 Copying a File: cp

The UNIX command `cp` copies one file to another. If the destination file already exists, `cp` overwrites it with the contents of the file being copied. OpenVMS, in contrast, creates a higher version number of the existing file. UNIX provides two ways to prevent unwanted erasure and replacement of existing files. First, when creating a valuable file, you can set the file permission at no write for all users, including yourself (see `chmod`, Section 8.4.1). Second, you can use the form `cp -i` for all copy operations to request confirmation on the copy when the destination file already exists (compare with the OpenVMS `COPY/CONFIRM` command). Novice UNIX users familiar with the multiple version numbers in OpenVMS should use this form for all UNIX copy operations by including an alias in `.cshrc` or `.profile`, as shown below. Note that the use of the shell variable `noclobber` has no effect here: `noclobber` prevents overwriting when redirecting output rather than copying files (e.g., `cat file1 > file2`).

OpenVMS	**UNIX**
Form:	
`$ COPY[/QUALIFIER(S)]`	`% cp [option(s)] input_file \`
`input-file -output-file`	`output_file`
Example:	`% alias cp 'cp -i' # C shell`
	`$ alias cp='cp -i' # Korn shell`

```
$ COPY/CONFIRM FILE1. FILE2.        % cp file1 file2
Copy DUA1:[USER]FILE1. to -         Overwrite file2?
DUA1:[USER]FILE2.? [N]
```

4.11   Renaming a File: mv

The UNIX command mv (move or rename) has the same function as the OpenVMS RENAME command.

OpenVMS	**UNIX**
Form:	
`$ RENAME[/QUALIFIER(S)]`	`% mv [option(s)] input_file \`
`input-file -output-file`	`output_file`
Example:	
`$ RENAME FILE1. FILE2.`	`% mv file1 file2`
`$ RENAME/CONFIRM FILE1. FILE2.`	`% mv -i file1 file2`
	`% mv -f file1 file2`
	`% mv - -vn foo`

In the same way that cp -i invoked interactive mode, mv -i prompts the user for permission to proceed with the move operation if a file with the new name already exists. Once again, novice UNIX users should include alias mv 'mv -i' in their .cshrc file or the equivalent command in their .profile file to prevent the inadvertent overwriting of wanted files.

You can negate the effect of the -i option with the command mv -f (force), as shown in the third example above. Assuming file2 already exists and mv is made mv -i with an alias, then mv -f file1 file2 overwrites file2 without comment.

The last example, mv - -vn foo, is particularly valuable to novice users. You can inadvertently create a file that begins with a dash when you intended the dash to precede an option. If this occurs, efforts to address this file with a variety of commands will fail because UNIX interprets the filename as an option. The mv - command indicates that the next argument is a filename beginning with a dash. In this example, the command renames the file -vn to foo, a favorite scratch filename of ancient renown.

Note that neither OpenVMS nor UNIX will allow you to rename a file across devices.

4.12   **Deleting a File: rm**

Section 4.6 discussed using rm -r to remove directories and their contents. You can also use rm to remove files. As with cp (copy file) and mv (rename file), using the -i option with rm invokes an interactive form of the command that prompts the user before taking action. As previously suggested, the novice UNIX user should alias the command to reduce the likelihood of destroying wanted files. Even with the alias set, you can override confirmation of file deletion with the -f option.

OpenVMS	UNIX
Form:	
$ DELETE[/*QUALIFIER(S)*]	% rm [*option(s)*] *file(s)*
file-spec[,...]	
Example:	
$ DELETE FILE1.;1	% rm file1
Example:	
$ DELETE/CONFIRM[-]FILE1.;	% rm -i ../file1 file2
1,FILE2.;1	Delete /usr/file1?
Delete DUA1:[USER]FILE1.;1? [N]	Delete /usr/file1?
Delete DUA1:[USER.TMP]FILE2.;1? [N]	
	Example:
	% chmod 000 file1
	% rm file1
	rm: Override protection 0 for file1?

The first two examples of the rm command are straightforward. The last example illustrates the relationship of file and directory protections to the rm command. The chmod 000 file1 command removes all access to file1 (see Section 8.4.1), and yet it can still be deleted by the owner and root. Note, however, that the system asks the user whether to override the file protection, which indicates that the file has a protection that renders it undeletable. If the directory containing file1 is protected against delete access by the owner, then the message "permission denied" appears. The protection of the directory containing file1 must then be changed by the owner with the chmod command before deletion can be accomplished. The UNIX command rm * is the equivalent of the OpenVMS command delete *.*;*.

4.13 Summary

A useful way of summarizing the basic commands introduced in this chapter is to present a scenario of a new UNIX user's first experience with file management. For the sake of brevity, we omit all but one intentional typographical error and all command abuses!

UNIX
```
% pwd
/group/george
% ls
%
% ls -a
.  ..  .cshrc  .login  .mailrc
% more .cshrc
...
% find ~sue -name magic.c -print
/group/sue/progs/magic.c
/group/sue/new/magic.c
% ls -l ~sue/progs/magic.c ~sue/new/magic.c
-rwxr-----  1  sue  adm  2344  10 Apr  12:20 /group/sue/progs/magic.c
-rwxr-----  1  sue  adm  2734  12 Aug  13:11 /group/sue/new/magic.c
% groups
adm payroll
% mkdir tusk1
% rmdir tusk1
% mkdir task1
% cp ~sue/new/magic.*  ~george/task1/.
% ls task1
magic.c magic.o
% rm task1/magic.o
% mv task1/magic.c task1/magic_wand.c
```

The user George, having logged on for the first time, issues the command `pwd`, which establishes his present working directory and home directory as `/group/george`. The command `ls` turns up a blank for this directory; it finds no files. George is sure that the system administrator said his account would contain some template files that would establish his user environment. He remembers that these are important files and, therefore, likely to be hidden. The `ls -a` command indeed reveals three hidden files, as well as the indicators for his current directory and one directory level higher. George then displays one of these files with the command `more .cshrc` and recognizes many of the features discussed in Chapter 3 for establishing a user environment.

George plans to modify and run a C program, `magic.c`, originally written by Sue. Since he has no idea where Sue keeps the file, George uses `find`

~sue -name magic.c -print to search Sue's directories for the file and to print the path to any file magic.c that the system finds. Two versions of the file are found. George uses the long form of the ls command, ls -l, to display the dates that the files were last modified. Since /group/sue/new/magic.c was modified most recently and this version of the file is larger, George assumes that this is the file he needs to begin his project. George also notes that only other members of the group adm can read the file. By issuing the groups command, George discovers that he is a member of the group adm, which is also the group assigned to the file. Therefore, he can read the file. Before copying the file, George decides the application should reside in a separate subdirectory. Using mkdir, George inadvertently creates subdirectory tusk1; he meant to call the directory task1. George uses the rmdir command to remove the subdirectory and uses mkdir again to create task1. Note that George could have renamed the directory file with the mv command.

George copies the file to the newly created subdirectory using a wildcard; cp ~sue/new/magic.* ~george/task1/.. A directory lookup, ls task1, indicates that two files have been copied. The magic.o file contains object code, indicated in UNIX filenames by .o. Contrast with OpenVMS, where DIRECTORY TASK1.DIR does not give the contents of the subdirectory, but the details of the directory pointer file. The UNIX command ls task1 corresponds to the OpenVMS command DIRECTORY [.TASK1]. Since George plans to make changes to the source code immediately, the object file has no value, and George deletes it with the command rm task1/magic.o. Finally, to distinguish his application from Sue's, George issues the command mv task1/magic.c task1/magic_wand.c to rename the original C source file.

Editing

5

5

Editing

One half of the world cannot understand the pleasures of the other.

—*Jane Austen*

Now that you are familiar with enough file-management commands to perform simple tasks, we turn to the next major hurdle in mastering a new operating system: the editor. What alternatives does UNIX offer to the OpenVMS user familiar with EDT, TPU, or EVE? As you might expect, the alternatives are many and varied. The editors `edit`, `ed`, `ex`, `Emacs`, and `vi` provide interactive editing; `sed` provides noninteractive editing; and `awk`, a more sophisticated, hence more complex, noninteractive editor, provides pattern matching and subsequent file modification useful for extensive file reformatting.

These seven "standard" editors provided in UNIX represent only the tip of the editing iceberg, as you might guess from the chapter quote. There are dozens of text editors available as freeware, shareware, and commercial products.

To the new UNIX user, this chapter may appear to cover a bewildering amount of material. Most readers will feel more comfortable concentrating on a subset of commonly used `ex` and `vi` commands, leaving `sed` and `awk` for later. This is entirely appropriate, as `sed` and `awk` are meant for whole-file manipulation, more in the manner of programming languages. You need only become familiar with one editor, which you can do only with practice, to move on to subsequent chapters. The user who is ready to develop an application may return to `sed` and `awk` if the use of powerful string-handling utilities seems appropriate. Often they are used as part of a pipeline interactivity or in shell scripts.

The editors `edit`, `ed`, and `ex` are line editors, whereas `vi` (visual editor) is a screen editor. The line editor `ex` (Section 5.1) contains the features of both `edit` and `ed`, plus some of its own. OpenVMS users who are predominantly EDT line-mode users need only learn a new syntax when learning `ex`. The same cannot be said of `vi` (Section 5.2), which is designed to work on a variety of terminals and does not depend on a keypad, arrow keys, or VT compatibility. Edits that require a single keystroke in EDT keypad mode may require one or more keystrokes in `vi`, often a combination of the standard keyboard keys and the <CTRL> and <ESC> keys. The implications of using the standard keyboard keys are discussed in Section 5.2.

A powerful, programmable editor popular on UNIX systems, `Emacs` (Section 5.3) is to editors what UNIX is to operating systems. `Emacs` (or `Xemacs`, the X Windows version) comes preinstalled on many UNIX systems and is available for free for virtually all popular operating systems, including Windows and Macintosh. Of particular interest to the TPU/EVE user, `Emacs` shares much of the same look and feel, has a built-in emulation of EDT- and TPU-style keypad editing keys, and can even be set to create files with version numbers automatically, similar to the OpenVMS file system. Unlike `vi`, `Emacs` does not require switching between an input and editing mode, which, at least initially, makes it an easier editor to learn for most people.

Since `vi` and `Emacs` are the two most popular visual editors available on UNIX systems, in any UNIX community it is easy to find adherents of each editor who will tell you why one is superior to the other. The `vi` versus `Emacs` debate is a religious battle that has been raging for literally decades within the UNIX community. We can hardly expect to end this debate within these pages, but we can offer the following general guidelines: The `vi` editor tends to be favored by UNIX system administrators because it is available on virtually every UNIX operating system as a standard utility and requires modest resources to execute. This can be important when dealing with a fresh installation of an operating system or when fixing a crippled one. The `Emacs` editor tends to be favored by computer programmers and wordsmiths because it comes with built-in modes for editing programming-language source code (such as C, Fortran, Perl, etc.), as well as documentation texts. It is also itself programmable and easily extended by writing modules using its own programming language. Since `Emacs` is very feature rich, however, it demands significantly more system resources than an editor like `vi`, which makes it a poor choice for a machine with limited power or that is otherwise not intended for routine interactive computing.

Appendix B summarizes the commands available to the ex, vi, and Emacs user and compares them to EDT's line and keypad commands. It is not necessary to document each of these features here. Rather, we will introduce the general principles of ex, vi, and Emacs and tabulate the common commands in Tables 5.1 through 5.12. The editing required to port an OpenVMS application or write a UNIX application from scratch provides the reader with more than enough opportunity to learn the command syntax outlined in Appendix B.

As with the OpenVMS editors, ed, vi, and Emacs place the contents of the file you are editing in a buffer. When terminating an OpenVMS editing session, the editor writes the contents of the buffer to a file with the same name, but with a version number increased by one. By default, ex and vi write the contents of the buffer back to the same file, overwriting the old version of the file. In contrast, Emacs automatically renames the original file to a backup version before saving the buffer to the original file name. By default, Emacs only maintains a single backup copy, which is replaced after each editing session. But it can be made to maintain multiple file versions automatically, similar to the OpenVMS file system. To prevent overwriting, the novice ex, vi, or Emacs user should always direct the buffer contents to a file with a new name or copy the original file before editing to preserve the old and the new versions. Both the OpenVMS and the UNIX editors periodically save the contents of the buffer, so that in case of system failure you can recover the majority of your edits from the temporary file.

One can also program vi keys to work in much the same manner as the EDT keypad, a subject beyond the scope of this book. Finally, there are several commercial and shareware editors with the look and feel of OpenVMS editors. Some implement a file versioning scheme.

In the noninteractive editor sed (Section 5.4), you do not open a file, move around within it, make changes, see the effects of the changes, and save the changes. Rather, changes to the file are specified externally. You do not see the changes to the file as they are made, only the end result. The changes to be made are specified as part of the sed command line or contained in a separate file. The sed editor uses the same syntax as ex to specify changes to a file. You should use sed on large files and when making the same changes to a number of different files.

The awk editor (Section 5.5) extends the features of sed, but maintains the same principles: awk scans each line in a file to detect a pattern and performs an action when it finds the pattern or reaches a specified range of lines. The editors awk and sed perform different types of actions: awk sup-

ports complex actions, and users often think of its C-like syntax as more of
a programming language than a UNIX utility.

5.1   Line-Mode Editing: ex

Like OpenVMS EDT, ex functions in line mode. It addresses a line by its
line number, or a range of lines by its starting and ending line numbers, and
then performs some function.

You can abbreviate the ex commands that specify functions to single
letters, as shown in Table 5.1, which compares the ex commands to their
EDT counterparts and finds them quite similar. Nevertheless, note the following features of the ex editor:

- The ex editor uses the current line as the default (as does EDT).

- The ex editor uses one or two characters to specify commands.

- The ex editor, by default, does not display line numbers (compare
  with EDT, which displays line numbers): ex uses the command n to
  display line numbers for a specific command, and set number and
  set nonumber to toggle line numbering on and off.

- The w (write) command writes the whole file back to disk. If w is not
  followed by a filename, it overwrites the original version of the file.
  Once w writes the file, you may quit (q) the editor. During a long
  editing session, you should write the file periodically, even though ex
  periodically saves the buffer in case of system failure (see Section
  5.1.6). The command sequence wq writes the file and then quits the
  editor, an example of command grouping.

- If you attempt to quit (q) without writing the file, ex gives you a
  warning and refuses to quit. The command q! overrides this warning, quitting the editor and leaving the original file unchanged.

- The period (.) signifies the current line (compare with the use of the
  period in EDT).

- The dollar sign ($) signifies the last line of the file (compare with the
  EDT command END). This use of a metacharacter to help define a
  string is called a regular expression. Regular expressions are used in
  each of the utilities described in this chapter, although the capabilities
  and exact syntax vary.

- Unlike EDT, ex automatically resequences the line numbers after each command. EDT resequences only when you save the modified file or issue the RESEQUENCE command. For example, if you add a line between lines 1 and 2, EDT refers to the new line as 1.1, but ex refers to it as 2 and changes the original line 2 to line 3.

- The ex prompt is a colon (:). Compare with OpenVMS, which uses an asterisk (*).

Table 5.1   *Summary of ex Commands*

ex **Command**	**EDT Equivalent**	ex **Meaning**
a (append)		Appends lines after the current line
c (change)	CHANGE	Changes specified lines
d (delete)	DELETE	Deletes specified lines
e (edit)		Sets edit buffer to contain a specified file and overwrites original contents
f (filename)		Displays a specified file
g (global)	ALL	Applies command to whole file
i (insert)	INSERT	Inserts lines before the current line
j (join)		Joins two lines to make one
m (move)	MOVE	Moves lines to a new place (cuts and pastes)
n (number)	(default)	Includes line numbers
p (pointer)	TYPE	Displays specified lines
q (quit)	QUIT	Leaves editor without saving changes
r (read)	INCLUDE	Reads a file into the editing buffer
s (substitute)	SUBSTITUTE	Substitutes a new character string for an old one
t (transfer)	COPY	Copies lines to a new location
w (write)	EXIT	Writes contents of edit buffer to file
W (write)		Appends buffer contents to alternative existing file
=		Shows current numeric value of . or $

5.1.1   Displaying Lines

The following examples illustrate the display of lines using the ex editor. Note that ex uses the command p (position pointer and display lines) for this purpose (see Table 5.1). The p command is the default: If you enter only the line numbers, the editor assumes p.

OpenVMS   UNIX
Form:
```
* COMMAND [RANGE]                : [range] command
```
Example:
```
$ EDIT/EDT MYFILE.DAT            % ex myfile.dat
1 This is line 1 "myfile.dat"   59 lines, 1971 characters
*                                :
```
Example:
```
* T 5                            : 5 p              # display line 5
```
Example:
```
* T 5:10                         : 5,10             # display lines 5 to 10
```
Example:
```
* T WHOLE                        : 1,$              # display whole file
```
Example:
```
* T.:END                         : .,$              # display from current
```
Example: # line to end
```
* T 1:5;10:20                    : 1,5              # display lines 1 to 5
```
Example: # and 10 to 20
```
* T -1:END-10                    : 10,20: .-1,$-10  # display from one before
                                                    # the current line to
                                                    # the tenth from the
                                                    # last line
```

The above examples are straightforward. Note the following ex features:

- The ex syntax requires that the command follow the target range of lines; EDT places the command before the range of lines.

- When ex displays a range of lines, the current line is the last line in the display field (in EDT, it is the first).

- The ex editor uses minus (–) and plus (+) to indicate lines before and after the current line respectively, and a period (.) to indicate the current line, exactly as in EDT. Thus, `.-5` is five lines before the current line and `.+5` is five lines after the current line.

5.1.2   **Inserting, Appending, and Deleting**

The following examples illustrate inserting, appending, and deleting lines using ex.

OpenVMS	UNIX	
Example:		
`*INSERT`	`: I`	`# insertion occurs`
`This is one new line`	`This is one new line`	`before the current`
`This is two new lines`	`This is two new lines`	`line`
`<CTRL>Z`	`.`	
`*`	`:`	
	`: a`	`# append occurs`
	`This is one new line`	`after the current`
	`This is two new lines`	`line`
	`.`	
	`:`	
Example:		
`* DELETE`	`:d`	`# delete current line`
Example:		
`* D 1:3`	`: 1,3 d`	`# delete lines 1 to 3`
Example:		
`* R -1:. + 1`	`: .-1,. + 1 c`	`# delete one line`
`This line replaces 3`	`This line replaces 3 old`	`above current to one`
`old`		`line below current`
		`and insert`

As you study these examples, note the following:

- The command `a` (append) inserts text after the current line, and `i` (insert) inserts text before the current line.

- Insert mode is terminated by typing a period as the first character of a new line (compare with `<CTRL>-Z` in EDT), whereupon the ex prompt is returned.

- After appending or inserting text, the current line is the last line entered.

The command c (change) changes existing text, that is, a deletion immediately followed by an insertion (compare with the EDT command REPLACE).

5.1.3 Search and Replace

The following examples illustrate string searching and string substitution.

OpenVMS	UNIX	
Example:		
`* T "`*`STRING`*`"`	`: /`*`string`*`/`	`# display line below` `containing string`
Example:		
`* T-"`*`STRING`*`"`	`: ?`*`string`*`?`	`# display line above` `containing string`
Example:		
`* T "`*`STRING1`*`":"`*`STRING2`*`"`	`: /`*`string1`*`/,/`*`string2`*`/`	`# display lines` `between` *`string1`* `and` *`string2`*
Example:		
`* S `*`STRING1`*`/`*`STRING2`*`/1:5`	`: 1,5 s /`*`string1`*`/` *`string2`*`/`	`# substitute` *`string1`* `for` *`string2`* `in lines` `1 to 5; first` `occurrence only`
Example:		
`* S /`*`STRING1`*`/`*`STRING2`*`/` `1:END`	`/: 1,$ s/`*`string1`*`/` *`string2`*`/g`	`# substitute` *`string1`* `for` *`string2`* `in lines` `1 to 5; all` `occurrences`
Example:		
`* S ?/?slash?`	`: s/\//slash/`	`# precede with` `backslash if to be` `taken literally`
	`: s//`*`string2`*`/`	`# use last defined` *`string1`*

These examples illustrate the following ex features:

- The ex editor uses a slash to delimit a string; if the string itself contains a slash, precede the slash with a backslash to tell the editor to read the slash as a character instead of a delimiter (compare with EDT, where alternative delimiters may be used).

- If a forward search fails to find the string in the latter part of the file, ex will "wrap" the search to the beginning of the file (compare with EDT, where the search terminates at the end of the file). Hence, the line on which the string is found may precede the current line in the file. Similarly, in a backward search, the line containing the string may follow the current line in the file. If ex does not find the string, it will return a question mark. If the file does not contain the search string, the current line does not change; otherwise, the line containing the first occurrence of the search string becomes the current line.

- The s (substitution) command replaces only the first occurrence of a string in a line; the g (global) command substitutes all occurrences of the string in a line.

5.1.4 Cut and Paste

The m (move) command deletes text from one location in the file and places it elsewhere. The co (copy) command duplicates text in another location in the file.

OpenVMS	UNIX	

`* MOVE-3:. TO END`
`4 lines moved`
	`: -3,. m $`
	`last line moved here`
		`# move 4 lines`
		`(minus 3 to current`
		`inclusive) to the`
		`end of the file`

`* COPY 10:20 TO 31`	`:10,20 co 30`	`# copy lines 10 to` `20 after line 30`

`* COPY- "string1'":"`
`"string2'"`
`- TO . +1`
	`: /string1/,/string2/ \ co.`	`# copy lines between`
		`the first occurrence`
		`of string1 and`
		`string2,`
		`respectively after`
		`the current line`

Note the following:

- Remember that `co` is an abbreviation for the copy command, whereas `c` is an abbreviation for the change command.

- The `co` command copies a range following the specified line number; the EDT `COPY` command copies a range preceding the specified line number.

5.1.5 External File Handling

The `ex` command `r` (read) adds all or part of an external file to the file being edited (compare with the EDT `INCLUDE` command). The `w` (write) command writes part or all of the file being edited to a new file (compare with the EDT `WRITE` command). The `e` (edit) command reads an external file into the file being edited and discards the original contents of the file being edited (compare with the EDT commands `DELETE 1:END` followed by `INCLUDE`).

OpenVMS   **UNIX**

Example:
```
* WRITE NEWFILE 1:10     : 1.10 w newfile    # write the first 10 lines
                                             of the file being edited to
                                             newfile
```

Example:
```
* INCLUDE MYFILE.DAT     : r myfile.dat      # include myfile.dat after
                                             the current line
```

Example:
```
* DELETE 1:END           : e myfile.dat      # include myfile.dat,
* INCLUDE MYFILE.DAT                         deleting any original file
```

5.1.6 Recovering an Editing Session

In the event of system failure or inadvertent termination of an editing session—for example, with <CTRL>-C—the `ex` editor `-r` option recovers the file being edited (compare with the OpenVMS command `EDIT/RECOVER`). In this example, `ex -r myfile` recovers the editing session inadvertently terminated with <CTRL>-C.

OpenVMS	UNIX
`MYFILE.DAT`	`% ex myfile`
`$ EDIT/EDT MYFILE.DAT`	`[changes made here]`
`[changes made here]`	`<CTRL>-C`
`<CTRL>-Y`	
`$ EDIT/EDT/RECOVER`	`% ex -r myfile`

5.2   UNIX Screen Editor: `vi`

The UNIX editor `vi` (visual) corresponds to TPU or EDT when used in keypad mode. Rather than addressing a file by line number, `vi` addresses the file by the position of the screen cursor.

EDT functions mostly on VT-series terminals and makes extensive use of the keypad found on all such terminals; `vi` functions on virtually any video terminal. For the OpenVMS user faced with learning `vi`, this situation is both good and bad. It is good because its flexibility has led to `vi` being distributed as part of almost every version of UNIX (it was originally part of BSD). On different versions of UNIX and on different types of terminals, `vi` functions identically. It is bad because special keys, which may be terminal-specific, are not assigned to editing functions, making editing more cumbersome. For example, the character `d` deletes the word at the cursor. But what if you wish to insert the character *d* into the file? You must change from command mode to insert mode by pressing `i`. EDT in keypad mode is always in insert mode, because it does not manage editing commands with the printable character set.

Remembering to toggle between command and insert modes is the major hurdle for the OpenVMS user learning `vi`. All too frequently the novice `vi` user enters insert mode, adds text, and then strikes the arrow key to move the cursor to another location. Rather than moving the cursor, `vi` inserts the character mapping of the arrow key in the file because the user forgot to press the `<ESC>` key to change back to command mode.

We must note two further points before getting started with `vi`. First, `ex` is to `vi` what EDT in line mode is to EDT in keypad mode; that is, you can invoke many of the `ex` commands from the `vi` editor. Second, `vi` is a complex editor possessing over 100 commands that you can combine in many ways. We will discuss only a few commands that you are likely to need on a regular basis. Appendix B contains a listing of these commands.

5.2.1   Getting Started

The command `vi file1 [...]` starts a `vi` editing session. For example, `vi file1 file2` starts a `vi` editing session on `file1`. When you leave `file1`, `file2` will be opened for editing, and so on. If the file you call for does not exist, `vi` will create a new file. New files and short files that do not fill the screen cause `vi` to display a tilde (~) in column one of every screen line. The tilde is not part of the file and disappears as you add lines. Compare with EDT keypad mode `[EOB]`, the end of buffer symbol found at the end of each file. The tilde distinguishes blank lines in a file from no lines.

When you open a file for editing, `vi` begins in command mode: You may move the cursor and delete text, but you may not insert until you explicitly enter insert mode.

5.2.2   Cursor Movement

Table 5.2 introduces a subset of commands that move the cursor. Note the following:

- Movement commands typically require one or two keystrokes.
- Delimiters defining cursor movement in `vi` are similar to those used by EDT in keypad mode: Characters, words, lines, and screens all delimit movement.
- In EDT keypad mode, you can precede keystrokes with [4][1] or [5] to set the direction to forward or backward movement, respectively. The `vi` editor uses different commands to define forward and backward movement.
- Both `vi` and EDT keep internal records of line numbers. You can move to a particular line number with the `vi` command #G.
- You may combine `vi` movement commands with `vi` action commands (Section 5.2.4).

5.2.3   Action Commands

Action commands change the contents of a file in some way. Table 5.3 summarizes the commonly used `vi` action commands. Note the following:

---

1.   Keypad characters appear in square brackets throughout this chapter and in Appendix B.

Table 5.2   *Cursor Movements with `vi`*

`vi` **Command**	`vi` **Meaning**
`arrow keys`	Move the cursor right, left, up, or down
`$`	Moves to the end of the line
`^ or 0`	Moves to the beginning of the line
`H`	Moves cursor to top of screen
`L`	Moves cursor to bottom of screen
`M`	Moves cursor to middle of screen
`<CTRL>-F`	Scrolls file forward one screen
`<CTRL>-B`	Scrolls file backward one screen
`<CTRL>-D`	Scrolls file forward half a screen
`<CTRL>-U`	Scrolls file backward half a screen
`#<CTRL>-F`	Scrolls file forward # screens
`#<CTRL>-B`	Scrolls file backward # screens
`W`	Moves forward one word
`B`	Moves backward one word
`#w`	Moves forward # words
`#b`	Moves backward # words
`E`	Moves to last character of current word
`F`*n*	Moves forward to next character *n*
`B`*n*	Moves backward to next character *n*
`;`	Repeats search for *n* in the current line
`)`	Moves forward one sentence
`(`	Moves backward one sentence
`/`*string*	Searches forward for *string*
`?`*string*	Searches backward for *string*
`#G`	Moves to line number #

- Action commands are usually denoted by a single character.

- Commands that permit input must end with <ESC> (F11 on many terminals) to return the editor to command mode. It is common for the EDT keypad-mode user to forget this.

- In some instances, the single-letter command name, when doubled, applies to the whole line. For example, dd deletes the line at the cursor, then moves the cursor to the beginning of the next line.

- The vi editor does not use reverse video to highlight text.

Table 5.3   *Action Commands with* vi

vi **Command**	vi **Meaning**
i	Inserts text before the cursor
I	Inserts text at beginning of current line
a	Appends text after the cursor
A	Appends text after end of current line
o	Opens blank line after current line
O	Opens blank line before current line
<ESC>	Terminates input mode
x	Deletes character at cursor
X	Deletes character before cursor
D	Deletes starting at the cursor
Db	Deletes word backwards
Dd	Deletes current line
r	Overwrites single character
R	Overwrites until terminated by <ESC>
p	Pastes deleted or yanked text after cursor
P	Pastes deleted or yanked text before cursor
y	Yanks (copies) text into alternative buffer
yy	Yanks (copies) current line into alternative buffer

5.2.4   **Combining Action and Movement Commands**

You may combine action and movement commands to produce a vast number of possible effects. Table 5.4 summarizes a commonly used subset. Note that the movement command follows the action command. Thus, d (delete) followed by w (move the cursor from its current location to the end of the current word) deletes all characters from the current cursor location to the end of the word.

Table 5.4   *Common vi Commands Combining Movement and Action*

vi **Command**	vi **Meaning**
dw	Deletes from cursor to beginning of next word
#dw	Deletes from cursor # words
d)	Deletes from cursor to end of sentence
d(	Deletes from cursor to beginning of sentence
d$	Deletes from cursor to end of line
#dd	Deletes # lines
cw	Deletes word and inserts
cc or S	Deletes current line and inserts
c$	Deletes to end of line and inserts

5.2.5   **Invoking ex from vi**

The OpenVMS EDT keypad-mode user may issue a line-mode command by striking the keypad keys [PF1] [7]. Similarly, when the vi user enters a colon in command mode, a colon prompt appears at the bottom of the screen, and the user may enter an ex command. The most important uses of ex commands are to write (w) the contents of the editing buffer to a disk file and to terminate (q) the editing session.

Other common uses of ex commands include inserting the contents of another file into the current file and writing all or part of the current file to a new file. The command r *filename* issued at the colon prompt inserts the contents of the filename immediately before the cursor. You can write a section of the current file to a new file. The ex command requires line numbers to delimit the text you wish to write. The ex command set number displays lines in vi with line numbers. You may use *n,m* w *filename* to write lines *n* through *m* to the file *filename*. The `ex` command `set non-umber` turns off line numbering.

Table 5.5 lists these and other useful `ex` commands issued from `vi`. Note the following:

- The command `!`*command* executes a UNIX shell command. For example `!ls` displays the contents of the current directory. Press `<CR>` to redisplay the current file.[2]

- The `set shiftwidth = ` *n* command defines temporary right and left margins. The default margin is eight columns.

Table 5.5   *Common ex Commands Issued from `vi`*

Ex **Command**	`vi` **Meaning**
`r` *file*	Includes an external file
`!`	Enters a shell command
`set number`	Turns on line numbering
`set nonumber`	Turns off line numbering
`set autoindent`	Indents text following the cursor
`set noai`	Turns off indenting
`set sw = ` *n*	Sets shift width to *n* characters (default = 8)
`w`	Writes edit buffer to disk
`q!`	Quits editing without saving changes
`wq`	Writes edit buffer to disk and quits, saving changes

5.2.6   **Miscellaneous Commands**

Perhaps the most important command in this category is the `u` (undo) command. You may undo either the last command (`u`) or a number of sequential commands affecting a single line (`U`).

---

2.   Section 7.3 describes how the C shell user may suspend the editing session, issue UNIX commands, and then return to the editor.

Another important command in this category is the period (.), which repeats the last action command—a convenient shorthand for repeating editing commands.

You may use > (greater than, right shift) and < (less than, left shift) to move lines. Right and left shift move text right or left the number of columns specified by the *shiftwidth parameter* (see the command set shift-width = *n* in Table 5.5). Text will not be truncated if an attempt is made to move it beyond the left margin; rather the command is ignored. Similarly, the text wraps if moved beyond the right margin. The commands >> and << shift single lines right and left respectively.

A powerful feature of vi not available in EDT is *filtering*, the ability to pass all or part of a file to a UNIX command such as sort (see Section 8.4.6), spell (the UNIX spell checker), or nroff for text formatting. The following example illustrates the use of a sort filter.

```
UNIX
Example:
vi myfile.list
jill
jack
adam
~
....
: 1,$! sort
adam
jack
jill
~
....
:wq
%
```

The colon gets the attention of the ex editor, which accepts a range of lines (1, $) and passes them to the sort command with the construct !sort. The command sort without options uses the first field as the *sort key*, rearranges the text, and redisplays the screen. The command :wq, write followed by quit, saves the modified file.

5.2.7   Ending an Editing Session

You may terminate vi by issuing the ex commands to save the editing changes or quit leaving the file unchanged. The vi command zz issued from command mode will also terminate the vi session, saving any changes that you have made.

5.2.8   Recovering an Editing Session

In Section 5.1.6 we saw how to recover an ex editing session in the event of system failure or accidental termination of an editing session with an interrupt. You can recover vi editing sessions with the command vi -r *filename*.

5.3   UNIX Screen Editor: Emacs

The GNU software editor Emacs (editor macros) is one of the most powerful editors for UNIX and other operating systems. There are versions of Emacs for all flavors of UNIX and Linux, as well as for OpenVMS, DOS, and Macintosh. Appendix E provides references to further information about GNU Emacs.

In many ways Emacs resembles the EVE/TPU editor for OpenVMS systems. In fact, the EVE/TPU editor was modeled on Emacs. Figure 5.1 shows a sample Emacs session.

Emacs can be invoked from the command line, and you can issue commands using a sequence of keystrokes. Alternatively, an X Windows version of Emacs, called Xemacs, allows you to issue commands using menus. This chapter concentrates on the commands and options for the command-line version of Emacs.

The Emacs editor allows you to do much more than simply edit a file. It can also be used to do the following:

- Compile programs
- Send and receive mail
- Run a spell check on a file
- Execute a single-shell command
- Run a shell in an Emacs window

When you use Emacs to edit a file, you work on a temporary copy of the file in a buffer. The original file is not modified on disk until you write the

Figure 5.1
A sample Emacs
session.

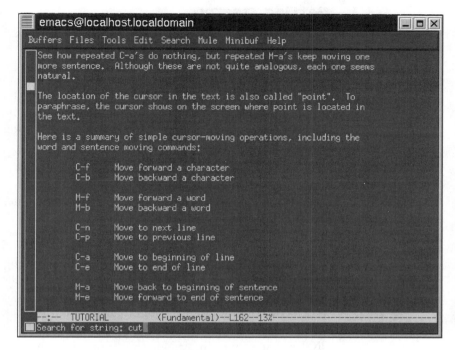

```
emacs@localhost.localdomain                        _ □ ☒
Buffers Files Tools Edit Search Mule Minibuf Help

See how repeated C-a's do nothing, but repeated M-a's keep moving one
more sentence.  Although these are not quite analogous, each one seems
natural.

The location of the cursor in the text is also called "point".  To
paraphrase, the cursor shows on the screen where point is located in
the text.

Here is a summary of simple cursor-moving operations, including the
word and sentence moving commands:

        C-f     Move forward a character
        C-b     Move backward a character

        M-f     Move forward a word
        M-b     Move backward a word

        C-n     Move to next line
        C-p     Move to previous line

        C-a     Move to beginning of line
        C-e     Move to end of line

        M-a     Move back to beginning of sentence
        M-e     Move forward to end of sentence

--:--  TUTORIAL         (Fundamental)--L162--13%------------------------
Search for string: cut
```

file with Emacs. And like EVE/TPU, Emacs allows you to open multiple buffers and edit them in separate windows.

Emacs has different operating modes, which allow Emacs to operate differently based on the contents of the file being edited. There are both major and minor modes. Some examples of major modes include the following:

- Text mode—for writing text

- Picture mode—for creating line drawings

- C mode—for writing C programs

- FORTRAN mode—for writing FORTRAN programs

Modes are available for all well-known programming languages and even text-document formats such as HTML and nroff. In this book, we concentrate only on the editing functions of Emacs. There is a wealth of printed and online documentation on Emacs available from bookstores and on the Web. See Appendix E for a list of general Emacs resources.

5.3.1   Getting Started

The command for starting an editing session is emacs *[options]* *file*. If you do not enter a file name, a scratch buffer is displayed, which contains the current Emacs version information and a short help text aimed at new users. (This includes instructions on how to start an interactive tutorial for learning Emacs right in the editor.) You can run Emacs in the current terminal window, or start a new window on X Windows or some other GUI.

There are a number of options that can be entered with the emacs command. One such option is the -u option to load a user's initialization file containing predefined functions. For example, to start an Emacs session using the initialization file belonging to user herb, you would enter

```
emacs -u herb
```

Much like TPU/EVE, Emacs divides the screen into distinct regions. The contents of a buffer are represented on the screen by a window and its associated status or "modeline" line. (Do not confuse the Emacs use of the word "window" with the separate overlapping windows of a GUI interface.) The modeline provides useful information about the buffer and serves as a separator between multiple Emacs windows when more than one buffer is displayed at a time. To distinguish it from the buffer itself, the modeline is displayed in reverse video. Information displayed in the modeline includes the following:

- The name of the buffer (which is usually the name of the file being edited)

- The current major editing mode (e.g., "Fundamental," "Text," "Fortran")

- The relative position of the cursor within the buffer, expressed as a percentage

- Indicators showing if the buffer contents have been modified yet, or if the buffer is read-only

At the very bottom of the screen, the last line is reserved for the "minibuffer." Like TPU/EVE, pressing a special key sequence allows English-like editing commands to be entered. The minibuffer is the command-line window where these commands are displayed as they are typed. It is also used to display brief messages from the editor.

5.3.2 Emacs **Commands**

Emacs has hundreds of available commands. The commands used most frequently are bound to specific keys. For example, many of the cursor movement commands are invoked using a combination of the Control key and a character key. Some other commands are invoked in combination with the Escape key.

There is a concept called the *meta* command that you will find in the GNU Emacs documentation and online help. Emacs recognizes the Escape key as the META key, and the documentation represents it as "M-" You can execute any meta command by pressing the Escape key followed by a given command-key sequence. In this book, we will refer to the meta commands by <ESC>.

As mentioned above, frequently used commands are bound to specific keys for convenient use. But all Emacs commands can also be entered by pressing <ESC>-X and then typing the command name, followed by a <CR>. This is similar to using the DO key with EDT and TPU/EVE in Open-VMS. In fact whatever key you already use as the DO key on your terminal or terminal emulator will most likely also be recognized by Emacs for this command function as well. But for portability between different desktop systems, you may want to get in the habit of using <ESC>-X, which should work on any keyboard.

5.3.3 **Cursor Movement**

Table 5.6 introduces a subset of commands that move the cursor.

Table 5.6   *Cursor Movements with* Emacs

Emacs **Command**	Emacs **Meaning**
arrow keys	Move the cursor right, left, up, or down
<CTRL>-E	Moves to end of line
<CTRL>-A	Moves to beginning of line
<ESC>-<	Moves cursor to top of buffer
<ESC>->	Moves cursor to end of buffer
<CTRL>-V	Scrolls file forward one screen
<ESC>-V	Scrolls file backward one screen

Table 5.6   *Cursor Movements with* `Emacs` *(continued)*

`<ESC>-F`	Moves forward one word
`<ESC>-B`	Moves backward one word
`<CTRL>-S` *string*	Searches forward for *string*
`<CTRL>-R` *string*	Searches backward for *string*
`<ESC>-X goto-line` *n*	Moves to line number *n*

The `<CTRL>-S` command works in a similar fashion as pressing the FIND key with a OpenVMS editor, but with an interesting twist. This key is bound to the `emacs` command "isearch-forward" where the "i" stands for incremental. Pressing `<CTRL>-S` causes `Emacs` to prompt with the string "`I-search:`" in the minibuffer. As you enter each character of your target string, the cursor will jump forward in the buffer to the next matching string. For example, when searching for the word "emacs," entering the letter "e" would cause the cursor to jump forward to the next letter "e" found in the text. Entering "m" would jump to the next "em" sequence, say in the word "them." Entering the next letter, "a," would jump the cursor forward again to the next occurring sequence of "ema," perhaps found in the word "thematic," and so on. Finally, entering the letter "s" would jump the cursor to the next occurrence of the word "emacs" in the text. And much like pressing the FIND key twice, entering `<CTRL>-S` twice will tell `Emacs` to search forward again for the previous target string.

5.3.4   **Marking Text**

You can use `Emacs` to mark regions to which you can subsequently apply another operation, such as copying or deletion. Table 5.7 introduces commands that mark text.

Table 5.7   *Marking Text with* `Emacs`

`Emacs` **Command**	`Emacs` **Meaning**
`<CTRL>-SPACE`	Sets mark at cursor position
`<CTRL>-X <CTRL>-X`	Swaps position of point and mark
`<ESC>-@`	Sets mark after end of next word

Table 5.7   *Marking Text with* Emacs

<ESC>-H	Sets mark at end of a paragraph and moves cursor to beginning of paragraph
<CTRL>-X <CTRL>-P	Marks page
<CTRL>-X H	Marks entire buffer

Pressing <CTRL>-SPACE (or <CTRL>-@) is similar to pressing the SELECT key when using a OpenVMS editor. Moving the cursor forward or backward, using any method, will cause the traversed text to be progressively selected. With Xemacs the selected text will be highlighted as the cursor moves over the text, in a similar fashion as with an OpenVMS editor. Unfortunately GNU Emacs does not do this; you have to remember where you started your selection. When selected in this fashion, marked text can then be operated on using commands that act upon a text "region." For example <CTRL>-W would be equivalent to pressing the CUT key, and in a similar fashion to EDT and TPU/EVE, the cut text is stored in a temporary buffer. The <CTRL>-Y (yank) command is used to paste the contents of this temporary buffer back, starting at the current cursor position, again, in a similar fashion to the PASTE key with an OpenVMS editor.

5.3.5 Action Commands

Table 5.8 lists some of the Emacs action commands.

Table 5.8   *Action Commands with* Emacs

Emacs **Command**	Emacs **Meaning**
<CTRL>-D	Deletes character at cursor
BACKSPACE	Deletes character before cursor
<ESC>-D	Deletes word at the cursor
<ESC>-<BACKSPACE>	Deletes word backwards
<CTRL>-K	Deletes from cursor to end of line
<ESC>-K	Deletes sentence the cursor is on
<CTRL>-K <BACKSPACE>	Deletes previous sentence
<CTRL>-Y	Restores last deletion

Table 5.8   *Action Commands with* Emacs *(continued)*

Emacs **Command**	Emacs **Meaning**
<CTRL>-W	Deletes a marked region
<CTRL>-X <CTRL>-O	Deletes all but one consecutive blank line
<ESC>-SPACE	Deletes all but one space before and after point
<ESC>-u	Uppercases word
<ESC>-l	Lowercases word
<ESC>-c	Capitalizes word
<CTRL>-X <CTRL>-u	Uppercases region
<CTRL>-X <CTRL>-l	Lowercases region
<ESC>-X capitalize region	Capitalizes region

Note that the "kill" command (<CTRL>-K), as well as similar commands that remove text, will store the deleted text into a temporary buffer. A quick way to move a contiguous chunk of text is to repeatedly use the <CTRL>-K command to delete several lines of text, then after repositioning the cursor, to use the "yank" command (<CTRL>-Y) to paste that text back into the file's buffer.

5.3.6   Executing a Shell Command from Emacs

Table 5.9 shows some Emacs shell commands you can run while in an editing session.

Table 5.9   Emacs *Shell Command*

Emacs **Command**	Emacs **Meaning**
<ESC>-!	Execute a shell command
<ESC>-shell	Start a shell in a window called shell
<ESC>-x |	Run a shell command on the region

The Emacs shell commands are analogous to the DCL command in EVE/TPU. When executed, the current buffer window is split to provide a new window where the command and the output it generates are displayed. (See Section 5.3.9 for information on how to work with multiple windows.)

5.3.7 Recording Keyboard Macros

With Emacs you can record *macros*, a set of commands and key sequences, that can be executed again, as many times as desired. Table 5.10 lists some Emacs keyboard macro commands.

Table 5.10 Emacs *Keyboard Macros Commands*

Emacs **Command**	Emacs **Meaning**
`<CTRL>-x (`	Start recording a keyboard macro
`<CTRL>-x )`	End recording a keyboard macro
`<CTRL>-x e |`	Execute last defined macro
`<CTRL>-u <CTRL>-x (`	Append to last defined macro
`<ESC>-x name-last-keyboard-macro`	Assign name to macro last defined

The Emacs keyboard macro commands are analogous to the EVE/TPU "learn" command, if maybe not quite as convenient to use. It is also possible to save keyboard macros for future use, or to even examine and edit the "program" that was created by the sequence of keystrokes used to create the macro.

5.3.8 Working with Files

Various Emacs commands allow you to manipulate files, such as inserting, saving, and so on.

Table 5.11 *Operating on Files with* Emacs

Emacs **Command**	Emacs **Meaning**
`<CTRL>-X <CTRL>-C`	Exit Emacs; asks if you want to save buffers
`<CTRL>-X <CTRL>-S`	Saves buffer
`<CTRL>-X <CTRL>-W` *file*	Writes buffer to *file*.
`<CTRL>-X <CTRL>-F` *file*	Finds *file* and reads it
`<CTRL>-X I file`	Inserts *file* at cursor
`<CTRL>-X <CTRL>-R`	Open buffer read-only

The Emacs find-file command (bound to <CTRL>-X <CTRL>-F) prompts in the minibuffer for the name of a file to edit. The selected file's buffer is then displayed *in place* of whatever file was previously being displayed. However, the original file's buffer and changes are *not* lost, the buffer itself is simply no longer visible. In contrast, the insert-file command (bound to <CTRL>-X I) inserts the file you specify into the current buffer at the current cursor position. With either command, Emacs provides automatic filename completion. When the command is first entered, Emacs will prompt with the directory path it assumes you want to use for the file. This will be the same directory that the contains the file you are currently editing. You can edit this path, if necessary, then enter the first few characters of the desired filename, and press the Tab key. If there is a unique match for that string, Emacs will complete the entire filename. Pressing <CR> will confirm the entry. If the string is not unique, Emacs will display as much of the filename as possible up to the point where the matched files diverge in their spelling. You can either enter a few more characters and press Tab again to continue the autocompletion, or pressing the Tab key twice will cause Emacs to display all available matching filenames in a separate (and temporary) window. When the file selection is completed and confirmed with a <CR>, the temporary file selection window will automatically disappear.

5.3.9   **Working with Windows in Emacs**

With Emacs, you can split your screen into multiple windows. This is useful if you want to work with several files at a time, for example, to cut and paste text between windows. Table 5.12 lists common Emacs windows commands.

Table 5.12   Emacs *Windows Commands*

Emacs **Command**	Emacs **Meaning**
<CTRL>-x 2	Splits current window into two vertically
<CTRL>-x 5	Splits current window into two horizontally
<CTRL>-x o	Moves to other window
<CTRL>-x 0	Deletes current window
<ESC>-X buffer-menu	Displays selection list of all open buffers
<ESC>-X shrink-window	Makes window shorter
<CTRL>-x ^	Makes window taller

Table 5.12   Emacs *Windows Commands*

Emacs **Command**	Emacs **Meaning**
<CTRL>-x 4 b	Selects a buffer in other window
<CTRL>-x 4 f	Finds a file in other window
<CTRL>-x 4 m	Composes mail in other window

In Section 5.3.8 we mentioned that the find-file command (<CTRL>-X <CTRL>-F) replaces the current buffer window with a new buffer for the file just selected. The buffer-menu command (<ESC>-X buffer-menu) is an easy way to call back any buffer to the display. The names of all the currently open buffers are displayed with useful information such as the size of the buffer, the associated filename, the editing mode, and an indication of whether the buffer contents have been changed since the last time it was saved. The cursor keys can be used to select the desired buffer and pressing the <CR> on that buffer's entry line will bring that buffer back into view for editing.

5.3.10 Error Recovery and Recovering an Editing Session

As with any editor, it's easy in Emacs to accidentally enter a wrong command or keystroke or to make an unintended change to your file. Then there is the problem of having an editing session interrupted by a computer or network crash. There are four basic recovery techniques that can be used to get yourself back on track or to repair the damage.

1. Use <CTRL>-G (the keyboard-quit command) to cancel any Emacs command currently in progress. For example, suppose that you press <ESC>-X to enter a command, but change your mind. Pressing <CTRL>-G will cancel the command entry and return the cursor to the file buffer window. Anytime you find yourself with Emacs asking you an unexpected question or to input information before you are ready, use <CTRL>-G to cancel the dialog and its associated operation.

2. Use <CTRL>-_ (Control + underscore) to invoke the "undo" command. This command can be executed repeatedly to walk back through the most recent changes to the buffer. This includes not

only reversing commands that perform large changes, such as cutting and pasting text, but even small incremental changes, such as typing text into the buffer. You'll probably want to use the undo command to try backing out of your mistake every time you find yourself saying "oops."

3.   The revert-buffer command (`<ESC>-X revert-buffer`) is used to return the contents of the buffer to the last saved version. This would be the most recent of either the original version of the file at the start of the editing session, or the last version you explicitly saved to disk using the save-buffer command (`<CTRL>-X <CTRL>-S`).

4.   The recover-file command (`<ESC>-X recover-file`) is used to restore and resume editing a file that was interrupted by a computer crash or network outage. As with the OpenVMS editors, Emacs keeps a record of the keystrokes you enter during an editing session. The recover-file command can be used to replay the editing session and recover most, if not all, of the changes you made to the file before the interruption. Note that if you start a new editing session on a file that was interrupted, Emacs will automatically detect this and suggest doing a recover-file operation.

5.3.11   TPU-EDT Mode and Automatic File Versions

The `tpu-edt` command activates the binding of Emacs commands to terminal keypad function keys similar to the command bindings used by TPU/EDT. To activate this mode, press `<ESC>-X` and then enter the command `tpu-edt` in the minibuffer. Pressing the [PF2] key should now bring up a diagram of the function-key assignments and a summary of available control-key functions.

As an aside, we should point out that there are advantages and disadvantages to making a text editor you are not familiar with emulate one that you already know. On the plus side, emulation can make you productive with the new editor almost immediately. But emulations are rarely perfect. You may find that using something that works in a similar, but not exactly the same fashion, is in the end more frustrating then just learning something new. An emulation can be like using a slightly broken version of an editor you are already fluent with, which can make the transition back and forth between the two more difficult.

Emacs can be made to maintain separate versions of files you edit with Emacs automatically, much in the same way that OpenVMS does for all programs and utilities. The easiest way to do this is to create a file named

.emacs in your home directory and place in that file the following Emacs initialization commands:

```
(setq version-control t)        ; Turn on file versioning.
(setq kept-new-versions 5)      ; Set 'window' of versions
(setq kept-old-versions 5)      ; to keep.
(setq delete-old-versions nil); On exit, ask before purging.
```

These are elisp commands, the programming language of Emacs. These commands turn on the built-in Emacs file-versioning system and set various control values. With these settings in place, here is what the file versions will look like in a typical editing session:

UNIX

Example:
```
% emacs myfile.for
(enter some text into a new file)

% ls myfile.for*
myfile.for

% emacs myfile.for
(make some edits to the file)

% ls myfile.for*
myfile.for   myfile.for.~1~

% emacs myfile.for
(make last edits to the file)

% ls myfile.for*
myfile.for   myfile.for.~1~   myfile.for.~2~
```

With the first invocation we create the initial file. Editing the file causes, on exit, the original file to be renamed with the file type .~1~, and the modified buffer is saved as the original filename. Editing the file again creates a second version, etc. Like OpenVMS, the higher the number, the later the version, *but* unlike OpenVMS, the latest version has no number at all. A final note: since file version numbers are not a part of the UNIX file system, outside of Emacs, no other utilities in UNIX "understand" these file versions. In place of the OpenVMS purge command, we instead use Emacs options in the `.emacs` initialization file to provide semiautomatic purging of old versions.

5.4   The Stream Editor: sed

The editor sed, which has no direct OpenVMS equivalent, is useful for editing large files or for making the same changes to a succession of files. In its simplest form, sed uses line numbers in the same way as ex to delimit the text to be edited. The real power of sed is its use of *regular expressions* to specify the text to be edited. For example, it is a simple matter in sed to edit the last word of each line in a file. The awk editor, discussed below, builds on this concept to permit complex string manipulation. Although awk is more powerful than sed, it is also more complex; its authors consider awk a high-level language.

We start by introducing sed with some simple examples.

UNIX
Form:
```
% sed [-n] [[-e command]...] [-f] file
```
Example:
```
% sed s/this/that/ file1
```
Example:
```
% sed s/this/that/p file1
```
Example:
```
% sed -n s/this/that/p file1
```
Example:
```
% sed -n s/this/that/ file1
```

Each of these examples performs an identical substitution in file1, but displays the results differently. The command sed s/this/that/ file1 displays the entire modified file. The command sed s/this/that/p file1 displays the entire modified file, as well as all the lines you have modified (p). The command sed -n s/this/that/p file1 displays only the lines that you have modified (n). Finally, sed -n s/this/that/ file1 (without p) displays nothing.

These examples illustrate that the syntax used by sed for string substitution is identical to the syntax that ex uses. Learning sed, therefore, should be straightforward for anyone who has mastered ex.

UNIX

Example:

```
% sed 3,4d file1
```

Example:

```
% sed -e s/this/that/ -e/for/d file1
```

Example:

```
% sed -e s/this/that/g -e /for/d file1
```

Example:

```
% cat writefile

1.2w filea
/the/w fileb
s/this/that/w filec
% sed -n -f writefile file1
```

The command sed 3,4d file1 deletes lines 3 and 4 from file1 and displays the modified file. The command sed -e s/this/that/ -e/for/d file1 illustrates the use of the -e option to specify multiple editing commands: sed makes two passes through the file, first changing the first occurrence of "this" to "that" on every line containing "this," then deleting all lines that contain "for." The command sed -e s/this/that/g -e /for/d file1 performs the same operations, except for globally substituting "this" for "that."

The last example illustrates the use of a file containing sed commands. The command sed -n -f writefile file1 modifies file1 based on the edit commands contained in writefile (-f); as the command cat writefile shows, one edit command is given per line. The result of this command is as follows: filea contains lines 1 and 2 of file1, fileb contains all lines of file1 that have "the" in them, and filec contains all lines of file1 in which "this" has been changed to "that."

In the examples given so far, sed has based line selection on the line number or a character string contained in the line. The sed editor can also use operator characters common to a number of UNIX commands that *fil-*

Table 5.13   *Operator Characters Used with* sed

Character	Meaning	Example
.d	Signifies any single character	d. Any two-character string beginning with "d"

Table 5.13   *Operator Characters Used with* sed *(continued)*

Character	Meaning	Example
$	Signifies end of line	d$ Any lowercase d which occurs at the end of a line
"	Delimits operator characters to prevent interpretation	"fred." fred followed by a period, not fred followed by any character
\	Turns off special meaning of a single character	fred\. fred followed by a period, not fred followed by any character
*	Matches zero or more characters	fr* Matches fr, fred, frog, and so on
[]	Specifies character classes	[A-Za-z0-9] Uppercase letters, lowercase letters, and digits
		[^0-9] All characters except 0 through 9
		[0\-9] The three characters 0, -, and 9
^	Matches only if string is at the beginning of the line	^"new line" Matches the string "new line" only if it is at the beginning of the line

ter text to expand these selection criteria, thereby creating a regular expression. Table 5.13 summarizes operator characters. Some simple examples of regular expressions using these operators appear below.

UNIX
```
% sed -n/^The/p file1
% sed -n/""p[a-z]/p file1
% sed s/". "/"."/gp file1
```

The command sed -n/^The/p file1 displays any line beginning with "The." The command sed -n/" "p[a-z]/p file1 displays any line containing a blank followed by a "p" and any other lowercase character of the roman alphabet. Finally, sed s/". "/". "/gp file1 substitutes a period followed by two blanks for any occurrence of a period followed by a single blank, then displays those lines of file1 that have changed. Note that the double quotes insure that sed reads the string literally.

These are very simple examples of a complex, yet powerful, syntax.

5.5 Pattern Matching and Processing: awk

The awk editor extends the features of sed. Features of awk include the following:

- Field-oriented processing
- Predefined variables
- Variable assignment
- Logical operations
- Arithmetic expressions
- Flow control
- Formatted output
- String operators
- Mathematical functions
- Redirected output
- Scalar variables and arrays
- Output redirection and piping

Like sed, awk does not have an OpenVMS equivalent. To achieve the functionality of awk, the OpenVMS user would most likely write a high-level-language program or use the string-handling capabilities of DCL.

Users often feel more comfortable mastering the basic features of UNIX before turning to awk. Users should decide whether to attempt awk based on the amount of difficulty they have experienced thus far and on the extent to which they need to make complex file modifications.

The awk editor searches each record in a file for a pattern and performs some action when it finds that pattern.[3]

UNIX
Form:
```
% awk [-Fsep] 'pattern {action} pattern {action} ...' \
filename(s)
% awk [-Fsep] -f pattern-action file filename(s)
```

---

3.   Recall that a UNIX record is an arbitrary number of bytes terminated by a newline character.

To awk, each record consists of a number of fields; awk uses the -F option to define a *field separator*. By default, the field separator is any number of blanks between fields. However, you can set the field separator to be any character string. For example, recall the /etc/passwd file introduced in Section 3.1, which contains a record for each UNIX user and uses a colon to separate fields in each record.

To prevent interpretation by the shell, single forward quotes (') delimit the complete pattern-action combination from the *file(s)* on which to perform the awk function. Curly braces ({ }) surround actions. You may store pattern-matching and action strings that you use repeatedly in awk scripts, which are files invoked with the -f option.

Let us now turn our attention to the available patterns and actions. Table 5.14 outlines the general features of the patterns and subsequent actions available to the awk user. At first glance, these strings are somewhat intimidating, so we will start with some simple examples.

UNIX
Example:
% awk -F: '/smith/{print $0}'/etc/passwd
Example:
% awk -F: '$4 ~/ 51/{print $0}'/etc/passwd
Example:
% awk -F: '$1 ~/^h*/{print $0}'/etc/passwd

The command awk -F: '/smith/{print $0}'/etc/passwd displays any records from the /etc/passwd file that contain smith in any field. Note that the field delimiter is a colon rather than the default (one or more blanks).

Table 5.14   awk *Patterns and Actions*

Pattern	Meaning
BEGIN {*statement*}	Executes statement before pattern matching
END {*statement*}	Executes statement after pattern matching
/*regular expression*/	Finds pattern containing a regular expression

Table 5.14   awk *Patterns and Actions (continued)*

Pattern	Meaning
relational expression	Finds pattern containing relation operator(s)
pattern && *pattern*	Boolean "and"
pattern || *pattern*	Boolean "or"
(*pattern*)	Finds single pattern
!*pattern*	Boolean "not"
pattern,*pattern*	Finds two patterns
if (*expression*) *statement* [else *statement*]	Conditional if statement
while (*expression*) *statement*	While an expression is true, performs statement
for (*expr1*:*condition*:*expr2*) *statement*	For each occurrence formulated from *expressions1* and *2* that obey the specified condition, executes the statement
break	Exits immediately from a for or while loop
continue	Forces next iteration of a for or while loop
next	Skips to next input record and begins processing from first pattern
exit	If found as part of BEGIN, terminates without execution of END
	If found in main body of script, branches and executes END
	If found at END, causes immediate termination
variable = *expression*	Equates *variable* to *expression*
print [*expression1*] > [*expression2*]	Redirects expression1 to expression2
print [*expression1*] |[*expression2*]	Pipes expression1 to expression2
for (*variable in array*) *statement*	For each array element, executes *statement*

The search pattern is `smith`, and the action is to display (`print`) the whole record. As we shall see in the following section, `$0` is a *predefined variable* that denotes the complete record.

The command `awk -F: '$4 ~ /51/{print $0}'/etc/passwd` displays the record for any user belonging to group `51`. That is, `awk` displays the record if the fourth field (`$4`) matches (`~`) the string "`51`".

The command `awk -F: '$1 ~ /^h*/{print $0}'/etc/passwd` displays the records of all users whose usernames begins with "h." The pattern is the expression `$1 ~ /^h*/`. The command searches for the first field (`$1`), which in the file `/etc/passwd` is the username. The tilde matches the username to the regular expression `^h*`, which is any string that starts with "h" at the beginning of a record.

The three examples given above illustrate the most commonly invoked action command: printing. In the following section, we will use this action command to illustrate some predefined variables available to the `awk` user.

5.5.1   Predefined Variables

Table 5.15 shows a subset of predefined `awk` variables. Several appear below, again using the `/etc/passwd` file. For the sake of brevity, the examples show only a sample of the output.

UNIX
Example:
```
% awk -F: '{print length}'/etc/passwd
46
63
...
```

Example:
```
% awk-F:'{print NR, NF}' /etc/passwd
17
27
...
```

Example:
```
% awk -F.'{print NR, $1}'/etc/passwd
1 root
2 sysop
3 daemon
...
```

The command `awk -F: '{print length}'/etc/passwd` displays the number of characters (`length`) in each record. The command `awk -F:`

Table 5.15   *Predefined* awk *Variables*

Variable	Function	Example
$0	The entire input record	awk '{print $0}' file
$*n*	The *n*th field of the input record	awk '{print $2, $1}' file
length	Length of the current input record	awk '{print length ($0), $0}' file
FILENAME	Name of the current input file	awk '{print FILENAME}' file
NR	Number of the current record; first input record is 1	awk '{print NR, $0}' file
NF	Number of fields in the current record	awk '{print NF}' file
RS	Input record separator (default = new line)	awk '{RS=":"; print NR}' file
OFS	Output field separator (default = blank)	awk '{OFS=":"; print $1 OFS $2}' file
ORS	Output record separator (default = new line)	awk '{ORS=":"; print $0}' file
OFMT	Output format for numbers (default = %.6g)	awk '{OFMT="%.5g"; print $2}' file

'{print NR, NF}'/etc/passwd   displays the number of the record (NR) and the number of fields (NF). Finally, awk -F: '{print NR, $1}'/etc/passwd displays the number of the record followed by the first field ($1), which in the /etc/passwd file is the username.

5.5.2   **Variable Assignment**

Accompanying the predefined variables are variables that the user may assign. You may assign variables according to context using the form variable name = integer or string value; that is, you do not have to declare a variable as a string or integer value as in many high-level languages.

UNIX
```
x = "3" + "4"
x = "some" + "thing"
```

These two examples illustrate the use of addition (+), first to equate the variable x to the integer 7, then to the character string "something".

5.5.3　Logical and Arithmetic Operators

Table 5.16 gives the operators available to the awk user in order of decreasing priority.[4] Operators grouped together have the same priority. The number of operators given in Table 5.16 suggests both the power and the complexity of awk. We will use a number of these operators in subsequent sections.

Table 5.16　awk *Operators*

Operator	Meaning
++a	Increments a's value before using it
A++	Increments a's value after using it
--a	Decrements a's value before using it
a--	Decrements a's value after using it
*	Multiply
/	Divide
%	Remainder (modulo)
+	Add
–	Subtract
	No operator between two variables implies catenation; for example, $1$2 catenates first two fields
>	Greater than
> =	Greater than or equal to
<	Less than
< =	Less than or equal to
= =	Similar to
! =	Not similar to
~	Match; for example, $1~/A|B|C/ matches if a, b, or c is in the first field

---

4.　Priority indicates the order in which awk executes the operators if used without parentheses.

Table 5.16	awk *Operators (continued)*
! ~	No match; for example, $1 !~/A|B|C/
!	Negate value of expression
&&	Boolean "and"
| |	Boolean "or"
=	Equal to
+=	i + = 2 compressed form of i = 1 + 2
- =	i - = 2 compressed form of i = i − 2
* =	i* = 2 compressed form of i = i*2
/ =	i/ = 2 compressed form of i = i/2
% =	i% = 2 compressed form of i = i%2

5.5.4 Scripts

Many users can meet their needs with single-line awk commands. However, to use the extended features of awk or to save awk commands for subsequent use, you must use an awk script. Before looking at how to use operators and variables in awk, we will consider the rules that govern the awk script.

UNIX
Example:

```
% cat awk_test
BEGIN {nw = 0}
{nw + = NF
    }
            END {print "number of words = ",nw
                }
                % awk -F: -f awk_test/etc/passwd
                number of words = 1031
```

The string BEGIN {nw = 0} signifies the beginning of an awk script. The BEGIN statement precedes a statement that sets the variable nw (number of words) to 0. The string {nw += NF} then increases (+=) the value of nw, adding the predefined variable NF (number of fields) as awk processes each record of the file /etc/passwd. After awk processes all records, control passes to the END statement, and the action command {print "number of words = ",nw} displays the number of fields. You must include the BEGIN and END commands only if you require some action before or after record processing, for example, to set a variable or print the value of a variable.

5.5.5 **Flow Control**

Table 5.17 summarizes the awk flow-control statements. Some of these statements are illustrated below.

> **UNIX**
> **Example:**
> ```
> { for (x = 1; x<= NF; x + + ) print $x }
> ```
> **Example:**
> ```
> { for (x in text) {print x, text[x]} }
> ```
> **Example:**
> ```
> { i = 1
>    while (x <= NF) {
>    print $x; + + x}
> }
> ```
> **Example:**
> ```
> for (x = 1; x<= NF; x + +) {
>    if ($x = = "halt") break
> }
> ```
> **Example:**
> ```
> for (x = 1; x<= NF; x + +) {
>    if ($x = = "end") continue
> }
> ```
> **Example:**
> ```
> for (x = 1; x<= NR; x + + ) {
>    incr + = 1
>    if (incr >100) exit
> }
> ```
> **Example:**
> ```
> for (x = 1; x<= NF; x + + ) {
>    if (NF <4) getline
> }
> ```
> **Example:**
> ```
> for (x = 1; x<= NF; x + + ) {
>    if (NF = = 1) next
> }
> ```

The statement { for (x = 1; x<= NF; x ++) print $x } will increment x from 1 to the number of fields per record and display each field,

Table 5.17   awk *Flow Control Statements*

Statement	Meaning
for (*expr1*:*condition*:*expr2*) *statement*	For each occurrence formulated from expressions 1 and 2 that obeys the specified condition, executes the statement
for (*i element in array*) *statement*	For each element of the array, executes the statement
if (*condition*) *statement1* [else *statement2*]	Performs a conditional if statement
while (*condition*) *statement*	While the specified condition holds, executes the statement
Break	Exits immediately from a for or while loop
Continue	Forces next iteration of a for or while loop
Exit	If found as part of BEGIN, terminates without execution of END
	If found in main body of script, branches and executes END
	If found at END, causes immediate termination
Getline	Forces processing to move to the next record
Next	Skips to next input record and begins processing from the first pattern

one per line. The statement { for (x in text) {print x, text[x]} } displays the element number x and its value in array text (see Section 5.5.6). The statement { i = 1 while (x <= NF) {print $x; ++ x} } has the same effect as the first example, printing each field of the record, one per line. The statement if ($x = = "halt") break uses if (for while) to stop processing records when field x is equal to the character string halt. The statement if ($x = = "end") continue stops processing the current record when field x is equal to the character string end. The statement if (incr >100) exit passes control to the END statement of the awk script when the value of the variable incr is greater than 100. The statement if (NF <4) getline continues processing the next record of the file, from the current point in the awk script, if the number of fields is less than 4. The statement if (NF == 1) next skips to the next input record if the number of fields in the current record is 1, but begins processing from the beginning of the awk script.

5.5.6 Using Arrays

In contrast to most high-level languages where array elements are explicitly assigned a data type (e.g., integer, real, or character), awk assigns array elements implicitly. That is, each awk array element assumes a data type according to the assigned value. For example, record[NR] = $0 assigns the NRth element of an array record to the current input record: a character string. Note that array elements are enclosed in square brackets.

UNIX

Example:
```
% cat awk_script
{ record[NR] = $0 }
END { for i = NR; i>0; i--) print record[i] }
% awk -f awk_script myfile
```

The statement { record [NR] =$0} enters each record of the file into the array record using the predefined variable NR (record number) as the counter. The statement { for i = NR; i>0; i--) print record[1] } displays the contents of the array record from record[NR] to record[1]; that is, it displays the records of the file myfile in reverse order.

5.5.7 Formatting Output

The awk printf statement, which resembles that found in the C programming language, formats awk output.

UNIX

Form:
```
printf "format_statement" expression1, ...
```
Example:
```
{ printf "%8.2f", $i}
```
Example:
```
{ printf "%10d\n", $i}
```

Example:
```
{ printf "%s". $i}
```
Example:
```
{ printf "%.6g", $i}
```

Each example displays the variable i in a different format: "%8.2f" is a floating-point number of eight digits, with two following the decimal point; "%10d\n" is a 10-digit decimal number followed by a new line; "%s" is an alphanumeric string; and "%.6g" makes useful interpretations of numeric values. For example, 11111111 returns 1.11111e + 07; 1001 returns 1001; and 10.1 returns 10.1. A text string returns a value of 0.

5.5.8   String Operators

Chapter 10 discusses *shell programming*, the UNIX equivalent of writing OpenVMS command procedures. It will be seen from that discussion that UNIX does not offer the full functionality of the OpenVMS lexical functions when used for string-manipulation. That shortcoming is addressed by awk, which offers string manipulation features similar to OpenVMS lexical functions (see Table 5.18).

The function length(*string*) returns the length of a string. If *string* is omitted, the function length returns the length of the current record. The function substr(*string, position, length*) returns a substring of *string* that starts at *position* and is *length* characters long. For example, the statement { printf "%s\n", substr($0,1,10) } below prints the first 10 characters of each record as awk processes them. After awk processes all records, it displays the total number of characters (nc) in the file using length to determine the number of characters in each complete record.

UNIX
Example:
```
% cat awk_script
BEGIN {nc = 0}
    { printf "%s\n", substr($0,1,10) }
    { nc + = length ($0) }
END { print "Number of characters =", nc
```

The function index(*string, substring*) returns the starting position in *string* that contains *substring*. If *substring* is not found, the function returns a value of 0. The function split(*string, array, "separa-*

tor") separates *string* into elements of *array* according to a field separator. If you do not specify a field separator, awk uses the predefined variable FS (field separator).

Table 5.18   *Commonly Used* awk *Functions*

Function	Meaning
length(*string*)	Length of *string*
substr(*string*, *position*, *length*)	Substring of *string*, starting at *position* and *length* characters long
index(*string*, *substring*)	Starting position of substring in string; if not found, returns 0
split(*string*, *array*, "*separator*")	string separated into elements of array according to the field separator
int(num)	Truncated integer value of variable num
cos(x)	Cosine trigonometric function of variable x
sin(x)	Sine trigonometric function of variable x
log(x)	Natural logarithm of variable x
int(x)	Integer function of variable x
sqrt(x)	Square root of variable x

UNIX

Example:

```
% date
Sat Aug 3 03:07:48 EDT 2002
% cat awk_script
{ split($4, time, ":")
print time[1], "hours"
print time[2], "minutes"
print time[3], "seconds"
}
% date | awk -f awk_script
03 hours
07 minutes
48 seconds
```

For example, the statement date | awk -f awk_script pipes the output of the date command to awk for processing by awk_script. The command split($4, time, ":") splits the fourth field of the date output, 03:04:48, into three elements of the array time using the colon as a delimiter.

5.5.9 Mathematical Functions

Table 5.18 includes the common mathematical functions available to the awk user. The following example shows values returned by some of these functions.

UNIX

Example:
```
% cat foo
90 90 10 12.7 36
% cat awk_script
{
a = sin($1); b = cos($2); c = log($3); d = int($4); e = sqrt($5);
print a; print b; print c; print d; print e
}

% awk -f awk_script foo
1
0
2.30259
12
6
```

5.5.10 Redirecting Output

The following examples illustrate writing to a file, appending to a file, and piping the results of awk to another command.

UNIX

Example:
```
% awk -F: '{print $1 >"myfile.dat"}'/etc/passwd
```
Example:
```
% awk -F: '{file = "myfile.dat"; print $1 >>file}' /etc/passwd
```
Example:
```
% awk -F: '{print $1 |"mail fred"}' /etc/passwd
```

The statement awk -F: '{print $1 >"myfile.dat"}' /etc/passwd writes the first field of the file /etc/passwd to myfile.dat. The statement awk -F: '{file = "myfile.dat"; print $1 >>file}'/etc/passwd appends the first field of the file /etc/passwd to the variable file, defined as myfile.dat. Finally, awk -F: '{print $1 |"mail fred"}'/etc/passwd mails the first field of each record of the file /etc/passwd to the user fred.

5.5.11   **Putting It All Together**

The following example illustrates some of the features of awk introduced in the previous sections. This example checks one or more files for two identical adjacent words, a common typographical error.

UNIX

Example:

```
% cat textfile
test of awk awk program
test of same words on two lines
lines
% cat awk_script
FILENAME ! = prevfile
{ NR = 1
 prevfile = FILENAME
}
NF > 0 {
   if ($1 = = lastword)
   printf "double %s, file %s, line %d\n", $1, FILENAME, NR
   for (i = 2; i <= NF; i + +)
        if ($i = = $(i-1)
        printf "double %s, file %s, line %d\n", $1, FILENAME, NR
   if (NF > 0)
      lastword = $NF
}
% awk -f awk_script textfile
double awk, file textfile, line 1
double lines, file textfile, line 2
```

The following statements

```
FILENAME! = prevfile
{ NR = 1
prevfile = FILENAME }
```

effectively reset the record counter for each new file where two or more files are given as arguments to the script. The statement (if ($i = = $(i-1)) checks the *i*th field against the *i*th − 1 field for each nonblank (NF>0) record in the file. If the two words are identical, then the word, filename, and the line number are printed (printf "double %s, file %s, line %d\

n", i, FILENAME, NR). The last word of a record is retained as the variable lastword and compared to the first word of the following record (if ($1 = = lastword)). If they are identical, a message is also printed. After all records in a file have been processed, NR is reset to 1 and the process is repeated for any additional files specified.

5.6   Summary

This chapter describes the various ways a UNIX user may create or modify the contents of a file. Typical of UNIX are the variety and complexity of the editors and string handlers available. For example, the editors edit, ed, and ex are available for line editing: ex is a superset of edit and ed and the editor discussed; ex has similar functionality to EDT in line mode with the following three exceptions: First, ex does not display line numbers, but these may be turned on with the ex command set number. Second, ex resequences lines after each command, whereas EDT only resequences line numbers with the RESEQUENCE command. Third, whereas the EDT user places the line or range of lines after the command, the ex user places them before. For example, the ex command 9d deletes line 9 (compare with the EDT command D 9). Note that the ex command d9 deletes 9 lines starting at the cursor, so be careful, and be aware of the undo ex command.

The vi (visual) editor is the closest UNIX editor to EDT in that, like EDT, it is a visual editor with a built-in line-mode editor. However, you make changes to a file using the standard keyboard keys and not the keypad keys. Hence, there are two vi modes: command mode for moving the cursor and active mode for inserting and making changes to existing text. Remembering to toggle between command and active modes is the major problem encountered by the EDT keypad mode user. Command- and active-mode commands may be combined to provide a very extensive command set.

The Emacs editor is very similar to TPU/EVE and is commonly found on UNIX systems. The chances are excellent that it is already installed on the UNIX system you are using right now. The designers of TPU/EVE were obviously "inspired" by Emacs, so the two editors have a very similar look and feel. But like vi, the Emacs editor is designed to be terminal and thus keyboard-independent, so it does not rely on VT-terminal-specific function keys the way EDT and TPU do. While Emacs commands are certainly very different from EVE, for people familiar with OpenVMS editors, the editing environment of Emacs is much more similar and feels more natural than that of vi. And like TPU/EVE, Emacs is a very powerful and extensible editor.

The ex, vi, and Emacs editors are interactive editors; you are in a sense part of the file, moving about within it and making changes. The sed command and the awk utility, which have no OpenVMS counterparts, are batch editors—all changes are made externally to the file. The end result is the same as for the interactive editors, a single updated version of the file. The sed editor uses the same syntax as ex. The editor awk, although very powerful, has an extensive C-like syntax. If you don't need a complex string handler at this time, you should skip awk. If sed or awk commands are used repeatedly, or are very complex, they are stored in a script file for easy recall.

6

Communicating with Other Users

Communicating with Other Users

The reason I dread writing letters is because I am so apt to get to slinging wisdom and forget to let up.

—Mark Twain

The ability of users to communicate with each other is integral to any interactive operating system. UNIX, like OpenVMS, supports communications between users on the same computer (local host) or between users on different computers (remote hosts) connected via a network. This chapter covers two commands and one utility (that is, two relatively simple programs and one relatively complex one) whereby users can communicate with each other either on a local computer or on a local and a remote computer. This chapter concentrates on communication between users on the local computer only. Chapter 13 discusses communication with remote hosts.

Note that depending on the networking protocol that is installed, OpenVMS supports either a DECnet mail address of the form *NODE::USERNAME*, or the Internet mail form *user@host*. Most OpenVMS examples in this chapter use the DECnet mail addressing form.

Communication with other users may take place in interactive or batch mode. Interactive communication requires an immediate response from the user receiving the message, who must be logged on to receive it. Batch communications do not require an immediate response from the receiver. The commands `talk` and `write` (Section 6.3) apply to interactive communication (compare with the OpenVMS commands *PHONE* and *REPLY*), whereas the `mail` utility (Section 6.1) applies to batch communications (compare with the OpenVMS utility *MAIL*). Note that `talk` and `write` are commands, and `mail` is a utility. This distinction reflects the relative complexity, and hence versatility, of each program. As indicated above, `write` and *talk* are relatively straightforward: Each command performs one simple task. The *mail* utility, on the other hand, has a variety of functions and a more extensive command syntax.

There are many third-party mail clients available for UNIX and Linux systems (e.g., pine, KMAIL, and Netscape Mail). Each of these mail clients has its own set of commands or GUI. In this chapter, we concentrate only on the standard command-line mail programs for UNIX.

After reading this chapter, you should be familiar with reading, sending, replying to, forwarding, storing, and searching mail, as well as with communicating interactively with other users. Chapter 13 extends these principles with a discussion of communication with users on remote hosts.

6.1   Batch Communications: mail

The UNIX and OpenVMS mail utilities possess similar capabilities. Both use folders to organize stored messages, both permit the user to modify the mail environment, and both permit mailing to lists of users on both local and remote hosts. Most of the differences in the way UNIX and OpenVMS mail function internally are irrelevant to the average user and are therefore not discussed here. Appendix D provides some discussion of the internal organization of the UNIX mailer. This section discusses differences in command syntax important for everyday use.

A UNIX mail message can be any text. When a user receives a mail message, the system stores it in the file */var/spool/mail/user*, known as the *system mailbox*. The command *mail* accesses this file and displays one line of header (address) information for each unread message. The header includes the sender's username, remote computer (if applicable), time the message was sent, and the subject of the message. The *from* command also displays header information, but does not permit further access to the system mailbox; it serves as a simple method of listing new mail headers without invoking the *mail* utility. You may wish to place the *from* command in the *.login* or *.profile* hidden files (see Sections 3.2.1 and 3.2.3), where it will automatically display the headers of any new mail messages you have received since your last terminal session.

The system mailbox functions like the OpenVMS *NEWMAIL* folder. A user may read, reply to, forward to, delete from, or store messages in the system mailbox. Once the user reads a message, *mail* moves it to the user's own mailbox; by default, this is the file *~user/mbox* (the file *mbox* in the home directory of *user*). This file is equivalent to the OpenVMS *MAIL* folder, the default storage bin for messages that have been read. OpenVMS users can gain access to messages contained in the *MAIL* folder only with the *MAIL* utility. The UNIX file *~user/mbox*, on the other hand, is an ordinary file that stores mail messages after they have been read. Users can call up this file using the *mail* utility; users can also use any UNIX command that manipulates ordinary files (see Chapters 4 and 8). It is not advisable to edit this file, since changes may render it unreadable by the *mail* utility. However, users may read, search, print, and otherwise manipulate it like any other file. Once messages have been read, they may also be moved to files or folders other than *~user/mbox*.

A feature of the UNIX mail utility not found in OpenVMS is the *dead.letter* file in the user's home directory. Pressing *<CTRL>-C* twice stores the incomplete draft of a message in the file *dead.letter* instead of sending it. The file *dead.letter* stores the aborted message until the user aborts a second message, at which time the second message overwrites the first.

6.1.1   Sending Mail

Users send mail by including either login names or a *mail alias* for a mailing list on the command line.

OpenVMS	UNIX
Form:	
`$ MAIL[/QUALIFIER(S)]`	`% mail [option(s)] recipient`
`[file-spec] [recipient]`	
`$ MAIL`	`% mail user1 user2`
`MAIL>SEND`	`Subject:[subject entered here]`
`To: user1, user2 [message entered here]`	`cc: [additional recipients entered here]`
`Subject: [subject entered here]`	`%`
`Enter your message below....`	
`[message entered here]`	
`<CTRL>-Z`	
`MAIL >`	
`MAIL>SEND`	`% mail userslis`
`To: @USERS.LIS`	

The first example above illustrates how to send mail messages to two individuals, *user1* and *user2*. Note, unlike OpenVMS, the UNIX *mail* command issued without arguments or options does not produce the *mail* prompt unless you have unread mail messages. If you have no unread messages in the system mailbox, *mail* returns the shell prompt with "no," or just a short comment. When invoked with user names or an alias for a distribution list on the command line, *mail* responds with a prompt for the subject. You enter the subject, then the message beginning on the following line. Terminate the message with a period as the first character of a line, or with a *<CTRL>-D* (compare with the *ex* editor in Section 5.1). You can then carbon copy (*cc*) the message to additional users (see the discussion of *askcc* in Section 6.1.8) by entering additional user names. Press *<RETURN>* for no users or when done specifying additional recipients.

The second example illustrates sending a message to a distribution list of names contained in the file *userslis*. In OpenVMS, the distribution list is a file containing a list of mailing addresses, one per line. The UNIX distribution list is a mail alias established in the *.mailrc* hidden file (see Section 6.1.8). Note the similarity between using an alias within *mail* and using an *alias* within a shell program. While entering a message in UNIX, you can make changes to the characteristics of the message not possible using the OpenVMS *MAIL* utility. Table 6.1 summarizes the UNIX message modifiers. Changes begin with a tilde as the first character of a new line. For example, *~e* can be used to invoke the editor at any point during message input. Correspondingly, changes may be made to the subject of the message (*~s*) or the list of users who are to receive the mail message can be enlarged (*~t*). The editor used is defined by the mail environment variable *EDITOR* in the *.mailrc* or */usr/lib/Mail.rc* file (Section 6.1.8). In OpenVMS the editor can be invoked from the *MAIL>* prompt; it cannot be invoked from within the message itself.

Table 6.1   *mail Message Modifiers*

UNIX Modifier	OpenVMS Modifier	UNIX Function
~d		Include the *dead.letter* file
~e	*/EDIT*	Invoke the editor set by *EDITOR*
~v	*/EDIT*	Invoke the *vi* editor
~user(s)		Add user(s) to the list of people receiving the message
~s new_subject		Change the subject of the message

Table 6.1   *mail Message Modifiers (continued)*

UNIX Modifier	OpenVMS Modifier	UNIX Function
~p		Display entire message
~h		Optionally change all characteristics
~r filename	*INCLUDE FILENAME	Include a file in the message
~m message_n		Include the message number *n* in the message sent

6.1.2   Reading Mail

The mail system, by default, notifies you of any new mail messages received since your last terminal session. When you have new mail, *mail* displays the message "You have new mail" when you log on. If you have unread messages received prior to your last terminal session, *mail* displays the message "You have old mail." If both conditions apply, *mail* displays only the new mail message. Notification of incoming mail during a terminal session depends on the command *biff*, discussed in Section 3.2.1. The command *biff y* displays the message header, including sender and subject and the first few lines of the message, when new mail arrives (compare with the OpenVMS command *SET BROADCAST = MAIL*). This display interrupts any output from the current process at the current cursor location. The command *biff n* gives no notification (compare with the OpenVMS command *SET BROADCAST = NOMAIL*). You can use the command *from* to review the headers of unread mail messages.

OpenVMS

Example:

```
$ MAIL
You have 1 new message
MAIL> DIR
# From   Date   Subject
1SYSTEM Sun Dec 28 12:15   TEST
MAIL>
```

UNIX

```
% mail

"/usr/spool/mail/fred": 1 message 1
unread
>U 1 root Sun Dec 28 12:15 62/2434
"test"

&
```

The above example illustrates the effect of invoking *mail* when user *fred* has messages in the system mailbox */usr/spool/mail/fred*. The message header >U 1 root Sun Dec 28 12:15 62/2434 "test" indicates the following:

>	Current message pointer
U	Message status: U = unread, N = new, * = unsaved
	Blank = read, but not saved
1	Message number
root	Sender's user name
Sun Dec 28	Date message was sent
12:15	Time message was sent
62/2434	Number of lines/characters in message
"test"	Subject of message

The & is the *mail* prompt indicating that the *mail* utility is ready to receive commands (compare with the OpenVMS *MAIL>* prompt). Table 6.2 lists the responses you can make to the prompt. The simplest response is *<CR>*, which displays the active message. As discussed above, the active message is indicated by the > symbol. The response *n* displays the next message, and *<message list>* displays one or more messages identified by message number. For example:

1	Message 1
1 7	Messages 1 and 7
1-7	Messages 1 through 7
.-$	The current message through the last message

Table 6.2   *Interactive Mail Responses*

Response	Function
t *<message list>*	Type messages
n	Go to and type next message
e *<message list>*	Edit messages

Table 6.2   *Interactive Mail Responses (continued)*

Response	Function
f *<message list>*	Give header lines of messages
d *<message list>*	Delete messages
s *<message list>* file	Append messages to *file*
u *<message list>*	Undelete messages
r *<message list>*	Reply to messages (to sender and recipients)
R *<message list>*	Reply to messages (to sender only)
pre *<message list>*	Make messages go back to */usr/spool/mail*
m *<user list>*	Mail to specific users
q	Quit, saving unresolved messages in *mbox*
x	Quit, do not remove system mailbox
h	Print out active message headers
!	Shell escape
ch *directory*	Move to directory or home if none given

Messages are piped through *more* (see Section 4.8), and therefore appear on your terminal one screen at a time, as in the OpenVMS MAIL message display.

A *<message list>* consists of integers, ranges of same, or user names separated by spaces. If omitted, *mail* uses the last message typed.

A *<user list>* consists of user names or distribution names separated by spaces. Distribution names are defined in *.mailrc* in your home directory.

6.1.3   **Replying to Mail**

There are several ways to reply to a message (see Table 6.2). Use R to reply only to the originator of the message. Use r[1] to reply to the originator and all users who received the original message, including those cc'd. By default,

---

1.   Be careful of using r to reply! Replies you might intend for just the sender will be sent to all original recipients, including all members of any alias to get the original mail. Such a practice can lead to junk mail barrage.

r or *R* reply to the last message read. If the user wishes to reply to different mail messages, then a message list or individual message number should be included.

6.1.4 Forwarding Mail

The UNIX *mail* utility provides no specific command corresponding to the OpenVMS *MAIL* command *FORWARD/EDIT* for forwarding mail to other users. Nevertheless, the procedure for forwarding mail is relatively simple.

OpenVMS   **UNIX**

Example:
```
$ MAIL                                                % mail
You have 1 new message                                Mail version 2.18 5/19/83. Type ?
                                                      for help.
                                                      "/usr/spool/mail/fred": 1 message 1
                                                      unread
                                                      >U 1 root Wed Apr 27 11:13 9/146
                                                      "test"
```

Example:
```
MAIL>FORWARD/EDIT 1                                   & m user1
To: USER1                                             Subject: forward message
<CTRL>-Z                                              ~m 1
MAIL>                                                 &
```

The command *m user1* directs *mail* to send a message to *user1*, having entered a new subject (OpenVMS *MAIL* uses the subject of the message being forwarded). The *~m 1* command includes message 1 as part of the text of the current message, which can be further modified.

You can also forward your own mail. This is useful in situations when you have multiple usernames on one computer, or usernames on multiple computers, and desire one point of reference for mail. The hidden file *.forward* in each home directory of each username may contain a common address (see Section 13.1.1 for the format of network addresses) to which all your mail is forwarded. Rather than logging on to each username to check for incoming mail, you need only look under a single username on a single computer (compare with the OpenVMS *MAIL SET FORWARD*).

6.1.5   Saving and Deleting Mail

Once you read a message, *mail*, by default, saves it to the file *~user/mbox*, which you can access via the *mail* utility or any command used on ordinary files. You can also print or delete mail messages, append them to a file, or place them in a folder. Each of these options is discussed below.

OpenVMS	UNIX
	Example:
	`% mkdir ~jones/mail_folder`
	`% ex ~jones/.mailrc`
	`:a`
	`set folder = mail_folder`
	`.`
	`:wq!`
Example:	
`MAIL>DIR/FOLDER`	`& folders`
`Listing of folders in`	`bugs`
`DUA1:[USER]-`	
`MAIL.MAI;1`	
`Press CTRL/C to cancel listing`	
`BUGS MAIL`	
Example:	
`MAIL>MOVE BUGS`	`& s + bugs`
	`& s 4-6 + bugs`
Example:	
`$ MAIL`	`% mail -f`
`MAIL>SET FOLDER MAIL`	
Example:	
`$ MAIL`	`% mail -f ~jones/mail folder/`
`MAIL>SET FOLDER BUGS`	`bugs`
Example:	
`MAIL>PRINT 10`	`& s 10 foo`
	`& !lpr foo; rm foo`
Example:	
`MAIL>DELETE 4`	`& d 4`

In the first example, the user establishes a directory, *mail_folder*, in which *mail* stores folders. (You do not need to make a mail folder directory in OpenVMS, as OpenVMS maintains folders as part of the *MAIL.MAI* file.) Then the user appends the command *set folder = mail_folder* to the file *.mailrc* using the *ex* editor (see Section 5.1). The hidden file *.mailrc* customizes the *mail* environment (see Section 6.1.8) and, in this instance, tells *mail* in which directory to store mail folders. Each folder appears as a separate file. New messages are appended to these files, and, like *~user/mbox*, these folder files may be accessed by any UNIX command used on ordinary files.

The second example, *folders* (compare with the OpenVMS *MAIL* command *DIRECTORY/FOLDER*), displays existing folders. The third example, *s + bugs* (compare with the OpenVMS *MAIL* command *MOVE BUGS*) moves the current message to the folder *bugs*. The fourth example, *s 4-6 + bugs*, moves the fourth, fifth, and sixth messages in the message list to the folder *bugs*.

The fifth and sixth examples illustrate how to access old mail files. The shell command *mail -f* (without a file name) accesses the *~user/mbox* file. The command *mail -f ~user/mail_folder/bugs* accesses the folder *bugs*. The seventh example illustrates how to print a message list. First, message 10 is stored in the file *foo* with the command *s 10 foo*. Then, *foo* is sent to the default line printer and, once spooled, deleted with the command sequence *!lpr foo; rm foo*. Note that *!* informs the *mail* utility that the command that follows is to be interpreted by the shell rather than by *mail*.[2] By using pipes and input/output redirection, you can initiate complex sequences of commands from within *mail*.

The last example, *d 4*, deletes the fourth message in the message list. Note that until quitting or exiting *mail*, you may recover the last deleted message list with the *undelete* command.

You may also save messages as files, as the following examples illustrate.

OpenVMS	UNIX
Example:	
MAIL>EXTRACT MAILFILE.TXT	*& s mailfile.txt*
Example:	
MAIL>EXTRACT 4 MAILFILE.TXT	*& s 4 mailfile.txt*
	Example:
	% mail -f mailfile.txt

---

2.   The use of *!* to escape to the shell is common to a number of utilities.

In the first example, *s mailfile.txt* saves the message just read to the file *mailfile.txt* in the current directory. In the second example, *s 4 mailfile.txt* saves message 4 in the message list to the file *mailfile.txt*. In the last example, the command *mail -f mailfile.txt* presents a further example of the UNIX *mail* utility's ability to access ordinary files. Provided that the contents of the file *mailfile.txt* have not been changed, for example, by use of an editor to remove the message header, the *mail* utility treats it as a regular mail message. You cannot do this in OpenVMS *MAIL*, although you can use messages previously saved to a disk file with the *EXTRACT* command. The OpenVMS *MAIL* utility commands *REPLY/EDIT*, *SEND/EDIT*, and *FORWARD/EDIT* invoke an editor that is used to include the message contained in the disk file, but not until a list of recipients and a subject have been entered.

6.1.6   Searching Old Mail

The UNIX *mail* utility offers several mechanisms for searching messages to locate the sender or a keyword in the header that indicates sender, subject, time, or cc. Once you store messages in ordinary files, you can use the *grep* command (see Section 8.4.5) for searching.

OpenVMS permits you to search mail message headers with the *MAIL* command *DIRECTORY/EDIT*. UNIX *mail* does not have a feature equivalent to the OpenVMS *MAIL* command *DIRECTORY/SINCE*, which lets you preview the header information of messages received since a specified time.

OpenVMS	UNIX
Example:	
$ MAIL	*% mail -f*
MAIL>SET FOLDER MAIL	*& h*
MAIL>DIRECTORY	
	Example:
	& f user
	Example:
	& f /keyword
Example:	
MAIL>SEARCH STRING	*& !grep string ~jones/mbox*

In the first example, h displays one line of header information for each message stored in *~user/mbox*. Unlike the OpenVMS MAIL DIRECTORY command, h displays only the first 18 message headers. The command *+h* displays the next 18. Correspondingly, *-h* displays the previous 18. In the second example, *f user* displays messages sent by a specified user. In the third example, *f /keyword* displays headers of messages containing the keyword. In the last example, *!grep string ~jones/mbox* issues a shell command from within *mail* (by temporarily escaping to the shell and then returning to *mail*) to search the user mailbox for *string*.

6.1.7 Terminating Mail

Terminating mail represents the most fundamental and annoying difference between the UNIX and OpenVMS mail utilities. In OpenVMS MAIL, when a message is deleted, it is moved to a temporary folder called WASTEBASKET. By default, the command EXIT deletes the WASTEBASKET folder and terminates MAIL. The OpenVMS MAIL command QUIT, on the other hand, leaves the WASTEBASKET folder intact, so that deleted mail messages can be recovered in subsequent mail sessions by moving them from the WASTEBASKET folder. In UNIX, these functions are reversed: *exit* leaves the *mail* environment unchanged so that any deleted mail messages will reappear the next time *mail* is invoked. The command *quit* loses forever mail messages that were deleted.

6.1.8 Customizing the Mail Environment

Just as you can customize the shell to suit individual needs (see Section 3.2.2), so you can customize the mail environment. The system administrator can customize the mail environment for all users by modifying the file */usr/lib/Mail.rc*. You can further modify your own mail environment with the hidden file *.mailrc*. The following example represents a typical system and user environment.

OpenVMS   **UNIX**

Example:

```
$ COPY SYS$SYSTEM:MAILEDIT.COM              % cat /usr/lib/Mail.rc
MYMAIL.COM                                  set append dot save ask askcc \
$ EDIT MYMAIL.COM                           SHELL=/bin/csh \
*s?EDIT?EDIT/TPU?21                         EDITOR=/usr/ucb/ex metoo hold
* EXIT
$ DEFINE MAIL$EDIT MYMAIL.COM
```

The variables defining the `mail` environment are as follows:

append	Messages are appended to *~user/mbox* rather than prepended
. (dot)	A dot (.) alone on a line signifies end of message, and supplements *<CTRL>-D*
save	Saves mail messages in a file or folder
ask	Prompts for subject field
askcc	Prompts for the cc field
SHELL	Shell to use with *!* command
EDITOR	The editor to use while in *mail* (compare with the OpenVMS *MAIL* command *SET EDITOR*)
metoo	Includes sender in recipients (compare with the OpenVMS *MAIL* command *SEND/SELF*)
hold	Messages, once read, are not automatically passed to *~user/mbox*, but are kept in the system mailbox

A typical user-specific modification to this systemwide environment might be as follows.

UNIX

```
% cat ~jones/.mailrc
#   .mailrc - File to tailor mail environment
#
set folder=mail_folders       #define directory for folders
set crt=20                    #set number of message lines
set autoprint                 #automatically display next
                              #message after delete

set EDITOR=/usr/local/emacs   #define editor for mail

alias managers george fred    #aliases
alias cshell jack jill george dragon
alias gripe root
```

The command *set folder=mail_folders*, as we saw previously, defines the directory in which to store mail folders. The command *set crt=20* sets the number of lines displayed per screen to 20. The command *set auto-print* automatically displays the next message after a message is deleted.

The command *set EDITOR=/usr/local/emacs* defines an alternative editor while in *mail*. The command *alias managers george fred* defines a mailing list called *managers*, which currently specifies the two recipients *george* and *fred*.

6.2   Comparison of OpenVMS and UNIX Mail Commands

Table 6.3 compares the mail program subcommands available on Open-VMS with similar commands that can be issued within most UNIX mail programs.

Table 6.3   *Comparison of OpenVMS and UNIX Mail Commands*

OpenVMS **Mail** Subcommand	UNIX **mail** Command	Function
DELETE	d	Deletes message(s)
DIR	f [user] or h	Displays header lines [from user]
DIR/FOLDER	folders	Displays existing folders
EDIT	e	Edits message(s)
EXIT	q	Ends, saving unread message(s)
EXTRACT	s file	Stores message(s) in file
HELP	?	Gets help on mail commands
MOVE	s + folder	Moves message(s) to folder
NEXT	n	Goes to next message
QUIT	exit	Ends, leaving mail environment unchanged
READ	t	Reads message(s)
MAIL REPLY	r	Replies to all receivers
	R	Replies to sender only
SEND	m	Sends a mail message
MAIL/EDIT	~e	Invokes the editor defined by *EDITOR* in *.mailrc*
SET	.mailrc	Defines the mail environment

Table 6.3 *Comparison of OpenVMS and UNIX Mail Commands*

OpenVMS **Mail** Subcommand	UNIX **mail** Command	Function
SET FOLDER	*mail -f folder*	Uses the specified folder
	!	Issues a shell command
SELECT folder-name	*ch dir*	Changes directory to *dir* (default home)
	~d	Includes the *dead.letter* file
	~h	Optionally changes all characteristics
	~m #	Includes message number in current message
	~p	Displays entire message
	~r file	Includes *file* in message
	~t users	Adds users to those receiving message
	u	Undeletes messages
	~v	Invokes the *vi* editor

6.3 Interactive Communications: `talk` and `write`

This section covers two commands, *talk* and *write*, with which users can communicate with other users logged on to the same or a remote computer. You can use *talk* (compare with the OpenVMS PHONE command) to conduct an ongoing conversation to the exclusion of any other interactive computing. You can use *write* to exchange messages while performing other interactive tasks. Note the analogy to the OpenVMS REPLY command, which is available only to system operators (users with the OpenVMS OPER privilege). You may use *mesg* if you do not wish to be interrupted by *talk* or *write* requests (compare with the OpenVMS command SET NOBROAD-CAST). The command *mesg n* prevents the receipt of a *talk* or *write* request, *mesg y* (the default) reinstates the ability to receive *talk* and *write* messages, and *mesg* without arguments reports the current state of *mesg*.

OpenVMS	UNIX
Form:	
`$ PHONE[/QUALIFIER(S)] USER`	`% talk user [ttyname]`
Form:	

`$ REPLY[/QUALIFlER(S)] MESSAGE`	`% write user [ttyname]`
	`[message]`
	`<CTRL>-D`

Example:	`% talk fred tty17`
`$ PHONE FRED`	
Example:	`% write fred`
`$ REPLY/USER=FRED -` `"ARE YOU THERE?"`	`are you there?` `<CTRL>-D`

Notice that both `talk` and `write` accept a `ttyname` argument. You can use this argument to send messages to a specific terminal when the user is logged on at more than one location. In the first example, `talk fred tty17` attempts to establish communication with user `fred` logged on to `tty17`. Fred's terminal will display the following:

```
Message from TalkDaemon@sender_computer talk: connection
requested by sender_name@sender_computer talk: respond with:
talk sender_name@sender_computer
```

If Fred responds with `talk sender_name@sender_computer`, then communication is established. Just as with PHONE, the screen splits into two segments, so that what the sender types appears in one window and what the receiver types appears in the other. You can refresh the screen with `<CTRL>-L` (compare with `<CTRL>-W` in OpenVMS). Communications terminate when either user types `<CTRL>-C`.

In the second example, `write fred`, user `fred` sees the following:

```
Message from sender_computer!sender_name sender_ttyname
Are you there?
```

At this point, Fred can respond if he wishes.

6.4 **Summary**

The following scenario, typical of daily mail use, summarizes the material presented in this chapter. User Joyce returns from vacation and checks her e-mail.

UNIX

Example:

```
% mail
"/usr/spool/mail/joyce": 10 messages
```

Example:

```
& h
>1 root   Tue May 12 12:11 28/950 "System backup tonight"
2 MAILER-DAEMON Wed May 13 17 16:43 23/615 "Returned mail:\
Host unknown"
3 poisson  Thu May 21 11:20 16/506 "dcp"
4 youkha   Thu May 21 12:55 21/507 "rmf,peters and dly"
5 youkha   Tue May 26 14:21 19/451 "brookhaven files"
6 youkha   Wed May 27 00:12 33/731 "rcpvms"
7 pahler   Wed May 27 22:15 29/864 |
8 murthy   Thu May 28 10:24 17/487 "stream <lf> files"
9 horton   Sat May 30 14:38 17/512 "man utility"
10 cucard!root  Thu Jun 18 18:04 11/282 "Re: test"
```

Example:

```
& 2
From joyce May 13 16:43:43 1998
Received: by cuhhca.UUCP (4.12/4.8)
id AA12988; Wed, 13 May 87 16:43:41 edt
Date: Wed, 13 May 98 16:43:41 edt
From: MAILER-DAEMON (Mail Delivery Subsystem)
Subject: Returned mail: Host unknown
To: joyce
Status: RO
----- Transcript of session follows -----
550 reidar@cucard... Host unknown: Not a typewriter
----- Unsent message follows -----
Received by cuhhca.UUCP (4.12/4.8)
id AA12986; Wed, 13 may 98 16:43:41 edt
Date: Wed, 13 May 98 16:43:41 edt
From: joyce (Joyce Lastname)
To: reidar@cucard
Subject: test
Hopefully when u poll me u should get this???? Joyce
```

Example:

```
& m reidar@cucard
Subject: Resending message of May 13
~m 2
```

Interpolating 2
(continue)
<CTRL>-D
Cc:

Example:

& d

Example:

& 1
From root Tue May 12 12:11:28 1998
Received: by cuhhca.UUCP (4.12/4.8)
id AA05129; Tue, 12 May 98 12:11:26 edt
Date: Tue, 12 May 98 12:11:26 edt
From: root (System Administrator)
To: joyce|
Subject: rsh to/from sunos
Status: RO
Dear Joyce
I fixed the problem....

Example:

& s + vacation
"/usr1/joyce/mail_folders/vacation"[New file] 28/950

Example:

& 9
From horton Sat May 30 14:38:57 1998
Received: by cuhhca.UUCP (4.12/4.8)
id AA27943; Sat, 30 May 98 14:38:55 edt
Date: Sat, 30 May 98 14:38:55 edt
From: Horton (John Horton)
To: joyce
Subject: man utility
Status: RO
Joyce. help ... please contact me as soon as you return

Example:

& !who
horton   tty06 May 2 07:20
murthy   tty07 May 2 07:08
system   tty10 May 2 09:42
zhaoping ttyp0 May 2 09:16 (cuhhmd.hhmi.colu)
royer   ttyp1 May 2 09:21 (cuhhmd.hhmi.colu)
!

Example:

&q
Held 8 messages in usr/spool/mail/joyce

Example:

% write horton
are you there?

```
<CTRL>-D
%
Message from cuhhca!horton on tty06 at 11:36
yes.. let us "talk"
EOF
%
Message from Talk_Daemon@cuhhca at 11:37 ...
talk: connection requested by horton@cuhhca
talk: respond with: talk horton@cuhhca
% talk Norton
[Connection established]
----------------------------------------
```

Using the command *mail*, Joyce discovers that 10 mail messages have been sent to her system mailbox */usr/spool/mail/joyce* during her absence. Using the *h* (header) *mail* utility command, she displays a one-line summary of each message. Message *2* catches her eye; it is a response from the *mail* utility (*MAILER_DAEMON*) indicating that it was unable to deliver a message she sent prior to her departure. She enters *2* at the interactive mail prompt *&*, which displays the message. It is in fact a message she tried to send to *reidar@cucard* (a network address; see Section 13.1.1). She decides to send this message again, believing that the network connection is now functioning correctly. The command *m reidar@cucard* begins sending the new message by prompting for a subject, to which user Joyce responds with *~m 2* to include message *2* in the text of the new message. Joyce sends the message by pressing *<CTRL>-D*, then *<CR>* at the cc prompt. Joyce then deletes the original message with the *d* command and reads the first message by typing *1*. Having read the message, Joyce decides to save it (*s + vacation*) in the new folder *vacation*, which is a file in the directory */usr1/joyce/mail_folders*. She then turns her attention to message *9*. Since this message is a call for immediate help, she decides to use interactive communications. The string *!who* issues a command *who* to the shell (*!*) to determine if user *horton* is logged on and therefore capable of receiving interactive communications. Seeing that he is logged on, she quits *mail* (*q*), retaining her unread messages in the system mailbox. The command *write horton* then opens a dialog with user *horton*. As he is logged on only once, it is not necessary to include a terminal name in the *write* command. The dialog is terminated with *<CTRL>-D*. User *horton* responds by using the *write* command and requests a *talk* session (whereupon user *horton* would have entered *talk joyce*). Joyce responds with *talk horton*. The screen splits into two segments and a dialog takes place.

Devices, Queues, and *Background Processing*

Devices, Queues, and Background Processing

Who's on first?

—Bud Abbott and Lou Costello

This chapter covers the use of printers, magnetic tape drives,[1] and the UNIX equivalent to batch processing. At first glance, these topics may appear unrelated. What they have in common, however, is that each is an example of *multitasking*, the ability to perform two or more tasks simultaneously. OpenVMS users perform most multitasking activities through the use of queues and device allocation. One OpenVMS user queues a job to a printer and performs some other interactive task without having to wait until the job is finished printing. Another OpenVMS user reserves a magnetic tape drive for later use while performing an interactive task. A third OpenVMS user submits a CPU-intensive task to a batch queue and, while that is processing, edits a file.

This chapter discusses the extent to which UNIX accommodates multitasking features similar to those implemented in OpenVMS and then goes on to describe features of multitasking unique to UNIX. In UNIX, the printing of files (see Section 7.1) corresponds to OpenVMS: Both systems queue files and typically print them in the order received. The availability of printers to handle UNIX print requests is, of course, site-dependent. Section 7.1 also shows you how to determine the printers available on a UNIX system and how you can use them.

Section 7.2 describes the commands available for reading and writing magnetic tapes. As with printers, the availability of magnetic tape drives and their characteristics are site-dependent. This section also shows you

---

1.   Throughout this chapter, magnetic tape means any sequential tape medium, for example, 1/2-inch tape reels and 1/4-inch tape cartridges.

how to determine the magnetic tape drives available on a system and how you can use them for reading and writing files. Section 7.2 concludes with a discussion of methods for exchanging files between UNIX and OpenVMS.

Section 7.2 also reveals the shortcomings of UNIX in handling tape-drive requests. To be sure, UNIX offers the equivalents of the Open-VMS BACKUP and COPY commands for reading and writing magnetic tapes. However, it seems that the designers of the early versions of UNIX assumed that individual users would not need to read and write their own magnetic tapes and that only the system administrator or system operator would have access to tape drives. The result of this assumption is that *anyone can access any mounted magnetic tape in UNIX*. OpenVMS, in contrast, allocates a given tape drive to a single user process.

Section 7.3 introduces the concept of UNIX background and foreground processing, which shows multitasking at its best. Unlike Open-VMS, which frequently utilizes batch queues, UNIX implementations rarely support batch processing.[2] UNIX achieves multitasking through the use of concurrent foreground and background processing. UNIX users do not submit tasks to a queue, the characteristics of which (e.g., process priority or CPU limit) may differ from a user's interactive process. Instead, UNIX users run tasks as separate, detached background processes with the same characteristics as the foreground process. The only difference between foreground and background processes is that only foreground processes may receive input from the keyboard. However, you can easily interchange foreground and background processes, so that you can make any process receive input from the keyboard. We shall explore this UNIX alternative to batch processing in some detail.

7.1   **Using Print Queues**

Most versions of UNIX support a *print spooler* for queuing print jobs to one or more printers. The print spooler software may differ from one version of UNIX to another. However, the average user who needs access only to the commands that use the spooler need not be perturbed: The commands that queue files for printing are identical in all versions of UNIX. You need to examine the print spooler software only if you must determine the available printers and their characteristics. In the case of a BSD or Linux print spooler,

---

2.   If, by definition, spooling is regarded as batch processing, then printing and transmitting files via UUCP (see Section 13.3) are also.

you can determine the printers available by examining the `/etc/printcap` file, a typical example of which appears below.

UNIX

Example:

```
% cat /etc/printcap

# Printer Definition File 4.2 BSD
#       lp =      Epson printer
#       lp1 =     talaris t1500 laser printer
# definitions:
#       mx#0      unlimited file size
#       pl#66     page length (lines)
#       pw#80     page width (characters)
#       br#       baud rate
#       lp        device name for output
#       if        accounting text filter /usr/tbin/if
#       of        output filter /usr/tbin/of
#       sd        spool directory
#       lf        error logging filename
#       af        accounting file
#       fc        clear flag bits
#       xc        clear local bits mode
#       fs        like fc but set bits
#       xs        like xc but set bits
|lplocal line printer:\
        :af=/usr/adm/lpd-acct:if=/usr/lib/lpf:mx#0:\
        :lp=/dev/tty0f:sd=/usr/spool/lpd:lf=/usr/adm/lpd-errs:\
        :rf=/usr/lib/flpf:br#1200:fs#06320:\
        :sb=default Printer:
lp1|laser|laser printer:\
        :af=/usr/adm/laser:ms#0:pl#66:pw#80\
        :lp=/dev/tty12:sd=/usr/spool/laser:lf=/usr/spool/laser/\
        error:br#4800:fc=0:xc=0:fs=06320:xs=00460:
```

OpenVMS

Example:

```
$ SHOW QUEUE/DEVICE/FULL
Terminal queue TTA4, on TTA4, mounted form PORTRAIT/
BASE_PRIORITY=4
/CHAR = (0) /DEFAULT = (FLAG = ONE,FORM = PORTRAIT) /NOENABLE_ -
GENERIC
/LIBRARY = LN03 Lowercase /OWNER = [SYSTEM,POSTMASTER]
/PROTECTION= (S:E,O:D,G:R,W:W) /SEPARATE= (RESET = (RESET))
```

Note the similar formats of `/etc/printcap` and `/etc/termcap` (see Section 3.1). If you need information on the variables used to define the characteristics of each queue, display the online man page entry for `printcap`, consult your system administrator, or simply attempt to print a file on each of the available printers. To do the latter, you must know the name(s) your system uses to address each queue. The BSD version of UNIX and Linux provides this information in the /etc/printcap file.[3]

The sample /etc/printcap file above begins with a number of comment lines, identified as usual by # occurring as the first nonblank character of a record. Definitions of two printers follow. The backslash (\) at the end of a line indicates that the definition continues on the following line. Colons (:) separate the fields within each definition. The first field in each printer definition gives the printer's names; vertical bars (|) separate each name. In the above example, the first printer is addressed as either lp or "local line printer," and the second printer is either lp1, laser, or "laser printer." If the printer name is a phrase rather than a single word, you must surround the phrase with double quotes in all commands so that the shell can distinguish the queue name from the names of the files being printed. If the command line does not address a specific printer, the system defaults to lp (the same as lp0; compare with the OpenVMS logical name SYS$PRINT). You may modify the definition of the default printer with the environment variable PRINTER. The two sample printer definitions described in the /etc/printcap file will be used in examples of the print commands described below.

Printing files in UNIX differs from OpenVMS in two major ways. First, OpenVMS print queues may sequence jobs on the basis of size or other characteristics in addition to the order received.[4] UNIX, on the other hand, queues print jobs in the order received. Second, unlike OpenVMS, BSD UNIX does not support a *generic queue*, which places jobs in a single queue supporting more than one printer and prints them on the first available printer. UNIX print queuing is explicit; there is a separate queue for each printer.

7.2 **Submitting Print Jobs:** lpr

The commands lpr (offline print; available in all versions of UNIX) and print[5] (print to the line printer; do not confuse with Korn shell print) queue any files with a protection that renders them readable by the user for

---

3. Other versions of UNIX, for example, some implementations of System V, support a version of the BSD print spooler and therefore use an /etc/printcap file.
4. The OpenVMS system administrator may use the command INITIALIZE/QUEUE/ SCHEDULE=NOSIZE to override the default condition, thus printing jobs in the order received.
5. This is not available on all versions of UNIX or Linux.

printing (compare with the OpenVMS command PRINT).[6] The command
print may be a one-line shell script containing the command lpr -p, also
written as pr file | lpr. Both print and lpr -p invoke the pr com-
mand to format a file prior to printing. One function of pr, discussed in
Section 8.2.3, places a header at the top of each page (compare with the
OpenVMS command PRINT/HEADER).

The following examples illustrate the major options of the lpr command. The following discussion omits site-dependent features, such as
addressing different fonts on printers that support multiple fonts.

OpenVMS	UNIX
Form:	
$ PRINT[/*QUALIFIER(S)*] *file-spec*[,...]	% lpr [*option(s)*] *file(s)*
Example:	
$ PRINT FILE1.,FILE2.	% lpr file1 file2
Example:	
$ PRINT/COPIES=3/QUEUE=LASER FILEA	% lpr -Plaser -#3 filea
Example:	
$ PRINT/DELETE FILEB.	% lpr -r fileb
Example:	
$ PRINT/NOFLAG/QUEUE=LASER FILEC	% lpr -hPlaser filec
Example:	
$ DEFINE SYS$PRINT TTA4:	% setenv PRINTER laser
$ PRINT FILEZ.	% lpr filez
	Example:
	% lpr -s filee
	Example:
	% lpr -f filef

The command lpr file1 file2 queues two files to the default printer,
and lpr -Plaser -#3 filea queues three copies (-#3 option) of filea to
the printer named laser (-Plaser option) defined in the /etc/printcap
file. The command lpr -r fileb prints fileb on the default printer and
then deletes it (-r option). The command lpr -hPlaser filec queues
filec to the printer named laser and prints it without the banner page

---

6.   The term line printer is a historical quirk; today it means any kind of printer, including character and laser printers.

(-h option). The command setenv PRINTER laser establishes an environment variable that redefines the default system printer lp. All print requests that do not use the -P option are sent to the laser printer rather than lp.

The examples of lpr discussed thus far are similar to variations of the OpenVMS PRINT command; the following two are peculiar to UNIX. You can use lpr -s filee to print large files.[7] This command does not queue filee in the spool directory (defined as /usr/spool/lpd in the /etc/printcap file for the default printer), since the spool directory could reside on a file system with insufficient free disk space to accommodate it. Rather, lpr -s filee prints the file directly from the user's directory. If you use lpr -s to print a particular version of a file, and then later unthinkingly make changes to that file, lpr -s prints the latest version of the file available at the time the file begins printing. In other words, the printed file would incorporate any changes made to the file between the time you added the print job to the queue and the time the file actually prints. If the file had been spooled, that is, copied to the spool directory, the version printed would be the version that existed when you issued the print command.

The command lpr -f filef prints filef using any FORTRAN carriage control characters present in column 1. Without the -f option, UNIX ignores these control characters and prints them like any other characters.

7.2.1   Examining Print Queues: lpq

The lpq (line printer queue) command lists the contents of a print queue; that is, it displays a list of jobs that are printing or waiting to print (compare with the OpenVMS command SHOW QUEUE). Like lpr, lpq assumes the default queue unless you specify an alternative.

OpenVMS

Example:

SHOW QUEUE[/QUALIFIER(S)] queue-name

UNIX

% lpq [option(s)] [-Pprinter] [job #] [user]

---

7.   The -s option is not available on all versions of UNIX.

Example:
```
$ SHOW QUEUE LASER
Terminal queue laser, on tta4
Jobname   Username  Entry  Blocks  Status
-------   -------   -----  ------  ------
LOGIN.COM  SYSTEM   70   3    Printing
RESET.DAT  SYSTEM   71   3    Pending
```

Example:
```
%lpq -Plaser
Rank    Owner   Job Files      Total Size
active  root    70  .login      913 bytes
wnd     root    71  /tmp/reset 22 bytes
```

Example:
```
% lpq fred
```
Example:
```
% lpq 71
```

The command `lpq  -Plaser` displays information about the queue `laser`. By default, OpenVMS displays information only about those jobs owned by the user making the request.[8] UNIX, on the other hand, displays all jobs. As with the OpenVMS PRINT command, each UNIX `lpr` command constitutes a single job irrespective of the number of files specified on the command line. The command `lpq` displays jobs in the order in which they are to be printed (rank). For each job, `lpq` displays the owner, the job number, the file(s) to be printed, and the size of the job in bytes.

The command `lpq  fred` displays information only on those jobs owned by user `fred` in the default print queue; `lpq 71` displays information about job `71` in the default print queue.

7.2.2 Removing Queued Print Jobs: lprm

The command `lprm` (line printer remove) deletes one or more of your jobs from the print queue; you cannot remove other users' print jobs (compare with the OpenVMS commands DELETE/ENTRY and STOP/ABORT). The syntax for specifying an alternative print queue is consistent with that of the `lpr` and `lpq` commands. The job being deleted may be printing or pending.

The command `lprm  -Plaser 71` removes job `71` from the laser print queue. Unlike the OpenVMS DELETE/ENTRY command, `lprm` informs you of dequeued jobs. The command `lprm -`, which has no OpenVMS equiva-

---

8.   Most OpenVMS users invoke the SHOW QUEUE/ALL command to display all queued jobs.

OpenVMS

Form:

```
$ DELETE/ENTRY=entry-number queue-
name
```

Example:

```
$ DELETE/ENTRY=71 LASER
```

UNIX

```
% lprm [-Pprinter] [job #] [user]
```

Example:

```
% lprm -Plaser 71
dfA071cuhhca dequeued
cfA071cuhhca dequeued
```

Example:

```
% lprm -
dfA072cuhhca dequeued
cfA072cuhhca dequeued
```

lent, removes from the default printer queue all jobs owned by the user making the request. UNIX offers no mechanism to requeue a job; you must first delete the job from one queue and then submit it to another.

7.3   Using Tape Drives

It is common practice to use tape drives to make personal archives of important files or to import and export data. UNIX provides several commands for reading and writing magnetic tapes: tar (tape archiver) is the most frequently used for creating personal archives and for importing and exporting files between UNIX systems, since all UNIX systems support it. The command dd (convert and copy a file) reads and writes files in nonstandard formats. The command mt, although not specifically used to read or write magnetic tape data, positions a magnetic tape, writes an EOF mark on a magnetic tape, or places a magnetic tape offline. Finally, the system administrator uses the dump and restore commands (not discussed here) to archive and retrieve whole file systems. Note that restore is valid only for magnetic tapes written with the dump command; it will not read a magnetic tape written with tar. Like the OpenVMS BACKUP command, tar and dd can also perform disk-to-disk copying.

UNIX handles tape-drive requests clumsily. In OpenVMS, you can determine the availability of a tape drive, allocate the drive, and mount the magnetic tape for reading or writing; most versions of UNIX do not support these features. Without the ability to allocate a tape drive, UNIX has no mechanism to prevent a user from inadvertently (or purposefully) reading from or writing to another user's tape while it is on the tape drive and online! Not surprisingly, some versions of UNIX have been enhanced to permit the allocation of a tape drive to a specific user.

To determine which tape drives are available on a UNIX system, a principle introduced in Section 2.3 is brought into play. You use a special device file to address devices; that is, tape drives are accessed as if they were files. The address of each tape drive resides as a file entry in the directory /dev. A single tape drive may have multiple entries, each entry defining a different way to use the device [e.g., to read or write at different densities (compare with the OpenVMS command BACKUP/DENSITY) or to specify whether or not to rewind the tape after each read or write (compare with the OpenVMS command BACKUP/REWIND)]. Different versions of UNIX use different names for these device files, but most names include the string "mt".

UNIX

Example:

```
% ls -l /dev/*mt*
crw-rw-rw-  1 root  36,  12 May  2  15:26  /dev/nrmt0h
crw-rw-rw-  1 root  36,   4 May  2  15:26  /dev/nrmt01
crw-rw-rw-  1 root  36,   8 Jun 22  17:13  /dev/rmt0h
crw-rw-rw-  1 root  36,   0 May  2  15:26  /dev/rmt01
```

This example defines two devices, mt01 and mt0h. The device /dev/rmt0h is a raw character device (rmt): It processes input/output as a stream of characters. The device /dev/nrmt0h buffers character input/output (nrmt). Since raw character devices are commonly used in the reading and writing of UNIX tapes, we use them for the examples in this book. You can check the online man pages for each system for more information about raw character devices and their relation to disk devices.

Your system may have several device files, but there is no guarantee that each of these files represents a device available to users. You should therefore check with your system administrator for information on available tape drives, the device files with which to access them, and the default. To illustrate how to use different tape drives or different features of the same tape drive at the command level, we will use the two character device files /dev/rmt0h and /dev/rmt01 from the example shown above.

Each version of UNIX defines one of the available tape-device files as the default. You can define your own tape-drive default with the TAPE environment variable in the same way that you can define a specific printer as the default with the PRINTER environment variable. For example, the command setenv TAPE /dev/rmt01 changes the default tape drive to rmt01.

7.3.1 **Archiving Files:** tar

The UNIX tar command (compare with the OpenVMS BACKUP command) reads and writes personal archive tapes and imports and exports files from one UNIX processor to another. Note the following contrasts and similarities:

- Unlike OpenVMS BACKUP/VERIFY, tar does not support file verification, which checks the files on the magnetic tape against the files on the disk.

- The tar command does not support writing to multiple magnetic tapes. In OpenVMS, BACKUP requests that additional magnetic tapes be mounted as necessary; the tar user, on the other hand, can archive only those files that fit on a single magnetic tape. If the target tape lacks the capacity to accommodate all the files you want to transfer, you must complete the copy operation by listing the contents of the first tape, mounting a second tape, and issuing a new tar command specifying the files that remain to be copied.

- In OpenVMS, BACKUP writes a directory hierarchy to a BACKUP save-set either on disk or magnetic tape, which you may then treat as a single file using OpenVMS file-manipulation commands. The command tar also copies directory hierarchies to magnetic tape and disk for treatment as a single file.

- You can append files to an existing tar magnetic tape as a separate tar file. You can use the mt command to skip tar files. In OpenVMS, BACKUP appends files as a separate save-set, with a separate header including the save-set name and the date it was written. The OpenVMS user then selects the save-set using the appropriate save-set name.

- Both OpenVMS BACKUP and tar are recursive when saving or extracting files if the appropriate file specification is given. That is, if the file specification for tar includes a directory, the contents of that directory and any subdirectories will also be included in the save or extract operation. In the simplest form, with no file specification, tar will save all files from the current directory and any subdirectories in a save operation or extract all files on the tape in an extract operation.

- Both OpenVMS BACKUP and UNIX tar support absolute and relative pathnames for naming files. If you write files to tape using absolute pathnames, the files must be copied from tape back to their original directories. If you use a relative pathname to save files, the files will be copied from tape to directories relative to the present working directory. As in the case of any command that writes files, you must have write access to the directory that is to contain the restored files.

- If you restore a file to a directory on disk that already contains a file of the same name, some versions of tar will overwrite the original file.[9] The behavior of the OpenVMS BACKUP command depends on the qualifiers you use. By default, if the file on the magnetic tape and the existing file on disk are identical, BACKUP will notify you that the file already exists and will not restore the file from magnetic tape.

UNIX users and system administrators who need to save whole file systems should use the command dump for saving files to magnetic tape and the command restore for restoring them to disk. The system administrator (user root) using the dump command can update the file /etc/dumpdates, which keeps a record of when a file system was last saved, either completely or in part. The header of a dump magnetic tape contains a listing of the files on the tape, including the directory hierarchy of the file system. The restore command is used, first to select files or directories to be restored, and then to extract the selected files from magnetic tape.

7.3.1.1 Writing Files to Tape

The following examples illustrate writing files to the beginning of a tape and appending files to a tar tape.

OpenVMS   **UNIX**

Form:

```
$ BACKUP[/QUALIFIER(S)]          % tar [option(s)] file(s)
file-spec[,...] - tape-
device:saveset
```

---

9.   The GNU tar command for Linux offers a -k option to specify that existing files should not be overwritten.

Example:

```
$ ALLOCATE MUA0: MYTAPE              % tar -cv ~fred
$ MOUNT/FOREIGN MYTAPE
$ BACKUP/REWIND/LOG/RECORD -
DUA1:[FRED...]*.*;*
MUA0:ARCHIVE.BCK
```

Example:

```
$ BACKUP/REWIND/LIST=NL:             % tar -ruv ~fred`
MUA0:ARCHIVE.BCK
BACKUP/NOREWIND/RECORD -
/SINCE = BACKUP/LOG
DUA1:[FRED...]*.*;* -
MUA0:ARCHIVE1.BCK
```

Example:

```
$ MOUNT/FOREIGN/DENSITY = 6250 MTA0   % tar -cf/dev/rmt0h file1 file2
$ BACKUP/REWIND/DENSITY = 6250 -
FILE1.,FILE2. MTA0:EXPORT.BCK
```

In the first example, `tar -cv ~fred` copies all the files of user `fred` to the beginning of the tape using the `-c` option. The `-v` option (verbose) informs the user as each file is copied. The files are written to tape using the default tape device.[10]

The second example, `tar -ruv ~fred`, illustrates the later incremental save of `fred`'s files. This command appends the new files following any existing files on tape (`-r` option); copies only files created or modified since the tape was originally written, that is, files that are different from the files already on tape (`-u` option); and once again informs the user as it copies files (`-v` option). Note the reference to the OpenVMS command BACKUP, which creates a new save-set after you position the tape at the end of the first save-set by listing the contents of the first save-set to the null device. Positioning the tape should not be necessary if the /NOREWIND qualifier (the default) is used with BACKUP. OpenVMS then selects files for copying to magnetic tape by looking for the backup recording date in the header record of each disk file.

The last example illustrates the use of an alternative tape device. The command `tar -cf /dev/rmt0h file1 file2` writes two files, assumed to be in the present working directory, to the beginning of a tape (`-c` option). Rather than using the default tape-device file specification, this command uses an alternative, defined by the `f /dev/rmt0h` option (that is, `f` followed

10.   Unlike most other UNIX commands, `tar` does not require a hyphen preceding options. However, for consistency, it is
      included here.

by a tape-device filename). This command could, for example, write to a tape drive that supports the reading and writing of tapes at a density of 6,250 bpi, rather than 1,600 bpi as indicated by the default tape-device file specification.

Note that the general form for the `tar` command is `tar [option(s)] file(s)`, but with `tar`, these options are not really optional. You must specify one or more optional arguments when entering the `tar` command.

7.3.1.2 Listing Tape Contents

The `-t` option lists the contents of `tar` tapes.

OpenVMS	UNIX
Example:	

`$ BACKUP/REWIND/LIST MUA0:SAVE.BCK`	`% tar -t`
	`/usr/file1`
	`doc/book.txT`
	`./myprog.f`
	`../oneup.c`

Example:	

`$ MOUNT/FOREIGN/DENSITY = 6250 MTA0:`
`$ BACKUP/LIST = -`
`SYS$PRINT MTA0:EXPORT.BCK`
	`% tar -tf /dev/rmt01	lpr`

In the first example, `tar -t` displays the files on the magnetic tape to the terminal. The listing shows file specifications for four different types of files: `/usr/file1` is an absolute file specification, `doc/book.txt` is a relative file specification; `./myprog.f` indicates a file from the present working directory; and `../oneup.c` is a file in a directory one above the present working directory. The implications of these different types of file specifications will become clear in the next section, which discusses restoring files from tape. In the second example, `tar -tf /dev/rmt01 | lpr` pipes the output of the `tar` display command to the default printer. The tape is mounted on device `/dev/rmt01`.

7.3.1.3 Extracting Files from Tape

The `-x` option of `tar` restores (extracts) files from tape.

OpenVMS	UNIX
Form:	

```
$ BACKUP/REWIND/LOG MUA0:SAVE.BCK*
```

```
% tar -xv
x /usr/file1
x ./doc/book.txt
x ./myprog.f
x ../oneup.c
```

Example:

```
$ BACKUP/REWIND/SELECT = MYPROG.FOR -
MUA0:SAVE.BCK*
```

```
% tar -xm ./myprog.f
```

In the first example, tar -xv without file arguments extracts (-x option) the contents of the whole tape, reporting on each file as it is restored (-v option). The file definition /usr/file1 is absolute; file1 is written specifically to /usr, overwriting any existing file with the same name. Only user root can issue this command, for usually /usr may not be written to by all users. The response ./doc/book.txt indicates that the file book.txt is being restored to a subdirectory doc of the present working directory. This present working directory can be different from the one from which the file was originally saved. The response ../oneup.c indicates that the file oneup.c is being restored to a directory one level higher than the present working directory. When restoring files with relative filenames, you should be in the correct working directory before you issue a tar restore command.

This example illustrates the flexibility of tar, which can use both absolute and relative pathnames. The use of absolute pathnames, however, is not recommended, particularly if you are going to export files to another UNIX computer. You may not have write access to the directory into which you wish to restore the files (assuming it exists), and even if you do, you may overwrite important files already in the directory.

In the second example, tar -xm ./myprog.f extracts the single file myprog.f. The -m option updates the file's modification date to the time the file was extracted. The default condition, like the OpenVMS command BACKUP, maintains the modification date that existed at the time the file was originally saved.

7.3.1.4 Disk-to-Disk Copying

You can use tar for disk-to-disk copying. It is particularly useful if you wish to maintain directory hierarchies during the copy operation.[11]

OpenVMS

```
$ BACKUP [FRED...]*.*;*
FRED.BCK -
/SAVE_SET
```

UNIX

```
% tar -cvf /tmp/tar_save
/usr/fred
```

OpenVMS

```
$ BACKUP [FRED...]*.*;* [JOHN...]*.*;*
```

UNIX

```
% cd /usr/fred ; tar -cf - . | (cd /usr/john ; tar -xf -)
```

The command `tar -cvf /tmp/tar_save /usr/fred` saves all files from `/usr/fred` down the directory hierarchy to the `tar` file `/tmp/tar_save`. You can restore files later from this `tar` file or list them with the command `tar -tf /tmp/tar_save`. Note that here the `-f` option indicates a `tar` file on disk. In the previous examples, the `-f` option points to a device special file, synonymous with a magnetic tape drive with a predefined set of characteristics.

The command construct `cd /usr/fred ; tar -cf - . | (cd /usr/john ; tar -xf -)` is more complex. First, it changes the directory `/usr/fred`. Then, rather than writing the files read by `tar` to magnetic tape, it pipes them to another command sequence (-), which first changes the directory to `/usr/john` and then extracts the files using the input from the previous command in the pipe. File `/usr/fred/filea` thus becomes `/usr/john/filea`, `/usr/fred/doc/fileb` becomes `/usr/john/doc/fileb`, and so on. An alternative method of copying directory hierarchies, the `cp -r` command, is discussed in Section 8.3.1.

The parentheses in this example place the enclosed commands in a separate environment from the rest of the pipeline. Changes in that environment, such as a different working directory, remain throughout the execution of the parenthesized commands, but vanish when the last command in the parentheses completes.

7.3.2 Special Tape Formatting: dd

The command `tar` writes files to magnetic tape in a specific format useful if you wish to read the magnetic tape on another UNIX processor, because all UNIX processors support `tar`.[12] If a non-UNIX processor will read the

---

11. UNIX applications and utilities are also commonly distributed in `tar` format file, which is then compressed with a file compression utility like `gzip`.

12. There are also free versions of `tar` that run on OpenVMS allowing `tar` archives to be packed and unpacked on OpenVMS systems.

tape, you can use dd to write the magnetic tape in a more generic format. Conversely, you can use dd to read magnetic tapes written on a non-UNIX processor. Section 7.3.4, which deals with the exchange of files on magnetic tape between UNIX and OpenVMS computers, discusses dd in detail. Three general examples are given here. Note that the format of the dd command is different from anything you have encountered before.

UNIX

Form:

```
% dd [option(s) = value(s)]
```

Example:

```
% dd if = myfile.dat of = /dev/rmt0h ibs = 3120 cbs = 80 conv = block
40 + 5 records in
10 + 1 records out
```

Example:

```
% dd if = /dev/rmt0h of = ~fred/ibm.dat ibs = 800 cbs = 80 cony =
ascii,lcase
40 + 5 records in
27 + 1 records out
```

Example:

```
% dd if = /dev/rmt01 of = /tmp/catfile ibs = 3120 cbs = 80 conv =
ascii,lcase files=3
1340 + 385 records in
4276 + 911 records out
```

The first example illustrates writing a file to magnetic tape with dd, and the latter two examples illustrate reading files from magnetic tape. The command dd if = myfile.dat of = /dev/rmt0h ibs = 3120 cbs = 80 conv = block writes the file myfile.dat to magnetic tape; if defines the input file; of = /dev/rmt0h defines the output file, which is the device file for the magnetic tape drive. Unlike tar, dd does not assume a default for input or output. The command ibs defines the block size, and cbs defines the record size.

The second example, dd if = /dev/rmt0h of = ~fred/ibm.dat ibs = 800 cbs = 80 conv = ascii,lcase, resembles the one given in the man page for dd. The string conv = ascii,lcase converts EBCDIC to ASCII and maps uppercase characters to lowercase.

Normally, you use dd to read or write a single file, but you can also append multiple input files on magnetic tape to a single output file, as shown in the third example. The command dd if = /dev/rmt01 of = / tmp/catfile ibs = 3120 cbs = 80 conv = ascii,lcase files = 3 reads the first three files from magnetic tape and combines them into a single output file, /tmp/catfile. As we shall see in the following section, the user can skip any number of files before reading files.

7.3.3   Tape Manipulation: mt

The command mt positions a magnetic tape, writes EOF marks on the tape, or rewinds a tape and places the tape drive offline. It is often used in conjunction with dd to position the magnetic tape while extracting files.

> **UNIX**
> **Form:**
> % mt [-f *tapename*] *command* [*count*]
> **Example:**
> % mt -f /dev/rmt01 rewind
> **Example:**
> % mt fsf 4
> **Example:**
> % mt offline

In the first example, mt -f /dev/rmt01 rewind completely rewinds the magnetic tape on the tape drive specified by the special device file /dev/rmt01 and leaves it online. In the second example, mt fsf 4 moves the magnetic tape on the default tape drive four files forward from the current position. These four files could be four tar files, each containing one or more files. You should issue the command in the final example, mt offline, the moment you have finished with the magnetic tape. Once rewound and placed offline, the tape is inaccessible to other users unless physically loaded and placed online again. Other useful mt command options include the following:

- eof [*count*]   Write *count* EOF marks at the current position
- fsr [*count*]   Move forward *count* records from the current position
- bsr [*count*]   Move back *count* records from the current position
- bsf [*count*]   Move back *count* files (as defined by EOF marks) from the current position

Each of these commands assumes that you know the current position of the magnetic tape relative to the files and the records it contains.

7.3.4   OpenVMS-to-UNIX Tape Exchange

To determine the most straightforward method of exchanging files written on magnetic tape between computers using OpenVMS and computers using UNIX, you should consult the system administrator of each computer. The version of UNIX that the computer uses and any locally written software will likely affect the choice of method. In any event, it is unlikely that you can read an OpenVMS BACKUP tape on a UNIX computer or that you can read a UNIX tar tape on an OpenVMS computer without third-party software to emulate BACKUP or Posix tar on OpenVMS. Nevertheless, the exchange of files written on magnetic tape is possible; this section describes one common method.

The dd command, available in all versions of UNIX, is used to read or write files with a fixed record length and block size. Use of dd assumes that the OpenVMS computer can read files with fixed block and fixed record lengths from, or write them to, a magnetic tape with no tape label. OpenVMS provides EXCHANGE/MOUNT/FOREIGN to accomplish this task. You can also write a simple high-level language program as detailed below.

The dd command is used to read files written on an OpenVMS computer or to write files to be read by an OpenVMS computer. Both applications use a fixed block length, a fixed record length, and no tape label.

UNIX

Example:

```
% dd if = /dev/rmt0h of = foo ibs = 800 cbs = 80\conv = unblock
40 + 5 records in
27 + 1 records out
```

UNIX

```
% dd if = /dev/rmt0h of = foo1 ibs = 800 cbs = 80  conv = unblock
files = 3
102 + 8 records I
65 + 3 records out
```

UNIX

```
% dd if = foo1 of = /dev/rmt0h ibs = 800 cbs = 80 conv = block
27 + 1 records in
40 + 5 records out
```

The command dd if = /dev/rmt0h of = foo ibs = 800 cbs = 80 conv = unblock copies the first file on tape to the file foo. The conversion conv = unblock converts fixed- to variable-length records. Without this conversion, UNIX will set the record length to the block size, which is dependent on the disk partition (Section 2.3) and may well be 512 bytes. If the tape is not rewound, you can repeat the command for additional files. As the command dd if = /dev/rmt0h of = foo1 ibs = 800 cbs = 80 conv = unblock files = 3 in the second example illustrates, you can use the files option to concatenate input files to form a single output file. In this example, the command concatenates three files on tape to form a single output file, foo1. Finally, dd if = foo1 of = /dev/rmt0h ibs = 800 cbs = 80 conv = block writes the file foo1 to the tape drive defined by /dev/rmt0h with fixed length records of 80 bytes (that is, as a card image) and 10 records per block. You could read the file foo1 from tape with a simple program like the one shown below, written in DEC FORTRAN:

OpenVMS
Example:

```
$ TYPE TAPEREAD.FOR
Template program to read fixed block and record magnetic tapes
Assumes: BLOCKSIZE = 800 bytes ; RECORDSIZE = 80 bytes ; No Label
C
C
CHARACTER LINES(10) * 80
C Open Input Tape File
OPEN(UNIT = 1, NAME = 'TAPE', RECORDSIZE = 800, BLOCKSIZE = 800)
C Open Output Disk File
OPEN(UNIT = 2, NAME = 'FOO1.DAT', CARRIAGECONTROL = 'LIST')
C Read a block of data from tape
5 READ(1,10,END = 1000) (LINES(JJ),JJ = 1,10)
10 FORMAT (<10>A80)
C Write a block of data to disk
WRITE(2,10) (LINES(JJ),JJ = 1,10)
C Go back for next tape block
GO TO 5
C File completely read so exit
1000 CLOSE (UNIT = 1)
CLOSE (UNIT = 2)
END
$ ALLOCATE MUA0: TAPE

$ MOUNT/BLOCKSIZE = 800 TAPE

$ RUN TAPEREAD
```

7.4   **Background Processing**

The C shell (csh), the Korn shell (ksh), the GNU Bourne-Again Shell (bash), but not the Bourne shell (sh), support *background processing*. A background process is a separate task, called a *job*, that may either be running or stopped. A user may have one *foreground job* and several *background jobs* running simultaneously, constituting a multitasking environment. A UNIX background job has all the features of a foreground job, with one exception: Only the foreground job can receive input from the terminal. This fact is not a restriction, as we shall see, since foreground and background jobs are easily interchangeable.

The analog to background processing in OpenVMS is the spawning of a subprocess (see Section 2.1.1). OpenVMS supplements spawning through the use of batch queues, which are not standard in UNIX. In UNIX it is very common practice to suspend the current interactive program, such as a text editor, to issue shell commands to print files, check queues, or even run a different interactive program like mail, and then later return to the suspended application exactly where you left off. In contrast, OpenVMS will allow you to suspend a job and issue DCL commands that do not start a new image, and then continue the suspended process with the CONTINUE command. However, if another image is loaded and executed, the suspended image is lost.

Background jobs in UNIX differ from jobs submitted to OpenVMS batch queues in two ways. First, UNIX background jobs can make the same demands on system resources as any of a user's interactive processes. They are not restricted by the same limitations imposed on an OpenVMS batch queue, such as lower priority, or a CPU time limit, although some implementations of the C shell reduce the priority of a background process that has been running for a predefined period of time (see the command `nice` in Section 12.3.3).

Second, OpenVMS batch jobs continue processing when you log out. What happens to UNIX background jobs when you log out depends on whether the background job is running or stopped. If you attempt to log out with stopped background jobs, the system responds with the message, "There are stopped jobs." You may attend to these background jobs or issue the `logout` or `exit` command again (or <CTRL>-D, depending on `ignoreeof`), which terminates all stopped background jobs. Background jobs that are running when you log out continue processing.[13]

If you log back in, the background job started in the previous terminal session no longer functions as a child process of the current parent shell; that is, it is not a background job of the current terminal session and cannot be manipulated or examined like other background jobs. However, you can treat it like any other process you own and can examine or modify it using the commands outlined in Chapter 12. Thus, you can issue the command

---

13.   This may differ for some versions of UNIX.

ps -aux | grep *user* to display the characteristics of the process (see Section 8.4.5 for a discussion of grep).

7.4.1 Moving Command Execution to the Background

To execute a command in the background, end the command with an ampersand (&). You can also stop a command that is running in the foreground by pressing <CTRL>-Z. In both cases, you receive a new copy of the shell with a unique process number for foreground processing. Note that jobs stopped with <CTRL>-Z remain inactive until you either restart them in the foreground or start them in the background (see Section 7.4.3).

The following examples, used again in subsequent sections, illustrate the use of background processing to perform interactive tasks in parallel.

UNIX

Form:
```
% command &
```

Example:
```
% find / -name myfile -print > find.out &
    [1] 15781
```

Form:
```
% command
<CTRL>-Z
```

Example:
```
% grep "hello again" /usr/file1 >grep.out
   <CTRL>-Z
   Stopped
% ps
PID   TT  STAT  TIME  COMMAND-csh[user] (csh)
15229 p2  S     0:04  find / -name myfile -print >find.out
15781 p2  R     0:02  grep "hello again" /usr/file1 >grep.out
15792 p2  T     0:01  ps
15804 p2  R     0:00
```

The first example, find / -name myfile -print > find.out & starts a background job. The system returns a job number, identified by square brackets, and a process number. In the second example, grep "hello again" /usr/file1 >grep.out was already running when stopped with <CTRL>-Z. In this case, the system does not report the process number and the job number.

The ps command (see Section 12.1.3) issued at this point displays four processes: the parent process csh and three child processes, two for the background jobs and one for the ps command itself. The state field (STAT) indicates that the ps and find processes are running (R), the shell process (csh) has been inactive for a few seconds (S), and the grep process is stopped (T).

Note the use of the > metacharacter to redirect the output of the background process to a file. Without this redirection, the system outputs the results of the background jobs to stdout, the terminal (compare with the OpenVMS logical name SYS$OUTPUT). The simultaneous display of output from foreground and background jobs can be confusing. By redirecting the output to a file, you can easily review it at a later time. Another method for preventing the simultaneous display of output from multiple jobs is to issue the shell command stty tostop. With this command set, background jobs about to display output will stop processing until brought to the foreground. Of course, this method is less efficient than the first, inasmuch as it interrupts the processing of background jobs. The default stty -tostop negates the effect of stty tostop.

If background processes are likely to generate error messages, you should also redirect them from stderr, the terminal (compare with the OpenVMS logical name SYS$ERROR), to the same file capturing stdout >& by using the redirection syntax >& which redirects both standard output and error messages to the same file.

The system notifies you when a background job is completed. By default, the system notifies you just before the shell prompt reappears, that is, at the completion of a foreground command. C shell users can receive immediate notification by setting notify. The command notify without arguments toggles notification on and off. You can set notify in the .cshrc file to have it be in effect for every process generated.

7.4.2   Examining Background Jobs

You can use the jobs shell command to examine the status of any background jobs started by the current parent shell.

UNIX

Example:
```
% jobs
[1] - Running     find / -name myfile -print >find.out
[2] + Stopped     grep "hello again" /usr/file1 >grep.out
```

The fields displayed by the jobs shell command are as follows:

- `[1]`   Job number
- `+/-`   Job status: current/next-to-current
- `Running/Stopped`   State of each job
- `find / -name....`   Command being executed

Note that "current" does not imply processing order, but relates to the order in which jobs are affected by the foreground process. The current background job is the last one affected by the foreground process, and the next-to-current background job is the one prior to the current background job that was affected by the foreground process. The following section explains how to manipulate background jobs using either the *job number* or the *job status*.

7.4.3 Manipulating Background Jobs

In the following example, we have added to the two background jobs described in the previous example a C language compilation (`cc`), a file edit (`vi`), and the display of a file (`more`). We will use this so-called *job stack* to illustrate the manipulation of background and foreground jobs.

UNIX
Example:
```
% jobs
   [1] - Running  find / -name myfile -print >find.out
   [2] + Stopped  grep "hello again" /usr/file1 >grep.out
   [3] Running  cc /usr/progs/calc.c >& errlog
   [4] Stopped  vi users.lis
   [5] Stopped (tty output)  more test.f
```
Form:
```
% %job_number &
```

Example:
```
% %2 &
   [2] grep "hello again" /usr/file1 >grep.out
```
Form:
```
% % job_number or fg job_number
```
Example:
```
% %5
more test.f
```

Form:
```
% stop %job_number
```
Example:
```
% stop %3
[3] + Stopped cc /usr/progs/calc.c >& errlog
```
Form:
```
% kill job_number
```
Example:
```
% kill %4
[4] Terminated vi users.lis
```

The `jobs` command displays the current job stack. Note the additional information displayed for job 5 (`[5]`): `tty output` indicates that the `more` command was sending output to the terminal at the time it was stopped.

In the second example, `%2 &` changes the status of a background job (`[2]`) from stopped to running. The command `bg 2` (background 2) has the same effect. In the third example, `%5` brings job 5 to the foreground; `fg 5` (foreground 5) has the same effect. The commands `bg` and `fg` issued without arguments place the current job (+) in the background or bring it to foreground, respectively. In the fourth example, `stop %3` changes the status of the third background job from running to stopped.

Note that when you change the status of a background job as in each of the above examples, that background job becomes the current job (+). Note also that if you change directories after submitting a background job, when you bring that job to the foreground, the shell returns to the directory from which you issued the command to submit the background job. Once that job is completed, the directory to which you moved will once again become the current directory.[14]

In the fifth example, `kill %4` removes the fourth background job completely. Note the analogy to `kill` (see Section 12.3.1) for removing a process according to its process identification number.

7.5   Batch Processing

The fact that you can simultaneously execute a number of interactive tasks in UNIX, but cannot do so easily in OpenVMS, reflects a basic difference in the typical use of each operating system. The OpenVMS user is usually content with one interactive process and a number of batch jobs running in queues configured to prevent the degradation of interactive response time.

---

14.   See the discussion of the `at` command in Section 12.3.2.

The majority of UNIX versions do not have batch-processing capability. Rather, the user can simultaneously run a foreground process and a number of background processes. A large number of background processes should not adversely affect interactive response time, because in most versions of UNIX the shell automatically lowers the priority of processes running in background for a system-defined period of time. The UNIX method puts the system administrator at a disadvantage, because he or she cannot easily exert the same level of control over the jobs running on the system as is possible in OpenVMS when defining the many characteristics of a batch queue. Note that while at and cron are not the same as batch queues, they provide many of the same scheduling functions as OpenVMS batch queues. See Section for 12.3.2 for more information on these commands.

7.6   Summary

The following scenario illustrates the practical use of some of the commands introduced in this chapter.

User Jack receives a tape written at 1,600 bpi in ASCII format with no tape label, a record size of 80 characters, and a block size of 3,120 characters. The magnetic tape contains two files that are versions of the same program, one written in C and one in FORTRAN.

```
UNIX
Example:
% pwd
/usr/jack
% mkdir newprog; cd newprog
% dd if=/dev/rmt0h of=prog.c ibs=3120 cbs=80 conv=unblock
40 + 5 records in
27 + 1 records out
% mt rewind
% mt fsf 1
% dd if=/dev/rmt0h of=prog.f ibs=3120 cbs=80 conv=unblock
40 + 5 records in
27 + 1 records out
% ls
prog.c prog.f
% mt offline
% lpr prog.c prog.f
% lpq
Rank  Owner  Job  Files   Total Size
1st   root   70   .login  913 bytes
2nd   george 71   /tmp/T1500_reset   22 bytes
3rd   joyce  72   /usr/joyce/bigjob  4598376 bytes
4th   jack   73   /usr/jack/myprog   94738 bytes
```

```
% lprm -
dfA73 cuhhca dequeued
cfA73 cuhhca dequeued
% lpr -P fastprint prog.c prog.f
% lpq -P fastprint
Rank  Owner  Job  Files  Total Size
Printing  jack  831  /usr/jack/myprog94738 bytes
% cc -o progc.exe prog.c >& c.err &
[1] 73682
% f77 -o progf.exe prog.f >& f.err &
[2] 73688
% jobs
[1] - Running  cc -o progc.exe prog.c >& c.err
[2] + Running  f77 -o progf.exe prog.f >& f.err
```

First, Jack makes a subdirectory to contain the programs. Then he makes the subdirectory the present working directory with the command sequence mkdir newprog; cd newprog. Jack places the magnetic tape on the drive and online and reads the first file from the tape into the file prog.c with the command dd if=/dev/rmt0h of=prog.c ibs=3120 cbs=80 conv=unblock, which includes the block and record size specification of 3,120 and 80 bytes, respectively. Since Jack is not sure whether the tape-device file causes the magnetic tape to rewind after each command, he uses the mt rewind command to reposition the tape at the beginning, moves forward one file with the mt fsf 1 command, and reads the second file from magnetic tape into the output file prog.f with the command dd if=/dev/rmt0h of=prog.f ibs=3120 cbs=80 conv=unblock. Jack uses the ls command to verify that the two files have been copied. He then rewinds the tape and places the drive offline with the mt offline command.

Jack decides to make a printed listing of the two programs. He uses lpr prog.c prog.f to send the two files to the default printer. Using the lpq command to display the contents of the default printer queue, Jack discovers that a large job, /usr/joyce/bigjob, is queued in front of his job. While wishing that print queue ordering were based on job size rather than time of submission, Jack decides to delete his own job and send it to another print queue to achieve a faster turnaround. He removes the print job from the default queue with lprm -. Since Jack knows that this is the only job he has queued, he uses this shorthand form of print job deletion, which removes all of his print jobs from the queue. Jack queues the job to a queue called fastprint with the command lpr -P fastprint prog.c prog.f. The command lpq -P fastprint verifies that the job is now printing in that queue.

While his file is printing, Jack compiles each program in background with the commands `cc -o progc.exe prog.c >& c.err &` for a C compilation and `f77 -o progf.exe prog.f >& f.err &` for a FORTRAN compilation (see Section 9.1). For both background jobs, Jack redirects standard output and standard error to appropriate files. Finally, Jack verifies that the two program compilations are running in the background with the `jobs` command.

8

File Management Revisited

8

File Management Revisited

> *One never notices what has been done; one can*
> *only see what remains to be done.*
>
> —*Marie Curie*

Chapter 4 introduced UNIX commands and options for file management that a novice user might need in the first few terminal sessions. Now we turn our attention to more complex and diverse commands and options. Although used less frequently, they are important for the management of files and directories. Once you understand the commands and options presented here, you will be ready to consult the man pages to obtain further information. Tables 4.1 and 4.2 summarize most of the UNIX commands used in file management and the subset discussed in this book, respectively. This chapter follows the organization of Table 4.2: It divides commands into those that relate to directories and those that relate to individual files; it further divides them into commands that display directory and file contents and those that modify directories and files. One of the features presented here is unique to the C shell: the creation of a *directory stack* that simplifies movement between commonly used directories.

Once you have read this chapter and experimented with the commands discussed, you should be ready to perform any file-management task required by the average UNIX user. The UNIX features discussed herein include the following:

- Displaying files in new ways (Section 8.2)

- Copying whole directory structures (Section 8.3.1)

- Simplifying access to files in different directories (Section 8.3.2)

- Changing a file's permissions (Section 8.4.1)

- Changing the group ownership of files (Section 8.4.2)

- Comparing files (Section 8.4.3)

- Finding and managing files in new ways (Section 8.4.4)

- Searching the contents of files (Section 8.4.5)

- Sorting file contents (Section 8.4.6)

- Updating a file's modification date (Section 8.4.7)

- Translating characters in a file (Section 8.4.8)

- Counting file contents (Section 8.4.9)

- Creating multiple references to a file (Section 8.4.10)

8.1   Advanced Directory Display Commands

Chapter 4 covered most of the frequently used options of the `ls` command for displaying directory contents. Here we discuss some extended features of `ls`.

8.1.1   `ls` Revisited

The command `ls -F` displays the name of the file followed by a flag describing the file type. It offers a condensed listing, rather than the long listing generated by `ls -l`, which is useful when you only need information about file type.

UNIX

Example:

```
% ls -F
myfile.txt  program.f*  tmp/     zfoo@
```

An asterisk (*) indicates that the file is executable. This does not mean that the file is an executable image (an `.EXE` file in OpenVMS terminology), but merely that the file has a file permission rendering it executable. For example, a file that contains a list of shell commands may be readable, but the shell program will not interpret the contents unless the file is also executable. The default permission on a file created with UNIX does not usually include execute access. You must explicitly make the file executable with `umask` (see Section 3.2.1) or `chmod` (see Section 8.4.1). In OpenVMS, the default file protection usually renders the file executable by the owner and other members of the group.

A forward slash (/) following the file name indicates that the file is a pointer to a directory; @ signifies a *symbolic link* (see Section 8.4.10); and = signifies a *socket* (see Section 13.1).

The final four ls options that we will discuss refer not to the features of a file to be displayed, but rather to the display format, which the following options modify.

OpenVMS	UNIX
Example:	
$ DIR/COLUMN = 1	% ls -1
Example:	
$ DIR/PRINTER	% ls -C | lpr
	Example:
	% ls -t
	Example:
	% ls -r

In the first example, ls -1 lists files at the terminal one per line rather than in multiple columns. The default gives multiple columns for terminal display and one file per line for output sent to any nonterminal device, including the printer. In the second example, ls -C | lpr illustrates how to override the printer default. The -C option forces multiple column output, which is piped to the default printer. In the third example, ls -t sorts the file listing by date last modified rather than alphabetically, displaying the most recently modified file first. In the last example, ls -r displays files in the reverse of whatever sorting order is in effect—in this case, since nothing else is specified, alphabetical order. Were the command ls -tr, the files would be listed in reverse chronological order. You can generally combine options to achieve their cumulative effect.

8.2 **Advanced File Display Commands**

In Section 4.8, we introduced the commands cat (catenate and print) and more, also called page (display a file a page at a time), for the display of file contents. We will now discuss the extended features of the more command and introduce the additional file display commands od, head, tail, and pr.

The command od displays file contents in various formats and is useful in searching for nonprintable characters, such as control characters and tabs. The OpenVMS command DUMP offers the same functions. The commands head and tail, as their names suggest, display the beginning and end of a file, respectively. The command pr does some simple page formatting that is useful for files you wish to send to a printer.

8.2.1   more Revisited, less Introduced

In Section 4.8, we compared the UNIX more command to the OpenVMS command TYPE/PAGE, which displays the contents of a file one screen (by default, 24 lines) at a time and allows you to scroll through several screens of information. Using more, you can advance the file one screen by pressing <SPACEBAR>, or one line by pressing <CR>. Additional responses include the following:

i	Set default scrolling so that *i* lines is a page
*i*f	Skip *i* screens and print a screen
*i*s	Skip *i* lines and print a screenful of lines
i%	Go directly to the line at the specified percentage of the file
d	Scroll forward one half screen
u	Scroll backward one half screen (not on GNU Linux)
q or Q	Terminate file display
i/*expr*	Search forward for the *i*th occurrence of the expression
:f	Display the current file name and line number
i:n	Skip to the *i*th next file listed on the command line
!*command*	Invoke a shell and execute the command
.(dot)	Repeat the previous command
h or ?	Display the above information on more options

As you can see, more offers some of the functions of a line editor when you use it in read-only mode.

Of course, since users always want more features, many implementations of UNIX now include less. (A linguistic purist might argue that it should have been called `fewer`, but that takes one extra character to type.) While `less` includes all of the features (and more) of `more`, the commands to invoke each differ in many cases. Corresponding, and then adding, to the list above of `more` commands, `less` has the following:

i	Set default scrolling so that *i* lines is a page
f	Skip screen and print a screenful
*i*g	Skip to line *i* and print a screenful of lines
i% or *i*p	Go directly to the line at the specified percentage of the file
d	Scroll forward one half screen
u	Scroll backward one half screen
q or Q	Terminate file display
i/*expr*	Search forward for the *i*th occurrence of the expression
:f	Display the current file name and line number
i:n	Skip to the *i*th next file listed on the command line
!*command*	Invoke a shell and execute the command
. (dot)	Repeat the previous command
h	Display the above information on `more` options
<down-arrow>	Scroll forward one line
<up-arrow>	Scroll backward one line
i?*expr*	Search backward for the *i*th occurrence of the expression
{	Find closing curly bracket corresponding to one on top display line
(	Find closing parenthesis corresponding to one on top display line
[	Find closing square bracket corresponding to one on top display line
m	Prompt for lowercase letter to serve as bookmark of current position
'	Prompt for lowercase letter, then go to that bookmark

8.2.2   **Dump a File:** od

The UNIX command od (octal, decimal, hexadecimal, ASCII dump) corresponds to the OpenVMS DUMP command. You can use od to examine the contents of files in various formats and to locate control and other non-printable characters. The OpenVMS DUMP command is most useful for determining the format of magnetic tapes, whereas od is usually used on disk files that may have been read from tape with the dd command (see Section 7.3.2).

OpenVMS	UNIX
Form:	
$ DUMP[/*QUALIFIER(S)*] -	% od [*option(s)*] *file*
file-spec	
Example:	
$ TYPE FILE.	% cat file1
line 1	line 1
$ DUMP FILE.	% od -a file1
...	0000000 ht l i n e sp 1 nl nl
$ DUMP/OCTAL FILE.	% od -o file1
...	0000000 066011 067151 020145 005061 000012
$ DUMP/HEXADECIMAL FILE.	% od -h file1
...	0000000 6c09 6e69 2065 0a31 000a

These examples, od -a, od -o, and od -h, display the contents of file1, in this case a single line consisting of a tab followed by the phrase "line 1" in character, octal, and hexadecimal, respectively. Note that od -a denotes spaces with "sp," new lines with "nl," and tabs with "ht".

If a file is mostly printable text, cat -net is a popular alternative to od. cat -net shows the beginnings and endings of lines and control characters. The less command can also do this and will display control characters in reverse video.

8.2.3   head, tail, and pr

The command head displays the beginning of a file, and tail displays the end. The head command has no OpenVMS equivalent. The command pr formats one or more files that, without redirection or piping, appear at the terminal with page headers and page breaks. OpenVMS achieves some features of the `pr` command with the `PRINT/HEADER` command.

OpenVMS	UNIX
Form:	
`$ TYPE /TAIL file-spec`	`% head [-count] file(s)`
`$ PRINT[/QUALIFIER(S)] file-spec[,...]`	`% tail [option(s)] file(s)`
	`% pr [option(s)] file(s)`
	Example:
	`% head -30 /usr/test`
Example:	`% head *.txt >> index`
`$ TYPE /TAIL=30 TEST.`	`% tail -30 /usr/test`
	`% tail -r /usr/test	lpr`
Example:	
`$ PRINT /HEADER FILE.DAT`	`% pr file.dat`
	`% pr -m file1 file2`
	`% pr -2 file1`

In the first example, `head -30 /usr/test` lists the first 30 lines of the file. In the second example, `head *.txt >> index` lists the first 10 lines (default) of all the files ending in `.txt` and redirects the output to the file `index`. Note the use of `>>` redirection (compare with `>`), which appends the result of each `head` operation to the file index, rather than overwriting it. The entry for each `.txt` file in `index` is separated from the next file by a line which looks like "==>*filename*<==". In the third example, `tail -30 /usr/test` displays the last 30 lines of the file. The command `tail -r /usr/test | lpr` reverses the order of the last 10 lines (default); that is, it displays the last line first, the second-to-last line second, and so on. The command pipes the result to the default printer.

The first example of printer formatting is the command `pr file.dat` without options, which formats `file.dat` for printing using the default file formatting characteristics. The default sets each page to a length of 66 lines and prints the filename, date, and page number on each page with a five-line header and a five-line trailer. The command `pr -m file1 file2` prints `file1` and `file2` side by side, which is useful for comparing file contents. As with all forms of `pr`, this command truncates long lines rather than wrapping them, so files are more likely to remain synchronized when displayed together. Finally, `pr -2 file1` prints `file1` in two columns, which is useful for saving paper when printing narrow files.

8.3   Advanced Directory Management Commands

Sections 4.4 through 4.6 introduced commands for creating, deleting, and moving between directories. We now look at the last step in directory management: copying the contents of a whole directory structure. We will also introduce two extensions of the C shell with which you can simplify access to files located in a variety of different directories.

8.3.1   Copying Whole Directories: `cp  -r`

Used with the `-r` option, the `cp` (copy) command accepts directories as arguments. You can use `cp -r` to graft one directory structure onto another. This use of `cp -r` corresponds to using the OpenVMS BACKUP command to copy directory structures from disk to disk, rather than from disk to a backup save-set on magnetic tape.

OpenVMS   **UNIX**

Example:

```
$ BACKUP[/QUALIFIER(S)] -
input-specifier output-specifier
```

```
% cp -r [option(s)] directory1
directory2
```

Example:

```
$ BACKUP [USER1...] -
[USER2.USER1...]
```

```
% cp -r  /user1  /user2
```

The result of the command in this example is illustrated in Figure 8.1. Both directory structures remain intact, and the command grafts the directory /user1 and associated subdirectories onto /user2 so that /user1 becomes an additional subdirectory of the directory /user2.

If you want to merge the contents of /user1 and /user2 while maintaining the lower-level directory structure—for example, changing /user1 /bin, /user1/source, and /user1/tmp to /user2/bin, /user2/source, and /user2/tmp, respectively—you would use the `tar` command (see Section 7.3.1).

8.3.2   Directory Navigation

Both the C shell and the Korn shell offer extensions to the shell-independent command `cd` for changing the current directory. The C shell provides the shell variable `cdpath` and the directory stack, whereas the Korn shell

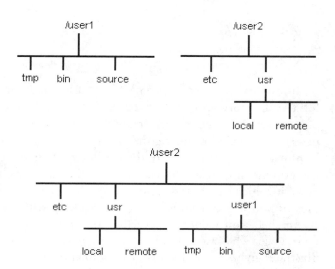

Figure 8.1
*Grafting
directories.*

includes CDPATH and OLDPWD. The Bourne-Again shell both recognizes CDPATH and OLDPWD and includes a directory stack. The variables cdpath and CDPATH let you move easily to a commonly used directory, irrespective of the current directory. In other words, you can move from the present working directory to a directory defined by cdpath or CDPATH without regard to the relative or absolute pathname required to get to that directory. The Open-VMS DEFINE command achieves a similar result, with one notable difference: DEFINE establishes a pointer to a specific directory, whereas cdpath and CDPATH establish a search list to potential parent directories of any sub-directory that is used frequently.

OpenVMS	UNIX (C shell)
Form:	
`$ DEFINE logical-name -`	`% set cdpath = directory-spec`
`equivalence-name[,...]`	
Example:	
`$ DEFINE TEST DUA2:[USER.TEST]`	`% set cdpath = /user/test`
`$ SHOW DEFAULT`	`% pwd`
`DUA3:[PROGRAMS.NEW]`	`/programs/new`
`$ SET DEFAULT TEST`	`% cd temp`
`$ SHOW DEFAULT`	`% pwd`
`DUA2:[USER.TEST]`	`/user/test/temp`

Example:
```
$ DEFINE DOC DUA2:[USER.DOC]          % set cdpath = (/user/doc /user/com)
$ DEFINE COM DUA2:[USER.COM]
```

In the first example, OpenVMS's DEFINE establishes a synonym, TEST, for the directory specification DUA2:[USER.TEST]. The UNIX command set cdpath = /user/test establishes a pointer to all subdirectories of /user/test. Hence, changing the directory to temp via a relative file definition makes /user/test/temp the present working directory irrespective of the current directory. The exception is the existence of /programs/new/temp, in which case that directory would have been preferentially made the present working directory. If you are working with the Korn or Bourne-Again shell, you would achieve the same results by defining CDPATH as /user/test. The last example, set cdpath = (/user/doc /user/com), illustrates giving multiple directory arguments to cdpath by enclosing them in parentheses and separating them with a blank. The Korn and Bourne-Again shells separate each directory with a colon (just as they do the directories in the PATH variable) and omit the enclosing parenthesis.

A directory stack is a list of directory specifications retained by the C and Bourne-Again shells for the current terminal session only. Directory specifications can be made part of the stack and recalled as required. The present working directory is always at the top of the directory stack. The following scenario illustrates the use of a directory stack.

UNIX (bash and C shell)
Form:
```
% pushd dir
% pushd +n
```
Example:
```
% pwd                              # Push /user2/programs/new onto the
/user2/programs/new                # stack and make /usr the current
% pushd /usr                       # directory
/usr /user2/programs/new
```
Example:
```
% dirs                             # Display the directory stack
/usr /user2/programs/new
```
Example:
```
% pushd /etc                       # Push /usr onto the stack and move to
/etc /usr /user2/programs/new      # /etc
```

Example:

```
% pushd +1                          # Rotate the stack n times
/usr /user2/programs/new /etc
```

Example:

```
% popd                              # Discard /usr from directory stack,
/user2/programs/new /etc            # change to next on stack, /usr2
% pwd                               # /programs/new
/user2/programs/new
```

Example:

```
% cd /tmp                           # Replace top entry on stack with /tmp
% dirs                              and set working directory there
/tmp /etc
```

The examples begin in the directory `/user2/programs/new`. The command `pushd /usr` places (pushes) the directory `/usr` onto the directory stack and makes it the present working directory. Note that the `pushd` command displays the directory stack; other commands that manipulate the stack also display it. Note also that `pushd` without arguments (not shown) switches the top two entries of the stack. The C shell command `dirs` interrogates the contents of the directory stack. Further use of the `pushd` command (`pushd /etc`) deepens the stack, and `/etc` becomes the present working directory. The command `pushd +1` makes the first directory stack entry the last, and the last the first; that is, it rotates the stack +1 (one) time. The `popd` command discards the top of the directory stack (the present working directory) and makes the second entry in the stack the new present working directory. Note the use of `cd /tmp`, which changes the top entry in the stack to `/tmp`, but does not change other entries in the stack.

While the Korn shell has no such elaborate directory stack, it does keep a record of the most recent previous working directory in the `OLDPWD` variable. You can thus go back and forth between two directories simply using the command `cd $OLDPWD`. The Korn and Bourne-Again shells use a directory sequence, `~-`, as equivalent to the variable. Thus, the command `cd ~-` is the same as the command `cd $OLDPWD`. Similarly, the two shells interpret `~+` as a reserved variable for the current directory, `PWD`.

8.4   Advanced File-Management Commands

Section 4.2 described the various characteristics of UNIX files. This section discusses commands that change those characteristics and introduces other file-management commands (see Table 4.2) that you may require from time to time.

8.4.1 **Change File Permission: chmod**

In OpenVMS, one has file protections, but in UNIX one has file permissions. No matter the name, they serve the same purpose. The UNIX command chmod, like the OpenVMS SET PROTECTION command, changes the permissions assigned to a file or directory. The command chmod provides two methods for specifying a change in file permission, as shown in the following examples.

OpenVMS   UNIX

Form:

```
$ SET PROTECTION = -
```
                                                  `% chmod v file(s)`
```
(CLASSIFICATION:LEVEL) file-spec[,...]
```

Example:

```
$ SET PROTECT=(O:RWED,G:RE,W:RE) A.DAT
```
                                                  `% chmod 755 a.dat`

                                                  `% chmod +x a.dat`

Example:

```
$ SET PROTECT=(O:RWED,G,W) A.DAT
```
                                                  `% chmod g-w,o-w a.dat`
                                                  `% chmod u=rwx,g=,o= a.dat`

The first example illustrates the *absolute form* for specifying a file's permissions. A level of protection is specified using an octal representation for each of the three types of user—owner, group, and world (in that order): where

```
user (owner)        group (group)        other (world)
rwx                 rwx                  rwx
421                 421                  421
```

Hence,

```
7 = 4 + 2 + 1       Read, write, and execute
6 = 4 + 2           Read and write
5 = 4 + 1           Read and execute
```

```
4 = 4              Read only
3 = 2 + 1          Write and execute
2 = 2              Write only
1 = 1              Execute only
```

Note that specifying the levels of file permission with chmod is *inverse* to the umask command, where 7 implies no access, 1 implies read and write access, but not execute access, and so on. The command chmod 755 a.dat changes the permissions of the file a.dat to give the owner read, write, and execute access, group members read and execute access, and the world read and execute access.

The second and third examples introduce the *symbolic form* of the chmod command. The command chmod +x a.dat adds execute access to all types of users, that is, to the user owning the file, group members, and all others. The command chmod g-w,o-w a.dat removes write access from group members and all others. Note that the symbolic forms of chmod use + (plus) and – (minus) to add and subtract levels of permission, but do not change the permission for classes of users or permission levels not specifically addressed. That is, the second example gives execute access to the owner, group, and all others, but does not change previously established read and write levels of permission. The equals sign (=) assigns permissions absolutely. The last example, chmod u=rwx a.dat, illustrates absolute permission assignment by giving the user owning the file read, write, and execute access to a.dat and removing all access from the group and all others.

You should also note from the table a critical difference in nomenclature between OpenVMS and UNIX. OpenVMS deals with a file's owner, the owner's group, and the rest of the world (ignoring for the moment the system protection). UNIX deals with the file user, the user's group, and all others. It's unfortunate that the OpenVMS abbreviation for owner, *o*, is the same as the UNIX abbreviation for all others. Be careful how you abbreviate when using the symbolic form of chmod!

For all uses of the chmod command, you must own the file for which you request a change in permission. Only the superuser may change the protection of files owned by other users.

8.4.1.1   Change Group Ownership: chgrp

The command chgrp changes the group ownership of a file. It corresponds to changing the ACE for an OpenVMS file, except that an OpenVMS file can have multiple ACEs, whereas a UNIX file can belong to only one group. To change group ownership, the UNIX user requesting the change must be the owner of the file and must be a member of the group being assigned to the file.

OpenVMS

Form:

```
$ SHOW SECURITY[/QUALIFIER(S)] file-spec
```

Example:

```
$ SHOW SECURITY FILE1
DUA3:[PARNIGONI]FILE1.;1 object of class FILE
Owner: [PROJECTA,PARNIGONI]
Protection: (System: RWED, Owner: RWED, Group: RE, World)
Access Control List:
  (IDENTIFIER=PROJECTA,ACCESS=READ+WRITE+DELETE+CONTROL)
```

Form:

```
$ SET SECURITY[/QUALIFIER(S)] object-name
```

Example:

```
$ SET SECURITY /ACL=(IDENTIFIER=[ADMIN], -
ACCESS=READ+WRITE+DELETE+CONTROL) DUA3:[PARNIGONI]FILE1
```

UNIX

Form:

```
% groups [username]
% chgrp [-f] group file(s)
```

Example:

```
% groups; ls- lg file1; chgrp hmwrk file1; ls -lg file1
hmwrk projecta
-rw-rw-r--  2  melvin  projecta  15 Feb 25 13:58  file1
-rw-rw-r--  2  melvin  hmwrk     15 Feb 25 13:58  file1
```

In the above example, the groups command indicates that the user (in this instance, melvin) belongs to the groups hmwrk and projecta. The command ls -lg file1 indicates that user melvin owns file1 and is therefore entitled to change the group from projecta to hmwrk. The command line chgrp hmwrk file1 changes the group ownership of the file file1 from projecta to hmwrk, which is verified by again issuing the command ls -lg file1.

8.4.2 **Compare File Contents:** `cmp`, `diff`, **and** `dxdiff`

The UNIX commands `cmp`, `diff`, and `dxdiff` serve the same function as the OpenVMS command DIFFERENCES for reporting the differences between two files. The command `cmp` reports only the first difference found between two files; it is a useful quick-check to determine whether two files are identical. The `cmp` command is also useful for reporting the first difference found in two non-ASCII files. The command `diff` reports all the differences between two files or the contents of two directories. The `dxdiff` command handles the differences between two files, but does so in a graphical way, most similar to DIFFERENCES /PARALLEL. The OpenVMS user familiar with the simple output of the DIFFERENCES command may find the output of the `diff` command difficult to interpret: DIFFERENCES displays the differences it finds, whereas `diff` displays the editing commands necessary to make the two files identical to one another. (Does anyone remember DIFFERENCES /SLP?)

OpenVMS

Example:

```
$ TYPE FILE1.,FILE2.
Maine
Montana
Nebraska
Illinois
Iowa
SYS$DISK:[BRUCE]FILE2.;1
Texas
Montana
Illinois
Alabama
Maine
```

UNIX

```
% pr -m file1 file2
Maine    Texas
Montana    Montana
Nebraska    Illinois
Illinois    Alabama
Iowa    Maine
```

OpenVMS

Form:

```
$ DIFFERENCES [/QUALIFIER(S)] file1
[file2]
```

Example:

```
$ DIFFERENCES FILE1. FILE2. -
/MAXIMUM_DIFFERENCES=1 -
/MATCH=1
************
File SYS$DISK:[BRUCE]FILE1.;1
   1  Maine
******
```

UNIX

```
% cmp [option(s)] file1 file2
```

```
% cmp file1 file2
file1 file2 differ: char 1 line 1
```

```
File SYS$DISK:[BRUCE]FILE2.;1
   1  Texas
************
Number of difference sections found: 1
Number of difference records found: 1

DIFFERENCES=1/MERGED=0-
    SYS$DISK:[BRUCE]FILE1.;1-
    SYS$DISK:[BRUCE]FILE2.;1
%DIF-W-MAXDIF, max number of difference records encountered - DIF aborted

OpenVMS
$ DIFFERENCES /PARALLEL /MATCH=1 FILE1. FILE2.
-------------------------------------------------------------------------------
File SYS$DISK:[BRUCE]FILE1.;1              | File SYS$DISK:[BRUCE]FILE2.;1
-------------------------- 1 -------------------------------------- 1 ----------------
Maine                                     | Texas
-------------------------- 3 -------------------------------------- 3 ----------------
Nebraska                                  |
-------------------------- 5 -------------------------------------- 4 ----------------


Iowa                                      | Alabama
                                          | Maine
-------------------------------------------------------------------------------
Number of difference sections found: 3

Number of difference records found: 4
DIFFERENCES /IGNORE=()/MATCH=1/PARALLEL-
    SYS$DISK:[BRUCE]FILE1.;1-
    SYS$DISK:[BRUCE]FILE2.;1
```

OpenVMS	UNIX

OpenVMS

Form:

```
$ DIFFERENCES [/QUALIFIERS] -

file-spec [file-spec]
```

Example:

```
$ DIFF/MATCH=1 FILE1 FILE2
************
File SYS$DISK:[BRUCE]FILE1.;1
    1    Maine
    2    Montana
******
File SYS$DISK:[BRUCE]FILE2.;1

    1    Texas
    2    Montana
************
************
File SYS$DISK:[BRUCE]FILE1.;1
    3    Nebraska
    4    Illinois
******
File SYS$DISK:[BRUCE]FILE2.;1
    3    Illinois
```

UNIX

Form:

```
% diff [option(s)] file1 file2


% diff [option(s)] dir1 dir2
```

Example:

```
% diff file1 file2
1c1
<Maine
---
>Texas
3d2
Nebraska
5c4.5
<Iowa
---
>Alabama
>Maine
```

```
* * * * * * * * * * * *
* * * * * * * * * * * *
File SYS$DISK:[BRUCE]FILE1.;1
    5   Iowa
* * * * * *
File SYS$DISK:[BRUCE]FILE2.;1
    4   Alabama
    5   Maine
* * * * * * * * * * * *
Number of difference sections found:
3
Number of difference records found:
4
DIFFERENCES /IGNORE=()/MATCH=1/
MERGED=1-

    SYS$DISK:[BRUCE]FILE1.;1-
    SYS$DISK:[BRUCE]FILE2.;1
```

<pre>$ DIFFERENCES/SLP/OUT=TT:
FILE2. FILE1.
-     1,   1
Maine
-     2
Nebraska
-     4,   5
Iowa
/</pre>
	<pre>% diff -e file1 file2
	5c
	Alabama
	Maine
	.
	3d
	1c
	Texas
	.
	% diff -r directory1 directory2</pre>

Example:
```
$ DIRECTORY/BRIEF/COLUMNS=1-
[DIR1...]*.*;* /OUTPUT=DIR1.LIS
$ DIRECTORY/BRIEF/COLUMNS=1-
[DIR2...]*.*;* /OUTPUT=DIR2.LIS
$ DIFFERENCES DIR1.LIS DIR2.LIS
```

In the first example, cmp file1 file2 finds the first difference in the two files in the first character of the first line. This equates roughly to the MAXIMUM_DIFFERENCES=1 qualifier, which instructs DIFFERENCES to terminate after finding one different record.

Older implementations of UNIX include no character cell equivalent to DIFFERENCES /PARALLEL; in GNU Linux diff --side-by-side --width provides the capability. In addition, some manufacturers offer an alternative based in the X Windows System. Tru64 UNIX calls its differences program dxdiff. For those who prefer to see differences in parallel, dxdiff offers additional clarity and emphasis over its rival character cell version. For example, dxdiff highlights difference sections in reverse video and forms the correspondence between those sections using lines to join their top lines and their bottom lines. You can also scroll through the files in synchrony or step from one difference section to the next. The dxdiff program will align the difference sections as they approach the center of the window.

The command diff file1 file2 reports each difference it finds, accompanied by up to four lines of information describing the changes required to make file1 identical to file2.

Line 1:	Three fields describing the change:
	1. The line number or range of line numbers in the first file prior to the change
	2. A character to describe the type of change:
	a = append
	c = change
	d = delete
	3. The line or range of line numbers after the change
Line 2:	The lines from the first file, if appropriate, identified by <
Line 3:	A delimiter (---) between the items of the first and second file, if appropriate
Line 4:	The lines from the second file, if appropriate, identified by >

The output of the second UNIX example, diff file1 file2, indicates the following: Change Maine for Texas in file1; line 1 remains line 1; delete line 3 (Nebraska) from file1 so that line 3 becomes line 2; and change line 5 in file1 from Iowa to two lines, Alabama and Maine, so that line 5 becomes lines 4 through 5. Note the similarity to the OpenVMS /SLP qualifier, which formerly was used as input to the Open-VMS SLP editor to maintain edit histories on files. The -e option produces just this sort of output; diff -e file1 file2 displays the commands that you must give to the ed editor to make file1 identical to file2.

In the last example, diff -r directory1 directory2 compares whole directories, rather than individual files, and reports either the existence of a file in only one of the two directories (as determined by its name rather than its contents) or the differences found in files with the same name. The -r (recursive) option compares all subdirectories of directory1 and directory2.

8.4.3 **find Revisited**

Section 4.7 introduced the find command for locating files anywhere in the system and illustrated its power to perform file-management functions on any files it finds. We now continue our discussion of find by introducing more complex examples of finding files and executing commands on them. The syntax of the find command differs from most other UNIX commands in that options consist of more than one character and are position-sensitive.

OpenVMS	UNIX
Form:	
`$ DIRECTORY[/QUALIFIER(S)]-` `file-spec`	`% find pathname_list criterion` `action`
Example:	
`$ DIR/FULL[*...]MYFILE.`	`% find / -name myfile -exec file {} \;` `/user1/bin/myfile: executable` `/usr/local/myfile: directory` `/etc/myfile: empty` `/user3/myfile: ascii text` `/user4/data/myfile: data` `/user5/scripts/myfile: commands`
Example:	`% find /user1 -mtime +45 -print`
`$ DIR/MODIFIED/SINCE=-45-00 -` `[USER1...]`	
	Example:
	`% find /user1 -name '*.f' -atime -45 -print`

UNIX

Example:

`% find /usr/fred -name '*.f' -o (-mtime -3 -atime -6) -exec rm {} \;`

In the first example, find / -name myfile -exec file {} \; not only locates all occurrences of files named myfile, but also displays information about the file type. The construct -exec file {} \; executes the command file on each file myfile found. In contrast to find, file is a simple command that accepts a filename as an argument (in this example, passed from find as the open and close curly brackets), examines the contents of that file, and returns the file type. The example shows some typical file types returned by the file command. The semicolon terminates the executed command, but note that it must be escaped with a backslash for it to be passed to find, rather than interpreted by the shell.

In the second example, find /user1 -mtime +45 -print displays all files down the directory hierarchy from /user1 that were last modified (mtime) more than (+) 45 days ago. In the third example, find /user1 -name '*.f' -atime -45 -print displays all files that end in .f (FORTRAN source files) and have been accessed (atime) in the last (-) 45 days. Note that "modified" implies "written to", whereas "accessed" implies "read from." OpenVMS has mechanisms to determine whether a file was modified (written) or created, but not when it was read.

The final example, find /usr/fred -name '*.f' -o (-mtime -3 atime -6) -exec rm {} \;, introduces -o, which functions as a Boolean "or" operator: It deletes each file found from /usr/fred down the directory hierarchy that ends in .f and has been modified in the last three days or accessed in the last six.

8.4.4   **Search File Contents:** grep

The UNIX command grep (compare with the OpenVMS command SEARCH) searches one or more files for a string of characters. Although grep has some powerful features, including the use of regular expressions (introduced in Chapter 5 for the ex, sed, and awk editors), older versions lack two features commonly used with the OpenVMS SEARCH command: the /WINDOW qualifier for displaying records before and after the search string, and Boolean operators, available with the /MATCH qualifier.

As with every other UNIX command, the search string when using grep is case-sensitive by default. This is not true of the OpenVMS SEARCH command unless you use the /EXACT qualifier. OpenVMS users familiar with SEARCH often reverse the syntax of the UNIX grep command, in which the search string precedes the file specification.

OpenVMS	UNIX
Form:	
`$ SEARCH[/QUALIFIER(S)] -` `file_spec string`	`% grep [option(s)] string file_spec`
Example:	
`$ SEARCH/EXACT FILE1. "hello` `there"`	`% grep 'hello there' file1`
`hello there, what a nice day`	`hello there, what a nice day`

`$ SEARCH FILE*.TEXT -`
`"HELLO THERE"`
	`% grep -i 'hello there' file*.txt`
	`file1.txt: hello there, what a nice`
	`day`

```
*****************************          file2.txt: Hello there, what a
SYS$DISK:[BRUCE]FILE1.TXT;1           horrible day
hello there, what a nice day
*****************************
SYS$DISK:[BRUCE]FILE2.TXT;1
Hello there, what a horrible day
```

Example:

```
$ SEARCH/NUMBERS FILE3. GOODBYE       % grep -n Goodbye file3
12 Goodbye and have a nice day        12:Goodbye and have a nice day
```

Example:

```
$ SEARCH/STATISTICS FILE3.-           % grep -c Goodbye file3
GOODBYE                               1
Files searched: 1        Buffered
I/O count: 5


Records searched: 12   Direct I/O
count: 5
Characters searched: 28  Page
faults: 104
Records matched: 1
Elapsed CPU time: 0 00:00:00.16
Lines printed: 1  Elapsed time: 0
00:00:00.73
```

Example:

```
$ SEARCH/MATCH=NOR FILE3.-            % grep -v goodbye file3
GOODBYE
```

Example:

```
$ SEARCH/WINDOW=0 *.FOR INCLUDE       % vi 'grep -l "include" *.f'
                                      % grep mode$ file4
                                      % grep "^ the" file5
                                      % ls -l | grep "^d"
```

In the first example, grep 'hello there' file1 searches file1 for all records that contain the string "hello there" and lists them. The single quotes, although not always necessary, delimit the string and ensure that metacharacters are passed to the command, rather than being interpreted by the shell. Some quoting is necessary in this example, because the search string includes a space. Omitting the quotes would have caused a search for just the word "hello," and the word "there" would have been interpreted as the name of the first file to be examined. The OpenVMS `SEARCH` command uses the `/EXACT` qualifier to make the two commands equivalent.

In the second example, `grep -i 'hello there' file*.txt` uses the `-i` option to make the command case-insensitive. OpenVMS users may feel more comfortable defining an alias such that `grep -i` becomes the default. Because the command references more than one file, it lists records that match the search string preceded by the name of the file containing the string.

In the third example, `grep -n Goodbye file3` searches for all records in `file3` that contain the string "`Goodbye`". The `-n` option displays the line numbers of records containing this string. In this example, the command found a single occurrence of the string on line 12.

In the fourth example, `grep -c Goodbye file3` once again searches for all records in `file3` that contain the string "`Goodbye`". In this case, the `-c` option displays the number of times the string was found. As you can see, this command supplies less statistical information resulting from a search than does the OpenVMS command `SEARCH/STATISTICS`.

In the fifth example, `grep -v goodbye file3` displays all lines in `file3` except those that contain the string "`goodbye`" (not shown). The sixth example, `vi `grep -l "include" *.f``, uses `grep` to extract filenames for further processing. The `-l` option returns only the filename of any file `*.f` that contains the word `include`. The `vi` editor then edits any files found.

The final three examples illustrate simple regular expressions: `grep mode$ file4` displays those lines of `file4` that end with the string "`mode`"; `grep "^the" file5` displays the records of `file5` containing `the` at the beginning of the line; and `ls -l | grep "^d"` lists those entries in a directory that are directory pointer files (that is, directory entries with `d` as the first character on the line).

The version of `grep` distributed with GNU Linux includes features corresponding to the OpenVMS `SEARCH` command qualifier `/WINDOW`.

Sections 5.4, `sed`, and 5.5, `awk`, discuss other situations where regular expressions appear. You should be aware that regular expressions can be extremely complex and have nuances and capabilities that vary not only between different commands, but even within the same command, depending on the switches! There are whole books devoted to `sed`, `awk`, and the use of regular expressions. If you plan to make more than minimal use of their power, you owe it to yourself to buy one.

OpenVMS	UNIX (GNU Linux)
Form:	

```
$ SEARCH WINDOW=(before,after) file -
string
$ TYPE FILE1.
Maine
Montana
Nebraska
Illinois
Iowa
Texas
New Jersey

$ SEARCH/WINDOW=(1,2) FILE1. Nebraska
Montana
Nebraska
Illinois
Iowa
```

```
% grep -A count -B count
pattern file

% cat file1
Maine
Montana
Nebraska
Illinois
Iowa
Texas
New Jersey
% grep -B 1 -A 2 Nebraska file1
Montana
Nebraska
Illinois
Iowa
```

8.4.5   Sort and Merge Files: sort

The sort command sorts the contents of individual files or merges the contents of two or more sorted files. There are two major differences in the way OpenVMS and UNIX sort files. First, OpenVMS accepts more data types as sort keys. Second, you can define UNIX sort keys using any predefined delimiter, whereas in OpenVMS you must define fields by fixed positions within the record.

OpenVMS	UNIX
Form:	

```
$ SORT[/QUALIFIER(S)] -
input_file output_file
```
```
% sort [option(s)][+pos1][-
pos2] file(s)
```

Example:
```
$ SORT FILE1. SYS$OUTPUT
```
```
% sort file1
```

Example:
```
$ MERGE FILE1. FILE2.
SYS$OUTPUT
```
```
% sort file1 file2
```

Example:
```
$ SORT FILE1. FILE.OUT
$ SORT/COLLATING_SEQUENCE= -
```
```
% sort -o file.out -n file1
```

```
MULTINATIONAL FILE1. 1.TMP
$ SORT/COLLATING_SEQUENCE= -
MULTINATIONAL FILE2. 2.TMP
$ MERGE 1.TMP 2.TMP SYS$OUTPUT       % sort -f file1 file2
                                     % sort +2 -4 file1
                                     % sort -t: + 3n -5 + 2n -4 /
                                     etc/passwd
```

The first example, sort file1, illustrates the simplest sort possible, using default settings for all characteristics: The sort key is the whole record for characters and the first digit for numbers; the ordering priority is the same as for listing files with the ls command (numbers first, uppercase before lowercase); and the sorted list is written to stdout. In the second example, sort file1 file2 functions the same way, but merges the sorted lists for each file into a single display. In the third example, sort -o file.out -n file1 uses the -o option to direct output to the file file.out. The -n option sorts in strict ascending numeric order, using the whole number and not just the first digit. In the fourth example, sort -f file1 file2 sorts, then merges, the contents of file1 and file2, disregarding the case of the alphabetic characters (-f option).

The fifth example, sort +2 -4 file1, illustrates the use of an alternative sort key to the default. In this instance, the sort key begins after (+) the second field (2) and ends (-) before the fourth field (4); that is, it uses the third field. By default, blanks delimit sort fields; that is, each word in a sentence constitutes a field. You can use other field separators, as in the sixth example, where sort -t: +3n -5 +2n -4 /etc/passwd sorts records in the password file. As we saw in Section 4.2, fields in the password file are separated by a colon. The -t option indicates that the separator is a colon, rather than a blank. The sixth example specifies two sort fields: +3n -5, the numeric field (n) beginning after the third field and ending before the fifth, namely the fourth or group field; and +2n -4, the numeric field (n) beginning after the second field and ending before the fourth, namely the third field, which represents the numeric identifier unique to each user.

It can be very useful to combine the sort and uniq commands:

UNIX

Example:

```
% cat file1
New Hampshire
North Carolina
```

```
        Texas
        Maine
        South Carolina
        Montana
        New Hampshire
        New Hampshire
        North Carolina
        Nebraska
        Illinois
        Iowa
        North Carolina
        Texas
        New Hampshire
        New Jersey
        New Hampshire
```
Example:
```
% sort file1 | uniq -c
      1 Illinois
      1 Iowa
      1 Maine
      1 Montana
      1 Nebraska

      5 New Hampshire
      1 New Jersey
      3 North Carolina
      1 South Carolina
      2 Texas
```

In this example, we not only sort the names of the states, but we create a count of the number of times each state name appears. A practical use of this technique could start with a list of student addresses, use the awk command (Section 5.5) to pick out the state names, pipe the result into sort and uniq, and come up with a geographical distribution of the students.

8.4.6   **Create or Update a File:** touch

The command touch updates the modification date of a file by reading a character from the file and writing it back. In other words, touch edits the file without actually changing it. If the file you specify does not exist, touch will create it, unless you have used the -c option. The touch command has special significance when used with the make utility, as we will show in Section 9.2.

Creating empty files with touch can be very useful when experimenting with UNIX commands like those described in this chapter; touch always creates files with the same attributes because, as we saw in Section 2.3, having only one type of file structure is indigenous to the operating system. All UNIX files have the same attributes: a string of bytes with the block size defined by a given partition. Therefore, UNIX has no concept of a file definition language (FDL) like that found in OpenVMS.

OpenVMS

Form:

```
$ CREATE[/QUALIFIER(S)] file-spec[,...]
```

Example:

```
$ CREATE TEMP.
<CTRL>-Z
```

UNIX

```
% touch [option(s)] file(s)
```

```
% touch temp
```

Example:

```
% touch -c temp
```

8.4.7   Translate Characters: tr

The tr command provides a simple mechanism for translating specified characters in a file into different characters without using an editor to perform a global edit. In the examples below, tr translates uppercase characters into lowercase or vice versa.

UNIX

Form:

```
% tr [option(s)] string1 [string2]
```

Example:

```
% tr A-Z a-z < file1 > file2
```

Example:

```
% tr -c A-Za-z '\012' < file1 > file2
```

In the first example, tr A-Z a-z < file1 > file2 translates the alphabetic characters A through Z from file1 to their lowercase counterparts and writes the output to file2. Characters already lowercase in file1 are copied unchanged to file2. In the second, more complex example (taken from the tr man page), tr -c A-Z a-z '\012' < file1 > file2 performs the same translation, but outputs each word in file1 on a separate line in file2. The -c option indicates that each string of characters in file1 will be followed with the delimited string 012, the octal notation for a new line. As we have seen, the \, acting as a metacharacter, prevents immediate interpretation by the shell; instead, the command itself performs the interpretation. In sum, the command takes each word (anything containing characters A through Z or a through z) from `file1`, follows each word with a new line, and outputs each word to `file2`.

8.4.8 Word Count: `wc`

We introduced `wc` in Section 2.5 to illustrate how different UNIX commands interpret wildcards. By default, `wc` lists the number of lines, words, and characters in a file.

UNIX

Form:

```
% wc [option(s)] file(s)
```

Example:

```
% wc chapter3
723 7281 56388 chapter3
```

In this example, `wc chapter3` indicates that the file `chapter3` (an early draft of Chapter 3 in this book) consisted of 723 lines, 7,281 words, and 56,388 characters.

8.4.9 Multiple References to a File: `ln`

A *link* provides a mechanism for assigning different names to the same file. The link does not create a separate copy of the file, but a directory entry, providing different pathways to the same information. Since the same file can have multiple links, different users could, for example, read from a single file, each using a different file name, but accessing the same information.

This use of links raises issues concerning the maintenance of a file's integrity, for example, when two processes from the same or different users write to the file simultaneously. This issue relates to the broad subject of *file locking*, which OpenVMS and UNIX handle differently. In OpenVMS, a file by default is open for writing to only one process at a time. This safeguard is usually not a limitation to an authorized user, since OpenVMS users usually do not generate many processes at any one time. In UNIX, on the other hand, many different processes are likely to be running simultaneously, and files therefore must be accessible to a variety of processes. This situation increases the likelihood that a file could be corrupted inadvertently and makes recovery of a corrupted file more difficult.

There are two types of links: a *hard link* (default) and a *soft*, or *symbolic, link*. A hard link maintains a directory entry, which renders the link file indistinguishable from the original file except that it has a different name. Changing the permissions on one link to a file causes the permissions to change on another link. Similarly, using `touch` (Section 8.4.7) on one link updates the access date on any other link. If the original directory entry were deleted, the link directory entry would still exist and could be accessed in the same way as the original. When a user makes a hard link to a file, the link count (see Section 2.3) for that file increases by one, preventing deletion of the file itself until the last hard link is gone.

A symbolic link simply provides a path, or pointer, to the original file. If the original file were deleted, the link would still exist (often called a *stale link*), but there would be no way of accessing the original file. A symbolic link does not increase the link count. Links are often used to associate data files to be read or written by programs.

Hard links may neither span file systems nor refer to directories, whereas symbolic links may do both.

A symbolic link in UNIX assumes the same role as the OpenVMS `DEFINE` or `ASSIGN` commands, with two notable exceptions. First, the OpenVMS commands without qualifiers place an entry in the process name table and remove it when the process terminates; they exist only in process address space. Symbolic links, because they are actual disk files, remain in effect until the link file is removed, that is, longer than a single terminal session. Second, OpenVMS `ASSIGN` and `DEFINE` are often used with the qualifier `/USER_MODE`, which maintains the assignment, not for the duration of the terminal session, but only for as long as it takes to run a single executable image. UNIX links have no equivalent feature.

In the first example, `ln file1.dat foo` establishes a hard link between `file1.dat` and `foo`, so that writing to or reading from `foo` is identical to writing to or reading from `file1.dat`. As both files reside in the same directory, a simple long listing of the directory contents reveals two identical files. Compare this with the link count of two with the count of one for the nonlinked file. The first link is always to the directory in which the file resides.

In the second example, `ln -s file2.dat foo` establishes a symbolic link between `file2.dat` and `foo`. Note the different format of the display provided by `ls -l` when the link is symbolic; the first column under `foo`

OpenVMS	UNIX
Form:	`% ln [-s] `*`name1`*` [`*`name2`*`]`
`$ DEFINE[/`*`QUALIFIER(S)`*`] -`	
`logical-name equivalence-name``[,...]`	
Example:	
`$ DIRECTORY/PROTECTION/SIZE/DATE/`	`% ls -l`
`NOTRAIL`	`-rw-rw-r-- 1 system 15 Feb 25 13:58`
`FILE1.DAT;1  1  25-APR-1997`	`file1.dat`
`13:58:02.10`	`% ln file1.dat foo`
`$ SET FILE/ENTER=FOO FILE1.DAT`	`% ls -l`
`$ DIRECTORY/PROTECTION/SIZE/DATE/`	`total 1`
`NOTRAIL`	
`FILE1.DAT;1  1  25-APR-1997`	`-rw-rw-r-- 2 system 15 Feb 25 13:58`
`13:58:02.10`	`file1.dat`
`FOO;1        1  25-APR-1997`	`-rw-rw-r-- 2 system 15 Feb 25 13:58`
`13:58:02.10`	`foo`
Example:	
`$ DEFINE FOO FILE2.DAT`	`% ln -s file2.dat foo`
`$ SHOW LOGICAL FOO`	`% ls -l`
`"FOO"="FILE2.DAT"`	`total 1`
`(LNM$PROCESS_TABLE)`	`-rw-rw-r-- 1 system 15 Feb 25 13:58`
	`file2.dat`
	`lrwxrwxrwx 1 system 25 Feb 25 14:27`
	`foo->file2.dat`

contains `l` to indicate a symbolic link and displays the actual link at the end of the record as `foo1 -> file1`.

8.5   Summary

The following series of examples summarizes the commands introduced in this chapter.

UNIX
```
% grep '/bin/csh' /etc/passwd | sort | awk -F: \
'{print $1}' > Cusers
```
Example:
```
% cp -r /george/applic1 /usr/public/applic1
% chmod 775 /usr/public/applic1/*
```

```
% chgrp admin /usr/public/applic1/*
```
Example:
```
% find /usr/public -name "*.f" -exec head -1 {} \; | sort > index
% grep -i fft index
```

The first example comes from a UNIX user who has grasped the concept of complex command constructs built from relatively simple components. It pipes together three commands and then redirects the output to produce a file, Cusers, which lists all users who invoke the C shell by default at login time. This file could, for example, serve as a mailing list to relate information of importance only to C shell users. The construct grep '/bin/csh' /etc/passwd searches the password file for all records that define the C shell as the default. Recall that the file passwd contains one record for each user on the system and that /bin/csh defines the default shell as the C shell. The command passes these records to sort, which sorts on the whole record since it has no arguments. Since the login name is the first entry of the record, sort sorts the records alphabetically by login name. The command then passes the sorted list to awk -F: '{print $1}', which uses a colon as the field separator, as does the /etc/passwd file. The awk utility prints the first field of each record, which is redirected to the file Cusers.

In the second example, user George copies a set of files residing in the directory /george/applic1 to a public area where all users can access them. George can do this since he is the owner of the directory /usr/public. If any subdirectories of /george/applic1 existed, they would become subdirectories of /usr/public/applic1. George then changes the protection of all files so the owner and the group have full access and all users can read and execute the files. Lastly, George changes the group ownership of the files so that members of the group admin can read, write, and execute the files.

In the last example, the find command locates all files in the public directories /usr/public that end in *.f, that is, FORTRAN source files. The command pipes the first line of each file it finds through sort and redirects the sorted output to the file index. If all programs use the first record to declare the program name, then index contains a sorted list of all the programs on the system regardless of their file names. The command grep -i fft index searches this file index for all occurrences of the string "fft", irrespective of the case of the string (-i option).

Programming

9

9

Programming

The wave of the future is coming and there is no stopping it.
—Anne Morrow Lindbergh

This chapter introduces UNIX commands and utilities for compiling, debugging, profiling, and managing programs written in high-level languages. All the examples presented in this chapter use either the C or FOR-TRAN languages, although most features discussed here apply to any language for which a UNIX compiler is available. Readers who do not intend to use programming languages in the UNIX environment can skip this chapter.

Most versions of UNIX come with compilers for high-level languages. With OpenVMS, you must purchase compilers as separate products. BSD is distributed with FORTRAN, C, and PASCAL; other compilers are available in the public domain. The advantages of both the BSD and public-domain compilers are their low price—BSD itself is inexpensive to license—and their ability to run on any computer supporting BSD UNIX. Unfortunately, they do not use features of the hardware specific to each vendor. Consequently, they run compiled code slowly compared with native compilers that support such features as floating-point accelerators, multiple processors, and vector processing units. The FORTRAN and DEC C compilers, available for both the OpenVMS and Tru64 UNIX operating systems, are examples of compilers taking advantage of specific hardware, in this case the Alpha architecture. Readers who wish to determine what compilers are available on their systems should consult their system administrator or refer to online help using the command `man -k compile`.

In addition to specialized compilers, vendors may also offer proprietary software tools to assist in program development, such as language-sensitive editors, debuggers, and profilers. Irrespective of any additional proprietary software development tools, all versions of UNIX possess programming tools, tools for which UNIX is well known, although even these will vary slightly for different distributions of UNIX. Table 9.1 summarizes these tools, a few of which we discuss in this chapter. Some of the OpenVMS tools listed above are available as layered products.

Table 9.1 *Summary of UNIX Programming Tools*

UNIX Tool	OpenVMS Equivalent	Function
ar	LIBRARIAN	Archives and maintains and library
as	MACRO	Compiles assembler language
awk		Performs pattern matching and action
bc		Is an arbitrary precision mathematical language
cb		Beautifies C programs
cc	CC	Compiles C language
cflow		Analyzes application files and builds a graph that charts the external references made in the application
ctags		Locates functions within a C or FORTRAN program
cxref		Analyzes a set of C application files and builds a cross-reference table listing all the symbols used in the application.
dbx	/DEBUG	Debugs at the source level
dc	DECalc2	Serves as an arbitrary precision desk calculator
dis		Disassembles object files into machine instructions
error	/LIST	Analyzes and disperses in source compiler-error messages
f77	FORTRAN	Compiles FORTRAN-77 language
file		Reads one or more files as input, performs a series of tests on the files, and determines their types

Table 9.1 *Summary of UNIX Programming Tools (continued)*

UNIX Tool	OpenVMS Equivalent	Function
fpr	PRINT	Prints files with FORTRAN carriage control
fsplit		Splits a multiroutine FORTRAN program into individual files
gcore	ANALYZE/ PROCESS	Gets core image
gprof	PCA	Profiles program execution
indent		Indents and formats C programs
ld	LINK	Serves as loader (linker)
lex		Generates programs used in lexical analysis of text
lint		Verifies C program
ln	ASSIGN	Links two files for reading or writing
lorder		Finds ordering relationship for an object library
make	DEC MMS	Maintains groups of programs
mkstr		Creates a C error message file
nm	LINK/ SYMBOL_TABLE	Prints the name list (symbol table) of an object file
odump		Displays information about an object file, archive file, or executable file
pc	PASCAL	Compiles PASCAL
pdx	/DEBUG	Debugs PASCAL
pixie		Reads applications, partitions them into basic blocks, and counts the execution of the basic blocks
pixstats		Analyzes the output from pixie
pmerge		Merges PASCAL files
prof	PCA	Profiles program execution
px		Interprets PASCAL
pxp		Profiles PASCAL execution

Table 9.1   *Summary of UNIX Programming Tools (continued)*

UNIX Tool	OpenVMS Equivalent	Function
pxref		Serves as PASCAL cross-reference program
rabnlib	LIBRARIAN	Randomizes libraries
sccs	DEC CMS	Serves as source code control system
size		Displays size of an object file
stdump		Displays detailed symbol table information for an application or object
strings		Displays ASCII strings in a binary file
strip		Removes symbols and relocation bits
symorder		Rearranges name list
time	SHOW PROCESS /ACCOUNTING	Determines system, user, and elapsed times
xstr		Extracts strings from C programs
yacc		Serves as a compiler writing assistant

In this chapter, first we describe the steps involved in producing executable code using both the FORTRAN and C compilers. Next, we introduce the make utility (compare with the OpenVMS layered product MMS), a powerful UNIX tool for managing large programs that you need to compile repetitively. We do not discuss sccs or cvs (Source Code Control System and Concurrent Versioning System respectively; compare with the OpenVMS layered product CMS), utilities that extend the capabilities of make. Both maintain the revision history and other features of a large program, typically coded by more than one programmer.

Next, we discuss the debugging of programs. You can find errors in syntax using the error command (compare with the /LIST qualifier of any OpenVMS compiler), and errors in program logic using the interactive debugger dbx (compare with the OpenVMS qualifier /DEBUG). We then turn to improving program efficiency with the profiling commands prof and gprof, which indicate where and how the code uses CPU time (compare with the OpenVMS layered product VAX Performance and Coverage Analyzer).

Finally, we discuss the command `ar` (archive), the UNIX analog to the OpenVMS `LIBRARIAN` for maintaining groups of files. Of particular interest here is the use of `ar` for the creation and maintenance of object libraries to be included when linking.

9.1   Compiling and Linking

You invoke the BSD FORTRAN and C compilers with the commands `f77` and `cc`, respectively. Used without options (and assuming that no errors are found), these commands perform all the steps shown in Figure 9.1 to produce an executable image. Unlike OpenVMS, you do not have to explicitly link the object code.

The filenames used in UNIX compilations traditionally carry file extensions. However, unlike OpenVMS, UNIX uses such names only for file recognition purposes (the extensions are not assumed when used with commands). For example, in OpenVMS, you can use the command `CC MYPROG` or `CC MYPROG.C` to compile the program contained in the file `MYPROG.C`; in UNIX, you must use the command `cc myprog.c`, for `cc myprog` will produce a "file not found" error. Some UNIX systems require a `.c` file type and will not work with your source unless it is both appropriately and explicitly named.

C++ files often have `.cc` and `.cxx` suffixes. But be careful when copying `MYPROG.C` from OpenVMS to `MYPROG.C` on UNIX, as some compilers will assume it's a C++ file due to the uppercase "C"! C++ code is compiled and loaded in exactly the same manner as C code, except for differences in running the compiler. Often the same command can compile both C and C++ code.

The first step in producing an executable image invokes a *preprocessor*, which ignores all lines except those beginning with a comment indicator. Refer to documentation on the compiler (e.g., `man f77` or `man cc`) for a discussion of preprocessor instructions. Preprocessor instructions include the following:

- `#include "filename"`, `#include <filename>`, useful for including additional user-written code shared by a number of programs or for including a system routine (usually kept in subdirectories of `/usr/sys`). Angle brackets are used for including system files, quotation marks for code written by the programmer.

Figure 9.1   *Steps in program compilation.*

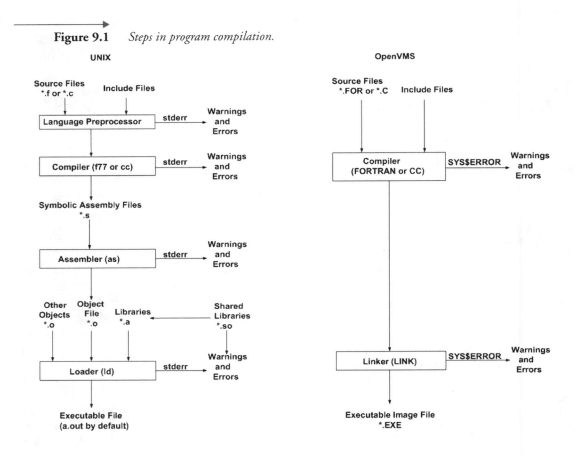

- ■ #define, for replacing one string of characters with another.

Often the task of the preprocessor is to include headers files, which have the suffix .h. (Note that in the most recent C++ specification, the default system header files no longer have any suffix.) These header files contain declarations of functions contained within other source files and allow the inclusion of shared functions across multiple files.

The second step in creating an executable image invokes the compiler proper to produce a *symbolic assembly file* with the file extension .s. The third step passes the symbolic assembly file to the assembler to produce an object file with an extension of .o (compare with the OpenVMS extension .OBJ). Note that BSD symbolic assembly code is independent of the language compiler that produced it; that is, the BSD assembler can interpret assembly code no matter what language compiler generated it. This feature has a number of benefits, including simplifying the writing of a new compiler and making applications more portable. If the system successfully produces an object file, by default it deletes the symbolic assembly file (.s). The system then passes the object code and any other objects, either files or library entries, to the *loader* (*linker* in OpenVMS), which produces an executable image retaining the object code (.o). Unless you call for an alternative file specification, the file containing the executable image is always named a.out (compare with the OpenVMS file extension .EXE). This last step is arcane and unimaginative. It may also be counterproductive if the novice UNIX user inadvertently overwrites an a.out file created during an earlier compilation of a different program.

The following examples illustrate the steps involved in producing an executable image and introduce options that you can use to retain intermediate files or produce executable files with more imaginative names. All the options presented in these examples apply to both the FORTRAN and C compilers.

OpenVMS	**UNIX**
Form:	
$ FORTRAN[/*QUALIFIER(S)*] *source-file(s)*	% f77 [*option(s)*] *source-file(s)*
Form:	
$ CC[/*QUALIFIER(S)*] *source-file(s)*	% cc [*option(s)*] *source-file(s)*
Example:	
$ FORTRAN MYPROG.FOR	% f77 myprog.f
$ LINK MYPROG.OBJ	% chmod 755 a.out
$ RUN MYPROG.EXE	% a.out
Example:	
$ FORTRAN MYPROG.C	
$ LINK/EXECUTABLE = NEWNAME.EXE - MYPROG.OBJ	% cc -o newname.exe myproc.c
Example:	
$ FORTRAN MYPROG.FOR	% f77 -c myprog.f
	% cc -S myprog.c
Example:	
$ FORTRAN MYPROG.FOR,[PUBLIC]*.FOR	% f77 -l/usr/public myprog.f
$ LINK MYPROG,[PUBLIC]*.OBJ	

Example:

```
$ CC MYPROG.C                             % cc myprog.c -lplotlib
$ LINK MYPROG, -
SYS$LIBRARY:PLOTLIB.OLB/LIB
```

In the first example, f77 myprog.f without options produces an executable file a.out, to which the command chmod 755 a.out (see Section 8.4.1) gives an executable file protection. The file is executed simply by giving the path to the file. (Like any other UNIX command, whether you can simply name the file or must supply an explicit path, or whether another command of the same name is executed in place of your file, is determined by the PATH environment variable.) In the second example, cc -o newname.exe myprog.c also produces an executable file, but with the name newname.exe (-o option). You should use this option and a unique filename in all compilations to prevent inadvertently overwriting executable files from prior program compilations.

In the third example, f77 -c myprog.f suppresses the loading stage (-c option), producing an object file myprog.o. In the fourth example, cc -S myprog.c generates symbolic language code in the file myprog.s, but stops there (-S option). In the fifth example, f77 -I/usr/public myprog.f uses the -I option to include an additional directory in the search path that the preprocessor uses to resolve references to #include files; usually, the preprocessor searches only /usr/sys. In the last example, cc myprog -lplotlib resolves references to calls to subroutines contained in the object code library plotlib.a (see Section 9.5). Note that this is a rare example where the file type (.a) is assumed. By default, the preprocessor searches the directories /lib, /usr/lib, and usr/local/lib in sequence to resolve references (compare with the OpenVMS logical name SYS$LIBRARY).

Subsequent sections introduce additional options for the f77 and cc commands.

9.2   **Simplifying Compilation: make**

Like the OpenVMS layered product MMS, the UNIX utility make manages a group of files in some way dependent on each other. We will discuss the most common use of make: to maintain large programs. But you can also, for example, use make to maintain a large document set, where changes in one document require corresponding changes in related documents.

In simple terms, `make` "remembers'" which part of a program must be recompiled after you make a change. OpenVMS users usually maintain a single large source file, which they must recompile after making even a small change to a single routine or function. This programming practice is wasteful of both user time and system time. UNIX users, on the other hand, can maintain a number of smaller files, use `make` to remember which files have been changed since the creation of the last executable image, and recompile only those parts of the program that were changed.

Instructions for `make` are stored in a *makefile*; `make` searches for makefiles with the names `makefile` or `Makefile`. Before looking at the rules that govern a `makefile`, let us consider the sequence of events that takes place when porting an OpenVMS high-level language program to the UNIX environment. (Section 9.6 gives a specific example of porting a FORTRAN program from OpenVMS to UNIX.)

1.   Split the source code into smaller interdependent parts using the UNIX command `fsplit`, which splits FORTRAN source files into subroutines and functions.

2.   Write a makefile to manage the programs.

3.   Run `make` to create an up-to-date executable file.

4.   Run the program.

You would repeat the last two steps each time you make a change to the program, recompiling only those subroutines and functions containing the code that you changed. If you wish to recompile all files, use the `touch` command (see Section 8.4.7) to update each file's modification date so that `make` includes it.

Some terms used in describing a makefile appear below. Note that we will not use all of these terms in the examples that follow.

- *Commands*: Actions make is to take on a target file (e.g., compilation)

- *Dependencies*: Relationships between files (e.g., the executable image is dependent on a number of object files, which in turn are dependent on a number of source-code files)

- *Targets*: Files produced as a result of commands and dependencies (e.g., an executable image)

- *Flags*: Strings of command options (e.g., options for the f77 or cc commands)

- *Macros*: Shorthand means of specifying dependencies or commands; the macro name is made equal to a string once, and then used in subsequent references to the string

- *Suffixes*: Filename extensions that infer certain actions to be performed

- *Prefixes*: List of directories to be searched

- *Comments*: Any information preceded by # and ending with a new line

These terms follow the syntax rules listed below:

`<tab>`	Designates the beginning of a command line following a dependency line
`<tab>-`	Designates the beginning of a command line following a dependency line; if an error is found in this line, make will not stop
`=`	Assigns a name to a macro
`@`	At the beginning of a command line, causes the command to execute silently, that is, without displaying output on the screen
`:`	Separates a list of targets from a list of dependent files
`a(b)`	Indicates that filename b is stored in archive (library) a
`a((b))`	Designates b as an entry point in a file stored in archive a
`s1.s2`	Designates a second-level dependency; that is, files whose names end in s2 depend on files whose names end in s1 (e.g., .c.o: files that have the file type o depend on files that have the file type c)
`\`	Continues a command line or variable assignment onto the next line (quotes the new line)

The following example illustrates a simple makefile to print a long directory listing (ls -l) of the files residing in the directory /usr/fred. The listing resides in the file list.out, which is recreated only if the contents of the directory have changed since the last invocation of make.

UNIX

Example:

```
% cat makefile
# Macro definitions:
FILES = /usr/fred
# Target definitions:
Print: list.out
   lpr list.out
# Second level dependency
list.out: $(FILES)
   ls -l $(FILES) > list.out
```

Example:

```
% make -n
ls -l /usr/fred > list.out
lpr list.out
```

Example:

```
% make
ls -l /usr/fred > list.out
lpr list.out
% make
lpr list.out
```

The line FILES = /usr/fred defines a macro for a *second-level depen-dency*. Dependencies are nested; that is, a first-level dependency is first dependent on a second-level dependency. The command line ls -l $(FILES) > list.out substitutes the value for the macro. The parentheses are obligatory. Compare this substitution to a shell substitution (see Section 10.2), where $FILES would be valid. Since it follows a dependency, the ls command line is indented by a tab, indicating that the listing depends on the value associated with the macro. Similarly, the target Print depends on list.out. The lpr command, indented by a tab, follows the first-level dependency. lpr prints the directory listing on the default printer. make -n displays the commands that will be executed without actually executing them (-n option), verifying that the makefile will function correctly. The second invocation of make creates the file list.out, a long listing of the files that reside in the directory /usr/fred, and sends it to the default printer. In the third invocation, make determines that the contents of the directory /usr/fred have not changed since the listing file was made and, therefore, prints the listing without recreating the file list.out.

Let us complete our discussion of make by introducing a *predefined symbol*. Predefined symbols, which begin with a period, appear in uppercase, and end with a colon, are names that signify a special function, as the following examples illustrate:

.DEFAULT:	Indicates that a target depends on a file for which there are no specific commands or built-in rules to describe the dependency
.IGNORE:	Prevents make from halting when a command returns a nonzero status (see Section 10.8.12 for a discussion of error handling)
.PRECIOUS:	Prevents the target from being deleted if make is interrupted
.PREFIXES:	Lists directories to be searched to resolve a reference to a file
.SILENT:	Executes commands without printing them to the screen
.SUFFIXES:	Lists filename suffixes that have defined prerequisites in make (e.g., .c, .f, .s, .o, and .out)

The following example illustrates a makefile for compiling a group of C programs. This example and the makefile described in Section 9.6 may be used as templates for your own applications.

UNIX
Example:

```
% cat Makefile
# macro definitions
CSOURCE = a.c b.c c.c d.c
OBJECTS = a.o b.o c.o d.o
CFLAGS = -c -w -a
# target definitions:
prog.out: $(OBJECTS)
|    cc -o $@ $(OBJECTS)
clean: $(OBJECTS
     rm -f $(OBJECTS)
touch: $(CSOURCE)
     touch $(CSOURCE)
# second level dependencies
.c.o: $(CSOURCE)
     cc $(CFLAGS) $?
# definitions
.SUFFIXES: .out .o .c
```

```
.PRECIOUS: prog.out
```

Example:
```
% make
cc -c -w -a a.c
cc -c -w -a b.c
cc -c -w -a c.c
cc -c -w -a d.c
cc -o prog.out a.o b.o c.o d.o
% ex b.c
:...
:wq
```
Example:
```
% make
cc -c -w -a b.c
cc -o prog.out a.o b.o c.o d.o
```
Example:
```
% make clean
rm -f a.o b.o c.o d.o
% make touch
touch a.c b.c c.c d.c
```

The makefile maintains four files containing C source code, which it compiles and loads into the executable image file prog.out. In the first example, make compiles each of the four files and creates an executable image. The second example invokes make after modifying one of the source code files using the ex editor; make recompiles only the source-code file b.c, which has been modified, and uses the loader to create a new executable image file. The third example, make clean, illustrates the concept of *alternative entry points:* If the executable image file is current, it removes all object (.o) files; if the executable image is not current, it generates a current executable image and then removes all object files.

The last example, make touch, illustrates an important use of make: to force compilation even if a source file is up-to-date. The command touch updates the modification date of the file, thus causing make to recompile the source. Here, touch is invoked from the makefile using an alternative entry point. The source files could just have easily been touched with the UNIX command touch *.c, for example.

9.3   **Debugging Programs:** error **and** dbx

Table 9.1 lists several UNIX tools for debugging programs. Here, we consider two source-level debugging tools, the error command and the dbx utility.

The command error inserts error messages generated by incorrect syntax into the source-code file. Compare with the /LIST qualifier used by the OpenVMS compilers, which provide a separate file (.LIS) locating syntax errors and displaying other useful information. The error lines appear in the source-code file as comments and therefore do not affect subsequent compilations. Since numerous messages make the source code difficult to read, you should make a copy of the source code before invoking error or perform a global edit and delete when the source code is completely debugged. For example, the command sed /^C###/d myprog.f removes all comments generated by error from the FORTRAN source code file myprog.f (see Section 5.3).

OpenVMS	UNIX
Form:	
`$ FORTRAN/LIST source-file`	`% f77 source-file |& error`
`$ CC/LIST source-file`	
Example:	
`$ TYPE MYPROG.FOR`	`% cat myprog.f`
`     READ (5,*) A`	`     read (5,*) a`
`     WRITE (6,*] A`	`     write (6,*] a`
`     END`	`     end`
`$ FORTRAN/LIST MYPROG.FOR`	`% f77 myprog.f |& error`
`%FORT-F-MISSDEL Missing operator`	`1 file contains errors \`
`or delimiter [write (6,*]] in module`	`File "myprog.f" (1)`
`MYPROG$MAIN at line 3`	`File "myprog.f" has 1 error.`
`...`	`1 of these errors can be inserted`
	`into the file`
	`You touched file(s): "myprog.f"`
Example:	
`$ TYPE MYPROG.LIS`	`% cat myprog.f`
`...`	`(5,*]a`
`0001      READ (5,*) A`	`C# [f77] Error on line 2 of myprog.f`
`0002      WRITE (6,*] A`	`\`
`%FORT-F-MISSDEL. Missing operator`	

```
or -                                   Syntax Error at   "]"%%%
delimiter                              write (6,*] a
...                                    ...
```

The command `f77 myprog.f |& error` performs a FORTRAN compilation of `myprog.f`, piping error messages to the `error` command, which inserts them at the appropriate places in the source code. Each error begins with `C###` followed by the line number, interpreted as a comment in later compilations (compare with `/*###...*/` for C programs).

`dbx` is a BSD source-level interactive debugger for the C, FORTRAN, and PASCAL languages (compare with the OpenVMS utility `DEBUG`). Table 9.2 compares OpenVMS and UNIX interactive debugger commands. Users of the OpenVMS debugger may be disappointed with `dbx`. The OpenVMS and UNIX debuggers offer similar functionality, albeit using a different syntax, although not all features of `DEBUG` are in the UNIX debugger. For example, in UNIX, without a windowing interface, you cannot use a split screen to display simultaneously the values of variables and the section of code that generated them.

Table 9.2   *Subset of* dbx *Commands*

UNIX **dbx**	OpenVMS **DEBUG**	Function
Execution and Tracing		
run [*args*]	GO [*address-expression*]	Begins executing
rerun [*args*]	GO [*address-expression*]	Restarts execution
trace [*trace*] [if]	SET TRACE[/*QUALIFIER(S)*]- [WHEN.. DO]	Traces execution of a line, procedure, change to a variable, or print expression when line is reached
stop [if. at. in]	SET BREAK- [/*QUALIFIER(S)*]- [WHEN.. DO]	Stops execution at some point
status	SHOW BREAK - [/*QUALIFIER(S)*]	Displays active stop points
	SHOW TRACE - [/*QUALIFIER(S)*]	Displays active trace points
delete	CANCEL BREAK - [/*QUALIFIER(S)*]	Removes active stop points

Table 9.2   *Subset of* dbx *Commands (continued)*

UNIX dbx	OpenVMS DEBUG	Function
	CANCEL TRACE - [/*QUALIFIER(S)*]	Removes active trace points
cont	GO	Continues execution
step	STEP	Executes one source line
next		Steps to next line, executing calls
call [*proc*]		Executes object code associated with procedure
Printing Variables and Expressions		
dump [*proc*]	SHOW SYMBOL	Displays names and values of variables in procedure
print	EXAMINE [/*QUALIFIER(S)*]	Displays variables
whatis	SHOW TYPE	Displays declaration of variable (e.g., real)
where	SHOW MODULE	Prints active procedure and function
Source File Access		
/pattern/	SEARCH [/*QUALIFIER(S)*]	Searches forward or backward for pattern
edit [*file*]	EDIT [MODULE__NAME\LINE]	Invokes editor
file *file*	SET SOURCE	Changes current source file (or returns name if no argument is given)
func *function*	SET MODULE	Changes current function (or returns current function if no arguments are given)
list [*line1,line2*]	TYPE *line1:line 2*	Displays lines of text (default 10)
use dirs		Searches directory for source files
Aliases and Variables		

Table 9.2 *Subset of* dbx *Commands (continued)*

UNIX **dbx**	OpenVMS **DEBUG**	Function
alias [chars *string*]	DEFINE [/*QUALIFIER(S)*]	Defines chars to be an alias for string
set *var* [=*expr*]	DEPOSIT [/*QUALIFIER(S)*]	Defines value for a variable
unalias chars	UNDEFINE [/*QUALIFIER(S)*]	Removes an alias
unset var		Removes a variable
Miscellaneous		
help	HELP	Calls online help
quit	EXIT	Quits the debugger
sh *command*	SPAWN	Passes command to shell for execution
source *file*	@*file-spec*	Reads and executes commands from a file

The following example illustrates a simple use of the debugger: The user invokes the debugger, lists source code, sets a breakpoint, examines a variable, changes the variable at the breakpoint, and runs the program.

The dbx utility invokes the debugger (compare with the OpenVMS command RUN/DEBUG) provided you previously compiled and loaded the source code with the -g option, which produces additional symbol table information needed by the debugger. The debugger uses the file a.out if you specify no other executable image. The debugger issues the (dbx) prompt (compare with the OpenVMS prompt DBG>) when ready to receive commands; list 1,7 (compare with the OpenVMS DEBUG command TYPE 1:7) lists the first seven lines of the source file; stop at 4 (compare with the OpenVMS DEBUG command SET BREAK %LINE 4) sets a break point at line 4; run <hkl.in (compare with the OpenVMS DEBUG command GO) executes the program. Rather than accepting input from the keyboard (stdin), the debugger reads input from the file hkl.in. When execution stops at the breakpoint, print nref displays the value of the variable nref (compare with the OpenVMS DEBUG command EXAMINE NREF); assign nref = 4 changes this value (compare with the OpenVMS DEBUG command DEPOSIT NREF = 4); and the cont command continues program execution (compare with the OpenVMS DEBUG command GO).

OpenVMS	UNIX
Form:	
`$ FORTRAN/DEBUG/NOOPT -`	`% f77 -g [source-file]`
`[source-file]`	
`$ LINK/DEBUG [object-file]`	
`$ RUN [executable-file]`	`% dbx`
`DEBUG Version V4.7-1`	`dbx version 2.0 of 4/2/87 22:10.`
`%DEBUG-I-INITIAL, language is -`	`Type 'help' for help.`
`FORTRAN.module set to`	`enter object file name (default is`
`IFCONVERT$MAIN`	`'a.out'):`
`DBG>`	`reading symbolic information`
Example:	`(dbx)`
`$ ASSIGN HKL.IN FOR005`	
`$ RUN FCONVERT.EXE`	`% dbx fconvert.exe`
`DBG> TYPE 1:7`	`(dbx) list 1,7`
`1    integer h`	`1    integer h`
`2    dimension fii(10)`	`2    dimension fii(10)`
`3    nref = 0`	`3    nref = 0`
`4    read (5,2) nsf`	`4    read (5,2) nsf`
`5    write (6,2) nsf`	`5    write (6,2) nsf`
`6 10 read`	`6 10 read,2,end=100)h,k,l,fo,sigf,`
`(5,2,end=100)h,k,l,fo,sigf, -`	`\`
`     stol, (fii(i),i= 1.nsf)`	`     stol,(fii(i),i= 1.nsf)`
`7write (6,2)`	`7    write (6,2)`
`h,k,l,fo,sigf,stol,(fii(i),i=1.nsf)`	`h,k,l,fo,sigf,(fii(i),i= 1.nsf)`
`DBG> SET BREAK %LINE 4`	`(dbx) stop at 4`
	`[1] stop at 4`
`DBG> SHOW BREAK`	
`breakpoint at FCONVERT$MAIN\`	
`%LINE 4`	`(dbx) status`
`DBG> GO`	`[1] stop at 4`
`break at FCONVERT$MAIN\%LINE 4`	`(dbx) run <hkl.in`
`4:  read (5,2) nsf`	`[1] stopped in MAIN at line 4`
`DBG> EXAMINE NREF`	`4  read (5,2) nsf`
`FCONVERT$MAIN\NREF 0`	`(dbx) print nref`
`DBG> DEPOSIT NREF = 4`	`0`
`DBG> EXAMINE NREF`	`(dbx) assign nref = 4`
`FCONVERT$MAIN\NREF 4`	`(dbx) print nref`

```
DBG> GO                                    4
...                                        (dbx) cont
                                           ...
```

9.4   Profiling: prof and gprof

Profiling enables a programmer to determine how a program is spending its execution time. Profiling is useful if the programmer wishes to improve the efficiency of program code. Different versions of UNIX provide different utilities that work in different ways. The optional layered product VAX Performance and Coverage Analyzer (PCA) provides profiles for OpenVMS users.

We will discuss two utilities available to BSD users, prof and gprof. The prof utility provides a subset of the information available with gprof. Use the following steps to obtain profile data with prof or gprof:

1.   Compile the program with either the p (prof) or pg (gprof) options.

2.   Run the program to create the file used in profiling: by default, mon.out (prof) or gmon.out (gprof).

3.   Invoke pbrof or gprof.

We will use the same program with which we illustrated dbx in the previous section to illustrate the use of gprof with default options. You should consult the man page on gprof for producing alternative profiles. Each time you invoke gprof, the output includes a description of each file displayed, as shown in the following example.

UNIX
Form:
```
% cc [-p or -pg] myprog.c
% f77[-p or -pg] myprog.f
% a.out
% prof (or gprof)
```
Example:
```
% f77 -pg fconvert.f
% a.out <hk1.in> /dev/null
% gprof
%time   cumsecs   seconds   calls   name
 42.7     2.71      2.71             mcount
```

```
      9.6        3.32       0.61      9172   _s_wsfe
      7.3        3.78       0.46      1091   _rd_ned
      6.9        4.22       0.44      8969   _ _flsbuf
  ...
[continued below]
```

The command `f77 -pg fconvert.f` produces an executable image file, `a.out`, which contains the information necessary to produce profile data. The command `a.out <hkl.in> /dev/null` runs the program, reading input from the file `hkl.in` and sending output to `/dev/null`. Recall that `/dev/null` (compare with the OpenVMS logical name `NL:`) is called the *bit bucket* and discards unwanted output. The command `gprof` displays profile data by reading the default files `a.out` and `gmon.out`. The first part of the `gprof` display is the so-called *flat profile*, also produced by `prof`. This section of the display does not describe the interrelationships between function—for example, how often function `a` calls function `b`—but reports in descending order the percentage of total run time spent in each routine. The fields indicate the following:

`%time`	The percentage of the total running time of the program that this function uses
`cumsecs`	A running sum of the number of seconds used by this function and those listed above it
`seconds`	The number of seconds used by this function alone: the major sort for this listing
`calls`	The number of times this function was invoked, if profiled; otherwise blank
`name`	The name of the function: the minor sort for this listing

The second part of the display is unique to `gprof` and describes the interrelationships among the various program functional units. There are three types of records in this display:

1.   One or more parent records for each function (listed first)

2.   A single record for each function (listed second)

3.   Multiple child records for each function called by the parent (listed last)

The definition for each field in each of the three types of record is given below, reading from left to right.

```
[gprof display continued ...]
                                    called/total   parents
                                    called + self  name index
     index  %time  self  descendants  called/total  children
                                                   <spontaneous>
     [1]    100.0  0.00  3.63                       start [1]
                   0.00  3.63                  1/1  _main [2]

     --------------------------------------------------

                   0.00  3.63                  1/1  start [1]
     [2]    100.0  0.00  3.63                  1    _main [2]
                   0.03  3.58                  1/1  _MAIN_ [3]
                   0.00  0.01                17/17  _signal [28]
                   0.00  0.01                  1/1  _f_init [33]
                   0.03  3.58                  1/1  _main [2]
     [3]     99.5  0.03  3.58                  1    _MAIN_ [3]
                   0.20  3.03            2183/2384  _do_fio [4]
                   0.01  0.15             101/101   _e_wsfe [19]
                   0.01  0.15             100/100   _e_rsfe [20]
                   0.01  0.01            101/9070   _s_wsfe [7]
                   0.00  0.00            101/9120   _s_rsfe <cycle 1>[14]
                   0.00  0.00                  1/1  _exit_ [50]
```

The function entries indicate the following:

index	The index of the function in the call-graph listing as an aid to locating it (shown in square brackets)
%time	The percentage of the total time of the program accounted for by this function and its descendents
self	The number of seconds used by this function itself
descendents	The number of seconds used by the descendents of this function on behalf of this function
called	The number of times this function is called (other than recursive calls)
self	The number of times this function calls itself recursively
name	The name of the function, including its membership in a cycle, if any

The parent listings indicate the following:

`self`*	The number of seconds of this function's self-time due to calls from this parent
`descendents`*	The number of seconds of this function's descendent time due to calls from this parent
`called`†	The number of times this function is called by this parent; acts as the numerator of the fraction that divides the function's time among its parents
`total`*	The number of times this function was called by all of its parents; acts as the denominator of the propagation fraction
`parents`	The name of this parent, including the parent's membership in a cycle, if any
`index`	The index of this parent in the call-graph listing as an aid in locating it

*These fields are omitted for parents (or children) in the same cycle as the function. If the function (or child) is a member of a cycle, the propagated times and propagation denominator represent the self-time and descendent time of the cycle as a whole.
†Static: only parents and children are indicated by a call count of 0.

The children listings indicate the following:

`self`*	The number of seconds of this child's self-time due to being called by this function
`descendent`*	The number of seconds of this child's descendant's time due to being called by this function
`called`[2]	The number of times this child is called by this function; acts as the numerator of the propagation fraction for this child
`total`*	The number of times this child is called by all functions; acts as the denominator of the propagation fraction
`children`	The name of this child, including its membership in a cycle, if any
`index`	The index of this child in the call graph listing as an aid to locating it

The cycle as a whole is listed with the same fields as a function entry. Below it are listed the members of the cycle and their contributions to the time and call counts of the cycle.

9.5   **Maintaining Libraries: `ar` and `ranlib`**

UNIX offers features similar to the OpenVMS LIBRARIAN utility for maintaining files in an organized manner for easy access. As we shall see, the UNIX user has to do a little more work and become familiar with more than one command. The command `ar` (archive and library maintainer) creates libraries, adds files, replaces files, deletes files, and so on. Once you create or modify the library, you usually randomize it with the command `ranlib`. Randomization creates a table of contents to assist in the location of files. The table of contents is available to the loader to speed up the loading of files. This performance gain is useful in the main function of libraries: the storage of object files used by a variety of different programs at load time.

The following example illustrates the creation, manipulation, and subsequent use of an object library using the commands `ar` and `ranlib`.

OpenVMS   UNIX

Form:

```
$ LIBRARIAN[/QUALIFIER(S)] -        % ar [option(s)] [position] archive
LIBRARY-FILES                          file(s)
```

Example:

```
$ LIB/CREATE PLOT.OLB -             % ar cr plot.a start.o stop.o move.o
START.OBJ,STOP.OBJ, MOVE.OBJ,-        draw.o
DRAW.OBJ
$ LIB/LIST PLOT.OLB
Directory of OBJECT library -
FOO:[SCRATCH]-
PLOT.OLB;1 on 19-SEP-1997 18:49:34
Creation date:  19-SEP-1997 18:48:20
Creator:  VAX-11 Librarian V04-00
Revision date:  19-SEP-1997 18:48:21
Library format:  3.0
Number of modules:  1
Max, key length:  31
Other entries:  1
Preallocated index blocks:  49
Recoverable deleted blocks:  0
Total index blocks used:  2
Max. Number history records:  20
Library history records:  0
DRAW
```

```
MOVE
START
STOP
```

Example:
```
$ LIB/INSERT PLOT.OLB SYMBOL.OBJ
```

Example:
```
$ LIB/REPLACE PLOT.OLB -
SYMBOL.OBJ
```

Example:
```
$ LIB/EXTRACT=MOVE -
/OUTPUT=MOVE.OBJ PLOT.OLB
```

```
% ar t plot.a
start.o
stop.o
move.o
draw.o

% ar q plot.a symbol.o
% ar mb start.o plot.a move.o

% ar r plot.a move.o


% ar x plot.a move.o
```

In the first example, `ar cr plot.a start.o stop.o move.o draw.o` creates a library, `plot.a`, containing four object files (c option means create; r option means replace). Unlike the majority of UNIX command options, `ar` options are not preceded by a hyphen. (GNU implementations of UNIX are more liberal here, permitting a hyphen for the first argument.) Note that `.a` is the default file extension for libraries (compare with the OpenVMS extensions `.OLB` for object libraries and `.HLB` for help libraries). Unlike all other UNIX file types, compilers assume `.a`: For example, `cc myprog.c -lplot` is valid; `cc myprog.c -lplot.a` is not.

In the second example, `ar t plot.a` lists the contents of the library (t option). Unlike the OpenVMS LIBRARIAN, `ar` does not store files alphabetically, but in the order they are received. Files added at a later date, therefore, will appear at the bottom of the library listing.

In the third example, `ar q plot.a symbol.o` adds the file `symbol.o` to the library (q option); `ar` does not perform a check to see if the file already exists in the library, but it simply appends the file. If you inadvertently add a second file with the same name to the library, how do you delete the unwanted version? The answer to this question lies in the use of the positional parameter, as shown in the form of the command and illustrated in the fourth example.

The command `ar mb start.o plot.a move.o` uses a positional parameter to move (`m` option) `move.o` before (`b` option) `start.o`. The library entry to be moved is placed at the end of the command string; the library entry marking the move point immediately follows the command option. The order now becomes `move.o`, `start.o`, `stop.o`, `draw.o`. The positional parameter can also pinpoint the file to be deleted, for example by indicating a file after (`a` option) another file in the library.

In the fifth example, `ar r plot.a move.o` replaces the existing file `move.o` with a new version of the same file (`r` option) and places the new version at the end of the library.

In the final example, `ar x plot.a move.o` extracts a copy of the file `move.o` (`x` option); that is, the file remains in the library, but a copy is extracted and placed in the current directory.

Once you are satisfied with the contents of an object library, you should randomize it with the `ranlib` command to improve the loader's access time when it loads the library with other source code files.

OpenVMS	UNIX
	Form:
	`% ranlib library`
Example:	
`$ LINK MYPROG.OBJ,PLOT.OLB/LIBRARY`	`% ranlib plot. a`
	`% cc myprog.c -lplot`

The command `ranlib plot.a` randomizes the library created above for use by the loader. You should perform a randomization whenever you make a change to the library. The command `cc myprog.c -lplot.a` compiles and links the C program `myprog.c`, using object code from the library `plot.a` to resolve any external references. The compiler searches the directory paths specified by the shell variable path for the object library file. The directories `/lib` and `/usr/lib` contain system libraries (compare with the OpenVMS directory defined by the logical name `SYS$LIBRARY`). Site-dependent libraries usually reside in the directory `/usr/local/lib/`.

9.6   Summary

This summary once again uses examples from everyday use. The first example takes a FORTRAN program `prolsq.f`, copied from an OpenVMS system and compiles and runs it.

UNIX

Example:

```
% fsplit prolsq.f
prolsq.f already exists, put in zzz000.f
symmin.f
recip.f
....
rtest.f
% ls
bcnvrt.f  disref.f  plnref.f  symmin.f  typescript
bref.f    ellips.f  polar.f   symref.f  vdwref.f
calc.f    expv.f    prolsq.f  teref.f   zzz000.f
cgsolv.f  freeze.f  recip.f   torref.f
chiref.f  matinv.f  rtest.f   torshn.f
cross.f   matmul.f  scale.f   toss.f
det3.f    plane.f   sfref.f   trig.f
% mv prolsq.f prolsq.orig
% mv zzz000.f prolsq.f
% cat Makefile
#
OBJ = prolsq.o symmin.o recip.o sfref.9 calc.o \
  trig.o expv.o disref.o plnref.o plane.o \
  chiref.o det3.o vdwref.o bref.o teref.o \
  ellips.o bcnvrt.o torref.o torshn.o cross.o \
  symref.o toss.o polar.o matinv.o cgsolv.o \
  matmul.o scale.o freeze.o rtest.o
f77 =  f77 -v
  .f.o:
  $(f77) -c $*.f
  MAIN:  $(OBJ)
  $(f77) -o MAIN $(OBJ)
% make -n
  f77 -v -c prolsq.f
  f77 -v -c symmin.f
  ....
  f77 -v -c rtest.f
  f77 -v -o MAIN prolsq.o symmin.o .... rtest.o
```

The command `fsplit prolsq.f` breaks the large FORTRAN source code file into routines and functions to be managed by `make`. Because `prolsq.f` already exists, the main program cannot be called `prolsq.f`, so the command renames it `zzz000.f`. The user then renames `prolsq.f` as prolsq.orig, and zzz000.f as prolsq.f. The command cat Makefile displays the makefile written to maintain this group of routines. The command OBJ = . . . defines a macro OBJ for the object files; note that the backslash denotes the continuation of the macro definition. Next f77 = f77 -v defines a macro for the compilation that includes the -v option to display the version number of the compiler. The .f.o: command defines the dependency; that is, the existence of an .o file depends on the existence of an .f file. The dependency is followed by the command $(f77) -c $*.f, beginning after a tab; the -c option suppresses the loading phase. A further dependency, MAIN, appears, which depends on the OBJ macro. The command $(f77) -o MAIN $(OBJ) (after a tab) loads the object files into an executable image file MAIN. The command make -n then displays the commands that make will execute without actually executing them.

UNIX

Example:

```
% make
  f77 -v -c prolsq.f
  Berkeley F77, version 1.0
  prolsq.f
  MAIN prolsq:
  Error on line 45 of prolsq.f Declaration error. .
  . . .
% f77 prolsq.f | & error
  1 non-specific errors follow
  [unknown] MAIN prolsq:
  [unknown] Error. No assembly.
  1 file contains errors "prolsq.f" (1)
  File "prolsq.f" has 1 error
  1 of these can be inserted in the file
  You touched file(s): "prolsq.f"
% more + 45 prolsq.f
  DATA DMIN /5.0,3.0,2.5,2.0/
  C###45 [f77] Error on line 45 of prolsq.f Declaration \
  error . . .
```

Once make is functioning correctly, the program can be debugged. The make command without options invokes the makefile called Makefile and compiles each routine; make finds only one error, in the parent program prolsq.f. This parent program is compiled again, external to make, with the command f77 prolsq.f | & error. The error message generated by the compilation is piped to the error command, which embeds the error message at the appropriate place in the source file. The command more +45 prolsq.f displays the file beginning at line 45, since the compilation indicated that the error was at line 45. Assuming the error was fixed, a further invocation of make would compile just the prolsq.f file and create an executable image file called MAIN from all the object files.

Once the program is compiled and running, the user decides to profile a typical execution to determine where the program uses most of its CPU time. The user plans to recode the most CPU-intensive parts of the program, thus improving its efficiency.

UNIX

Example:

```
% ex Makefile
:/-c/
$(f77) -c $*.f
:s/-c/-c -pg/
$(f77) -c -pg $*.f
:wq
% touch *.f; make
% cat run
#
In IDISK fort.3
In JDISK fort.4
In . ./protin/ATMDST.8 fort.10
In SHIFT.IN fort.15
In SHIFT.OUT fort.16
In . ./fconvert/prolsq.hkl fort.20
In FOFC.OUT fort.31
In XYZBG.OUT fort.32
date
time MAIN ;ltdata
date
rm -f fort.
% run
% gprof MAIN gmon.out
```

First, the user modifies the makefile with the ex editor to include the option pg for each compilation. The command touch *.f; make updates the modification dates of all the FORTRAN source files (*.f) so that the subsequent make will recompile each file with the profile options (pg). The user runs the program with the script file named run, which assigns data files to the various FORTRAN unit numbers and runs the program. Notice that a hard link assigns files to FORTRAN unit numbers. In the example, writing to FORTRAN unit number 3 would, by default, write to the file fort.3, but the link causes data to be written to the file IDISK. After the program runs, the user removes the hard links with the command rm -f fort.*. Recall that if the user had set soft links, the IDISK file would have also been deleted. (Different UNIX FORTRAN compilers use different methods for assigning data files.) The user then invokes gprof with the executable file defined as MAIN in the makefile and gmon.out, the default profile produced at run time. The example does not show the output of gprof, but it would look similar to the output shown in Section 9.4.

10

Shell Programming

10

Shell Programming

> *Civilization advances by extending the number of important operations that can be performed without thinking of them.*
>
> —*Alfred North Whitehead*

Shell programming involves grouping together a number of shell commands and constructs into a file (called a shell script) to perform a routine task. The analog in OpenVMS is the creation of a DCL command procedure. If you are versed in DCL command procedures, you should be aware that achieving equivalent functionality in UNIX requires becoming adept at writing shell scripts. The syntax of a shell script varies according to the shell in use; in this chapter, we will give examples of C shell (csh), Bourne-Again shell (bash), and Korn shell (ksh) syntax. The Korn shell is an extension of the original Bourne shell (sh), adding interactive convenience features; bash likewise extends Bourne shell functionality while also borrowing liberally from csh. It is important to note that a shell script written using just sh syntax and features should be executable under ksh or bash without modification. In contrast, only the simplest csh scripts would be compatible with sh or ksh and, to a slightly greater extent, bash. Another shell, tcsh, is an extension of the C shell.

Since the man pages are terse, this chapter explains a few features of shell programming in greater detail. For more than the basics though, you should invest in a book dedicated to the shell you plan to use. The following comparisons will help to orient the OpenVMS user to shell programming in UNIX.

- Both shell scripts and DCL command procedures use only commands and constructs that the standard operating system can interpret. Use of a high-level language compiler is not necessary.

- As a general rule, shell scripts execute faster than DCL command procedures.

- The debugging of scripts and DCL command procedures relies on the error-reporting features of the shell and command-language interpreter, respectively. Error reporting by the shell is uninformative.

- DCL command procedures may utilize comprehensive string-handling capabilities. The C shell has limited string-handling capabilities, the Korn shell somewhat more; you will likely supplement them with the extensive string-handling capabilities of `tr`, `awk`, and `sed`.

- Some string-handling concepts of DCL do not map directly to those present in the various shells. You may need to rethink the implementation of command procedures; a simple translation may not be possible.

- Compared to a high-level language, both the shells and DCL are slow in performing integer arithmetic.

- Neither the C shell nor DCL is capable of noninteger arithmetic. On some systems, the Korn shell has built-in double-precision floating-point arithmetic.

- UNIX has an extensive set of commands and utilities that you can incorporate in scripts.

- C shell scripts are similar to C; if you can program in C, then you will find its shell programming easy.

In recent years, other scripting languages have become popular, notably Perl. Perl is available on many computer architectures and operating systems. Because it has gained popularity with UNIX, we will include equivalent Perl constructs in several of our examples. In contrast to the standard UNIX shells, Perl incorporates very powerful string-handling functions and data types, which can make it a better choice than a shell script for creating complex applications.

Figure 10.1 illustrates the various components of shell programming and indicates the organization of this chapter. The guts of a shell script are the UNIX commands and utilities, many of which we have discussed already. Script programming adds string manipulation, flow control, argument handling, error handling, and the like to help you use UNIX commands more effectively. The features of script programming are built into the shell.

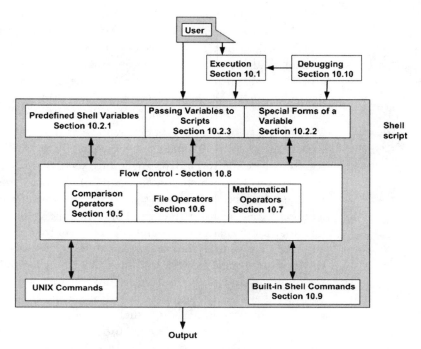

Figure 10.1
Shell programming
overview.

While UNIX commands are readily available via Perl, many more operating system calls and constructs are directly available within the language.

Section 10.1 presents the execution of scripts. Beginning with execution may seem premature, but remember that a script need not be complex. A script might be no more than a shorthand notation for a single command string, many of which we have discussed already. We are therefore more than ready to execute our first script. Section 10.2 describes how scripts handle variables. Section 10.3 describes how they handle filename modification, and Section 10.4 describes how they handle variable expansion. Sections 10.5 to 10.7 describe the various types of operators available. Section 10.8 discusses flow control, and Section 10.9 discusses built-in commands useful in shell programming. Finally, Section 10.10 discusses how to debug the mess we have created.

10.1 Executing Scripts

In OpenVMS a DCL command procedure is executed by preceding the filename with the special @ metacharacter. If no file type is specified, DCL will assume the file has a .COM extension. In contrast, if certain conventions are followed, UNIX scripts can be invoked in the same way as any built-in shell command or executable binary program. In addition, the file containing the script is not expected or required to have any particular extension. A UNIX shell script can be invoked as a command if it is protected as both readable and executable (rx) for the user. If the directory containing the script is not explicitly specified as part of the file name, the shell will automatically use a "search path" to try to locate the specified program. The path (csh) or PATH (bash, ksh, Perl) shell variable contains the set of directories that is to be searched for executable files. Thus, the first executable file (binary or script) that is matched is invoked by the shell. Typically, a user's search path contains standard directories, such as /usr/sbin and /usr/bin (see Section 2.3), which contain many of the programs and scripts that make up the UNIX command set. A common convention is also to specify a period (.) as the last path entry. This forces the shell to search the current directory for the script or program as well. Contrast this with DCL, which automatically assumes the current default directory is to be used if no directory path is specified. While automatically searching the current directory for programs and scripts is a great convenience for the average user, it is considered a security risk for privileged users and thus should not be done on the root account. Special shell initialization files (.login, .cshrc, .bash_profile, or .profile) are used in a similar fashion as the DCL LOGIN.COM file for presetting environment features such as the search path variable (see below).

Like all UNIX commands that are not part of the shell, the script file normally executes in a child shell forked by the parent shell (see Section 10.9.4 for an exception). Normally, this child shell takes on all the predefined variables assigned to the parent shell, as well as those defined by the user in the files .login, .cshrc, .bash_profile, or .profile (themselves shell scripts) or the script indicated by the Korn shell ENV environment variable (see Section 3.2.3). However, #!/usr/bin/csh -f, appearing as the first line of the script file, invokes a fast start of the C shell and does not execute the commands in .cshrc. This line could represent significant time savings if the .cshrc file is long and complex or if the programmer wants to prevent settings made in the .cshrc file from affecting his or her script. The following example illustrates a simple shell script.

OpenVMS

@MYSCRIPT[.COM]

UNIX

myscript

Perl

```
% cat test.pl
#!/usr/bin/perl -w
# Test Perl script
```

```
system('who');
exit;

% chmod  o+x  test.pl
% test.pl
system ttyp0 Aug 6 09:00
```

OpenVMS	**UNIX (C shell)**

`$ TYPE TEST.COM`	`% cat test.csh`
`$!`	`#!/usr/bin/csh -f`
`$! Test command procedure`	`# Test C shell script`
`$ SHOW USERS`	`who`
`$ EXIT`	`exit`
`$ SET PROTECTION=O:RWED`	`% chmod o+x test.csh`
`$ @TEST`	`% test.csh`
`OpenVMS Interactive Users`	`system ttyp0 Aug 6 09:00`
`Total number of interactive users = 1`	
`SYSTEM _RTA1: 000004AE RTA1:`	

Note the following:

- Commands in scripts are not preceded by the shell prompt (compare $ for DCL command procedures).

- The script file is first made executable with the chmod command. This is necessary if the script file has not already been given a file permission rendering it executable by the owner, as is usually the case (see the discussion of umask in Section 3.2.1).

- The procedure is terminated with the exit command (compare with the OpenVMS DCL command EXIT), which returns control to the parent shell. Since the exit command is assumed by default if an EOF is reached, it is not essential in this example.

- The C illustrates the use of the csh fast start (-f) option.

- DCL assumes a .COM file type when executing a command procedure. UNIX has no such structure, although, as this example shows, many programmers follow the convention of using the shell name in place of a file type.

- Anything following # in a command line is interpreted as a comment (compare ! in OpenVMS). An exception is the so-called shebang[1] notation (#!) when it is used as the very first line of the script. A script usually executes using the same shell as the process that invokes

---

1.   See http://www.uni-ulm.de/~s_smasch/various/shebang/.

it. You can control which shell executes a script by using that first line comment to specify the full path to the shell after the #! symbol—a very powerful technique that frees the script user from having to know which shell or script language to use and the script writer from having to know which shell is in use by the user.

10.2 Variables

You can assign variables in bash and Korn shell scripts with a statement that resembles a DCL symbol assignment. C shell scripts use the set command. Note the following differences in assigning values to variables and returning variable values between shell scripts and DCL command procedures.

The C shell does not make the same distinction as OpenVMS between defining variables for the duration of the command procedure and defining variables for the duration of the terminal session (that is, globally). The set command always assigns variables for the current process. Including the variable assignment in the .cshrc file gives the equivalent of global definitions, because this file is usually executed each time a shell (process) is started, that is, for each command or script file executed. The exception, as noted above, is a fast start of the C shell. You can use the C shell setenv command to set environmental variables.

The bash and Korn shells do distinguish between variables local to a script or shell and those accessible to child processes. You may use the export command or an equivalent shell option to make variables accessible.

Perl provides several different scoping mechanisms for its variables, but Perl variables are separate and distinct from variables in the user's interactive shell. A Perl program can read the parent's shell variables if desired, but cannot change them.

The C shell makes no distinction in defining a shell variable as an integer or a text string (compare with the OpenVMS = and :=). In the Korn shell, all variables are string variables (even if the string happens to look like an integer) unless explicitly declared as integer variables using the typeset -i or integer (an alias for typeset -i) commands. You may perform integer arithmetic on string variables, but arithmetic will be faster using integer variables. On today's processors, the speed you gain is unlikely to make a noticeable difference in shell execution time. Perl provides a scalar variable type, which may contain either a string or number (integer or floating-point) and will automatically convert a string to a number in the appropriate context.

UNIX always treats uppercase and lowercase strings differently. Open-VMS translates lowercase to uppercase unless the text string is surrounded by double quotes. Similarly, variable names are case-sensitive under the bash, C, and Korn shells and in Perl.

Use the $ character to force a shell variable to be dereferenced and replaced with its value. This is directly analogous to the use of single quotes to force dereferencing of a DCL symbol.

Once you have assigned a name to a variable, you can use the bash or C shell command echo or the Perl and Korn shell equivalent print (compare with the OpenVMS command WRITE SYS$OUTPUT) to write to stdout (standard output), returning either the numeric or text string value of a variable. The commands /usr/bin/env and /usr/bin/printenv perform roughly the same function as the OpenVMS command SHOW SYMBOL, listing the values of all symbol assignments.

OpenVMS

Form:

```
$ VARIABLE_NAME = local_integer/text
$ VARIABLE_NAME == global_integer/text
$ VARIABLE_NAME := local_text
$ VARIABLE_NAME :== global_text
```

Example:

```
$ SAMPLE = 1
$ WRITE SYS$OUTPUT "Number ''sample'"
Number 1
$ WRITE SYS$OUTPUT "Number sample"
Number sample
$ STRING == "hello there"
```

UNIX (C shell)

Form:

```
% set variable_name = value
% setenv variable_name [value]
```

Example:

```
% set sample = 1
% echo "Number $sample"
Number 1
% echo "Number sample"
Number sample
% set string = "hello there"
```

UNIX (Bash and Korn shells)

Form:

```
$ variable_name=value
$ export variable_name
```

```
$ typeset -i variable_name
$ integer variable_name
```

Example:

```
$ first_sample=1
$ integer second_sample
$ second_sample=9
$ print Number $first_sample
Number 1
$ print Number first_sample
Number first sample
$ print Number $second_sample
Number 9
$ ((sum=$first_sample + $second_sample))
$ print Sum $sum
Sum 10

$ string="hello there"
```

Perl

Form:

```
$variable_name = value;
local $variable_name [= value];
my $variable_name [= value];
```

Example:

```
$ perl -e '
> $first_sample = 1;
> $second_sample = 9.5;
> $third_sample = "nine point 5";
> print "Number $first_sample\n";
> print "Number first_sample\n";
> print "Number $second_sample\n";
> print "Sum ", $first_sample + $second_sample, "\n";
> print "Result ", $first_sample + $third_sample, "\n";
> '
Number 1
Number first_sample
Number 9.5
Sum 10.5
Result 1$
```

These examples follow their respective shell prompt, indicating that they were issued as commands and not executed as part of a script.

In the C shell example, set sample = 1 assigns a value of 1 to the variable sample. Note that the $ metacharacter forces the value of the variable to be returned. In the second example, set string = ''hello there'' equates the variable named "string" to a text string. Unlike OpenVMS, the C shell makes no distinction between equating a variable name to an integer or a text string.

Contrast the Korn shell examples. In the first, a string that looks like the digit 1 is assigned to `first_sample`, a string variable, while the number 9 is assigned to `second_sample`, an integer variable. The two variable types print the same way and can be mixed in arithmetic. Attempting to assign to `second_sample` anything that does not look like an integer would cause an error. Double parentheses surrounding a command indicate integer arithmetic.

The above Perl example is a little contrived. While a Perl script can indeed be entered "on the fly" as shown here, Perl is not itself an interactive shell environment like csh, ksh, or bash, and its own variables are not available to the user's shell environment. However, expert Perl users often do enter short programs on the command line to quickly perform some task more easily done with Perl. A Perl variable that starts with a $ is called a *scalar* and may contain either a string or a number. Depending on the context, Perl will automatically treat a variable's contents as a string or a number as appropriate. If a numeric operation is attempted on a scalar that contains a string that cannot be converted to a number, the value zero is used, rather than causing an error. Finally, note that both floating-point numbers and integers are supported.

10.2.1 Predefined Shell Variables

Section 3.2 introduced predefined shell variables, the most common of which appear in Table 10.1; Table 3.1 has a more complete list. When using the C shell, you can display a complete list online using the `set` command without arguments. The bash and Korn shells will print the environment variables via the `/usr/bin/printenv` command. The OpenVMS analog to predefined shell variables consists of the symbol definitions found in the system logical name table. You should avoid using predefined shell variable names when defining your own variables.

Table 10.1 *Predefined Shell Variables*

C Shell Variable	Bash and Korn Shell Variable	OpenVMS Equivalent	UNIX Meaning
user	USER	F$GETJPI("", "USERNAME")	Username
path	PATH	logical name defined as searchlist	Current path specification
home	HOME	SYS$LOGIN	Home directory of user

Table 10.1   *Predefined Shell Variables (continued)*

C Shell Variable	Bash and Korn Shell Variable	OpenVMS Equivalent	UNIX Meaning
shell	SHELL	F$GETJPI("", "CLINAME")	Pathname of current shell
term	TERM	F$GETDVI(''TT:'', ''DEVTYPE'')	Terminal type
status	?	$STATUS	Status returned by last command: 0 = no error, 1 = error

The variable term returns an alphanumeric string, whereas F$GETDVI returns an integer value. The values of the variables status, ?, and $STATUS are redetermined each time a command is executed. Compare the UNIX definition to OpenVMS, where a return value with the low bit set implies no error and a return value with the low bit clear implies an error (Section 10.8.12). The following examples illustrate typical values returned for common predefined shell variables.

OpenVMS

Example:
```
$ WRITE SYS$OUTPUT -
'F$GETJPI("","USERNAME")'FRED
```

Example:
```
$ SHOW LOGICAL SYS$SYSTEM
    ...
```

Example:
```
$ SHOW LOGICAL SYS$LOGIN
"SYS$LOGIN" = "SYS$DISK3:[FRED]"
(LNM$JOB_802B0A50)
```

Example:
```
$ SHOW TERMINAL
Terminal: TTA4: Device_type VT100-
Owner: FRED...
```

Example:
```
$ SHOW SYMBOL $STATUS
STATUS == "%X00000001"
```

UNIX (C shell)

```
% echo $user # username
fred
```

```
% echo $path # command reference
/usr/fred/bin /usr /bin /usr/bin
```

```
% echo $home # login directory
/usr/fred
```

```
% echo $term # terminal type
vt100
```

```
% echo $status # success condition
0
```

Perl

Example:

```
$ cat environ.pl
#!/usr/bin/perl -w
# Accessing shell environment vars from a Perl script

print <<ENDBLOCK;
    user = $ENV{USER}
    path = $ENV{PATH}
    home = $ENV{HOME}
    term = $ENV{TERM}
ENDBLOCK
$status = system("date");
print(" return status = $status\n");

$ ./environ.pl
    user = fred
    path = /usr/fred/bin:/usr:/bin:/usr/bin
    home = /usr/fred
    term = vt100
Wed Nov 20 22:09:50 EST 2002
return status = 0
```

The discussion of error handling in Section 10.8.12 will illustrate the importance of status.

10.2.2 Special Forms of a Variable

Table 10.2 illustrates the special forms of a variable. You can break the value of a variable into separate elements, where each element is separated by a blank. The shell can then conveniently address these elements. What if you wish to define elements of a variable other than those delimited by blanks? You cannot do this easily with C shell commands, for the C shell does not offer the convenience of the OpenVMS lexical functions to manipulate strings—for example, F$EXTRACT to decompose a variable according to the position of each character in a string, and F$CVSI, F$CVUI, and F$FAO for integer-to-character string conversions. The bash and Korn shells provide a mechanism with the IFS variable and the $* operator. In general, however, you may find it more convenient to work with awk (Section 5.5), the pattern-matching and action utility, which can decompose a string in ways beyond the OpenVMS lexical functions. Perl, which, by the way, is an acronym for Practical Extraction and Report Language, is also an excellent choice for doing string manipulation, providing a large array of powerful and flexible operators and functions for dealing with strings.

Table 10.2 also lists the `$<` construct in the C shell and the `read` command in the bash and Korn shells (compare with the OpenVMS command `INQUIRE`) for entering the value of a variable to a shell script from `stdin`.

Table 10.2　　*Special Forms of a Shell Variable*

C Shell Form	bash and Korn Shell Form	OpenVMS Form	UNIX Meaning
`$?name`		`F$TYPE(NAME)`	Returns 0 if variable name is not defined; 1 if defined
	`${name:?word}`		Returns value of name if set and non-null; otherwise prints word
`$#name`	`${#name[*]}`	†	Returns integer specifying the number of elements of variable name
`$name[m-n]`		†	Returns elements m through n of variable name, where m and n are integers
`$name[m-]`		†	Returns elements m through the last element of variable name, where m is an integer
`$name[*]`	`${name{*}}`	†	Returns all elements of variable name
`$name[$]`		†	Returns last element of variable name
`${0}`	`$0`	`F$ENVIRONMENT ("PROCEDURE")`	Returns name of script being executed
`$?0`			Returns 0 if name of current script is known; 1 if not
`$n` or `$argv[n]`	`$n` or `${n}`	`Pn`	Returns nth variable passed to script

Table 10.2   *Special Forms of a Shell Variable (continued)*

C Shell Form	bash and Korn Shell Form	OpenVMS Form	UNIX Meaning
$*	$* or $@		Returns all variables passed to script
$$	$$	F$GETJPI("", "PID")	Returns process numbers of current shell
$<	read	INQUIRE	Takes input from terminal keyboard

†This information is not directly obtainable, but may be obtained by decomposing a variable into its elements with the **F$ELEMENT** lexical function.

The following shell script illustrates some of the features named above.

OpenVMS
Example:

```
$ TYPE TEST.COM
$! Special forms of a variable
$!
$ INQUIRE NAME "Enter text string:"
$!
$ WRITE SYS$OUTPUT "This is called -
''F$ENVIRONMENT(""PROCEDURE"")'"
$ WRITE SYS$OUTPUT -
"Processed by PID ''F$PID(A)' "
$ NUM = 0

$ LOOP:
$ LABEL = F$ELEMENT(NUM," ",NAME)
$ IF (LABEL .EQS. "") THEN GOTO END
$ COUNT = NUM + 1
$ WRITE SYS$OUTPUT "Word ''COUNT' =
''LABEL' "
$ NUM = NUM + 1
$ GOTO LOOP
$ END: WRITE SYS$OUTPUT -
```

UNIX (C shell)

```
% cat test_script
# Special forms of a variable
#
echo -n "Enter text string:"
set name = $<
echo \
"This script is called ${0}"
echo \
"Processed by PID $$"
echo "The first word is $name[1]"
echo "The last word is $name[$]"
echo "The string entered has \
$#name elements"
exit
```

```
"The string entered has ' 'COUNT'
elements"
$ EXIT

$ @TEST
Enter text string: -
test of string manipulation
This is called TEST.COM
Processed by PID 00000043
Word 1 = test
Word 2 = of
Word 3 = string
Word 4 = manipulation
The string entered has 4 elements
```

Perl

Example:

```
$ cat test_script
#!/usr/bin/perl -w
# Special predefined vars and string edits
#
print "Enter text string: ";
$input = <STDIN>;
chomp($input);
@myarray = split(/ /, $input);
print "This script is called $0\n";
print "Processed by PID $$\n";
print "The first word is $myarray[0]\n";
print "The last word is $myarray[$#myarray]\n";

print "The string entered has ", scalar(@myarray), " elements\n";
exit;

$ chmod 744 test_script
$ test_script
Enter text string: test of string manipulation
This script is called test_script
Processed by PID 27183
```

```
% chmod 744 test_script
% test_script
Enter text string:
test of string manipulation

This script is called test_script
Processed by PID 27183
The first word is test
The last word is manipulation
The string entered has 4 elements
```

```
The first word is test
The last word is manipulation
The string entered has 4 elements
```

Note the variation in the use of echo. The -n option prevents skipping to the next line (print -n when using the Korn shell), allowing you to enter a response after the string echoed (the default condition for the Open-VMS command INQUIRE). You can equate the string entered to the variable name with set name = $< and then manipulate it using the definitions outlined in Table 10.2; that is, the variable name consists of four elements, the words "test of string manipulation." The Korn shell allows a more elegant, one-step command to accomplish the entire task of prompting and reading a response, read name? prompt, which closely parallels the OpenVMS INQUIRE command. Unlike INQUIRE, read allows more variable names to follow the prompt and will assign one word of the response to each variable, stuffing any remainder into the last variable. An unquoted prompt may look to the Korn shell as though successive words are variable names! Recall from Section 5.5.8 that the awk construct substr($name,1,6) could have been used to return, for example, an element of "test o," a substring of name starting at character one and six characters long. Thus, we have an element that includes blanks, but is not delimited by blanks.

In the Perl example, we read from the automatically opened file handle STDIN into a scalar variable named $input. The chomp() function is used to remove any line terminator from the string. Perl provides a very powerful set of string-manipulation functions, one example of which is the split() function, used here to parse the string on space boundaries and load the resulting words into our array variable @myarray. In Perl, the first character indicates the variable type, @ is used to denote an array, and $ denotes a scalar as already noted above. When referencing the elements of an array, you use the starting symbol that indicates the type of the *element* of the array. This is why the first element of the array is referenced as $myarray[0] and not @myarray[0], because the content of that element is a scalar value (a string). The $# notation is used to return the element number of the last element of the named array. If an array variable is evaluated where a scalar is expected, the count of array elements is returned. In this example, we forced a scalar context by using the scalar() function.

Notice that Perl has borrowed the meaning of the special C shell variables $0 and $$. Perl syntax borrows liberally from all of the common Unix shells, as well as popular UNIX utilities like grep and awk, and from programming languages like C, BASIC, Pascal, Lisp, and FORTRAN.

And finally, it is interesting to note that this sample Perl script will run without modification on an OpenVMS system that has the OpenVMS version of Perl installed. With some care, it is possible to write Perl scripts that are portable across UNIX and OpenVMS systems.

10.2.3 Passing Variables to Scripts

Table 10.2 illustrates how values are passed to scripts from the command line. The C, Korn, and bash shells use numeric variable names as the most common way of referencing the parameters passed to a script: $1, $2, etc. In addition, the C shell reserves the variable name argv for a vector of arguments entered on the command line. Thus, argv[1] is the first argument (a synonym for $1; compare to P1 in OpenVMS). Further, $$ provides the current process number (the lexical function call F$GETJPI(0,"PID") is the OpenVMS equivalent). You must enclose any argument passed to a script that contains a blank or a shell metacharacter in single or double quotes. OpenVMS limits the number of variables (parameters) that you may pass to a command procedure to eight. UNIX has no such restriction; that is to say, the number of variables that you may pass to a script file is so large that the average user will never reach it. However, for syntactic reasons, if you wish to reference variable n, where n is greater than 9, you must use the argv[n] form of reference for the C shell, or the ${$n$} form for the Korn and bash shells. To learn more about this and other restrictions, refer to the man pages for csh, bash and ksh. Perl uses the $1, $2 notation for a different purpose unrelated to command-line arguments, but does borrow the C shell (and C language) notion of preloading the special @ARGV array with the values specified on the command line.

OpenVMS	UNIX (C shell)
Example:	
`$ TYPE TEST.COM`	`% cat test_script`
`$! return parameters passed to procedure`	`# return variables passed to script`
`$ WRITE SYS$OUTPUT P1`	`echo "$argv[1]"`
`$ WRITE SYS$OUTPUT P2`	`echo "$2"`
	`echo "$argv[$#argv]"`
`$ WRITE SYS$OUTPUT P3`	`exit`
`$ EXIT`	
`$ @TEST [DIRECTORY] TEST "hello there"`	`% chmod 744 test_script`

```
[DIRECTORY]                              % test_script "[directory]" test \
TEST                                     "hello there"
HELLO THERE                              [directory]
                                         test
                                         hello there
```

Perl   **UNIX (Korn shell)**

```
$ cat test_script                        $ cat test_script
#!/usr/bin/perl -w                       # return values passed to script
# return parameters passed to script    print "${1}"
print "$ARGV[0]\n";                      print "$2"
print "$ARGV[1]\n";                      eval last=\${$#}
print "$ARGV[$#ARGV]\n";                 print "$last"
exit;                                    exit

$ chmod 744 test_script                  $ chmod 744 test_script
$ test_script "[directory]" test         $ test_script "[directory]" test \
"hello there"                            "hello there"
[directory]                              [directory]
test                                     test
hello there                              hello there
```

The above example illustrates the passing of literal string parameters to a script. As with OpenVMS, space delimited "words" are treated as individual parameters, but quoting can be used to pass a string with embedded spaces as a single parameter. With the UNIX shells and Perl, strings can be quoted using either single quotes (`'string'`) or double quotes (`"string"`). However, it can definitely make a difference which you use. If you are a bash or C shell user, entering the command `echo 'hello there!'` will do what you would expect, while `echo "hello there!"` will cause an error because the exclamation point (a.k.a. "bang") is a shell metacharacter. Section 10.4 covers the different quoting styles and how and when they are used, but as a simple rule, when in doubt, use single quotes when you need to quote command-line parameter values.

10.3 Filename Modifiers (C Shell Only)

Filename modifiers cause the system to return portions of an absolute or relative filename, as defined in Table 10.3. OpenVMS users familiar with the `F$PARSE` lexical function, which calls the `$PARSE` RMS service for extracting portions of a file specification, can achieve similar results using a shell script with filename modifiers. UNIX has no direct way of modifying filenames on a remote UNIX computer. Compare the OpenVMS command `F$PARSE(file-spec ... "NODE")`. However, as we shall see in Section 13.2.7, you can pipe a remote file lookup to a filename modifier to return portions of the filename, but not the remote host name.

Table 10.3   *Filename Modifiers*

C Shell Modifier	OpenVMS Equivalent	UNIX Meaning
`:r`	`F$PARSE(file-spec..."NAME")`	Returns portion of file-name preceding a period; if filename does not contain a period, returns complete file-name
`:e`	`F$PARSE(file-spec..."TYPE")`	Returns portion of file-name following a period; if filename does not contain a period, returns null
`:h`	`F$PARSE(file-spec..."DEVICE")+` `F$PARSE(file-spec..."DIRECT")`	Returns head (path) of file specification
`:t`	`F$PARSE(file-spec..."NAME")+` `F$PARSE(file-spec..."TYPE")`	Returns tail of file specification, excluding path

In the example below, which illustrates the use of the filename modifiers outlined in Table 10.3. We are reading a filename entered on the command

OpenVMS

Example:

```
$ TYPE FPARSE.COM
$! Return portions of a filename
$ WRITE SYS$OUTPUT P1
$ N = F$PARSE(P1,,,"NAME")
$ T = F$PARSE(P1,,,"TYPE")
$ D = F$PARSE(P1,,,"DIRECTORY")
$ F = N + T
$ WRITE SYS$OUTPUT "Name = ''N'"
```

UNIX (C shell)

```
% cat fparse
# Return portions of a filename
echo "$1"
set n="$1:r"
set t="$1:e"
set d="$1:h"
set f="$1:t"
echo "Name = $n"
echo "Type = $t"
echo "Dir = $d"
```

```
$ WRITE SYS$OUTPUT "Type = ''T'"          echo "File = $f"
$ WRITE SYS$OUTPUT "Dir = ''D'"           exit


$ WRITE SYS$OUTPUT "File = ''F'"          % fparse ~/program.c
$ EXIT                                    /usr/fred/program.c
                                          Name = program
                                          Type = .c
$ @FPARSE PROGRAM.C                       Dir = /usr/fred
PROGRAM.C                                 File = program.c
Name = PROGRAM
Type = .C
Dir = [FRED]
File = PROGRAM.C
```

Perl   **UNIX (Korn shell)**

Example:

```
$ cat fparse.pl                           $ cat fparse
#!/usr/bin/perl -w                        echo "$1"
# Return portions of a filename           n=`basename $1`
use File::Basename;                       n=${n%%.*}
print "$ARGV[0]\n";                       t=${1##*.}
($n, $d, $t) = fileparse($ARGV[0],        d=`dirname $1`
'\..*');                                  f="$n.$t"
$f = $n . $t;                             print "Name = $n"
print "Name = $n\n";                      print "Type = $t"
print "Type = $t\n";                      print "Dir = $d"
print "Dir = $d\n";                       print "File = $f"
print "File = $f\n";                      exit
exit;
                                          $ fparse ~/program.c
$ fparse  ~/program.c                     /home/fred/program.c
/home/fred/program.c                      Name = program
Name = program                            Type = c
Type = .c                                 Dir = /home/fred
Dir = /home/fred/                         File = program.c
File = program.c
```

line and breaking it up into the component parts of the file's name, type (extension), directory, and finally the file-spec minus the directory. In the OpenVMS example, notice that we enter just the filename PROGRAM.C without any directory name. The F$PARSE is able automatically to determine the containing directory's name by finding out the current default directory from the system. Before we get into the details of the UNIX examples, notice that in each case the value we passed to the script was ~/program.c, which tells the shell to look for this file in the user's home directory. The first line of each script simply echoes what was passed. In the OpenVMS example, we see exactly what was entered, nothing more. But in the UNIX examples, the ~/ notation was automatically expanded into a directory path by the shell before the script was started. Why is this important? In all of the UNIX examples, we will be doing string manipulations on only what was passed to the script, nothing more. If we had not specified some sort of path information on the command line, there would have been no path information to extract. Instead, only a period or ./ would be returned, which in either case simply means the current directory. In other words F$PARSE can be used to fill in the missing parts of a file specification because it knows the context of where the file lives. In UNIX this type of expansion happens on the command line, but once the parameter is passed to the script, it is really just a string with no meaning or context other than what our script assigns to it.

The C shell provides very convenient operators to extract the parts of a file name. In contrast, we have to work a bit harder with the Korn shell. The programs basename and dirname make extracting the filename (with extension) and directory name fairly easy, but since these are programs, we have to use the backtick (`) operators to execute the programs, and the result, which would have gone to STDOUT, is instead assigned to our shell variables. To capture and remove the file extension, we use the Korn shell's pattern-matching facility to match all text found after the last period in the string. In one case, we keep only what was matched; in the other, we throw away what was matched.

Perl provides a built-in file-parsing routine that in many respects is similar to OpenVMS's F$PARSE function, but again, it must be stressed that if there is no directory information in the string being passed, the Perl functions will just return ./, meaning the current directory.

10.4 Variable Expansion

The result of variable expansion depends on whether the variable is surrounded by single forward quotes (a.k.a. strong quotes), double quotes (a.k.a. weak quotes), or single backward quotes (a.k.a. backticks). A string delimited with the single forward quote character prevents any kind of variable expansion or metacharacter interpretation (compare with the variable name only in OpenVMS). The variable name is returned literally, and alias or wildcard expansion does not take place. A string delimited with the double-quote character also groups characters or numbers into a single argument (as shown above), but it allows variable expansion, while still preventing wildcard expansion (compare with the double quotes in Open-VMS). A string delimited with the single backward quote character also performs variable expansion, but in addition, allows wildcard expansion and then causes the resulting string to be executed as a command (available under OpenVMS only if the symbol is the first word on a command line). The example below illustrates these three kinds of variable expansion.

OpenVMS
Example:

```
$ NAME =''DIR *.FOR''


$ WRITE SYS$OUTPUT ''NAME'' NAME
$ WRITE SYS$OUTPUT NAME
DIR *.FOR
$ 'NAME'
PROGRAM.FOR
```

UNIX (C Shell)

```
% set name = "ls *.f"
% echo $name
ls program.f
% echo '$name' $name
% echo "$name"
ls *.f
% echo `$name`
program.f
```

Perl
Example:

```
$ cat quotes.pl
#!/usr/bin/perl -w
# Quote demo
$name = "ls *.f";
print '$name', "\n";
print "$name\n";
print `$name`;
exit;

$ ./quotes.pl
$name
ls *.f
program.f
```

The command echo $name returns the variable substitution with the metacharacter expanded, whereas echo '$name' prevents any variable substitution and returns the variable name. The command echo "$name" returns the substitution for the variable name, which includes the nonexpanded metacharacter *. Finally, echo `$name` causes immediate command execution: The result of executing the command between backward quotes becomes part of the command line. The command ls *.f indicates that one file of the file type .f, program.f, resides in the present working directory. Quoting under the Korn and bash shells is the same as under the C shell. The Perl example is also very similar; only notice that for strong quotes we could not include the new-line metacharacter within the string, or it would have literally printed out as $name\n and would not have started a new line.

10.5   Comparison Operators

Table 10.4 illustrates the comparison operators supported by the C and Korn shells. We will encounter numerous uses of comparison operators in subsequent examples. We now introduce the if statement, discussed in greater detail under flow control in Section 10.8, to show how comparison operators function. The C shell uses the same operator for both text and integer variables, whereas Perl, Korn shell, and OpenVMS use a different comparison operator for each.

Table 10.4   *Comparison Operators*

C Shell Operator	Bash and Korn Shell Operator	Perl	OpenVMS Equivalent	UNIX Meaning
==	==	==	.EQ.	Equal to (arithmetic)
==	=	eq	.EQS.	Equal to (string)
!	!	!	.NOT.	Boolean "not" (negates other operators)
!=	!=	! ne	.NE. .NES.	Not equal to (arithmetic and string
&&	&&	&&	.AND.	Boolean "and"
||	||	||	.OR.	Boolean "or"
>	>	> gt	.GT. .GTS.	Greater than (arithmetic and string)
<	<	< lt	.LT. .LTS.	Less than (arithmetic and string)
>=	>=	>= ge	.GE. .GES.	Greater than or equal to (arithmetic and string)
<=	<=	<= le	.LE. .LES.	Less than or equal to (arithmetic and string)

The Bash shell also permits == as a string comparison operator for equality. Perl also supports the keywords or, and, and not as alternatives to ||, &&, and not, respectively, although there are important contextual differences in how these operators are evaluated. See documentation on Perl for more details.

OpenVMS
Example:
```
$! Equal to
$ IF (I .EQ. 10) THEN
$ IF (STRING .EQS. "Red") THEN
```
Example:
```
$! Not equal to
$ IF (I .NE. 10) THEN
$ IF (STRING .NES. "Red") THEN
```
Example:
```
$! Greater than 1 and less than 10
$ IF (I .GT. 1 .AND. I .LT. 10) THEN
```
Example:
```
$! Equal to 0 or 1
$ IF (I .EQ. 0 .OR. I .EQ. 1) THEN
```
Example:
```
$! Equal to Blue OR Red
$ IF (STRING .EQS. "Blue" .OR. STRING .EQS. "Red") THEN
```
Example:
```
$! Not less than or equal to 10
$ IF (.NOT. (I .LE. 10)) THEN
```
Example:
```
$! A zero-length (null) string
$ IF (F$LENGTH(STRING) .EQ. 0) THEN
$ IF (STRING .EQS. "") THEN
```

UNIX (C shell)
Example:
```
# equal to
if ($i == 10) then
if ($string == "Red") then
```
Example:
```
# not equal to
if ($i != 10) then if ($string != "Red") then
```
Example:
```
# greater than 1 and less than 10
if ($i>1 && $i<10) then
```

Example:

```
# equal to 0 or 1
if ($i == 0 || $i == 1) then
```

Example:

```
# equal to Blue or Red
if ($string == "Blue" || $string == "Red") then
```

Example:

```
# not less than or equal to 10
if (!($i <= 10)) then
```

Example:

```
# a zero-length (null) string
if (-z $string) then
```

UNIX (bash and Korn shell)

Example:

```
# equal to
if (( $i == 10 )) then
if [[ $string = "Red" ]] then
```

Example:

```
# not equal to
if (( $i != 10 )) then
if [[ $string != "Red" ]] then
```

Example:

```
# greater than 1 and less than 10
if (( $i > 1 && $i < 10 )) then
```

Example:

```
# equal to 0 or 1
if (( $i == 0 || $i == 1 )) then
```

Example:

```
# equal to Blue or Red
if [[ $string == "Blue" || $string == "Red" ]] then
```

Example:

```
# not less than or equal to 10
if (( ! ( $i <= 10 ) )) then
```

Example:

```
# a zero-length (null) string
if [[ -z $string ]] then
```

Perl

Example:

```
equal to
if ( $i == 10 ) then
if ( $string eq "Red" ) then
```

Example:

```
# not equal to
if ( $i != 10 ) then
if ( $string ne "Red" ) then
```

Example:

```
# greater than 1 and less than 10
if ( $i > 1 && $i < 10 ) then
if ( $i > 1 and $i < 10 ) then
```

Example:

```
# equal to 0 or 1
if ( $i == 0 || $i == 1 ) then
if ( $i == 0 or $i == 1 ) then
```

Example:

```
# equal to Blue or Red
if ( $string eq "Blue" || $string eq "Red" ) then
if ( $string eq "Blue" or $string eq "Red" ) then
```

Example:

```
# not less than or equal to 10
if (! ( $i <= 10 )) then
if (not ( $i <= 10 ) then
```

Example:

```
# a zero-length (null) string
if ($string eq "") then
```

Each example compares either the variable i to some integer value or the variable string to some text string, as described in the comment that precedes the command. The example `if (( ! ($i<=10) )) then` is noteworthy because it illustrates the nesting of comparison operators: Variable i is neither less than nor equal to 10; that is, it is greater than 10 (identical to `if ( $i>10 ) then`).

While parentheses are useful in OpenVMS and important in changing the order of operator precedence, by and large they are not needed. The UNIX shells require enclosing the expression to be evaluated. In the C shell, a single pair of parentheses is sufficient. Some old versions of the Korn shell permitted a single pair of parentheses; modern implementations require double parentheses around an arithmetic comparison and double square brackets around a string comparison or an expression that uses file operators.

The Korn shell is somewhat finickier than either OpenVMS or the C shell, requiring spaces surrounding the double square brackets and the operators in string comparisons. On the other hand, Korn shell permits white space in numeric comparisons; we have chosen to use it for readability. Similarly, Korn shell will substitute a variable name in a numeric comparison regardless of the preceding dollar sign, but we have again included it for readability and to show the parallelism between the syntactical forms. If a string variable evaluates to a numeric value, you may use that variable in a numeric comparison as though it were a numeric variable.

The example that tests for a zero-length string illustrates a different syntactic form, one that permits the shells to test many different properties of objects, not simply a string characteristic. Section 10.6 shows the syntax in a few other situations. In Perl this operator and others like it are reserved for file testing only. String operators, string functions, and regular expressions would be used instead for this type of string property testing.

Finally, bash and Korn shell string comparisons are actually instances of pattern matching. See Section 5.5 for a brief discussion of pattern matching. It should help give a sense of the power and complexity of Korn shell to say that pattern matching allows many of the capabilities one finds in OpenVMS lexical functions, and many more not present in them. Within a string comparison, the pattern must always appear to the right of the comparison operator. The quotes are optional if the pattern contains only letters and digits. If the pattern contains characters that may be further interpreted by the shell, you must enclose the pattern with quoting characters.

10.6 File Operators

Table 10.5 lists C and Korn shell operators that test the characteristics of a file. Perl liberally borrows this syntax from both shells and adds a few operators of its own. There is no analog to these file operators in OpenVMS, although you can use values returned by the F$FILE_ATTRIBUTES lexical function to determine the attributes of an OpenVMS file. The features returned by F$FILE_ATTRIBUTES do not translate into UNIX file operators because of the different ways in which OpenVMS and UNIX treat files. An OpenVMS file is highly structured, and F$FILE_ATTRIBUTES returns information about that structure. A UNIX file is nothing more than a string of bytes. Since a UNIX file has no file structure information, file operators only return features like file ownership and permissions.

With two exceptions, the bash and Korn shells have the same operators as the following examples, but use the string comparison syntax ([[-operator object]]) instead. Those two exceptions are -o, for which they use -O, and -z, for which -s is used (test is negated).

Table 10.5 *File Comparison Operators*

C Shell Operator	Perl	Bash and Korn Shell Operator	OpenVMS Equivalent	UNIX Meaning
		-a	*†	True if object is any kind of file
	-b	-b		True if file is a block-special file
	-c	-c		True if file is a character special file
-d	-d	-d		True if file is a directory
-e	-e	-e	*†	True if file exists
-f	-f	-f		True if file is a regular file
	-T			True if file is "text"
	-B			True if file is "binary"
	-s		F$FILE_ATTRIBUTES (,"EOF")	If file exists and is not empty, returns size in bytes (UNIX) or blocks (OpenVMS)
	-M			Returns modification age in days
	-A			Returns access age in days
	-C			Returns inode-modification age in days

Table 10.5 *File Comparison Operators (continued)*

C Shell Operator	Perl	Bash and Korn Shell Operator	OpenVMS Equivalent	UNIX Meaning
	-g	-g		True if file has its `setgid` bit set
		-G	F$GETJPI()‡	True if file's group matches group id of process
	-k	-k		True if file has its sticky bit set
-l	-l	-L		True if file is a symbolic link
-o	-o	-O	F$GETJPI()‡	True if executor of file is owner (note that shells use different case)
	-p	-p		True if file is a pipe or fifo special file
-r	-r	-r	‡	True if file is readable by executor
	-S	-S		True if file is socket
	-t	-t	F$GETDVI("TT:", "DEVTYPE")	True if file descriptor refers to a terminal
	-u	-u		True if file has its `setiud` bit set
-w	-w	-w	‡	True if file is writable by executor

Table 10.5   *File Comparison Operators (continued)*

C Shell Operator	Perl	Bash and Korn Shell Operator	OpenVMS Equivalent	UNIX Meaning
-x	-x	-x	‡	True if file is executable by executor
-z	-z	!-s	‡	True if file is empty (bash and Korn shells reverse sense of test)
		-nt	F$CVTIME()‡	True if one file is newer than a second
		-ot	F$CVTIME()‡	True if one file is older than a second
		-ef	F$FILE_ATTRIBUTES (,"FID")	True if two references are to the same file

*Same results could be achieved with an error handler.

†No OpenVMS equivalent to return the Boolean value described; use F$PARSE.

‡No OpenVMS equivalent to return the Boolean value described; use F$FILE_ATTRIBUTES alone or in combination with other lexical functions.

Remember that UNIX treats virtually every sort of object as a file: text and binary files to which you're accustomed from OpenVMS, devices, named pipelines, sockets, and so on. The third example uses the -f operator to check to see if the file is a *regular file,* a file similar to the OpenVMS notion of a file (as opposed to, say, a device-special file).

File comparison operators check whether a file is readable, writable, or executable by looking at the *protection mask,* that is, the permissions assigned to the file. In the following examples, /usr/fred/file will be reported as executable if its permissions render it such, irrespective of whether the file is an executable image, a shell script, or plain text.

OpenVMS	UNIX (C shell)

OpenVMS

Form:
```
$ IF F$FILE_ATTRIBUTES(file-spec,-
condition) THEN
```

UNIX (C shell)

Form:
```
% if (file_operator file) then
```

Example:
```
% if (file_operator file) then
```

Example:
```
$ IF (F$PARSE(file-spec) .NES.-
"") THEN
```

Example:
```
# true if /usr/fred is a directory
% if (-d /usr/fred) then

# true if /tmp/file1 exists
% if (-e /tmp/file1) then

# true if /usr/fred/text is a regular file
% if (-f /usr/fred/text) then
```

Example:
```
$ UIC = F$USER()
$ IF (F$FILE_ATTRIBUTES("FILE",-
"UIC") .EQS. UIC) THEN
```

```
% whoami
fred
# true if fred owns /usr/fred/file
```

Example:
```
$ IF (F$FILE_ATTRIBUTES("FILE",-
"PRO") .EQS. ...) THEN
```

```
% if (-o /usr/fred/file) then
# true if /usr/fred/file is readable
```

Example:
```
$ IF (F$FILE_ATTRIBUTES("FILE",-
"PRO") .EQS. ...) THEN
```

```
% if (-r /usr/fred/file) then
# true if /usr/fred/file is writeable
```

Example:
```
$ IF (F$FILE_ATTRIBUTES("FILE",-
"PRO") .EQS. ...) THEN
```

```
% if (-w /usr/fred/file) then
# true if /usr/fred/file is executable
```

Example:
```
$ IF (F$FILE_ATTRIBUTES("FILE",-
"EOF") .EQS. 0) THEN
```

```
% if (-x /usr/fred/file) then
# true if /usr/fred/file is empty

% if (-z /usr/fred/file) then
# prints string 'fred' to STDOUT
```

Perl

Example:
```
# true if /usr/fred is a directory
if (-d '/usr/fred') { ... }
# true if /usr/fred/text is a regular file
```

```
if (-f '/usr/fred/text') { … }
system('whoami');
# true if fred owns /usr/fred/file
if (-o '/usr/fred/file') { … }
# true if /usr/fred/file is readable
if (-r '/usr/fred/file') { … }
# true if /usr/fred/file is writeable
if (-w '/usr/fred/file') { … }
# true if /usr/fred/file is executable
if (-x '/usr/fred/file') { … }
# true if /usr/fred/file is empty
if (-z '/usr/fred/file') { … }
```

10.7 Mathematical Operators

We have seen that the C shell set command associates a value to a variable and that such values may be integers or text (e.g., set a = 1 or set a = "test"). The ksh and bash shells surround an arithmetic operation with double parentheses: ((a = 1)). Perl variable assignment statements closely model the syntax used in the C language (e.g., $x = 5 and $y++). OpenVMS uses = to equate a variable to an integer value and := or =... to equate a variable to a string value. The OpenVMS user can perform mathematical operations on either string or integer values. The UNIX C shell permits only mathematical operations on integer variables, whereas Perl and the Korn and bash shells permit arithmetic on string variables if the value of the variable equates to an integer. The C shell @ metacharacter equates a variable name to the result of a mathematical operation using integer variables. Table 10.6 lists mathematical operators used by the shells and Perl.

Table 10.6 *Mathematical Operators*

C Shell Operator	Bash and Korn Shell Operator	Perl	OpenVMS Equivalent	UNIX Meaning
Integers				
+	+	+	+	Add
–	–	–	–	Subtract
*	*	*	*	Multiply

Table 10.6   *Mathematical Operators (continued)*

C Shell Operator	Bash and Korn Shell Operator	Perl	OpenVMS Equivalent	UNIX Meaning
/	/	/	/	Divide
++	++	++		Increment by 1
--	--	--		Decrement by 1
%	%	%		Modulo
Bits				
>>	>>	>>		Right bit shift
<<	<<	<<		Lift bit shift
~	~	~		1's complement (invert bits)
!	!	!	.NOT.	Logical negation
|	|	|	.OR.	Inclusive OR
^	^	^		Exclusive OR
&	&	&	.AND.	AND

OpenVMS

```
$ TYPE TEST.COM
$ I = 15
$ J = 3
$!
$! Addition
$ K = (I + J)
$ WRITE SYS$OUTPUT "addition: ' 'K' "
$!
$! Subtraction
$ K = (I - J)
$ WRITE SYS$OUTPUT "subtraction: ' 'K' "
$!
$! Division
$ K = (I/J)
$ WRITE SYS$OUTPUT "division: ' 'K' "
$!
$! Multiplication
$ K = (I * J)
$ WRITE SYS$OUTPUT "multiplication: ' 'K' "
$!
```

UNIX (all shells, C shell syntax)

```
% cat test_script
set i = 15
set j = 3
#
# Addition
@ k = ($i + $j)
echo "addition: $k"
#
# Subtraction
@ k = ($i - $j)
echo "subtraction: $k"
#
# Division
@ k = ($i/$j)
echo "division: $k"
#
# Multiplication
@ k = ($i * $j)
echo "multiplication: $k"
#
```

```
$! Modulo                                         # Modulo
$ K = (I - ((I/J) * J))                           @ k = ($i % $j)
$ WRITE SYS$OUTPUT "modulo:' 'K' "                echo "modulo: $k"
$!                                                #
$! Right bit shift†                               # Right bit shift
$ K = (I/J)                                        @ k = ($i >> j)
$ WRITE SYS$OUTPUT "right bit shift:' 'K' "       echo "right bit shift by j: $k"
$!                                                #
$! Left bit shift†                                # Left bit shift
$ K = (I * J)                                      @ k = ($i << j)
$ WRITE SYS$OUTPUT "left bit shift:' 'K' "        echo "left bit shift by j: $k"
$!                                                #
$! Invert bits                                    # Invert bits
$ K = .NOT. I                                      @ k = (~$i)
$ WRITE SYS$OUTPUT "invert bits: ' 'K' "          echo "invert bits: $k"
$!                                                #
$! Logical negation                               # Logical negation
$ K = ((I .AND. 1) .NE. 1)                          @ k = (! $i)
$ WRITE SYS$OUTPUT "negation: ' 'K' "             echo "logical negation: $k"
$!                                                #
$! Bitwise inclusive OR                           # Bitwise inclusive OR
$ K = (I .OR. J)                                    @ k = ($i | $j)
$ WRITE SYS$OUTPUT "inclusive or: ' 'K' "         echo "bitwise inclusive or: $k"
$!                                                #
$! Bitwise exclusive OR                           # Bitwise exclusive OR
$ K = ((I .OR. J) .AND. .NOT. (I .AND. J))          @ k = ($i ^ $j)
$ WRITE SYS$OUTPUT "exclusive or: ' 'K' "         echo "bitwise exclusive or: $k"
$!                                                #
$! Bitwise AND                                    # Bitwise AND
$ K = (I .AND. J)                                   @ k = ($i & $j)
$ WRITE SYS$SOUTPUT "bitwise and: ' 'K' "         echo "bitwise and: $k"
$ EXIT                                            exit
$!                                                #!


$ @TEST                                           % test_script
addition: 18                                      addition: 18
subtraction: 12                                   subtraction: 12
division: 5                                       division: 5
multiplication: 45                                multiplication: 45
modulo: 0                                         modulo: 0
right bit shift: 3                                right bit shift by 2: 3
left bit shift: 60                                left bit shift by 2: 60
invert bits: -16                                  invert bits: -16
negative: 0                                       logical negation: 0
inclusive or: 15                                  bitwise inclusive or: 15
exclusive or: 12                                  bitwise exclusive or: 12
bitwise and: 3                                    bitwise and: 3
```

Perl

```
% cat test_script.pl
$i = 15;
$j = 3;
#
# Addition
$k = ($i + $j);
print "addition: $k\n";
#
# Subtraction
$k = ($i - $j);
print "subtraction: $k\n";
#
# Division
$k = ($i/$j);
print "division: $k\n";
#
# etc. …
```

†The OpenVMS example is an approximationof the Boolean operator present in the C and Korn shells. Arithmetic and logical operations treat the sign bit differently.

The above examples illustrate the use of the major mathematical operators. You should take care with the syntax used in these expressions; for example, in C shell syntax, @k is not the same as @ k (the space makes a difference), nor is ~$i the same as ~ $i (again, the space makes a difference). Spaces are not necessarily ignored in the C shell, although they may be sprinkled liberally to improve readability in Perl and the bash and Korn shells.

For readers unfamiliar with the characteristics of mathematical operators, we explain the above examples further. The definitions hold for OpenVMS as well as UNIX. Note that subscripts indicate the counting base: Hence, 3_{10} is 3 to the Base 10, and 1111_2 is 1111 to the Base 2 (binary).

DCL, Perl, and the bash, Korn, and C shells all perform *signed* integer arithmetic; that is, the underlying machine architecture understands and distinguishes positive and negative numbers.

Most implementations of the C shell and the Korn shell use 32-bit integer arithmetic. A few still use 16-bit integer arithmetic. With Tru64 UNIX from HP, Linux running on HP's Alpha processors, and with UNIX running on other 64-bit processors, the shells perform 64-bit integer arithmetic. Beyond this, Perl provides the Math::BigFloat math library, which provides arbitrary-length, floating-point arithmetic.

Division (i/j) returns an integer value rounded down. For example, 15/3 returns 5, and 15/4 returns 3.

Modulo (i % j) returns the remainder after division. For example, 15 % 3 returns 0, and 15 % 4 returns 3.

Bitwise right shift (i >> j) shifts i by j bits to the right, discarding the first j bits. For example, (15 >> 2) shifts 15 two bits to the right so that 1111_2 becomes 11_2, which is 3_{10}.

Bitwise left shift (i << j) shifts i by j bits to the left and pads with zeros. For example, (15 << 2) shifts 15 two bits to the left and pads with zeros, so that 1111_2 becomes 111100_2, which is 60_{10}.

The operator ~, 1's complement, changes 0s to 1s, and vice versa, including the sign bit; thus, it has the effect of making the integer value n become $-(n + 1)$. For example ~15 becomes -16.[2]

The operator !, logical negation, returns 0 for any result not equal to 0 and 1 for any result equal to 0.

The operator | signifies a bitwise inclusive or: A bit that is 1 in either variable returns 1.

For example, (15 | 3):

	Decimal Value	Binary Equivalent
	15_{10}	1111_2
	3_{10}	0011_2
(15 | 3) =	15_{10}	1111_2

The operator ^ performs a bitwise exclusive or: A bit that is 1 in both variables returns 0, and a bit that is 1 in only one of the variables returns 1. For example, (15 ^ 3):

	Decimal Value	Binary Equivalent
	15_{10}	1111_2
	3_{10}	0011_2
(15 ^ 3) =	12_{10}	1100_2

The operator & signifies a bitwise and: A bit that is 1 in both variables returns 1, and other bits return 0. For example, (15 & 3):

---

2. The substitution of the variable's values takes place before the Korn shell `print` command is interpreted. A variable that contains a negative value may appear in the `print` command to another switch, one which will not understand. To avoid an error message, you must indicate to `print` that all switches have been processed by preceding the variable with the `--` or the `-R` switch.

	Decimal Value	Binary Equivalent
	15_{10}	1111_2
	3_{10}	0011_2
(15 & 3) =	3_{10}	0011_2

Korn shell scripts may be subject to data-dependent errors. The substitution of a variable's value takes place before the Korn shell `print` command is interpreted. A variable that contains a negative value may thus appear to the `print` command to be another switch, one that the command will not understand. To avoid an error message, you must indicate to `print` that all switches have been processed by preceding the variable with the - - or the `-R` switches.

10.8   Flow Control

The statements IF-THEN-ELSE-ENDIF, GOSUB-RETURN, CALL, and GOTO provide flow control in OpenVMS command procedures. The UNIX C shell also offers `if` and `goto` and the additional statements `while`, `foreach`, `break`, `continue`, `switch`, `breaksw`, and `shift` to control the logical flow of a shell script. The Korn and bash shells provide `if`, `while`, `until`, `for`, `break`, `continue`, `case`, `select`, and `shift`. As with DCL command procedures, all three shells allow you to exert flow control in response to error conditions (see Section 10.8.12).

10.8.1   `if` (C, bash, and Korn Shells)

The `if` statement provides a one- or two-way conditional branch. You can nest `if` statements, as the more complex examples in Section 10.11 show.

The two Korn shell forms show a syntax that allows the `then` keyword to appear on the same line as the expression, a convention some programmers use, but the examples show `then` on a separate line, which others find more understandable. Like the Korn shell, bash requires that the `then` keyword be a separate statement, separated by either a new line or a semicolon from the test condition. The same requirements hold for the `fi` keyword. Like the C and Pascal programming languages, Perl statements are not line-oriented, but rather require semicolon statement separators. Because of this, the programmer has a great deal of flexibility in using line breaks and indenting to illustrate the structure of the code. The Perl examples above show two popular styles of indenting and brace placement. Which style to

OpenVMS	UNIX (C shell)

OpenVMS

Form:
```
$ IF expression
$ THEN
command(s)
$ ELSE
command(s)
$ ENDIF
```

Form:
```
$ IF expression THEN command
```

Example:
```
$ TYPE TEST.COM
$! Report a file's executable status
$ INQUIRE A "Enter filename: "
$ IF (F$PARSE(A,,,"TYPE") .EQS. -
".EXE")
$ THEN
$    WRITE SYS$OUTPUT A," is -
executable"
$ ELSE
$    WRITE SYS$OUTPUT A," is not -
executable"
$ ENDIF
$ TYPE TEST.COM
$! Display a non-empty file
$ IF (F$FILE_ATTRIBUTES-
(P1,"EOF") .EQ. 0) THEN GOTO EMPTY
$ TYPE /PAGE 'P1'
$ EXIT
$ EMPTY:
$ WRITE SYS$OUTPUT "File is empty"
$ EXIT
```

UNIX (C shell)

```
% if (expression) then
...
else
...
endif
```

```
% cat test_script
# Report a file's executable status
    echo -n "Enter filename: "
set a = $<
if (-x $a) then
    echo "$a is executable"
else
echo "$a is not executable"
endif
```

```
% cat test_script
# Display a non-empty file
if (-z $1) then echo "File is empty"
endif
more $1
exit
```

UNIX (Korn and Bash shells)

Form:
```
# Arithmetic expressions
$ if ((expression)) ; then
...
```

Perl

```
if (expression) {
...
} elsif (expression) {
...
```

```
elif ((expression)) ; then            } else {
...                                   ...
else                                  }
...
fi
```

Form:

```
# String and object
expressions
$ if [[expression]] ; then
...
elif [[expression]] ; then
...
else
...
fi
```

Example:

```
$ cat test_script                    $ cat test_script.pl
# Report a file's executable status  #!/usr/bin/perl -w
print -n "Enter filename: "          # Report a file.s executable status
read a                               print "Enter filename: ";
if [[ -x $a ]]                       $a = <STDIN>;  chomp($a);
then                                 if ( -x $a ) {
    print "$a is executable"             print "$a is executable\n";
else                                 } else {
    print "$a is not executable"         print "$a is not executable\n";
fi                                   }
                                     exit;
```

Example:

```
$ cat test_script                    $ cat test_script.pl
# Display a nonempty file            #!/usr/bin/perl -w
if [[ ! -e $1 ]]                     # Display a nonempty file
then                                 if ( ! -e $ARGV[0] )
    print "File does not exist"        {
elif [[ -s $1 ]]                         print "File does not exist\n";
```

```
then                                          }
    print "File is empty"             elsif ( (-s $ARGV[0]) == 0 )
fi                                            {
more $1                                           print "File is empty\n";
                                              }
                                          system("more $ARGV[0]");
                                          exit;
```

use is a matter of personal taste, but it is good practice to select one of the more common styles and use it consistently throughout the program.

In the first example, if (-x $a) then (in Korn syntax, if [[-x $a]]) defines a two-way branch that reports whether or not the file is executable (compare with the OpenVMS lexical function F$PARSE, which determines whether a file extension is .EXE, that is, if the file is likely to be executable). In the second example using C shell, if (-z $1) then defines a one-way conditional branch. If the file is empty, the fact is reported. Then, in both the empty and nonempty cases, the example displays the file with the more command; there is no else condition. The Korn shell version is a bit more complex. The C shell uses the -z operator to test both strings and files for zero length, but Korn uses -s on files. The example first tests to see if the file does not exist and only checks the length if it does. It makes use of the elif keyword, an optional construct, which allows a new condition in place of the list of statements usually introduced by else.

Finally, the Perl scripts closely parallel the Korn shell examples in basic structure. Notable differences include the use of the chomp() function to remove any end of line characters from the tail of the string and testing the numeric value returned by the -s operator. Unlike the Korn shell function, in Perl this operator returns the size of the file in bytes, not a logical TRUE/FALSE value. It would also be syntactically correct to have used instead the expression if (-s $ARGV[0]), but the sense of the test may be the reverse of what you might first expect. If the file is empty, the value returned by the expression will be 0. But zero is logically false, so the else branch is taken. Likewise Perl considers any nonzero numeric value to be logically true, so if the file is not empty, the then branch is followed. Of course, the zero test operator (-z) could have been used instead and probably would have been clearer.

10.8.2 `while` (C, bash, and Korn Shells)

Taken literally, the `while` statement means, "as long as a condition is in effect, perform a specific task."

OpenVMS

Example:
```
$ TYPE TEST.COM
$! Time waster
$ I = 1
$ LOOP:
$ IF (I .GE. 13) THEN EXIT
$ WRITE SYS$OUTPUT -
"No calendar available"

$ I = I + 1
$ GOTO LOOP
$ EXIT
```

UNIX (Korn shell)
Form:
```
# Arithmetic expressions
while ((expression)) ; do
...
done
```
Form:
```
# String and object expressions
while [[expression]] ; do
...
done
```
Example:
```
$ cat test_script
# Display calendar by month
integer i = 1
while (( $i != 13 ))
do
   cal $i 1998
   (( i = $i + 1 ))
```

UNIX (C shell)
Form:
```
while (expression)
...
end
```

```
% cat test_script
# Display calendar by month
set i = 1
while ($i != 13)
   cal $i 1998
   @ i = ($i + 1)
end
echo "Calendar complete"
exit
```

Perl

```
while (expression) {
...
}
```

```
$ cat test_script
#!/usr/bin/perl -w
# Display calendar by month
$i = 1;
while ($i != 13)
{
   system("cal $i 1998");
```

```
done                                    $i++;
print "Calendar complete"               }
exit                                    print "Calendar complete\n";
                                        exit;
```

The two Korn shell forms show a syntax that allows the `do` keyword to appear on the same line as the expression, a convention some programmers use, but the example shows `do` on a separate line, which others find more understandable. Like the Korn shell, bash requires that the `do` keyword be a separate statement, separated by either a new line or a semicolon from the test condition. The same requirements hold for the `done` keyword. Likewise, the Perl form shows a common style of brace placement, but the example illustrates an alternate block style.

This example shows a use of the `integer` alias (Section 10.2) and introduces the `cal` command, which displays a calendar for any given year. If you give only the year argument, `cal` displays the year with four months across the screen. The shell script `test_script` displays the months one after the other. By using the month option to `cal` (variable `i`), the script repeats the loop, increasing `i` by one each time. As long as `i` does not equal 13, the script continues. When `i` reaches 13, the script terminates.

10.8.3 `until` (Perl, bash and Korn Shells)

The `while` and `until` statements are virtually identical; `until` merely negates the value of the expression used to see if the loop should execute. The following uses `until` to achieve the same result as the `while` example above.

UNIX (bash and Korn shell)

Form:

```
# Arithmetic expressions
until ((expression)) ; do
...
done
# String and object expressions
until [[expression]] ; do
...
done
```

Example:

```
$ cat test_script  (Korn shell)
# Display calendar by month
```

```
integer i = 1
until (( $i == 13 ))
do
    cal $i 1998
    (( i = $i + 1 ))
done
print "Calendar complete"
exit
```

Perl

Form:

```
until (expression) {
…
}
```

Example:

```
$ cat test_script.pl
#!/usr/bin/perl -w
# Display calendar by month
$i = 1;
until ($i == 13)
{
  system("cal $i 1998");
  $i++;
}
print "Calendar complete\n";
exit;
```

10.8.4 foreach (C and Perl Only)

The `foreach` statement performs some function on a word (often a file name) in a list of words that meet a specified criterion. It sequentially defines each word that meets the specified criterion as a variable and performs some operation on it. This is similar to one form of the `for` command in the Korn shell (Section 10.8.5). In OpenVMS, you typically first create a list of files in a temporary file, then read back the temporary file, performing the appropriate operation on each file in the list.

The statement `foreach i (*.txt)` sequentially displays each `.txt` file in the current directory with the command `cat $i`. While `cat *.txt` would have the same effect as this script, one could include additional commands between the `foreach` and `end` statements, making the `foreach` the more powerful approach. The Perl statement `foreach $i (<*.txt>)` likewise is used to generate a list of all files that match the supplied pattern and assigns each filename in turn to the `$i` variable. Filename matching with the same semantics of the UNIX C shell is provided by Perl through the `glob()` function or the alternate `< >` syntax.

OpenVMS

```
$ TYPE TEST.COM
$! Type all .TXT files
$ DIR /COLUMN=1 /OUT=A.OUT
*.TXT
$ OPEN/READ INFILE A.OUT
$ READ INFILE SCRATCH
$ READ INFILE SCRATCH
$ READ INFILE SCRATCH
$ LOOP:
$     READ INFILE PROG
$     IF (PROG .EQS. "") THEN
GOTO END
$     TYPE 'PROG'
$ GOTO LOOP
$ END: CLOSE INFILE
$ EXIT
```

Perl

```
#!/usr/bin/perl -w
# Display all .txt files
foreach $i (<*.txt>)
   {
      system("cat $i");
   }
exit;
```

UNIX (C shell)
Form:

```
foreach variable (filelist)
...
end
% cat test_script
# Display all .txt files
foreach i (*.txt)
    cat $i
end
exit
```

10.8.5 `for` (bash and Korn Shell)

The Korn shell and bash provide two forms of `for` looping, a form similar to the `foreach` command in the C shell (universally available), and the more-or-less traditional three-argument incremental form (available only in some implementations). This first example dresses the `foreach` C shell example in Korn shell clothes. We repeat the OpenVMS example below so you can see the equivalency more directly.

The Korn shell form shows a syntax that allows `do` on a separate line, a convention some programmers use, but you may place the `do` keyword on

OpenVMS

Example:
```
$ TYPE TEST.COM
$! Type all .TXT files
$ DIR /COLUMN=1 /OUT=A.OUT -
*.TXT
$ OPEN/READ INFILE A.OUT
$ READ INFILE SCRATCH
$ READ INFILE SCRATCH
$ READ INFILE SCRATCH
$ LOOP:
$    READ INFILE PROG
$    IF (PROG .EQS. "")
         THEN GOTO END
$    TYPE 'PROG'
$    GOTO LOOP
$ END: CLOSE INFILE
$ EXIT
```

UNIX (Korn shell)
Form:
```
for variable in list
do
...
done
```
```
$ cat test_script
# Display all .txt files
for i in *.txt ; do
    cat $i
done
exit
```

the same line as the `for` command, which others find more understandable. Like the Korn shell, bash requires that the `do` keyword be a separate statement, separated by either a new line or a semicolon from the test condition. The same requirements hold for the `done` keyword.

The shell actually substitutes the names of all `.txt` files in the `for` command before the command begins execution; the `for` command itself has no understanding of the words that make up the list. Numbers or arbitrary strings (use quoting if they contain spaces or special characters) can be used in the list.

This second example shows the second form, in which three arguments provide initial, repetitive, and final expressions to evaluate. We emphasize that this form appears in bash, but not necessarily in all implementations of the Korn shell.

UNIX (bash shell)
Form:
```
for (( [expression1] ; [expression2] ; [expression3] ))
do
```

```
...
done
```

Example:

```
$ declare -i i
$ declare -i j
$ declare -i product=1
$ j=`ls | wc | awk '{ print $2 }'`
$ for (( i=$j ; $i ; i=$i-1 )) ; do
> (( product=$product*$i ))
> done
$ echo $j!=$product

$ cat linecnt
#!/bin/bash
# Graphically show line count.
for file in  *.txt; do
  lines=`wc -l $file | awk '{ print $1 }'`
  bar=""
  for (( i=$lines; $i; i=$i-1 )); do
     bar="$bar#"
  done
echo -e "$file\t$bar";
done
$ linecnt
bar.txt #############
foo.txt ###################################
```

Perl

Form:

```
for ( [expression1] ; [expression2] ; [expression3] ) {
...
}
```

Example:

```
$ cat forloop.pl
#!/usr/bin/perl -w
# Graphically show line count.
foreach $file ( <*.txt> )
  {
    $lines=`wc -l $file | awk '{ print \$1 }'`;
    chomp($lines);
    $bar="";
    for ( $i=$lines; $i > 0; $i-- )
      {
        $bar="$bar#";
      }
    print "$file\t$bar\n";
  }
exit;
$ forloop.pl
bar.txt #############
foo.txt ###################################
```

The bash form shows a syntax that allows do on a separate line, a convention some programmers use, but the example shows the do keyword appearing on the same line as the for command, which others find more understandable. Like the Korn shell, bash requires that the do keyword be a separate statement, separated by either a new line or a semicolon from the test condition. The same requirements hold for the done keyword.

While previous examples often show the execution flow commands in the context of a script, this example shows that they can be executed interactively. In this example, we calculate a factorial based on the number of files in the current directory. We begin by telling bash that the three variables are each integers, since that is how we plan to use them. We next count the files, first listing them, then obtaining a count of lines, words, and characters, and finally selecting the word count. We begin the calculation. The first expression in the for command, i=$j, sets up initial conditions and is only performed when the command first begins execution. The second expression, $i, is evaluated every time through the loop and before the looped commands execute. The final expression, i=$i-1, is also evaluated every time through the loop, but at the end. The loop terminates if the second expression ever equals zero. Within the loop we simply accumulate a product, using the mathematical operators in Section 10.7. Note that the bash shell uses the secondary command prompt [> by default (see Table 3.1)] within the loop. As in the previous syntax, the done command marks the end of the loop. Finally, we print the result.

10.8.6   break and continue (C, bash, and Korn Shells)

Although there are differences between the various shell versions of break, we've chosen to group these commands together because they are so alike conceptually. The break command leaves the current loop of a while, until, for, or foreach command. You may optionally specify an integer to exit multiple levels of looping when using the Korn or bash shells. The C shell allows you to achieve the same effect by repeating the break command on the same line. Perl uses the keyword last instead of break. Like the Korn shell, in Perl the last command by default will exit the innermost containing loop or block. To force an exit out of the outer loop, we gave that loop the label main and then explicitly told Perl which loop to jump out of by referencing that label.

This script lists each *.xtx file twice unless it finds a flag file. If the flag file is present, only those *.xtx files that come earlier in the alphabet get listed. The flag file tells the script to exit two levels of looping. Note that we have used indentation to try to make the nesting clearer.

UNIX (Korn shell)

Form:

```
break n
```

Example:

```
$ ls *.xtx
arthur.xtx george.xtx john.xtx
paul.xtx
$ cat test.ksh
for j in *.xtx ; do
  integer i=0
  while (( $i < 2 )) ; do
    (( i = $i + 1 ))
    if [[ $j = flag.xtx ]] ; then
      break 2
    fi
    ls $j
    done # with the while command
  done # with the for command
exit

$ test.csh
arthur.xtx
arthur.xtx
george.xtx
george.xtx
john.xtx
john.xtx
paul.xtx
paul.xtx
$ touch flag.xtx
$ test.ksh
arthur.xtx
arthur.xtx
$ # We're done
```

UNIX (C shell)

```
break
```

```
% ls *.xtx
arthur.xtx george.xtx john.xtx
paul.xtx
% cat test.csh
foreach j ( *.xtx )
  set i = 0
  while ( $i < 2 )
    @ i = $i + 1
    if ( $j == flag.xtx ) then
      break ; break
    endif
    ls $j
    end # of the while command
  end # of the foreach command
exit

% test.csh
arthur.xtx
arthur.xtx
george.xtx
george.xtx
john.xtx
john.xtx
paul.xtx
paul.xtx
% touch flag.xtx
% test.ksh
arthur.xtx
arthur.xtx
% # We're done
```

Perl

Form:

last [*label*]

Example:

```
$ ls *.xtx
arthur.xtx george.xtx john.xtx
paul.xtx
$ cat test.pl
#!/usr/bin/perl -w
main: foreach $j ( <*.xtx> )
   {
     $i = 0;

     while ( $i < 2 ){
         $i = $i + 1;
         if ( $j eq "flag.xtx" )
           {
               last main;
           }
         system("ls $j");
       } # of the while command
   } # of the foreach command
exit;
$ test.pl
arthur.xtx
arthur.xtx
george.xtx
george.xtx
john.xtx
john.xtx
paul.xtx
paul.xtx
$ touch flag.xtx

$ test.ksh
arthur.xtx
arthur.xtx
$ # We're done
```

The continue command behaves similarly in both shells. It jumps to the end of the current iteration of the loop without executing any further commands during that iteration. Perl also has a continue command, but it is not used in the same way as in the shell languages. Instead, the Perl next command would be directly analogous. Like the Perl last command illustrated above, a label can be specified if needed to force a jump out of a nested loop.

UNIX (Korn shell)

Form:

```
continue n
```

Example:

```
$ cat test.ksh
for j in 1996 1998 ; do
    integer i=0
    while (( $i < 12 )) ; do
        (( i = $i + 1 ))
        if (( $i > 6 && $i < 9
)) ; then
            continue
        fi
        cal $i $j > cal$j-$i
    done # with while command
done # with for command
exit
```

Perl

Form:

```
last [label]
```

Example:

```
$ cat test.pl
#!/usr/bin/perl -w
foreach $j ("1996", "1998")
  {
    $i = 0;
    while ( $i < 12 )
      {
        $i = $i + 1;


        if ( $i > 6 && $i < 9 )
          {
            next;
          }
        print("cal $i $j > cal$j-$i\n");
        system("cal $i $j > cal$j-$i");
      } # of while command
  } # of foreach command
exit;
```

UNIX (C shell)

```
continue
```

```
% cat test.csh
foreach j (1996 1998)
    set i = 0
    while ( $i < 12 )
        @ i = $i + 1
        if ( $i > 6 && $i < 9 )
then
            continue
        endif
        cal $i $j > cal$j-$i
    end # of while command
end # of foreach command
exit
```

Assuming a year off for good behavior, this example creates calendars for each of the months of the year during which school is in session. Again, we have used indentation to try to make the nesting clearer.

10.8.7   switch, case, and breaksw (C Shell Only)

The switch statement directs the flow of a script to a particular *case label*, a point in the script that matches the possible conditions defined by the switch statement. Don't confuse the C shell case, used in a case label, with the bash or Korn shell case statement (Section 10.8.8)! You may define a default condition default: should none of the switch statements match a case label. The breaksw statement directs flow to the statement following the endsw statement. Without breaksw, the C shell continues down the list of case labels searching for additional matches. If no condition is met and no default condition is defined, execution continues after the endsw statement. Sound confusing? The following simple example helps to clarify the use of switch.

OpenVMS

UNIX (C shell)

Form:

```
switch (string1)
case string2:
...
breaksw
case string3:
...
breaksw
default:
...
endsw
```

Example:

```
$ TYPE TEST.COM
$! Select a printer
$ ON WARNING THEN GOTO WRONG
$ WRITE SYS$OUTPUT "Select a -
printer"
$ INQUIRE PR "Enter 1 or <cr> for -
laser -
2 for plotter; 3 for character -
printer"
$ IF (PR .EQS. "") THEN GOTO 1
```

```
% cat test_script.csh
# Select a printer
#
echo "Select a printer"
echo "Enter 1 or <cr> for laser \
2 for plotter; 3 for character \
printer"
set p = $< ; if ( -z $p ) then
  set p = "1"
endif
switch $p
```

```
$ GOTO 'P1'                              case 1:
$ 1:                                        lpr -Plaser $1
$ PRINT/QUEUE = LASER 'PR'                  breaksw
$ GOTO DONE                              case 2:
$ 2:                                        lpr -Pplotter $1
$ PRINT/QUEUE = PLOTTER 'PR'                breaksw
$ GOTO DONE                              case 3:
$ 3:                                        pr -Pcharacter $1
$ PRINT/QUEUE = CHARACTER 'P1'              breaksw
$ DONE:                                  default:
$ EXIT                                      echo "Invalid entry"
$ WRONG:                                 endsw
$ WRITE SYS$OUTPUT "Invalid Entry"       exit
$ EXIT
```

Perl

Example:

```perl
#!/usr/bin/perl -w
# Select a printer
#
print "Select a printer\n";
print "Enter 1 or <cr> for laser\n",
      "2 for plotter; 3 for character printer\n";
$p = <STDIN>;
chomp($p);
$p = 1 if (not defined($p));
SWITCH: {

  if ($p =~ m/^1$/) {
    system("lpr -Plaser $ARGV[0]");
    last SWITCH;
  }
  if ($p =~ m/^2$/) {
    system("lpr -Pplotter $ARGV[0]");
    last SWITCH;
  }
  if ($p =~ m/^3$/) {
    system("pr -Pcharacter $ARGV[0]");
    last SWITCH;
  }
  print "Invalid entry\n";
}
exit;
```

In this example, the switch statement directs the printing of a file to a specific printer queue. The user issues a response of 1, 2, 3, or <cr> to choose a printer. The script directs flow to the appropriate case label corresponding to the user's response. The `lpr` command queues the file and passes control to the `endsw` statement. If the user enters the default condition `<cr>` or any character other than 1, 2, or 3, control passes to the default statement label, which prints the file on the default print queue. Compare this with OpenVMS, where to transfer to a handler automatically, you must introduce an `ON WARNING` condition to handle an erroneous character. Shell scripts also have error-handling capabilities, as we shall see in Section 10.8.12.

Note that nested `if-then-else` constructs could have exerted the same flow control. Where case labels are constants, however, `switch` is more convenient and usually easier to understand. Oddly enough, Perl does not provide a case statement, although there are several ways to simulate one. The example above is just one of many approaches commonly used. The `m//` is Perl's regular expression matching operator.

10.8.8   case (bash and Korn Shell)

The Korn and bash shells' `case` command is similar in concept to the C shell `switch` command with one important difference: It does not continue to look for a pattern match once it has found one and executed the accompanying statement. It's as though there were a C shell `breaksw` command automatically built into the statement accompanying the matched pattern.

A less dramatic difference, but one that greatly enhances the capabilities of the `case` command, is that each individual possibility is an expression, with the full generality and complexity allowed to expressions. Below is the Korn version of the printer selection example. We repeat the OpenVMS example so that you can see the equivalency more directly.

This `case` command does not need an explicit `default:` statement the way the C shell `switch` command does. Since the shell is looking for a pattern, you can set up a default value with `*`.

Korn and bash shell pattern matching allows us to expand the allowable responses to include the word for the printer name, as well as the number of the choice. Rather than have an `if` command to set up a legitimate default value, we can include the choice of an empty string for the default printer.

10.8.9   select (bash and Korn Shell)

The `select` command performs a simple, special case version of the `case` statement that is especially suitable for menu choices, such as the printer example used for `switch` and `case`. Given a list of words that are the possi-

OpenVMS

Example:

```
$ TYPE TEST.COM
$! Select a printer
$ ON WARNING THEN GOTO WRONG
$ WRITE SYS$OUTPUT "Select a
printer"
$ INQUIRE PR "Enter 1 or <cr> for
laser -
2 for plotter; 3 for character
printer"
$ IF (PR .EQS. "") THEN GOTO 1
$ GOTO 'P1'
$ 1:
$ PRINT/QUEUE = LASER 'PR'
$ GOTO DONE
$ 2:
$ PRINT/QUEUE = PLOTTER 'PR'
$ GOTO DONE
$ 3:
$ PRINT/QUEUE = CHARACTER 'P1'
$ DONE:
$ EXIT
$ WRONG:
$ WRITE SYS$OUTPUT "Invalid Entry"
$ EXIT
```

UNIX (bash and Korn shell)
Form:

```
case word in
pattern1) ... ;;
pattern2) ... ;;
...
esac
```

```
$ cat test_script.ksh
# Select a printer
print "Select a printer"
print "Enter 1 or <cr> for laser \
2 for plotter; 3 for character
printer "
read p
case $p in
  "1" | "laser" | "" )
    lpr -Plaser $1
    ;;
  "2" | "plotter" )
    lpr -Pplotter $1
    ;;
  "3" | "character" )
    lpr -Pcharacter $1
    ;;
  * )
    print "Invalid Entry"
  ;;
esac
exit
```

ble replies, select displays each word, preceded by a number. You are then prompted to respond with the number of the selection you want. The prompting repeats until the script exits or you explicitly exit with <CTRL>-C or <CTRL>-D. The prompt string may be the default value for the PS3 variable (see Section 10.2.1), or you may redefine PS3 as you wish.

UNIX (Korn shell)

Form:

```
select variable in list
do
...
done
```

Example:

```
$ cat test_script.ksh
# Select a printer
PS3="Please a select a printer"
select printer_choice in laser plotter "character printer"
do
  case $printer_choice in
    laser) lpr -Plaser $1 ;;
    plotter) lpr -Pplotter $1 ;;
    "character printer") lpr -Pcharacter $1 ;;
    *) exit ;;
  esac
done
exit
```

Note that `"character printer"` is quoted because it contains a space. The value of `printer_choice` is set to the text corresponding to the number of the choice you select. The value of the built-in variable REPLY is set to the response you typed. If you respond with a number that does not correspond to one of the choices in this example, `printer_choice` will be set to null. In such a situation, the Korn shell will reprompt with only the string in the PS3 variable, but bash will reprompt with both the list of choices and the string in the PS3 variable. Note that Perl has a `select()` function, but it is used for an entirely different purpose.

10.8.10   goto (C Shell and Perl Only)

You can use the UNIX C shell `goto` statement the same way as the Open-VMS GOTO statement to achieve flow control, by directing flow to a statement label ending with a colon. Shell script statement labels must appear on a line by themselves, unlike their OpenVMS counterparts, which may precede any valid DCL command line. Perl labels, by convention, are entered as uppercase. Labels may appear at the beginning of any statement, which is not necessarily the beginning of the line, although that is the convention most commonly used. However, while statement labels are commonly used in Perl programs, the `goto` statement is rarely seen in practice.

OpenVMS

Form:

```
$ GOTO LABEL
...
```

Example:

```
$ LABEL: [command]
$ TYPE TEST.COM
$ IF (P1 .EQS. "") THEN -
GOTO UNDEFINED
$ WRITE SYS$OUTPUT -

"The value of parameter 1 is: ''P1' "
$ EXIT
$ UNDEFINED:
$ WRITE SYS$OUTPUT "P1 is undefined"
$ EXIT
```

UNIX (C shell)

```
goto label
...
label:


% cat test_script
if ($1 == "") then
   goto undefined
endif

echo "The value of variable 1 is:
$1"
exit
undefined:
echo "Variable 1 is undefined"
exit
```

Perl

Example:

```
% cat test_script
#!/usr/bin/perl -w
if (not defined($ARGV[0])) {
   goto UNDEFINED
}
print "The value of variable 1 is: $ARGV[0]\n";
exit;
UNDEFINED:
print("Variable 1 is undefined\n");
exit;
```

In this example, if the value of the first variable passed to a script is undefined (null), the `goto` statement directs flow to the label `undefined:`.

10.8.11   shift (Perl and C, bash, and Korn Shells)

The `shift` statement does not direct the flow to a specific line in the script, but rather changes in a predictable way all the elements of a variable or of the positional parameters. The `shift` statement downgrades each element number by one, discarding element one. For example, in the C shell, using `shift` on variable `test` reassigns element n of test (`test[n]`) to element n-1 (`test[n-1]`). The element `test[2]` becomes `test[1]`, and the original `test[1]` is discarded. The action of the bash and Korn shells is the same, but applies only to the positional paramaters (`$1`, `$2`, ...), instead of an arbitrary variable. Thus, `$1` takes on the value of the former `$2`, `$2` takes on the value of the former `$3`, and so on. If no variable is named in the C shell version, it too operates on the positional parameters. In OpenVMS, you assign variable names to the elements of the original variable using the F$ELEMENT lexical function to decompose the variable into separate elements with blanks as delimiters, and then reassign the value of element to element-1 with a conditional loop.

By shifting argv (the alternate name for the C shell positional parameters), shift is particularly useful for performing the same operation on each of the arguments passed to the script file. Similarly the Perl shift operator works on the @ARGV array by default, but may be used on any array by explicitly referencing it. In this example, shift progressively decrements the elements of the variable z and echoes the result.

OpenVMS

Example:

```
$ TYPE TEST.COM
# Using shift
$ Z = "one two three"
$ NUM = 1
$ LOOP1:
$     EL'NUM' =F$ELEMENT(NUM-1," ",Z)
$     IF EL'NUM' .EQS. " " THEN GOTO
NEXT
$       NUM = NUM + 1
$       GOTO LOOP1
$ NEXT:
$ TOTAL = NUM - 1
$ WRITE SYS$OUTPUT -
"Start with ",TOTAL, " elements"
$! The ELn symbols each hold a word
$! of the string
$! Now begin the simulation of
"shifting" them.
$ NUM = 1
$ LOOP2:
$     WRITE SYS$OUTPUT EL1
$     IF NUM .EQ. TOTAL THEN GOTO END
$     I = 1
```

UNIX (C shell)

Form:

```
shift [variable]
% cat test_script
# Using shift
set z = "one two three"
echo "Start with $#z elements"
while ($#z > 0)
    echo "$z[1]"
    shift z
end
echo "After shift we have $#z elements"
exit
```

```
$ INNER_LOOP:
$    J = I + 1
$    EL'I' = EL'J'
$    I = J
$    IF I .LT. TOTAL-
$        THEN GOTO INNER_LOOP
$    NUM = NUM + 1

$    GOTO LOOP2
$ END:
$ WRITE SYS$OUTPUT "No elements left"
$ EXIT


$ @TEST
Start with 3 elements              % test_script
one                                Start with 3 elements
two                                one
three                              two
No elements left                   three
                                   After shift we have 0 elements
```

Perl

Example:

```
shift [@variable]
% cat test_script
#!/usr/bin/perl -w
# Using shift
@z = ("one", "two", "three");
print "Start with ", $#z + 1, " elements\n";
while ($#z >= 0) {
  print "$z[0]\n";
  shift @z;
}
print "After shift we have ", $#z + 1, " elements\n";
exit;
% test_script
Start with 3 elements
one


two
three
After shift we have 0 elements
```

Note that while Perl appears to have adopted the $# notation from the C shell, the meaning is significantly different. In Perl this operator yields the element number of the last element in the array. But that is not the same as the number of elements because Perl arrays, like the C language, start at 0 not 1. Thus, it follows that the value returned for an empty array would be −1, not 0.

10.8.12   Error Handling and Flow Control

OpenVMS uses the constructs ON WARNING THEN, ON ERROR THEN, and ON SEVERE_ERROR THEN to direct the flow of a DCL command procedure when it finds an error or warning condition. The error or warning condition applies to all command lines in the current procedure following the statement, until you introduce a new condition or turn error handling off entirely with SET NOON. UNIX handles errors on a command-by-command basis, using the built-in C shell variable status or its bash and Korn shell equivalent ?. When invoking external programs from within Perl, this same status code is captured by Perl and is available for examination. Thus, a Perl program can detect if an error has occurred and deal with it appropriately. However, native Perl statements themselves, in effect, return a status by always returning a value. And any Perl value can be used "logically," meaning that Perl treats undefined, 0, or blank strings as false, and nonblank or nonzero values as true.

You can also invoke error handling for Perl statements or shell commands using the comparison operators || and &&. The conditions that apply to these operators are as follows:

command 1 succeeds	operator	command 2 executes
Yes	||	No
No	||	Yes
Yes	&&	Yes
No	&&	No

We will illustrate each form of the operator with an example.

UNIX shell	Perl
Form:	`command1 || command2`
`% command1 || command2`	
Example:	
`% cc test.c >& err1 || mail fred < \` `err1`	`defined($x) || die("required value` `missing");`
Form:	
`% command1 && command2`	`command1 && command2`
Example:	
`% grep csh /etc/passwd >` `cusers && lpr cusers`	`-e $fspec && rename($fspec,` `  "$fspec.bak");`

In the shell example, the construct `cc test.c >& err1 || mail fred < err1` compiles a C program. If the compilation reports no errors, command execution stops. If an error occurs, the file containing the error messages is mailed to user `fred`. In the Perl example, the statement `defined($x) || die("required value missing")` tests to see if a value has been assigned or aborts the program.

In the shell example, the construct `grep csh /etc/passwd > cusers && lpr cusers` searches the `/etc/passwd` file for csh records that contain the names of users who use the C shell by default. If any such records are found, they are output to the file `cusers` and then printed on the default printer. If `grep` fails to find any entries, the `&&` condition fails and the null file is not sent to the printer. In the Perl example, the statement `-e $fspec && rename($fspec, "$fspec.bak")` tests if the file named in the variable exists, and if it does, renames it. Note that if the file does not exist or the variable itself is undefined, the `&&` condition fails and `rename()` is not executed.

Now we discuss the use of the predefined shell variable `status`. (Note that the name of the C shell variable is `status`; preceding it with the `$` meta-character indicates variable substitution. In OpenVMS, on the other hand, the symbol name is `$STATUS`; `$` is part of the symbol name.) The variable `status` is redetermined after the execution of any command or shell script. You can display it with the command `echo $status`. Unfortunately, the value it returns is not consistent from command to command, an artifact of the individual commands, rather than the shell. For example, `find /dir -name test -print`, which finds all files named `test` down the directory hierarchy from `/dir`, returns a status of 0 if `/dir` does not exist. The command `lpr file1`, on the other hand, returns a status of 1 if the file `file1` does not exist. Both commands return a nonzero status if the command syntax is incorrect. You should experiment with `status` values returned by commands before using the values as conditional branches in script files. You may find the following rule of thumb useful: 0 indicates that execution was successful; 1 indicates that there was nothing wrong with the command, but that it did not achieve what it set out to do; and any other value indicates that there is a problem with the command syntax. When using Perl to execute external programs, this exact same status value can be captured by your program and tested. Just keep in mind that when testing the success of Perl's own native statements, Perl evaluates the results returned in terms of true or false values, not success or failure per se.

OpenVMS

Example:

```
$ SEARCH MYFILE.DAT FRED
fred
$ SHOW SYMBOL $STATUS
$STATUS = "%X00000001"
```

Example:

```
$ SEARCH MYFILE.DAT JILL
%SEARCH-I-NOMATCHES, -
no strings matched
$ SHOW SYMBOL $STATUS

$STATUS = "%X08D78053"
```

Example:

```
$ SEARCH MYFIL.DAT FRED
%SEARCH-E-NOFILE, no file found
-RMS-E-FNF, file not found
$ SHOW SYMBOL $STATUS
STATUS = "%X08D7804A"
```

UNIX (C shell)

```
% grep fred myfile.dat
fred
% echo $status
0
```

```
% grep jill myfile.dat
%
% echo $status

1
```

```
% grep fred myfil.dat
myfil.dat: no such file or directory
% echo $status
2
```

Perl

Example:

```
% perl -e '$status = system("grep fred myfile.dat"); print "$status\n";'
fred
0


% perl -e '$status = system("grep jill myfile.dat"); print "$status\n";'
256
% perl -e '$status = system("grep fred myfil.dat"); print "$status\n";'
grep: can't open myfil.dat
512
```

These examples illustrate the above statement using the grep command. If the command executes correctly and finds the search string, it returns a value of 0. If the command executes correctly, but does not find the search string, it returns a value of 1. If the file itself is not found, the condition is more severe and a value of 2 is returned. Compare this with OpenVMS, where $STATUS returns an odd-numbered value if the command execution succeeded. In the Perl example, we saw the same value for success (0), but failure return values do not appear to be the same. This is because the value returned is not just the exit value: It includes the signal number (if any) that the process died from. In other words, the status actually contains two 8-bit values in one 16-bit number. The Perl statement $exit_value = $status >> 8 is an example of how the exit value could be decoded from the return status, yielding the exact same values seen in the shell example. However, there is other useful information that can be found in this whole return status value, so be sure to refer to the Perl documentation for more details on what other exit conditions can be detected.

We will now put this all together in a shell script. This example reports on the type of error found when using grep, based on the value of status.

OpenVMS

Example:

```
$ TYPE TEST.COM
$! Error handling
$ SET NOON
$ SEARCH 'P2' 'P1'
$ IF ($SEVERITY .EQ. 1) THEN
GOTO 1
$ IF ($SEVERITY .EQ. 2) .OR. -
($SEVERITY .EQ. 4) THEN GOTO 2
$ IF (SEVERITY .EQ. 3) THEN
GOTO 3
$ EXIT
$ 1: WRITE SYS$OUTPUT -
"Execution successful"

$ EXIT
$ 2: WRITE SYS$OUTPUT "Error"
$ EXIT
$ 3: WRITE SYS$OUTPUT "Nothing
- found"
$ EXIT
```

UNIX (C shell)

```
% cat test_script
# Error handling
grep $1 $2
set error = $status
if ($error == 0) then
    echo "Execution successful"
    goto end
endif
if ($error == 1) then
    echo "Nothing found"
    goto end
endif
echo "Severe error found"
end:
exit
```

Perl

Example:

```
% cat test_script
#!/usr/bin/perl -w
# Error handling
$status = system("grep $ARGV[0] $ARGV[1]");
$error = $status >> 8;
if ($error == 0) {
  print "Execution successful\n";
  goto END;
}
if ($error == 1) {
  print "Nothing found\n";
  goto END;
}
print "Severe error found\n";
END: exit;
```

10.9 Built-in Shell Commands

Within your shell of choice, you need not worry about the distinction between built-in shell commands and separate programs called by the shell. However, C shell users who invoke the bash or Korn shells, or Korn and bash shell users who invoke the C shell, will discover that some familiar commands are not available. Some built-in shell commands discussed elsewhere are dirs, pushd, and popd for manipulating the directory stack; fg, bg, and jobs for background processing; at, kill, and nice for affecting processes; shift, alias, export, and integer for controlling variables; and history for reviewing the history list. Regardless of which shell is used, Perl programs should only call other programs rather than trying to access shell built-in functions, which, even if available, may not work as expected. In most cases, Perl provides its own built-in equivalent, or the same functionality can easily be achieved by other means.

We now introduce several new built-in shell commands particularly useful in shell programming: onintr and trap, which redirect the control of a script when an interrupt is issued; eval, which executes a command built from variables (forces the current process to interpret any shell metacharacters before performing the variable substitution); time, which determines the execution time and elapsed (wall-clock) time of a command or shell script; and . (dot) and source, which force the execution of commands or shell scripts by the parent shell.

10.9.1   `onintr` (C Shell) and `trap` (bash and Korn Shell)

The C shell command `onintr` and the Korn shell command `trap` redirect the flow of a script following certain conditions. The C shell `onintr` mechanism is a <CTRL>-C interrupt, whereas the Korn shell `trap` is a general purpose signal handler. In contrast, the OpenVMS command ON CONTROL_Y is an intermediate interrupt handler. In the manner of `onintr`, ON CONTROL_Y is limited to responding to a single event, but in the manner of `trap`, ON CONTROL_Y has a wide range of possible responses. Interrupt redirection is particularly useful to the OpenVMS user writing captive command proc-edures, that is, procedures that do not let the user escape to the command-language interpreter. UNIX captive shell scripts cannot be created so easily, since the user always has the option to stop the current process with <CTRL>-Z and fork another copy of the shell.

All four examples below are intended to produce the exact same output. When executed, a `Please wait...` message is displayed and the script sleeps for five seconds, simulating some lengthy task being performed. If the user takes no action, the program will eventually exit, reporting a normal completion. But if the user gets impatient and causes an interrupt (typically by pressing <CTRL>-C), an interrupt handler is called. This would be our opportunity to do any housekeeping, such as cleaning up temporary files created during the run, as well as to let the user know that the program was not allowed to complete normally.

OpenVMS

Form:

```
$ ON CONTROL_Y THEN COMMAND
```

Example:

```
$ TYPE INT.COM
$! user interrupt trap demo
$ Say := WRITE SYS$OUTPUT
$
$ INT_HNDL: SUBROUTINE
$   Say "-- Task interrupted"
```

UNIX (C shell)

```
% onintr label
...
label:
```

```
% cat int.csh
#!/usr/bin/csh
# user interrupt trap demo

# Establish interrupt handler
```

```
$!  delete temp files, etc.           onintr int_handler
$   Say "Failure exit."               echo "Please wait..."
$   STOP
$ ENDSUBROUTINE                       sleep 5
$                                     echo "-- Task completed"
$! Establish interrupt handler        echo "Normal exit"
$ ON CONTROL_Y THEN CALL INT_HNDL     exit
$! Do some work...                    int_handler:
$ Say "Please wait..."                echo "-- Task interrupted"
$ WAIT 00:00:05                       # delete temp files, etc.
$ Say "-- Task completed"             echo "Failure exit"
$ Say "Normal exit"                   exit
$ EXIT
```

Perl

Form:

`$SIG{INT} = \&`*SUBROUTINE*

Example:

```
$ cat int.pl
#!/usr/bin/perl -w
# user interrupt trap demo

sub int_handler {
  print("-- Task interrupted\n");
  # delete temp files, etc.
  print("Failure exit.\n");
  exit;
}


# Establish interrupt handler
$SIG{INT} = \&int_handler;
print("Please wait...\n");
# Do some work...
sleep(5);
print("-- Task completed\n");
print("Normal exit\n");
exit;
```

UNIX (bash and Korn shell)

`$ trap` *action signal*

```
$ cat int.bash
#!/bin/bash
# user interrupt trap demo
function int_handler {
  echo "-- Task interrupted"
  # delete temp files, etc.
  echo "Failure exit"
  exit
}
# Establish interrupt handler
trap int_handler INT
echo "Please wait..."
# Do some work...
sleep 5
echo "-- Task completed"
echo "Normal exit"
exit
```

In all of the examples, except for the C shell, we created a subroutine to handle the interrupt since this is the most common technique used for interrupt processing in Perl, bash, and Korn shell. While we have not formally defined what subroutines are or how to code them, experience with DCL subroutines is easily translated to these other languages. In contrast the C shell does not provide a subroutine mechanism, but instead does an implied `goto`, jumping to the label specified. We could have written our DCL example with the exact same structure as the csh example by using the statement ON CONTROL_Y THEN GOTO LABEL, instead of calling a subroutine.

INT (the situation to which `trap` responds) is an example of a UNIX *signal*. UNIX includes many (often implementation-dependent) signals. Some, such as INT and KILL (Section 12.3.1), are universal, although the means of sending them to a process will vary. In Tru64 UNIX and Red Hat Linux, you may generate INT by pressing the <CTRL>-C key. The command `kill -1` will list the signals available in your version of UNIX. Under bash, `trap -1` will also list the available signals, giving both the numeric and symbolic ways of naming them. The bash and Korn shell command `trap -signal` restores the previous response to the signal.

10.9.2 `eval` (C, bash, and Korn Shells, and Perl)

A fundamental principle shared by OpenVMS's DCL and the UNIX shells is the need to perform metacharacter expansion on the command line before attempting execution. The idea is that the command processor first scans the command string looking for special characters, acts on them, and then attempts to execute the resulting command. But sometimes scanning a command once is not enough; the resulting string may require additional interpretation to yield the desired effect. As you might expect, DCL and the UNIX shells use different approaches to solving this problem. The OpenVMS approach is to scan the command line twice automatically, performing symbol expansion on both passes. To control the order of expansion, two different dereferencing syntaxes are used: The familiar 'VAR' notation is used to perform symbol expansion on the first pass, and the more rarely seen &VAR notation is used to force symbol expansion on the second. In contrast with the UNIX shells and Perl, the user must explicitly use the `eval` built-in command to force the shell to reexamine the command before attempting execution. In the following example we intentionally attempt to delete a nonexistent file to force the program to reveal what the command-line environment has passed as a value to the program.

In the example below, we first define a variable that contains the name of what will be a second variable. We then define that second variable and assign to it the name of a nonexistent file. The first time we attempt to use our "pointer" variable, its name is replaced with its value. But in each environment, the program just ends up receiving a literal string, because in this context the command-line processor is not expecting a variable, and there was no explicit dereferencing. In the second attempt, the contents of the pointer variable are revealed to be our second variable, and then the com-

OpenVMS
Example:
```
$ PTR = "MYVAR"
$ MYVAR = "NO-SUCH.FILE"
$ DELETE 'PTR';0
%DELETE-W-SEARCHFAIL, error searching for DISK:[FRED]MYVAR.;0
-RMS-E-FNF, file not found
$ DELETE &'PTR';0
%DELETE-W-SEARCHFAIL, error searching for DISK:[FRED]NO-SUCH.FILE;0
-RMS-E-FNF, file not found
```

UNIX (bash syntax)
Example:
```
$ ptr='$myvar'
$ myvar='no-such.file'
$ rm $ptr
rm: cannot remove '$myvar': No such file or directory
$ eval rm $ptr
rm: cannot remove 'no-such.file': No such file or directory
```

mand processor rereads the command again. This causes the second variable to be expanded, revealing its own value, which is passed to the program.

Of course, the obvious question is when would you want to do this? Using the variable name `ptr` (pointer) may give a hint to programmers who already have experience with languages, like C, that have pointer variables. A pointer variable is a variable that doesn't contain a value, but, rather, points to the location where the value can be found. In the example above, our pointer variable didn't contain the name of the file to be deleted, but rather indicated where to find the name of that file.

It's difficult to come up with a typical program example that would make sense for both OpenVMS and UNIX in demonstrating this principle because the problems this reevaluation mechanism is used to solve tend to be very different for each environment. In OpenVMS, DCL does not provide an array symbol type, so this technique is most often used as a way of simulating array structures. With the UNIX shells (and also in Perl), `eval` is commonly used to build command strings in a variable and then force the execution of that resulting string after all metacharacter expansion has already been performed. The `eval` command is also needed when it is necessary to force string evaluation within the context of the current process before a child process is launched. This is an issue that rarely comes up in OpenVMS.

The following examples demonstrate typical usage of command reevaluation in both OpenVMS and UNIX.

OpenVMS

Example:

```
$ INDEX = 0
$ LOOP:
$    INDEX = INDEX + 1
$    IF P'INDEX' .EQS. "" THEN GOTO ENDLOOP
$    APPEND/NEW  &P'INDEX'  SAVE.ALL
$    DELETE &P'INDEX';*
$    IF INDEX .LT. 8 THEN GOTO LOOP
$
$ ENDLOOP:
```

UNIX

Example:

```
$ cat myprefs
#!/bin/bash
echo "Current settings for personal preferences:"
for myvar in EDITOR VISUAL PAGER; do
  eval eval "echo $myvar = '$'$myvar"
done
$ myprefs
Current settings for personal preferences:
EDITOR =
VISUAL = emacs
PAGER = less
```

In the OpenVMS example, each file specified on the command line is appended to a master file and deleted until a blank parameter value is seen or all possible parameter values are exhausted. Remember that DCL automatically scans each line twice, so the first time it encounters `&P'INDEX'`, it replaces symbol INDEX with its value, let's say 5, and then rescans the line replacing the symbol `&P5` with its value, the fifth command-line parameter.

In the UNIX example, the name and value of three common environment variables are displayed. Using the VISUAL variable as an example, the first time the command is scanned by the shell, the string is rendered as eval eval echo VISUAL = '$'VISUAL; that is, the first variable substitution is made. The shell executes this result where the first eval causes the string to be rescanned, yielding eval echo VISUAL = $VISUAL, which removes the strong quotes. (Remember $$ is a built-in variable, which is why the strong quotes were needed to protect the first $.) The shell executes the result when the second eval rescans the string yielding echo VISUAL = emacs. This command is finally executed by the shell, echoing the result to the terminal. (It's left as an exercise for the reader to see how this line could be rewritten using just a single eval expression. Hint: Try use the \ instead of strong quotes to protect metacharacters.)

10.9.3 time

There are multiple implementations of the time command, /usr/bin/time, the C shell built-in time command, the bash built-in time command, and the Korn shell built-in command time. All most closely compare with the OpenVMS command SHOW STATUS.

The built-in C shell command time reports the time it takes commands and shell scripts to execute. If no argument is given, time reports the time used by the parent process and all the child processes it has generated since the beginning of the terminal session.

OpenVMS
Form:
```
$ SHOW STATUS
```
Example:
```
$ SHOW STATUS
...
$ @TEST.COM
$ SHOW STATUS
Status on 2-AUG-1998 15:30:37.97 Elapsed CPU: 0 00:41:56.73
Buff. I/O : 5216 Cur. ws. : 350 Open files : 0
Dir. I/O : 423 Phys. Mem. : 177 Page Faults : 7688
```
UNIX (C shell)
Form:
```
% time [command]
```
Example:
```
HP-UX (C shell)
% time myscript
0.2u 0.1s 0:22 33%
```

Tru64 UNIX (C shell)

Example:

```
% time
0.03u 0.07s 0.01 90% 0+3k 0+3io 1pf+0w
```

Linux (C shell)

Example:

```
% time ls
...
0.070u 0.110s 0:00.44 4.0%          0+1k 0+0io 178pf+0w
```

The first example is from an HP-UX system and shows how `time myscript` returns the time it takes to execute the script file `myscript`, as follows:

`0.2u`	0 minutes and 2 seconds of user CPU time
`0.1s`	0 minutes and 1 second of system CPU time
`0:22`	0 minutes and 22 seconds of wall-clock time
`33%`	33% of the available CPU resources

The second example, taken from a system running Tru64 UNIX, shows the output of `time` without arguments. There are three additional fields:

`0+3k`	1K of physical memory + 3K of the memory stack
`0+3io`	0 pages input + 3 pages output to the disk (1 page typically = 512 bytes)
`1pf+0w`	1 page faulted in + 0 pages faulted out

The third example shows output from `time` on a Linux system using the C shell. Note how the information displayed is system-dependent.

Tru64 UNIX (Korn shell)	**Tru64 UNIX (separate executable)**
Form:	
`$ time [command]`	`$ /usr/bin/time command`
Example:	
`$ time ls -l`	`$ /usr/bin/time ls -l`
...	...
`real    0m0.41s`	`real    0.1`
`user    0m0.03s`	`user    0.0`

```
sys     0m0.10s                      sys     0.1
$ time                               $ /usr/bin/time
real    0m0.00s                      usage: time [-p] command
user    0m0.00s
sys     0m0.00s
```

These examples from Tru64 UNIX show the similarity between the Korn shell built-in and the command implemented as an executable file. In the first example, the execution of `ls -l` is timed. We see the following:

```
real 0m0.41s        The total elapsed time for the command to run

user 0m0.03s        The time it actually took to execute the command

sys 0m0.10s         The time spent in the kernel
```

While the output from the first example shows that `/usr/bin/time` is less precise, you can see that the output has similar meaning. The second example shows the more significant difference between the two, `/usr/bin/time` requires an argument (that is, another command) to `time`, while the Korn shell built-in (like the C shell built-in) does not. If the argument is omitted, `time` returns the user and system time for the current shell and completed child processes.

The GNU version of `/usr/bin/time`, available primarily on systems running GNU Linux, is implemented to give far more information:

GNU
Form:
```
$ /usr/bin/time [command]
```
Example:
```
$ /usr/bin/time ls -l
...
0.03user 0.00system 0:00.03elapsed 83%CPU
(0avgtext+0avgdata 0maxresident)k
0inputs+0outputs (185major+31minor)pagefaults 0swaps
```

Here we see the following:

```
0.03user            The time it actually took to execute the command

0.00system          The time spent in the kernel
```

`0:00.03elapsed`	The total elapsed time for the command to run
`83%CPU`	Percentage of the CPU that this process got
`(0avgtext+0avgdata` `0maxresident)k`	Kilobytes of average total memory use; average size of the process's unshared data area; maximum resident size
`0inputs+0outputs`	Process file-system input and outputs
`(185major+31minor)page` `faults`	Hard (disk read) and soft (page still valid) page faults
`0swaps`	Count of times the process was swapped out

If the argument to any implementation of `time` is a pipeline, then the information returned reflects the entire pipeline, not just the first command. You should read the man pages on your system for the shell you plan to use to understand the output from the `time` command you will see.

10.9.4   source (bash and C Shell) and . (dot) (bash and Korn Shell)

You can nest scripts by including the name of a script file as a command line in the current script file. Compare with OpenVMS, where `@COMMAND_PROCEDURE` is a command line in the current procedure. The shell running the current script file usually forks a child process with its own set of characteristics for the nested script to execute in. At the end of the nested script, control returns to the current script. Any definitions made by the child process are not passed back to the parent (compare with OpenVMS's global definitions, which become part of the parent command procedure). Preceding the nested script with the built-in C shell command `source` or the Korn shell command . (dot) prevents the forking of a child process and forces the current process to perform the execution, so that any definitions that the nested script makes become active for the current script. Implementation is the same in bash, but it accepts both the . (dot) and `source` commands. Regardless of the shell you use, be sure you separate the . (dot) command by one or more spaces from the rest of the command line! Otherwise, it will look like part of the path to the command.

The following two examples illustrate other important uses of the `source` command.

OpenVMS	**UNIX (C shell)**
Form:	
`$ @command_procedure`	`% source [-h] script_file`
Example:	
`$ @LOGIN.COM`	`% source .cshrc`
Example:	
`$ RECALL/INPUT=COMMANDS.LIS`	`% source -h history_list`

In the first example, `source .cshrc` invokes definitions for the parent shell if they have just been made through modification to the `.cshrc` file. If `source` had not been invoked, the user would have had to log out of the C shell and log back in again for the new definitions to take effect in the parent process. If `.cshrc` were executed without the `source` command, the child process forked to execute the command would make the definitions, which would immediately be lost when control returned to the parent process. The analog exists in the Korn shell, where the equivalent command would be `. $ENV`, or in bash, where it would be `. .bash_profile`.

A special note about "sourcing" a script into the parent shell process: Since the script is executed within the context of the current process, if the script contains the `exit` command, it will cause that process, not just the script, to exit. This means that if you source a script from your login shell process and that script performs an `exit`, you will immediately be logged out!

In the second example, `source -h history_list` adds a predefined set of commands contained in the file `history_list` to the history list. You could have created the file `history_list` with the command `history -h 15 > history_list`, for example. Note that you may save a specified number of commands from the history list with the shell command `set save-hist n`, which retains the last *n* commands. The history list is saved in the hidden file `.history` and is automatically made part of the history list at the beginning of the next terminal session with the command `source -h ~/.history`, invoked by the shell at startup time. While the Korn shell variable `HISTSIZE` has the same meaning for the `.sh_history` file as the C shell `savehist` variable has for `.history`, there is no convenient analog to the `history -h` command.

10.9.5   exec (C, bash, and Korn Shells)

The first form of the `exec` command has similar meaning to all three shells. The command `exec` goes one step further than `source` or `.` (dot) in that it substitutes the command for the current shell. Note how that differs from typical command execution, which takes place in a forked process, and from `source` and `.`, where the parent shell remains in existence. In Open-VMS, there is no way a procedure or an executing image can replace an existing process; each user-mode image you run reuses the address space of the one prior, and none replaces the command line interpreter (CLI), which lives in a slightly different part of the continuing address space assigned to your process. Perhaps the closest analog in OpenVMS is use of the RUN command to create a new process. Such a process can exist without a CLI and will terminate immediately when the image completes execution.

UNIX (Korn shell)
Form:
```
$ exec file-spec
```
Example:
```
$ cat test_script
  ls -l exit

$ exec test_script
total 1
-rwxr-xr-x  1   user1 staff 1024 24   Aug 13:40   myfile.txt
-rwxrwx--x  1   user1 staff 512 10    Jul 1996    test_script
login:
```

As in most of the example scripts in this book, we end `test_script` with an `exit` command. But look what happens here! Instead of another shell prompt, we are faced with logging in again. The `exit` command acts as though you had typed it interactively, and the process to which you issued the `exec` terminates. In fact, we could have omitted the `exit` command and achieved the same effect. Just as an interactive end of file (<CTRL>-D) can terminate a login session, the end of a script terminates the script and, in this case, the process which `exec`'d the script.

The second form of the `exec` command is unique to the Korn shell. It associates a file with an input stream, a generalization of redirecting `stdin` or `stdout`.

In this example, we illustrate that we need not only interactive responses from the user, but also information from a file at the same time. The `exec 5< test.dat` command tells the Korn shell to read from `test.dat` when we ask for input from unit 5. The first `read` command, which does not specify a unit number, tells the shell to get its input from `stdin`. The second

OpenVMS	UNIX (Korn shell)
Form:	
`$ OPEN/READ ` *`logical-name file-spec`*	`$ exec ` *`number< file`*
`$ OPEN/WRITE ` *`logical-name file-spec`*	`$ exec ` *`number> file`*
`$ CLOSE ` *`logical-name`*	`$ exec ` *`number<&-`* ` # Close for read`
	`$ exec ` *`number>&-`* ` # Close for write`
Example:	
`$ OPEN/READ INP TEST.DAT`	`$ exec 5< test.dat`
`$ READ SYS$INPUT INTERACTIVE_LINE`	`$ read interactive_line`
`$ READ INP A_LINE_AT_A_TIME`	`$ read -u5 a_line_at_a_time`
...	...
`CLOSE INP`	`$ exec 5<&-`

read command specifies unit 5, test.dat. Finally, we disassociate unit 5 from test.dat. Note that there is no white space between the unit number and the redirection character <.

10.10 Debugging Shell Scripts

You can explicitly invoke the C, bash, or Korn shell programs using the commands csh, bash, or ksh, respectively, supplying one or more options and the name of a script at that time. Two of those options, -x and -v, provide debugging aid during execution of the script. The result is similar to using the OpenVMS command SET VERIFY, either prior to or as part of a command procedure.

OpenVMS	UNIX (C shell)
Form:	
`$ SET VERIFY`	`% csh [`*`option(s)`*`] `*`script_file`*
`$ @`*`command_procedure`*	
Example:	`% cat test_script`
`$ TYPE TEST.COM`	
`$ DIR /FULL 'P1'`	`'P1' ls -l $1`
`$ EXIT`	`exit`
`$ SET VERIFY`	`% csh -x test_script a`
`$ @TEST_SCRIPT A`	`ls -l a`
`$ DIR /FULL A`	`A -rwxr-xr-x 1 fred 32 Aug 8 19:19 a`
`[directory listing here]`	`exit`
`$ EXIT`	

Example:
```
% csh -v test_script a
ls -l $1
-rwxr-xr-x 1 fred 32 Aug 8 19:19: a
exit
```

The construct `csh -x test_script` a echoes the command lines after variable substitution (-x option), and `csh -v test_script` a echoes the command lines prior to variable substitution (-v option). Hence, the -x option is useful for locating problems in variable substitution, and the -v option is useful for locating the line on which a script file is failing. And of course, -xv can be used to turn both options on at the same time. The -x and -v options (not shown) extend the features of -x and -v to include the .cshrc file when you have not used a fast start of the C shell.

The Korn shell implementation of -x and -v is similar, but includes some useful extensions. The first allows you to set up the effect of -x or -v interactively, so that all commands you issue are traced, both those executed immediately and those in scripts you invoke. The second extension makes traced commands stand out more.

UNIX (Korn shell)

Form:
```
$ set -x # Turn on tracing with variable substitution
$ set -o xtrace # Same as set -x
$ set -v # Turn on tracing as commands are read in
$ set -o verbose # Same as set -v
```

Form:
```
$ PS4=string # Trace indication string
```

Example:
```
$ cat test_script
print "Listing directory $1"
ls -l $1
$ PS4="From test_script> "
$ set -o xtrace
$ test_script mathcounts
From test_script> print "Listing directory mathcounts"
Listing directory mathcounts
From test_script> ls -l mathcounts
-rwxr-xr-x 1 McK 65536 Jan 8 19:19 practice_examples
$ rm test_script
```

```
From test_script> rm test_script
$ set +o xtrace
```

In this example, we replace the default trace indication string, +, with one specific to our needs, From test_script>. We then enable tracing with variable substitution already performed. When we execute the script test_script, we first see each line, once variables have been substituted, as the line is ready for execution. The line is preceded by the trace indication string. We next see the result from executing that line. The setting remains in place even after the script completes. At this point, the trace indication string has little meaning, although it too remains unchanged. Finally, we turn off tracing using set +o xtrace.

Perl does not provide an analog mechanism for the shell -x and -v options because of the way it works; a Perl script is first translated into intermediate code format, which is then executed. This is done to optimize the execution speed for the script, but the resulting intermediate code is nothing a human would want to try to read. Perl, however, does provide a debug option (-d), which can be invoked either on the command line or from within the script. This is a powerful interactive debugger, similar to those available for compiled languages, which allows the user to step through the program source code, statement by statement, as it is executing. All of the typical program debugger functionality is available, such as the ability to set breakpoints and examine and set variables during execution. See the perldebug man page for more information.

10.11 Summary

A discussion of three annotated C shell script files and a Perl script summarizes the features presented in this chapter.

The first script file, run_program, solicits the user's response to a number of questions and creates a script file containing the commands necessary to run a program called prolsq. The flow of the script depends on whether the user includes arguments as part of the command line. If the user specifies no arguments, the system prompts for the appropriate input.

```
UNIX
% cat run_program
bin/csh -f
# run_program: Use symbolic links to associate data files to the
# program
# PROLSQ and then execute the program.
```

```
#
# Display banner message
echo "= = = = = = = = = = = = = = = = = = = = = = = ="
echo " Prolsq Submission Procedure"
echo "= = = = = = = = = = = = = = = = = = = = = = = ="
echo " "
if ($1 == "help") then  # redirect flow if help required
    goto info
endif
if ($1 == " ") then
    echo "Interactive input mode..."  # determine if 1st argument
defined
    # yes: assume all arguments defined
    echo " "  # no: interactively prompt for arguments
else
    echo "Predefined input mode..."
    echo " "
    if ($7 == " ") then  # exit if all 7 arguments not defined
        echo "Incorrect number of arguments"
        exit
    endif
    set card1 = $1  # assign variables to input arguments

    set card2 = $2
    set card3 = $3
    set card4 = $4
    set card5 = $5
    set card6 = $6
    set card7 = $7
    goto start_execution  # move to execution phase
endif  # begin interactive input phase
echo -n "CONTROL DATA FILE (<cr> = prolsq.dat):"
set card1 = $<  # prompt for each input variable
if ($card 1 == "") then  # and assign it offering a default
    set card1 = "prolsq.dat"
endif
echo -n "INPUT RESTRAINTS FILE (<cr> = atmdst.dat):"
set card2 = $<  # repeat for remaining 6 arguments
if ($card2 == "") then
    set card2 = "atmdst.dat"
endif
echo -n "INPUT SHIFTS FILE (<cr> = shift.in):"
set card3 = $<
if ($card3 == "") then
    set card3 = "shift.in"
endif
echo -n "OUTPUT SHIFTS FILE (<cr> = shift.out):"
set card4 = $<
if ($card4 == "") then
    set card4 = "shift.out"
endif
echo -n "REFLECTION INPUT FILE (<cr> = prolsq.hkl)"
set card5 = $<
if ($card5 == "") then
```

```
        set card5 = "prolsq.hkl"
endif
echo -n "STRUCTURE FACTOR OUTPUT FILE (<cr> = prolsq.fofc)"
set card6 = $<
if ($card6 == "") then
    set card6 = "prolsq.fofc"
endif
echo -n "COORDINATE OUTPUT FILE (<cr> = prolsq.outxyz):"
set card7 = $<
if ($card7 == "") then
    set card7 == "prolsq.outxyz"
endif
#
# start_execution:
# write all program parameters to a script file run_prolsq.scr
echo "#" > run_prolsq.scr   # open run_prolsq.scr
echo "cd $cwd" >> run_prolsq.scr   # append to run_prolsq.scr
echo "ln -s $card2 fort.10" >>run_prolsq.scr
echo "ln -s $card3 fort.15" >> run_prolsq.scr
echo "ln -s $card4 fort.16" >> run_prolsq.scr
echo "ln -s $card5 fort.20" >> run_prolsq.scr
echo "ln -s $card6 fort.31" >> run_prolsq.scr
echo "ln -s $card7 fort.32" >> run_prolsq.scr
echo "ln -s /stripe/idisk fort.3" >> run_prolsq.scr
echo "ln -s /stripe/jdisk fort.4" >> run_prolsq.scr
echo "time prolsq.exe < $card1" >> run_prolsq.scr   # $card1 is stdin
run-prolsq.scr   # run program giving the execution time
exit   # output is written to stdout
# helpful information
info:
echo " "
echo "Prolsq arguments:"
echo "argv(1)   control data file   (unit 5)   default prolsq.dat"
echo "argv(2)   input coordinates   (unit10)   default atmdst.dat"
echo "argv(3)   input shifts   (unit15)   default shifts.in"
echo "argv(4)   output shifts   (unit16)   default shifts.out"
echo "argv(5)   reflection list   (unit20)   default newrefs.dat"
echo "argv(6)   structure factor output   (unit31)   default \
fofc.out"
echo "argv(7)   coordinate output   (unit32)   default xyz.out" \
echo " "
echo "N.B., idisk (unit3) and jdisk (unit4) are scratch files \
written and"
echo " read in a stripe partition, i.e., simultaneously writes to \
2"
echo " filesystems"
exit
```

First, run_program tests for input arguments. If the first argument is
"help", control passes to the statement label info, which displays information on running the script and then exits. If the first argument is not
defined as "help", the script assumes that all arguments have been defined

on the command line and that interactive prompting is not required. Flow passes to a statement that checks whether all seven required arguments have been specified. If they have, control passes to the statement label `start_execution`. If all seven arguments have not been defined, the script terminates with an error message. If no arguments have been specified, the script prompts the user for the appropriate input, offering default responses.

Once the variables `card1` through `card7` have been defined in a script file, `run_prolsq.scr` is generated, containing the appropriate symbolic links to associate data files with FORTRAN unit numbers. Of course, how data files are associated with FORTRAN unit numbers depends on the version of UNIX and the version of the FORTRAN compiler. The program `prolsq.exe` then executes with the `time` command providing timing information; any program output is sent to `stdout`, the terminal.

The second example, `menu_script`, illustrates the use of a menu interface to access a simple database consisting of a number of files. Each file in the database contains a field called a recognition code at the end of each record, which is part of the name of the file. Each menu option that accepts a recognition code uses that code to point to one or more files.

```
UNIX
% cat menu_script
#!/bin/csh -f
#= = = = = = = = = = = = = = = = = = = = = = = = =
# menu_script: simple menu driven database lookup
#= = = = = = = = = = = = = = = = = = = = = = = = =
#
#
# retain original directory pointer and move to database directory
# pushd /data1/pdb
# present banner
echo " cuhhca Brookhaven Database Utility Program `date` "
# `(back quote) causes immediate execution of the date command
# to return the time the script was invoked
#
onintr menu  # on interrupt return to menu
menu:
echo " "  # present menu of options
echo " The following options are available:"
echo " "
echo " I list identity of the database"
echo " D list a directory of the database contents"
echo " SD search the directory listing for keywords"
echo " SF search full database for keywords"
echo " T list a database entry at the terminal"
echo " C copy database entry with possible format conversion"
echo " Q quit the database"
```

```
echo " "
echo -n "Option>"  # user enters option here
set command = $<
goto $command  # branch to option
#
# identity option---describes latest database update
#
I:   # account for upper and
i:   # and lowercase user response
echo "This database is the April 1986 release"
#
goto menu  # return to menu
#

# directory option---display a file summarizing all database
entries
#
D:
d:
echo " Type <ctrl>-C to return to menu"
echo " "
echo " Use the 4 character recognition code at the end of each
entry"
echo " to address entries with subsequent menu options"
# The file directory contains header information for each file in
# directory and was created with the command head -4 *.dat >> directory
#
cat directory
goto menu
#
# search directory for keywords using grep---records returned
# contain filename from where they were originally extracted with
# the head command
#
SD:
sd:
echo " "
echo -n "keyword(s).-"
set string = $<
grep -i "$string" directory  # disregard case or string (i)
goto menu
#
# search all files for string N.B. this is much slower than
# searching the file directory and should be used only after
# the search directory option has failed to return useful
# information
#
sf:
SF:
echo -n "Keyword(s):-"
set string = $<
grep -i $string *.dat  # search all data files
goto menu
#
```

```
# list a database entry
#
T:
t:
echo -n "Enter recognition code:-"  # code obtained from a search
option
set entry = $<
cat 'entry'
goto menu
#
# Copy entry---calls a program format.exe which will format a
# database entry suitable for editing. The user is
# prompted for the output file and appropriate symbolic links
# established for the input file (database entry) and output file
# (user file)
#
C:
c:
echo -n "Enter recognition code:-"
set temp_filein = $<
set filein = '/data1/pdb/pdb'$temp_filein
echo -n "Filename for output coordinates [/group/user/file]:"
set fileout = $<
ln -s $filein fort.1
ln -s $fileout fort.2
format.exe
rm fort.*  # remove symbolic links
goto menu
#
# FINITO---gracefully exit the script from the menu
#
Q:
q:
echo "Exit Brookhaven database utility program  `date` "
popd  # return user to original directory
exit
```

The script file menu_script presents a menu of options to the user. The user's response to the option list directs flow control. The script retains the present working directory for later recovery using pushd and popd. Files are searched with grep for strings specified by the user, entries are typed with cat, or the program program.exe is executed, performing a format conversion specified by the user.

In the next example, which locates the path to any commands given as arguments, provided the path is in the user's path list. The which command is useful for finding the directory in which a system program or user program resides. This example comes directly from the BSD version of UNIX, with additional comments for clarity.

UNIX

```
% cat /etc/ucb/which
#! /bin/csh -f
# fast start of the C shell
#
# @(#)which.csh 4.2 (Berkeley)  83/02/14
#
# which : locate the path to a command i.e. what directory it
# is in
#
set prompt  # pretend this shell is interactive -strike
set path2 = $PATH # save PATH in case it gets changed in.cshrc
# if .cshrc exists, execute it in the current shell to establish
# any aliases
if (-e ~/.cshrc) source ~/.cshrc
setenv PATH $path2 # restore PATH
# prevent variable name expansion
set noglob
#
# loop for each argument (i.e. command) given
#
foreach arg ($argv)
    set alius = `alias $arg`  # determine if the argument is an
alias
    switch ( $#alius )  # 0 = no; 1 = yes
        case 0:  # if so use the first real command name
            breaksw
        case 1:
            set arg = $alius [1]
            breaksw
        default :
            echo ${arg}:"  "aliased to $alius
            continue
    endsw
    unset found
    if ( $arg:h != $arg:t ) then  # if a path is specified
        if ( -e $arg ) then  # if file exists in current directory
      echo $arg
        else
      echo $arg not found
        endif
        continue
    else  # only command name given
        foreach i ($path)  # check for existence in each element of
path
      if (-x $i/$arg && ! -d $i/$arg) then
                echo $i/$arg
                set found  # found exists
                break
            endif
        end
    endif
    if (! $?found) then  # if found does not exist
        echo no $arg in $path
```

```
        endif
 end
```

The which BSD command script accepts multiple arguments (in this case commands). For each argument, which determines whether that command is an alias. If so, it uses the standard command name to determine the path. The which command then determines whether a path has been included as part of the argument. If so, the script determines whether the file exists in the directory specified (that is, it functions like the ls command) and then exits. If a path is not specified, foreach is used to check each directory in the path list. If the command is found, is not a directory, and is executable, the path is reported and the script exits or checks the next argument supplied. If, on the other hand, after exhausting the path list, the command is not found, that fact is reported, and the script exits or checks the next argument.

The last example, smart-rename, is a Perl script that attempts to redress a pet peeve many OpenVMS users have with UNIX. To make programs that deal with multiple files simpler to code, UNIX shells expand wild-carded filenames on the command line before executing the program and handing it its parameters. Since the program never sees the actual wildcard pattern used, it is limited in how smart it can be about what is being requested. For example, an OpenVMS user wanting to rename a set of files would think nothing of entering RENAME *.DAT *.DATA and would simply expect the right thing to happen. In contrast, the UNIX command mv *.dat *.data doesn't do what the OpenVMS user expects; all of the "dat" files are matched and expanded on the command line, the "data" spec probably matches nothing and drops away, the move command starts up and finds (if the user is lucky) three or more files and reports (if the user is lucky) that the last file is not a directory. In other words, when given more than two filenames, move expects that it is moving a set of files into a directory, not just changing their names.

This Perl script provides a very flexible method of file renaming, allowing OpenVMS-like renaming of sets of files, as well as some renaming tricks that would not be so easily done on that system.

Perl
```
$ cat smart-rename
#!/usr/local/bin/perl -w
#
#  Rename files using Perl regular expressions.

die("$0: Sorry - tested only under V5 of Perl\n") if ($] < 5.0);
```

```
#==========================================
# Check parameters and prompt for Perl expression.
#==========================================

die("usage:  $0  files... \n") if (@ARGV <= 0);
print(STDERR "  Enter Perl expression,\n or press [ENTER] for help
> ");
$op = <STDIN>;
chomp($op);
if ($op eq "")
   {
     print STDERR <<'HELP' ;
Enter a Perl expression that will transform the contents of the $_
variable from the names you have to the names you want. You will
be shown a list of all changes *before* they are made allowing you
to change your mind before committing.

Examples:

   (1) strip extension from all files matching *.bak

        s/\.bak$//

   (2a) append ".bak" to all specified files

        $_ .= ".bak"

   (2b) as above only using substitution

        s/$/.bak/

   (3) change all *foo*, *Foo*, and *FOO* files to *_bar_*

        s/foo/_bar_/i

   (4) translate uppercase names to lower case

        tr/A-Z/a-z/

   (5) rename  input_*.dat  output_*.dat

        s/input_(.*).dat/output_$1.dat/

HELP
     exit;
   } # if ($op eq "")
#==============================================
# For each file-spec, check to see if it exists and then determine
# and remember the resulting new name.
#==============================================
```

```
$changeCnt = 0;
@tempArray = @ARGV;
foreach (@tempArray)
  {
    if (not -f $_)
      {
        warn("$0: skipping non-plain file: $_\n");
        next;
      }
    die("\n$0: no such file: $_\n") if (not -e $_);
    $was = $_;
    if (not defined($spec{$was}))
      {
        $spec{$was} = "the specified file '$was'";      # never
# seen before, remember it
      }
    else  # uh oh, we've seen this name before.
      {
        die(" '$was' rename will collide with\n '$spec{$was}'\n",
            "$0: aborting, no files renamed\n",
          );
      }

    eval $op;
    die($@) if ($@);
    die("would have renamed '$was' to itself\n") if ($was eq $_);

    if (-e $_)
      {
        die("rename would have overwritten existing file:\n",
            "_         $_\n",
            "_ with $was\n",
          );
      }

    if (not defined($spec{$_}))
        { $spec{$_} = "'$_' (file that was renamed from $was)";
}
    else { die("renaming: $was\n_ will collide with $spec{$_}\n");
}

    $changeCnt++;
    print(STDERR "--existing--> $was\n will become: $_\n");
  }

#===========================
# Time to commit changes, maybe
#===========================

die("\n$0: no files would have been renamed\n\n")  if ($changeCnt
<= 0);
```

```
print(STDERR "$changeCnt files will be renamed\n\n",
            "   enter YES to commit changes> "
      );

$commit = <STDIN>;
chomp($commit);

if ($commit !~ m/^\s*YES\s*$/)
  {
    die("\n$0: no files will be renamed\n");
  }
else
  {
    $changeCnt = 0;
    foreach (@ARGV)
      {         $was = $_;
        eval $op;
        die $@ if ($@);
        next if ($was eq $_);
        rename($was,$_) or die("\n$0: unable to rename '$was' to
'$_'\n");
        $changeCnt++;
        print(STDERR "               $was\n renamed to: $_\n");
      }
      print(STDERR "$0: $changeCnt files renamed\n");
  }

exit(0);

#=======================
# EOF: smart-rename
#=======================
```

The Perl script starts out by checking to see if any filenames have been
entered on the command line and provides a short usage message if not.
Next, the user is prompted for a Perl expression that will transform each of
the filenames into the desired form, but a short help message with examples
is provided if the user enters nothing. With the preliminaries out of the
way, the script examines the specified files. Remember that UNIX treats
many things, such as devices, as if they were files, so we need to disregard
anything given to us that was not a "plain old file." For each file we perform
the proposed transformation, check to see if a file by that name already
exists, and then remember the new name. If it turns out the name is the
same as an already existing file, or if the next generated name is the same as
one that was already created from a previous file, this will cause a fatal error.
Finally, we show what the name transformations will be and ask the user to

give a final okay before making the changes. This script could be made more UNIX-like by accepting the Perl expression as the first parameter and by using command-line flags for things like committing the changes without confirmation or allowing existing files to be clobbered. These "improvements" are left to the reader to implement, based on his or her personal experience and confidence!

Administration

Administration

> *Though this be madness, yet there is method in't.*
> —*William Shakespeare, Hamlet, Act II, Scene ii*

This chapter introduces commands, utilities, and scripts used to administer UNIX systems by contrasting them with their OpenVMS counterparts. In this chapter, we assume a multiuser UNIX system that supports many users in a networked environment. The typical UNIX system is attached to other computers in corporate intranets, as well as to the Internet.

Administering systems and networks is a complex task. Quite often, vendors provide their own customized, proprietary tools and procedures for system and network installation. It is beyond the scope of this book to provide a detailed description of all the tasks that a system manager needs to perform. Instead, this chapter examines the following specific tasks, which are important to anyone managing operating systems like OpenVMS or UNIX:

- Installing software
- Starting up and shutting down the system
- Using system initialization files
- Managing groups and user accounts
- Backing up and restoring files
- Administering security
- Configuring networks

The traditional method for accomplishing these tasks on UNIX is to run a variety of scripts, commands, and utilities. Many vendors have developed unified administration applications to simplify matters. For example, Tru64 UNIX offers a graphical SysMan suite of tools that can be selected from the CDE front panel. HP-UX offers a similar tool, called the HP-UX System Administrator Manager, under its HP-VUE GUI. While these are a great help to the system administrator, such proprietary tools present quite different interfaces. Commands generally allow noninteractive processing, whereas GUIs do not. Therefore, this chapter stresses the command-line interfaces for administration that are common on many implementations of UNIX. Many of the UNIX examples show the command syntax used on Tru64 UNIX.

11.1   Installing Software

In OpenVMS, there are two methods for installing and upgrading software. The older method, developed for OpenVMS VAX systems, uses the VMSIN-STAL.COM command procedure. The newer, preferred method is the POLY-CENTER Software Installation (PCSI) utility. In addition to various improvements over VMSINSTAL.COM, the PCSI utility offers a choice of DCL- or Motif-style interfaces.

Because there are so many versions of UNIX available on a range of hardware platforms, there is really no standard installation procedure that applies to all systems. Each vendor provides tools and utilities for installing the operating system and optional software.

For example, to install UNIX software packages and applications for UNIX systems such as Solaris and UnixWare, use the pkadd utility. Linux from Red Hat Software uses the Red Hat Package Manager. Other applications use their own format or a tar archive format. Section 7.3.1.3 discusses how to extract files from tape using the tar utility.

On Tru64 systems, the setld command corresponds to VMSINSTAL.COM. The following examples illustrate the steps for installing an optional product.

In the first OpenVMS example, the PCSI utility subcommand PRODUCT INSTALL is used to install the latest version of FORTRAN. The second OpenVMS example uses the VMSINSTAL.COM procedure to install the product CALENDAR from the saveset CALENDAR020 on the CD-ROM device DKA400. The UNIX command loads the product OSFXMAIL from the subset OSFXMAIL100, which is from the CD-ROM device rz4c.

OpenVMS	UNIX
Form:	

```
$ PRODUCT INSTALL [product-name] --
[/qualifiers]
```

Example:

```
$ PRODUCT INSTALL FORTRAN
The following products have been
selected:
DEC AXPVMS FORTRAN V7.0 Layered
Product
Do you want to continue? [YES]
...
```

```
$ @SYS$UPDATE:VMSINSTAL -          % /usr/sbin/setld [options] \
product-name source-media -          [subset-name]
[OPTIONS options-list]
$ @VMSINSTAL CALENDAR020 -         % /usr/sbin/setld -l /dev/rz4c \
DKA400                               OSFXMAIL400
```

Both OpenVMS and UNIX provide the facilities for remote installation of software. The InfoServer Client for OpenVMS software enables clients running on an OpenVMS system to access virtual device services on a local-area network and perform a number of tasks, including software installation. Compare this with a facility available for Tru64 UNIX, the remote installation services (RIS) software: The ris utility configures, deletes, and displays software products that are available for installation.

11.2   Startup Procedures

It is not practical to describe all the bootstrap procedures for every implementation of UNIX, since there are so many types of hardware platforms available, and the bootstrap procedures will vary between them. Booting OpenVMS also varies depending on the VAX or Alpha model being used.

The command that you use to boot the UNIX kernel depends on several factors:

- The processor type
- The run level you want (described in Section 11.2.1)

- The location of the kernel that you are booting (on the boot disk or on a remote server)

- Whether any console environment variables are defined (Environment variables are similar in function to OpenVMS DCL symbols and logical names or SYSGEN parameters.)

- Whether you are booting the default kernel or an alternate kernel

Regardless of what computer is being used, the startup procedures for OpenVMS and UNIX cause a number of programs and scripts to run, and they perform such tasks as the following:

- Loading bootstrap programs into memory

- Configuring virtual address space

- Loading system images

- Starting system initialization

- Running startup procedures

Typically, when a UNIX system is booted, the system begins running processes associated with a particular initialization state (often called init state, or run level). The init process starts up processes based on the initialization states defined in the inittab file. The directory location of the inittab file will vary depending on the vendor. On some systems, this command is located in the /etc directory (e.g., Linux or Tru64); on other systems it may be in /sbin.

A typical UNIX system can operate in two different user modes: *single-user* and *multiuser*. Single-user mode is used when the administrator needs to perform system management operations without other users on the system.

11.2.1   Run Levels and System Initialization

A run level specifies the state of the system and defines which processes are allowed to run at that state. The primary Tru64 run levels are as follows:

- 0: the halt state

- s, S: single-user state

- 2: multiuser state without network services

- 3: multiuser state with network services, including X11

Other run levels exist, but they are left for definition at installation. Under Red Hat Linux, one has the following run levels:

- 0: the halt state
- 1, s, S: single-user state
- 2: multiuser mode without network services
- 3: multiuser mode with network services
- 4: unused
- 5: X11
- 6: reboot

The `/etc/inittab` file contains line entries that define the specific run levels and the `/rcn` command scripts that are associated with the run level *n*. When the `init` process starts, it reads the `inittab` file and executes the relevant `run` command scripts. The scripts, in turn, define which processes are to run at a specific run level and which processes are to be killed when the system changes run levels.

OpenVMS can be booted to states analogous to UNIX boot levels: stand-alone, multiuser without networking, and full timesharing with network access. The decision to boot stand-alone is made based on the contents of the SYSGEN parameter STARTUP_P1. If STARTUP_P1 contains MINIMUM, the OpenVMS system boots just far enough to allow you to log in at the operator's console.

11.2.2 Boot Sequence on UNIX

Figure 11.1 shows the typical sequence of events in the booting of a UNIX system.

11.3 System Initialization Files

A number of files establish the computing environment each time a UNIX system is booted.

Some applications require that certain elements be initialized when the system starts. Often, the applications have scripts in a run-state directory. Typically, the run-state directories on UNIX systems are hierarchies under

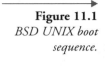

Figure 11.1
*BSD UNIX boot
sequence.*

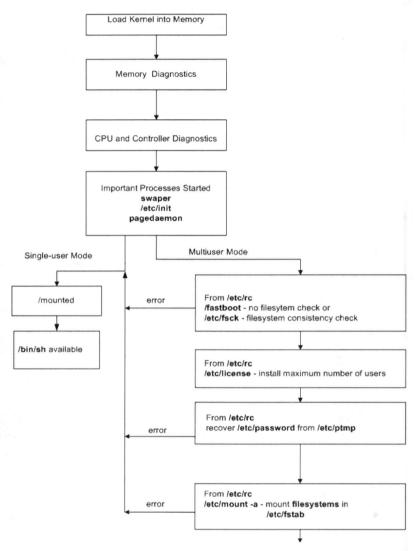

the /etc (e.g., Linux) or /sbin (Tru64) directory and are identified by
rc*n*.d, where *n* specifies a number corresponding to a run level. Run-state
directories include the following:

Figure 11.1
(continued)
BSD UNIX boot
sequence.

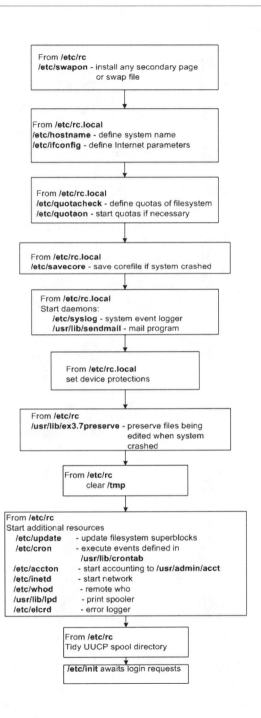

From **/etc/rc**
/etc/swapon - install any secondary page
                         or swap file

From **/etc/rc.local**
/etc/hostname - define system name
/etc/ifconfig - define Internet parameters

From **/etc/rc.local**
/etc/quotacheck - define quotas of filesystem
/etc/quotaon - start quotas if necessary

From **/etc/rc.local**
/etc/savecore - save corefile if system crashed

From **/etc/rc.local**
Start daemons:
     /etc/syslog - system event logger
     /usr/lib/sendmail - mail program

From **/etc/rc.local**
set device protections

From **/etc/rc**
/usr/lib/ex3.7preserve - preserve files being
                                       edited when system
                                       crashed

From **/etc/rc**
     clear **/tmp**

From **/etc/rc**
Start additional resources
     /etc/update   - update filesystem superblocks
     /etc/cron   - execute events defined in
                               /usr/lib/crontab
     /etc/accton   - start accounting to **/usr/admin/acct**
     /etc/inetd   - start network
     /etc/whod   - remote who
     /usr/lib/lpd   - print spooler
     /etc/elcrd   - error logger

From **/etc/rc**
Tidy UUCP spool directory

/etc/init awaits login requests

- rc0.d: contains startup scripts relating to the shut down and reboot states
- rc2.d: contains startup scripts relating to multiuser run states
- rc3.d: contains startup scripts relating to the networking run state

The files in these directories are linked to the commands in the init.d directory in the same hierarchy that the system executes when starting or changing a particular run level.

Table 11.1 describes some of the important system initialization files that are common on many UNIX systems, along with their OpenVMS counterparts. Note that locations and names will vary for some versions of UNIX. Appendix C lists additional important system files.

Table 11.1 *Comparison of System Initialization Files*

UNIX File Name	OpenVMS Equivalent	Description
/usr/sys/conf/SYSTEM-NAME	PARAMS.DAT VAXVMSSYS.PAR SYCONFIG.COM	Defines the components that the system builds into your configuration
/usr/sys/conf/param.c	PARAMS.DAT VAXVMSSYS.PAR MODPARAMS.DAT	Contains default values for some tunable system parameters used in building the system's kernel
/etc/sysconfigtab	VAXVMSSYS.PAR MODPARAMS.DAT SYS$CONFIG.DAT	Defines other dynamically tunable parameters
/etc/rc.config	PARAMS.DAT VAXVMSSYS.PAR MODPARAMS.DAT	Contains run-time configuration variables
/etc/fstab	SYSTARTUP_VMS.COM SYPAGSWPFILES.COM	Describes how to mount local and remote file systems and make them available to the system and users; also contains information about swap devices
/etc/inittab	SYSTARTUP_VMS.COM	Defines run levels and associated processes and administers terminals (see 11.2.1)

Table 11.1 *Comparison of System Initialization Files (continued)*

UNIX File Name	OpenVMS Equivalent	Description
/etc/init.d	SYS$STARTUP: SYSTARTUP_VMS.COM	A directory; contains start-up scripts for applications
/sbin/rcn.d	SYS$STARTUP: SYSTARTUP_VMS.COM	A set of individual directories; *n* specifies a number corresponding to a run level
/etc/ttys		Marks whether a given tty (terminal) line allows root logins; also configures and declares tty to the system
/etc/gettydefs		Contains entries to identify and define terminal line attributes
/etc/disktab		Describes the geometries and default partition sizes of the supported disks
/etc/passwd	SYSUAF.DAT	Contains information about local accounts
/etc/group	SYSUAF.DAT	Contains a list of valid groups along with the users who belong to each specific group
/etc/hosts	Network database	Contains information regarding the known hosts on the network
/etc/exports		Defines directories that are exported and may be mounted, using NFS, by other network hosts
/etc/printcap	SYCONFIG.COM SYSTARTUP_VMS.COM	Contains information about printer characteristics
/var/spool/cron/crontabs		A directory; contains the commands that run at pre-determined times
/etc/motd	SYS$ANNOUNCE.COM SYS$WELCOME.COM	Contains systemwide announcements

11.3.1 Shutdown Procedures

Shutting down a system is similar in OpenVMS and UNIX. The UNIX `/sbin/shutdown` command is analogous to the OpenVMS command procedure `SYS$SYSTEM:SHUTDOWN.COM`. Alternatively, many vendors have added a shutdown manager application to the CDE front panel.

We recommend that administrators use an "orderly shutdown" method to bring down any multiuser system, whether it be UNIX or OpenVMS. The important command-line steps in an orderly shutdown of a UNIX system include the following. Note that there are variations in the UNIX procedures, as there are with OpenVMS.

1. Prevent new logins using the `nologin` file; for example, `% /usr/bin/touch /etc/nologin` creates an empty file as a flag to the system to prevent any further logins. Compare this step with the SET LOGINS /INTERACTIVE=0 command on OpenVMS.

2. Issue the `shutdown` command, stating the amount of time before the shutdown, and notify all logged-in users. For example, the Tru64 UNIX command `% /sbin/shutdown +10 "System is going down to perform backups"` begins a shutdown of the system to single-user mode in 10 minutes and issues a message to all users.

    The equivalent under Red Hat Linux would be `% /sbin/shutdown -t 10 "System is going down to perform backups"`

3. Once in single-user mode, dismount all file systems; for example:

    ```
    # cd /etc
    # /sbin/umount -a
    ```

    Note that # is the prompt for single-user mode.

4. Synchronize disks (i.e., write cached data out to the disks), and halt the processor:

    ```
    # /sbin/sync
    # /sbin/halt
    ```

The `/sbin/shutdown` command on most UNIX systems performs steps 1, 3, and 4 automatically. Read the man page for `/sbin/shutdown` and compare it with the OpenVMS executable `SYS$SYSTEM:OPCCRASH.EXE`.

11.4   Managing User Accounts and Groups

An important task for the administrator of any multiuser system is to manage users and groups. On OpenVMS, the main tool for these tasks is the AUTHORIZE utility. Using AUTHORIZE, the administrator can perform a number of tasks, including adding or deleting users, defining default login directories, maintaining passwords, and assigning privileges. User account information is stored in the SYSUAF.DAT file.

On OpenVMS, the AUTHORIZE commands ADD, REMOVE, and MODIFY are used to add, remove, and modify users, respectively. For managing user accounts and groups from the command line, UNIX systems typically have a password file named /etc/passwd and a group file named /etc/group. To update these files, the administrator can edit the files directly, although this is not recommended since it presents a security risk, as well as the risk of corrupting the system. The password field in /etc/passwd is encrypted and is directly edited only to disable an account. On Tru64 UNIX systems, the administrator can also use the useradd, usermod, userdel, groupadd, groupmod, and groupdel commands.

As an alternative to command-line administration, many UNIX systems provide an integrated GUI to managing user accounts. For example, Solaris provides the admintool application. Tru64 UNIX provides user administration tools as part of the SysMan suite of graphics tools.

11.4.1   What Happens During Login on UNIX

Several files control the sequence of events that occur when a user logs in on a UNIX system. Some files, such as .profile, .login, and .cshrc, can be specified by the user for each shell (compare with OpenVMS's LOGIN.COM). The administrator is responsible for setting up and maintaining systemwide files, such as the /etc/passwd and /etc/group files.

A typical sequence of events (see Figure 11.2) for a login from a terminal on a UNIX system is as follows:

1.   The file /etc/passwd is accessed, and the password entered by the user is verified.

2.   The file /etc/group is accessed to provide primary and secondary group names.

3.   The user is placed in the home directory defined in /etc/passwd.

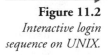

Figure 11.2
Interactive login sequence on UNIX.

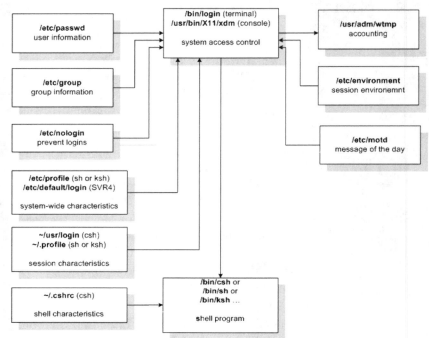

4.   The message specified in /etc/motd is displayed.

5.   Any systemwide /etc/profile and /etc/csh.login files are executed (see Sections 3.2).

6.   Any user-defined files such as .profile and .login are executed. The actual files executed depend on the shell defined as the default by the user (see Sections 3.2.1 through 3.2.3).

11.4.2 The /etc/passwd File

Data in the /etc/passwd file is used to verify that only valid users log in (compare with OpenVMS's SYSUAF.DAT file). If the NIS are used, the password file is located elsewhere, for example, /var/yp/passwd or the file /var/yp/*domain/passwd.byname.page*, and shared by multiple hosts.

The following is an example of an /etc/passwd file.

Example:

```
% cat /etc/passwd
root:ChKeDrL9y4lis:0:0:Superuser:/:/bin/sh
sys:nKqb19xOsGyiQ:0:0:Privileged account::/:
```

```
daemon:*:1:1:daemons:/:/dev/null
bin:*:2:2:System Tools Owner:/bin:
adm:*:5:3:Accounting Files Owner:/var/adm:
lp:*:9:9:Print Spooler Owner:/var/spool/lp:
nobody:*:60001:60001:SVR4 nobody uid:/dev/null:
noaccess:*:60002:60002:uid no access:/dev/null:/
operator:qfdc8TwxpXndA:99:99:Operator Account:/users/op/operator:/bin/csh
herb:0wdJc6aTRk5ZY:103:100:Herbert Johns:/users/op/herb:/bin/csh
consult:82TNaqLdftNqw:116:300:Consultant:/users/us/consult:/bin/ksh
smith:doS2uJm0s/Pvc:122:200:Wayne Smith:/users/sy/smith:/bin/csh
andym:ob9SMhVb2.84k:29286:400:Andy Menyhar:/users/u1/andym:/bin/csh
jwm:eFwZY4MMbOeIc:29288:998:Joseph MacMillan:/users/guests/jwm:/bin/csh
sylvia:Ay51tKNCqa/Ok:29289:998:Sylvia Hernandez:/users/guests/sylvia:/bin/csh
sml:FVy1wsFQobfnA:29500:200:Sarah Lilly:/users/sy/sml:/bin/ksh
```

For each user on the system, the /etc/passwd file contains a line with the following format:

name:*password*:*UID*:*GID*:*user-info*:*home-directory*:*shell*

The colon (:) is used to delimit fields of data—a practice common to a number of UNIX files. These fields contain the following information about the user:

- User name
- Password (encrypted)
- User identification number (UID)
- Group identification number (GID)
- Full name and additional information, such as telephone number
- Home directory
- Login shell

Unlike the OpenVMS file SYSUAF.DAT, access to which requires a specific utility, such as AUTHORIZE, the /etc/passwd file is a text file and is accessible to UNIX via commands such as cat, more, less, grep, and vi. What's more, in a throwback to the beginnings of UNIX, /etc/passwd is world-readable (but writeable only by the superuser). In fact, /etc/passwd is often use to illustrate the way the awk command can take apart and manipulate lines of data.

11.4.3 The /etc/group File

A *group* consists of a collection of users who are permitted access to specific files and directories. This concept is roughly the same on both UNIX and OpenVMS. On UNIX, the /etc/group file lists valid groups and the users belonging to those groups. The /etc/group file also specifies users permitted to become superusers by including those users in the system group.

Here is an example of an /etc/group file:

Example:

```
% cat /etc/group
system:*:0:root
daemon:*:1:root,daemon
bin:*:2:root,daemon
adm:*:3:root,adm,daemon
mail:*:4:root
kmem:*:8:root,adm
lp:*:9:
install:*:40:jpg,hutton,gross,terryh,julia
umich:*:50:georgec,sml,bec,jwm,herb,voris
class:*:512:mjb
vis550:*:550:
guests:*:998:dorisc,sarahm
```

Each line in the /etc/group file corresponds to a single group and contains the following fields:

- Group name
- Group password, represented by an asterisk (*)
- GID
- Group members, separated by commas

A user may be a member of multiple groups; that user is able to switch between those groups during a login session using the chgrp command and is thereby permitted access to different files, directories, and other processes.

A user's primary group is that which matches the GID in the `/etc/passwd` file; all others are secondary groups.

11.4.4 File Templates for Customizing a User's Environment

Once new users are added, they need to define an operating environment. Startup files, such as `.profile`, are provided for this purpose (see Section 3.2).

UNIX provides the concept of a skeleton user to simplify the building of configuration files for new users. Compare this with the DEFAULT account in the `SYSUAF.DAT` file on OpenVMS. The administrator can copy files created for the skeleton user to the home directory of a newly created user. The skeleton is located in the `/etc/skel` directory. On System V systems, this directory contains the following files:

- `.login`: defines the overall login environment
- `.cshrc`: defines the environment when using the C shell
- `.profile`: defines the environment when using the Bourne, Korn, and some other shells.

Remember that, unlike OpenVMS, which usually has only one command-line interpreter (DCL), UNIX offers a variety of shells. On some UNIX systems, the file `/etc/shells` lists the available shells.

11.5 Backing up and Restoring Files

On any operating system, it is a good idea to back up data frequently. On multiuser systems such as OpenVMS and UNIX, it is a necessity. To protect data and to be prepared for the need to restore it, the administrator must establish a routine for archiving files at frequent and regular intervals. Backup procedures include a number of tasks:

- Choosing a backup schedule
- Performing a full backup
- Performing an incremental backup

■ Performing a remote backup

On OpenVMS, the BACKUP utility is used to back up and restore files and data. On UNIX systems, the dump utility is the common tool for making backups, and the restore utility is the common tool for restoring files. Besides these utilities, there are also a number of archival applications available from third-party vendors for both OpenVMS and UNIX. One of the many online sources for finding third-party applications for UNIX is the UNIX Guru Web site (http://www.ugu.com).

An additional archival tool for UNIX is the tar utility. The main difference between tar and dump is that tar is more appropriate for making archives of selected files, rather than archives of entire file systems. Similarly, dd is a specialized command for reading and writing data files in specific formats. Refer to Chapter 7 for details on using tar and dd.

11.5.1   Backing up Files

Like the OpenVMS BACKUP utility, the UNIX dump utility is versatile: It can perform full or incremental backups. It can be used to archive individual directories or entire file systems. As with OpenVMS BACKUP, there are dozens of command options for the dump utility, and the administrator must become familiar with them.

There are variations in the dump utility among some versions of UNIX. On System V Release 4 systems, the command is called ufs-dump. The format of dump files across platforms is very similar, so it is usually possible to read dumps from one UNIX system on another. Tru64 UNIX has the vdump command, which works both on the Advanced File System (AdvFS) and UNIX File System (UFS).

The dump utility can access local or remote drives. On some systems, there is a second dump command, called rdump, which is used specifically for remote dumps (that is, for backing up a file system on a remote system using a tape device on the local system). Consider the following examples:

In the first example, the OpenVMS command BACKUP/IMAGE DUA0: MTA1: MTA1:DUA0IM.BCK backs up all files on device DUA0 to the saveset DUA0IM.BCK on tape device MTA1. The UNIX command dump -0uf /dev/rmt0 / produces a full dump of the root file system to tape device rmt0.

In the second example, the command BACKUP DUA1:[SALES...] MIA11:SALES.BCK backs up the contents of the directory tree [SALES] to the

OpenVMS	UNIX

Form:

```
$ BACKUP input-specifier -          # dump [options] [filesystem]
output-specifier [/SAVE_SET] -
[/LABEL=label]
```

Example:

```
$ BACKUP/IMAGE DUA0: -              # dump -0uf /dev/rmt0 /
MTA1:DUA0IM.BCK
```

Example:

```
$ BACKUP DUA1:[SALES...] -          # dump -0f /dev/rmt0 /projects
MIA11:SALES.BCK
```

SALES saveset on device MIA11. The UNIX command `dump -0f /dev/rmt0` `/projects` backs up the `/projects` directory tree to tape device `rmt0`.

As the administrator, you decide how frequently you should back up data and when you should do a full or partial backup. Generally, it is not necessary to back up an entire file system every time you do a backup. The `dump` command uses different dump levels to indicate whether full or incremental backups should be made. A dump level of 0 indicates a *full dump* of a specified file system. An *incremental* backup consists of only those files that have changed since the previous backup. Levels 1 to 9 indicate incremental dumps; that is, only files that have changed since the last dump of a lower dump level are backed up.

The level of an incremental dump is significant only in relation to other dumps. So, while dump level 0 backs up an entire file system, a dump level of 1 requests a backup of only those files that changed since the last level 0 dump, and a level 5 dump requests a backup of only the files that changed since the last lower level dump.

You can design your own backup strategy. Here are some examples:

Strategy 1   Monday level 0
                   Tuesday through Friday level 5

Strategy 2   Monday level 0
                   Tuesday level 1
                   Wednesday level 2
                   Thursday level 3
                   Friday level 4

Strategy 3

First month Monday level 0
First week Monday level 5
Tuesday through Friday level 9
Tuesday level 6
Wednesday level 7
Thursday level 8
Friday level 9

In these examples, strategy 1 takes longer to complete, but is simpler. Strategy 2 takes less time, but a complete restore will be more tedious. Strategy 3 might be a good solution for backing up a large collection of disks.

The `dump` utility records the date and level of prior dumps in the file `/etc/dumpdates`. For example:

`/usr`	0	Mon Oct 20	02:59:00 1998
`/root`	5	Wed Oct 22	03:19:00 1998
`/usr/user1`	0	Mon Oct 27	02:59:00 1998
`/usr/oracle 5`	5	Wed Oct 29	03:19:00 1998

In this example, full dumps (level 0) were made on each Monday, and incremental dumps (level 5) were made on each Wednesday.

11.5.2   Restoring Files

In OpenVMS, the BACKUP utility can be used to restore files from backup media (compare with the `restore` command in UNIX).

OpenVMS	**UNIX**
Form:	
`$ BACKUP save-set-specifier -`	`# restore [options] [file]`
`[/SELECT=(dir...)] output-`	
`specifier`	
Example:	
`$ BACKUP TAPE:MAR12SAVE.BCK -`	`# restore -x /usr/working/`
`DUA1:[JOE...]`	`old.file`

In the previous example, the OpenVMS BACKUP command restores files from the magnetic tape saveset MAR12SAVE.BCK to subdirectories of the directory DUA1:[JOE]:. The UNIX example restores the working/old.file file from the /usr file-system backup tape into your current directory.

The restore utility has an interactive mode that is useful for restoring selected files. To begin an interactive restore session, enter restore -i. The system responds with the restore> prompt and will accept command-line options.

UNIX

Example:

```
% restore -i
restore> ls
.cshrc bin/ lost+found/ tmp/ vmb.e
restore> cd bin
restore> ls
myfile
restore> add myfile
restore> ls
* myfile
restore> extract
You have not read any tapes yet.
Unless you know which volume your file(s) are on you should
start with the last volume and work forward towards the first.
Specify next volume %: 1
set owner/mode for "."? [yn] y
```

11.6   Security

When UNIX was first developed, the designers did not plan extensive security features. As commercial systems and computer networks have evolved, protection of systems and information has become a prime concern for planners and administrators.

Implementing security differs extensively on OpenVMS and UNIX. There are many implementations of UNIX, and different vendors have chosen different approaches to protecting data. OpenVMS was originally developed as a proprietary operating system, and Digital historically implemented its own security features.

However, in today's market, computer vendors are compelled to follow standards to meet the requirements of government and corporate contracts. For example, the National Computer Security Center (NCSEC) publishes the Trusted Computer Systems Evaluation Criteria (TCSEC), also known as the *Orange Book*. The growth of Internet commerce demands provisions for secure transactions. Most modern UNIX systems conform to strict security classifications, such as the C2 rating (described in Section 11.6.1), which has features such as auditing and improved password control. Both OpenVMS and Tru64 UNIX have been certified as C2-compliant, as have other operating systems from other vendors.

It is beyond the scope of this book to cover security in detail. This section gives an overview of the security concerns common to UNIX and OpenVMS.

11.6.1 Security Auditing Standards

The NCSEC publishes its evaluation criteria that specify the security standards that computer vendors must meet for certification for various government uses. This evaluation includes the following security levels:

Security Level	Explanation
D	*Minimal security*: The traditional desktop environment.
C	*Discretionary access control*: The operating system mediates access of objects by users and enforces a security model, but the actual access that any given object allows is at the discretion of the owner of the object and, hence, can be subverted by careless or malicious owners.
B	*Mandatory access control*: In addition to discretionary access control, the operating system supports access control that is mandatory and cannot be changed by the owner of the object. This is typically in the form of a security classification of the object. Only designated users (analogous to a superuser) can upgrade or downgrade the security classification of an object.
A	A formally specified security model and formally verified security model implementation within the operating system; this supplies the same functionality as level B.

Among the most important security criteria is C2 level. The C2 security classification requires that audit events be logged to track intrusions. OpenVMS and many vendors' UNIX systems have been certified as C2-compliant. Optional security packages for Open VMS and Tru64 UNIX provide features that comply with a stricter security classification, B1.

11.6.2   The Superuser

Unlike OpenVMS, which enables the administrator to assign a set of privileges selectively, UNIX provides only two privilege states. Superuser privilege (also called root) privilege allows you to do anything; regular users are restricted in the commands they can use and the files they can access. Superuser privilege is analogous to the privilege provided by the SYSTEM account or any account with BYPASS privilege assigned to any user on OpenVMS.

You use the su command to become superuser from a nonprivileged account, or you can log in directly as root. As is true of the OpenVMS SYSTEM account, judicious use should be made of the root account; this is even more true on a UNIX system. The /etc/group file defines which users can use the su command to become root.

11.6.3   User Authentication

Modern operating systems, including UNIX, OpenVMS, and Windows NT, require users to log in with a valid user name and password. It is up to the administrator to design and enforce effective password policies so that passwords are less obvious to someone wishing to compromise a system.

11.6.4   Permission Codes for Files

Section 4.2 describes the basic UNIX file permissions and compares these to OpenVMS file protections. In UNIX, the chmod command is equivalent to the SET PROTECTION command in OpenVMS. Section 8.4.1 describes how the chmod command can be used to change permissions on files, by granting combinations of r (read), w (write), and x (execute) permissions for three types of accessors: user (file's owner), group, and others. Don't confuse the abbreviation for "others," namely "o," with the file's owner!

An additional chmod command option allows the administrator to set special permission bits that establish temporary or restricted access to important files—files not normally accessible to other users. The s option sets the effective UID (setuid) or GID (setgid) to that of the owner or the group owner of the file whenever the file is run.

UNIX
Form:
```
# chmod [u, g]+s file
```
Example:
```
# chmod ug+s batchdoc
```

In this example, the chmod command uses the s option in combination with the u and g options to set the UID and GID modes for the file batch-doc, a command script that processes files in a database. Suppose that the owner of the batchdoc file is admin and that there is a user on the system named barbara. User barbara does not have permission to access any of the database files owned by admin. However, as a result of the chmod command shown in the previous example, she has permission to run batchdoc. When she does, her effective UID is temporarily changed to admin, so that the batchdoc command can access the data files owned by admin.

11.6.5 Monitoring Security Violations

Keeping a system secure begins with establishing a consistent practice of auditing the system. There are a number of commercial auditing tools available for various versions of UNIX. You can also use standard UNIX utilities. Figure 11.3 summarizes some of the events that you can monitor using basic BSD UNIX commands.

Figure 11.3   *BSD UNIX commands for monitoring security violations.*

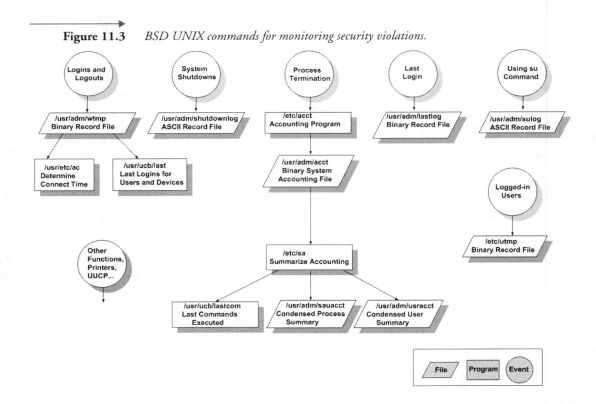

11.6.6 Security Checklists

If you are a system administrator for a UNIX system, consider the suggestions listed here.

Security Checklist—General

- Do not run a user-owned program as `root`.

- Be sure that your `PATH` (or `path`) environment variable will not get you into trouble by reaching a command with the right name in the wrong directory. Directories such as `/bin` and `/sbin` should be closer to the beginning. Many system administrators will not end `PATH` with the dot (current directory) because of the danger of executing a command inadvertently. It is a particularly good idea within a script to specify the absolute path to a command.

- Be wary of software from an unknown source.

- Run auditing.

- Ensure that the `/usr/adm/sulog` file is owned by `root`.

Security Checklist—User Accounts

- Develop a password policy and distribute it to all users.

- Avoid defining "captive" accounts.

- If not using enhanced security levels, then do the following:
  - Remove all "idle" guest accounts.
  - Remove all null password fields.

- Do not allow group accounts, that is, accounts intended for regular use by more than one person.

- Implement password controls, such as password "aging" and maximum and minimum length.

Security Checklist—Networks

- Ensure that `/etc/hosts.equiv` contains only local hosts.

- Decide whether `.rhosts` files are permitted.

- Do not export NFS file systems to the world.

- Do not include a "decode" alias in the aliases file.

- Ensure that modems and terminal servers handle hang-ups correctly.

- Decide whether to support anonymous `ftp`.

Security Checklist—File Systems

- Check protections and ownership of all system files.

- Do not allow `setuid` or `setgid` shell scripts.

- Have the proper `umask` value on the `root` account.

- Have correct protection modes on devices in `/dev`.

- When doing backups, be careful of ownership of restored files.

Security Checklist—Individual Users

- Do not run other user programs unless you own them.

- Maintain correct file and directory protections.

- Use file encryption for sensitive files.

- Take special care of hidden files such as `.profile`, `.cshrc`, and `.netrc`.

11.7 Network Configuration

There are many models for computer networks. The term *network* is itself rather vague, because it can mean a small collection of PCs or workstations, or something as complex as a corporate intranet composed of hundreds or thousands of mixed systems running a combination of protocols and operating systems. Designing, implementing, administering, and maintaining computer networks is a major task. We will confine our discussion of network configuration to the most basic TCP/IP model.

Networking on OpenVMS was originally accomplished using Digital's proprietary DECnet software. DECnet implemented the Digital Network Architecture (DNA), Digital's own networking model. On UNIX, a number of networking protocols evolved. Today, the most common networking protocol is known as TCP/IP. Modern networks that make up the Internet, now including OpenVMS, primarily support TCP/IP and related communications utilities.

11.7.1 Networking Products for OpenVMS

For OpenVMS, HP has made an effort to keep a high profile for "open" standards support. The latest versions of OpenVMS can support TCP/IP and DECnet, in addition to other network protocols.

DECnet Phase IV is the traditional networking product for OpenVMS systems. DECnet Phase IV supports the DNA network model. DECnet-Plus is the newer DECnet product. Formerly known as DECnet/OSI, DECnet-Plus incorporates standards from the Open Systems Interconnect (OSI) group.

The DECnet-Plus architecture follows a different model from DECnet Phase IV. DECnet-Plus network management is based on a director-entity model. DECnet-Plus uses the Network Control Language (NCL) as the primary tool for managing networks, rather than the Network Control Program (NCP).

OpenVMS also offers TCP/IP Services as an optional product. With this software installed, an OpenVMS system can operate as an active member of TCP/IP networks and use the same networking commands and utilities common on UNIX. You can also purchase TCP/IP add-ons for OpenVMS from third-party vendors.

The basic principles behind networking with DECnet and TCP/IP are the same. A computer identifies itself by both a name and a number and communicates with other hosts that are either defined locally or determined dynamically from the network.

11.7.2 TCP/IP Basics

The primary networking protocol used on the Internet today is referred to as TCP/IP. This is a suite of products and protocols that includes the following:

- *Internet Protocol (IP):* provides the underlying transfer layer

- *Transmission Control Protocol (TCP):* provides connection-oriented communication between processes and adds error detection and other services

- *User Data Protocol (UDP):* provides a low-overhead connectionless datagram protocol

- *Serial Line IP (SLIP):* supports networking over serial communication lines

- *Point-to-Point Protocol (PPP)*: supports networking over synchronous and asynchronous communication lines

- *Internet Control Message Protocol (ICMP):* supports messages such as those used by the `ping` utility

Programs called daemons, which are started at boot time and listen for network requests, control much of the work on networked systems. On OpenVMS, there are several background processes that are similar in concept to daemons, including NETACP and EVL. Some of the most important UNIX network daemons include the following:

- `inetd`: detects IP and UDP connection requests

- `rpcbind`: controls remote procedure call requests

- `routed`: detects network routing packets sent using the Router Interchange Protocol

- `gated`: handles multiprotocol routing for external network gateways

- `syslog`: detects messages and forwards them to other processes

- `nfsd`: detects requests for operations using NFS

- `ftpd`: transfers files between systems

- `telnetd`: controls remote login sessions

The master network daemon is `inetd`; it oversees all network activity on a UNIX machine connected to a TCP/IP network. It listens for connection requests. When it receives a connection request, it starts the appropriate daemons.

Some of the important files involved in this process are as follows (see Figure 11.4):

- At boot time, `/etc/inetd` reads the `/etc/inetd.conf` file, which defines the services that `inetd` should oversee.

- Next `/etc/inetd.conf` maps a service to a protocol and a daemon that starts it.

- The service is in turn mapped to an Internet port number in the `/etc/services` file.

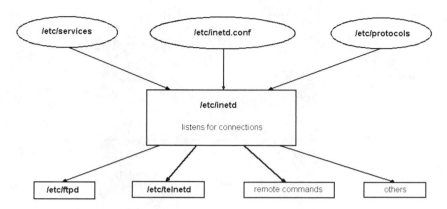

Figure 11.4
*TCP/IP
networking files
and daemons.*

- The service is further mapped to a specific protocol in the /etc/pro-tocols file.

11.7.2.1 Internet Addressing

In TCP/IP networks, each computer that is part of the network is called a *host*. Each host is identified by a unique host name in addition to a unique IP host address. The TCP/IP protocol translates the host name to the host address, as required by the IP protocol. Users can supply either the host name or IP address to UNIX networking commands.

The Internet uses distributed name and address mechanisms. The Domain Name Service (DNS) provides a hierarchy of host names to IP address mapping and distributes it across the network.

On TCP/IP networks, hosts are grouped hierarchically in domains. The top-level domain name in the hierarchy can represent an organizational domain or a geographical domain. Examples of organizational domains include .com for commercial organizations, .edu for educational institutions, and .gov for government institutions. Typically, there is one domain assigned to an entity. For example, hp.com is the domain assigned to HP, and umich.edu is the domain assigned to the University of Michigan. The top-level domain can be divided into subdomains that further identify the host. The subdomains are separated by periods. An example of a subdomain is music.umich.edu. Figure 11.5 illustrates this Internet domain example.

Associated with any computer on a TCP/IP network, referred to as a host, is an Internet address expressed in numeric form (e.g., 128.59.98.1). By comparison, in DECnet Phase IV networks, each host is identified by a unique, but nonhierarchical, host name (e.g., PLUTO) and a unique address consisting of its area number and node number (e.g., 1.121). Host name-

Figure 11.5
*Internet domain
structure.*

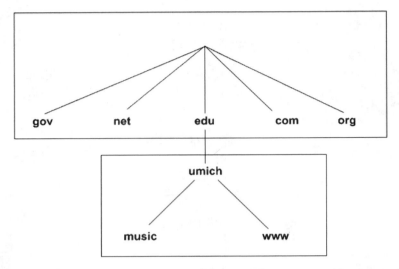

to-number mapping is not distributed. Users can supply either the host name or the host address where it is desired to specify a host.

See Section 13.2.5 for more information on Internet host naming.

11.7.3   Setting up Networks

The tools for setting up and managing networks on OpenVMS depend on the networking architecture adopted on the OpenVMS systems participating in the network. NCP is the primary tool for configuring DECnet Phase IV networks. You use NCP to define a database of nodes in the network, in addition to setting other network characteristics. DECnet-Plus uses NCL as its primary network management tool.

To configure a system for TCP/IP network user, the administrator needs to consider and configure a number of components. For example, on a Tru64 UNIX system these components are important:

- Network interfaces (Ethernet, FDDI, Token Ring, etc.)
- Static routes
- Network daemons
- IP router
- Hosts file (`/etc/hosts, /etc/.rhosts`)
- Networks file (`/etc/networks`)

In general, the network setup and configuration process is as follows:

1. Load the network software.

2. Specify which hardware interface(s) your system will use to access the network.

3. Set up your Internet address, host name, and domain information.

4. Start the `routed` daemon to obtain dynamic routing information or the `gated` daemon to go through gateways to other network sections.

5. Determine if subnetting is required, and use the `ifconfig` utility accordingly.

6. Start the Address Resolution Protocol (ARP) to convert IP addresses to Ethernet addresses.

7. Set up the `hosts` file.

8. Set up the `networks` file.

9. Modify the `rc.local` file to include changes at boot time.

10. Make pseudoterminal devices and include them in `/etc/ttys`.

11. Set up the `hosts.equiv` and `.rhosts` files.

Vendors supply special utilities or scripts to enable the administrator to configure the system. For example, Tru64 UNIX supplies both the `net-setup` command-line utility, and a graphical network configuration application (`netconfig`) available under CDE.

The following abbreviated example shows how to use the `netsetup` utility.

UNIX
```
# netsetup
**** MAIN MENU ****
1 Configure Network Interfaces
2 Enable/Disable Network Daemons and Add Static Routes
3 Add/Delete Host Information
4 Display Network Configuration
5 Exit
Enter the number for your choice: 1

***** CONFIGURE/DELETE NETWORK INTERFACES *****
.
.
```

```
.
Enter whether you want to "(c)onfigure" or "(d)elete" network
interfaces. If you are finished, press the RETURN key: c
You want to "configure" interfaces. Is this correct [yes]?
.

.

.
This machine contains the following network interfaces:
tu0
sl0
Which interface do you want to configure [tu0]:
You want to configure "tu0". Is this correct [yes]?
The hostname for the system is "grazie".
Is this correct [yes]?
Enter the Internet Protocol (IP) address for interface "tu0"
i dot notation []: 77.888.80.17
The IP address for interface "tu0" is "77.888.80.17".
Is this correct [yes]?
.

.

.
**** MAIN MENU ****
.

.

.
Enter the number for your choice: 4
***** DISPLAY NETWORK CONFIGURATION *****
Obtaining hardware and software configuration. Please wait...
Current network adapters on this system:
tu0
sl0
Current software configuration in /etc/rc.config:
HOSTNAME = grazie
NUM_NETCONFIG = 1
NETDEV_0 = tu0
IFCONFIG_0 = 77.888.80.17 netmask 255.255.255.0
RWHOD = no
ROUTED = no
ROUTED_FLAGS =
GATED = yes
GATED_FLAGS =
GATED_OLD = yes
ROUTER = no
MAX_NETDEVS = 24
Press RETURN to continue

**** MAIN MENU ****
.

.

.
```

```
Enter the number for your choice: 5
.

.

.
Do you want netsetup to automatically restart the network
services on this system [no]? y
Stopping Internet services on this system. Please wait...
kill: 250: no such process
Unmounting NFS filesystems
Internet services on this system are stopped.
Starting Internet services on this system. Please wait...
.

.

.
Internet services on this system are started.
***** NETWORK SETUP COMPLETE *****
```

11.7.3.1 The /etc/hosts and /etc/networks *Files*

The file `/etc/hosts` statically maps host names into IP addresses. This is comparable to the DECnet database on OpenVMS. The following is an excerpt from a sample `/etc/hosts` file on a UNIX system.

Example:
```
% more /etc/hosts
127.0.1. localhost
132.249.40.5 shark.sdsc.edu shark
132.249.40.6 marlin.sdsc.edu marlin
132.249.40.8 piranha.sdsc.edu piranha
132.249.40.9 goldfish.sdsc.edu goldfish
132.249.40.10 catfish.sdsc.edu catfish
132.249.40.11 tigerfish.sdsc.edu tigerfish
132.249.40.32 c90.sdsc.edu c90
132.249.40.34 g90.sdsc.edu g90
```

Because the Internet is so vast and dynamic, it is impractical to try to list all Internet addresses in this file. This file is reserved for local addresses, that is, those accessed most frequently for reasons of efficiency or security. Section 11.7.4 discusses ways to work around this problem by dynamically resolving addresses using hierarchies of hosts.

The `/etc/networks` file maps names of networks to the corresponding network numbers. This file differs from the `/etc/hosts` file in that only the network number portion is listed in the file. See the following example:

Example:

```
% more /etc/networks
loopback-net 127
sdscnet 132.249
cray-ymp 132.249.10
old-dmz 132.249.16
social-sciences 132.249.18
basement 132.249.19
computer-room 132.249.20
fddi-ring 132.249.40
atm-70 132.249.70
```

11.7.4   NFS, NIS, and BIND

Several network services have been developed over the years and are now common on most UNIX versions. NFS is software available for UNIX implementations and, optionally, for OpenVMS. It provides access to file systems from remote hosts. Section 13.2.8 provides more information on NFS.

NIS, formerly referred to as Yellow Pages, allows the sharing of such databases as users, passwords, groups, and network domain names between hosts that share administrative control. The Berkeley Internet Name Domain service (BIND) provides a host name and address lookup service for networked systems.

As with other network services, the procedure for configuring NFS, NIS, and BIND will vary depending on the vendor's version of UNIX. In addition to integrated network configuration tools, some vendors also provide command-line utilities. For example, many UNIX systems provide a generic terminal-based setup utility in /usr/sbin/setup. This utility provides a menu of most administrative setup functions. In turn, it calls nfssetup, nissetup, bindsetup, latsetup, lprsetup, and so on. This abbreviated example shows the nfssetup utility.

UNIX

```
# nfssetup
Checking kernel configuration
.
.
.
NFS locking to be enabled [y] ?
Will you be exporting any directories [n] ? y
Do you want to allow non-root mounts [n] ?
.
.
```

```
            .
Enter the number of TCP daemons to run (0 to 128) [8] :
Enter the number of UDP daemons to run (0 to 120) [8] :
            .

            .

            .
Would you like to run the property list daemon [n] ?
            .

            .

            .
Enter the number of block I/O daemons to run [7] :
            .

            .

            .
Would you like to run the PC-NFS daemon [n] ?
            .

            .

            .
Would you like to run the automount daemon [n] ?
You are now setting up your directory export list...
Enter the directory pathname:
Directory export list complete...
            .

            .

            .
Enter the remote host name: blabber
Enter the remote directory pathname: /usr3
Enter the local mount point: /usr3
/usr3: Directory does not exist, but will be created.
Is this a read-only mount [y] ? n
            .

            .

            .
Remote directory mount list complete...
Please confirm the following information which you have entered for
your NFS environment:
8 TCP server daemons, 8 UDP server daemons
7 nfsiod daemons
locking daemons installed
No directories (in addition to those already in /etc/exports)
exported
Remote directory mount list:
/usr3@blabber mounted on: /usr3, mount options are: rw,bg
Enter "c" to CONFIRM the information, "q" to QUIT nfssetup without
making any changes, or "r" to RESTART the procedure [no default]: c
Updating files:
/etc/rc.config
/etc/fstab
Creating local mount points:
/usr3
```

```
.
.
.
Would you like nfssetup to stop/start the daemons now [y]?
kill: 2368: no such process
NFS mount daemon started
NFS export service started NFS IO service started
NFS Locking: rpc.statd and rpc.lockd started
Mounting NFS filesystems
/usr3 on /usr3 type nfs (v3, rw, udp, hard, intr)
The NFS daemons for your machine have been started.
[Press the RETURN key to continue ]:
***** NFSSETUP COMPLETE *****
```

The following abbreviated example shows the `bindsetup` utility.

UNIX

```
# bindsetup
.

.

.
Berkeley Internet Name Domain (BIND)
Action Menu for Configuration
Add => a
Modify => m
Remove => r
Exit => e
Enter your choice [a]:
.

.

.
Enter the default BIND domain name []: pdh.ngh.com
Configuration Menu for domain "pdh.ngh.com"
Primary Server => p
Secondary Server => s
Caching Server => a
Slave Server => l
Client => c
Exit => e
Enter your choice [c]:
.

.

.
Enter the host name of a BIND server: alpha
Enter the Internet address for alpha.pdh.ngh.com []: 16.140.128.4
Would you like to add alpha to the /etc/hosts file (y/n) [n] ? y
Enter the host name of a BIND server: beta
Enter the Internet address for beta.pdh.ngh.com []: 16.140.144.7
Would you like to add beta to the /etc/hosts file (y/n) [n] ? y
```

```
Enter the host name of a BIND server:
Finished entering BIND server(s) (y/n) [n] : y
Updating files:
/etc/hosts
/etc/rc.config
/etc/resolv.conf
Bindsetup will now change the hostname from "grazie" to
"grazie.pdh.ngh.com".
Would you like bindsetup to change the hostname [y]?
Setting hostname to: grazie.pdh.ngh.com
.

.

.
Service Order Selection Menu
1) Query /etc/hosts before querying BIND for host information.
2) Query BIND first for host information.
3) Run svcsetup to customize service order selection.
Enter your choice [1]:
Updating files: /etc/svc.conf
***** BINDSETUP COMPLETE *****
```

11.8 Monitoring the Network

Both OpenVMS and UNIX provide commands and utilities for monitoring the network, as shown in Table 11.2. For more information about the `hostname` and `netstat` commands, see Sections 12.2.2 and 13.2.1.

Table 11.2 *Comparison of OpenVMS and UNIX Networking Commands*

OpenVMS Command	UNIX Command	Description
SHOW NETWORK	netstat	Displays network use
	ruptime	Displays uptime of remote hosts
SHOW LOGICAL SYS$NODE	hostname	Shows local host name
NCP TELL	ping	Tests ability to reach other hosts

11.9 Summary

Administering a computer system is a comprehensive job. Besides installing and configuring the operating system and layered products, the administrator must deal with a seemingly endless list of additional tasks—maintaining users and groups, establishing security policies, and setting up and maintaining network services. These and many other tasks are common to UNIX, OpenVMS, and other multiuser computer operating systems. Traditionally, administrators used commands, utilities, and scripts on UNIX and maintained several database files for host names, users, and groups. Newer versions of UNIX provide graphical tools to streamline these administration tasks. In addition, many third-party vendors sell "enterprise management solutions" intended to simplify administration.

12

Monitoring and Utilizing System Resources

12

Monitoring and Utilizing System Resources

> *I can't see who is ahead—it's either Oxford or Cambridge.*
> —*John Snagge*

This chapter discusses UNIX commands that analyze and affect the use of system resources such as the CPU, physical memory, virtual memory, and disk space. Monitoring system resources is of major concern to the system administrator in maintaining a balanced workload. Users become interested in this subject when, for example, the system responds sluggishly to terminal input or when they wish to estimate the running time of a particular application. Unfortunately, users can usually do nothing to improve the situation except to alter processes they own, which is often self-defeating.

Applications programmers may consider this position narrow-minded, reflecting only a system administrator's perspective. Indeed, programmers can examine how a particular application consumes resources and often see how to improve the performance of their code. This chapter, however, is not a lesson in programming and, therefore, offers no insight into how such improvements might be made. It simply describes the commands that monitor how processes utilize system resources and that affect the system resources devoted to processes.

UNIX users familiar with the OpenVMS commands MONITOR, SHOW, and ANALYZE and their easily understood output will likely be disappointed by the commands UNIX offers to analyze system-resource utilization due to the original UNIX design constraints. These constraints required that output be displayed as hard copy on slow Teletype devices. The designers of the original operating system could not, of course, avail themselves of the fast screen updating capabilities of today's video terminals. Some vendors of

UNIX systems now offer graphical output that is pleasing to the OpenVMS MONITOR user.

Despite differences in convenience, the principles for analyzing resource utilization in both OpenVMS and UNIX are the same. Figure 12.1 illustrates the common UNIX commands for monitoring and changing resource utilization. These commands apply either to single processes (discussed in Section 12.1) or to the sum of all processes (discussed in Section 12.2). Once resource utilization of your system has been analyzed, a community-conscious user (if such a creature exists) can modify his or her processes to reduce system-resource requirements (see Section 12.3).

We will begin by looking at the commands for monitoring system-resource utilization as they apply to a single process, a single user, or disk space.

12.1   Monitoring Users and Their Processes

Before examining how individual processes are consuming system resources, you should examine how many interactive users are logged into the system as a first indication of the workload. UNIX offers several commands—users, who, w, and rwho—for displaying a list of interactive users.

Figure 12.1
UNIX commands for monitoring and changing resource utilization.

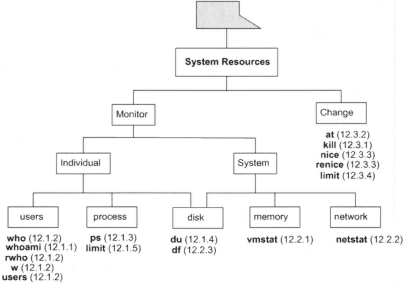

The casual user is advised to concentrate on the commands **who**, **ps**, **kill**, and **df**.

Many implementations of UNIX even have a command, whoami, to determine who you yourself are. Once you have determined the number and names of the interactive users on your system, you can list the processes that you and your fellow users are running with the ps command. If you need additional information, you can issue the du command to determine the amount of disk space consumed or the bash and ksh command ulimit (the csh command limit) to get information on the resource limits imposed on user processes.

12.1.1   Who Am I: whoami

The whoami command is not as ridiculous as it may at first appear. It is useful, for example, when you have different usernames on several frequently used UNIX computers. You may invoke whoami to determine your current username and, hence, which computer you are using. You might also use whoami when sharing a terminal with other users. If the shared terminal has been left unattended, you can issue whoami to list the name of the user who is currently logged in. You may then locate that user and ask him or her to end the terminal session. In OpenVMS, the corresponding command SHOW PROCESS returns the current user's username, as well as other useful information; whoami returns only the username.

OpenVMS	UNIX
Form:	
$ SHOW PROCESS[/*QUALIFIER(S)*] *process_name*	% whoami
Example:	
$ SHOW PROCESS	% whoami
29---JUN-1998 11:20:12.98 RTA3: User: SYSTEM	root
Pid: 00000219 Proc. name:_RTA3: UIC:	
[SYSEM,POSTMASTER]	
Priority: 4 Default file spec:	
SYS$SYSROOT:[SYSMGR]	

The BSD version of UNIX originated whoami. System V begat who am i, which returns the username, the terminal name, and the time the user logged in. Many implementations of UNIX (including both Tru64 and GNU Linux) now support both forms, returning the appropriate information for each.

12.1.2   **Monitoring Interactive Users:** users, who, w, **and** rwho

The UNIX commands users, who, and w provide information in increasing detail on interactive users using the local computer (compare with the OpenVMS command SHOW USERS). The command rwho provides information about interactive users using remote computers on the same network (see Chapter 13).

OpenVMS

Form:

```
$ SHOW USERS [/OUTPUT] [username]
```

Example:

```
$ SHOW USERS
VAX/OpenVMS Interactive Users
Total number of interactive users =
3
BEIGI          ALPHA       0000021
LTA40:
HENDW     HENDW     00000129    RTA1:
JAYARAM   JAYARAM   0000020D  LTA36:
```

UNIX

Form:

```
% who [file]
% users
% w [option(s)] [user]
```

Example:

```
% who
beigi        tty06    Jun 28 12:04
hendw        tty0c    Jun 27 19:15
jayaram      ttyp0    Jun 29 09:42
```

UNIX

Example:

```
% w
12:09pm up 14 days, 2:07, 3 users, load average: 0.78, 0.35, 0.20
User     tty     login@    idle    JCPU   PCPU   what
beigi    tty06   12:04pm   31:02   9      9      rlogin cuhhmd
hendw    tty0c   7:15pm    40:53   7      2      -csh[hendw] (csh)
jayaram  ttyp0   9:42am    2:27    3      1      -csh[jayaram] (csh)
```

Example:

```
% who /usr/adm/wtmp | grep fred | tail -4
fred    tty03    Feb 24    11:10
fred    tty03    Feb 24    12:03
fred    tty05    Feb 25    12:10
fred    tty05    Feb 25    15:09
```

The who command, which most closely resembles the OpenVMS SHOW USERS command, displays the name of the device to which the user's terminal is connected (e.g., tty06) and the login time (e.g., Jun 28 12:04). The users command returns only an alphabetical list of the usernames of inter-active users currently logged in. The w command also displays a header line with the time of day (12:09pm), how long the computer has been up (14 days, 2:07), the number of users (3), the system load, and the following information about each user:

idle	How long since the user last typed anything, in minutes
JCPU	The accumulated CPU time of all the user's processes since logging in, in minutes
PCPU	The CPU time used by any currently active processes, in minutes
WHAT	The program being executed by the current process

For example, user jayaram logged on at 9:42 A.M., has not touched the terminal connected to ttyp0 for 2 hours and 27 minutes, and is running the C shell program. Blanks in the fields idle, JCPU, and PCPU indicate a time of less than one minute.

The three values for system load indicate how busy the system was 1, 5, and 15 minutes ago. A load of 0.78 indicates that the system was oper-ating at 78% capacity; a load of 2.30 indicates that it would take 2.3 identical systems to process the current load efficiently. Stated another way, a single CPU-intensive application running at a system load of 2.30 will receive 1/2.3, or approximately 44%, of CPU resources.

The last example, who /usr/adm/wtmpc |grep fred | tail -4, illus-trates the use of who to interrogate a system accounting file rather than the default file /etc/utmp. The file /etc/utmp maintains information on users currently logged onto the system. The file /usr/adm/wtmp maintains infor-mation on all logins and logouts. Rather than displaying the contents of this file (the default), the example pipes the output to the grep command (compare with the OpenVMS command SEARCH in Section 8.4.5), which searches for records that indicate when user fred logged into and out of the system. The example, in turn, pipes this information to the command tail -4 (see Section 8.2.3), which displays the last four records: namely, the last two times user fred logged into and out of the system. This information is useful, for example, if you sent a mail message to user fred and wish to know when he is likely to read it. If user fred has logged in twice in the last couple of days, then you can assume that user fred uses the system fre-quently and will read the message in the near future. On the other hand, if user `fred` logged in only twice in the last two months, it is less likely that he will read the message in the near future.

The command `rwho` produces a display similar to the `who` command, but for users who are logged into other computers on the network.

UNIX

Form:

```
% rwho [option(s)]
```

Example:

```
% rwho
ari        cunixc:ttype      Jun 29 13:30
brown      sylvester:ttyp2   Jun 28 10:47        :52
glenda     zeno:tty17        Jun 29 11:46
gr         cunixc:tty56      Jun 29 12:50
heidi      cunixc:tty25      Jun 29 09:04        :06
system     cuhhmd:ttyp3      Jun 29 13:39        :07
zagorski   cuhhmd:ttyp0      Jun 28 12:04        :20
```

The command `rwho` displays the same information as `who`, as well as a name preceding the terminal name and the amount of time elapsed since the user last typed, in minutes. A blank field here indicates that the user has typed something within the last minute. The name preceding the terminal name is the *host name* of the remote computer (see Section 13.1). Open-VMS, in contrast, does not offer a convenient way to determine who is logged into a remote DECnet node. You may use the options -a and -h with `rwho`. The option -a reports on all remote users. Without the -a option only those users who have touched the terminal in the last hour are reported. The -h option sorts the output alphabetically by host name, rather than by username. On a large network, the system administrator may prevent the computer from broadcasting messages describing who is currently using the system in an effort to prevent the network from becoming overloaded. In this case, `rwho` would not detect a complete list of remote users.

12.1.3   **Monitoring Processes: ps**

The command `ps` (process status) shows the system resources being consumed on a UNIX system at any given time by one or more processes. The OpenVMS analog to `ps` is a combination of the SHOW SYSTEM and SHOW PROCESS commands. Although `ps` has many options, the subset described here will meet the needs of the average user.

OpenVMS

Form:

```
$ SHOW PROCESS[/QUALIFIER(S)] [process]

$ SHOW PROCESS
29-JUN-1998    15:08:38.91    RTA3:    User: SYSTEM
Pid: 00000219  Proc. name:_   RTA3:    UIC: [SYSTEM.POSTMASTER]
Priority: 4    Default file spec: SYS$SYSROOT:[SYSMGR.COM]

$ SHOW PROCESS/ALL

2-JUL-1998     11:03:46.85    RTA2: User: SYSTEM
Pid: 00000196  Proc. name:_   RTA2:  UIC: [SYSTEM.POSTMASTER]
Priority: 4    Default file spec: DUA3:[BOURNE.MASS11]
Devices allocated:    RTA2:
Process Quotas:
CPU limit: Infinite    Direct   I/O limit: 18
Buffered I/O byte count quota:  99904         Buffered I/O limit: 18
Timer queue entry quota:    20     Open file quota: 59
Paging file quota:   59063       Subprocess quota: 10
Default page fault cluster: 64  AST limit: 22
Enqueue quota: 30      Shared file limit: 0
Max detached processes:      0      Max active jobs: 0
Accounting information:
Buffered I/O count:          147    Peak working set size: 387
Direct I/O count: 55               Peak virtual size: 1159
Page faults: 1285                  Mounted volumes: 0
Images activated: 7
Elapsed CPU time: 0 00:00:09.35    Connect time: 0 00:00:40.75
Process privileges:
GRPNAM        may insert in group logical name table
TMPMBX        may create temporary mailbox
WORLD         may affect other processes in the world
NETMBX        may create network device
Process rights identifiers:
INTERACTIVE
REMOTE
Process Dynamic Memory Area
Current Size (bytes)  25600       Current Total Size (pages) 50
Free Space (bytes)    21648       Space in Use (bytes) 3952
Size of Largest Block 21568       Size of Smallest Block 8
Number of Free Blocks 4           Free Blocks LEQU 32 Bytes 2
Processes in this tree:
_RTA2: (*)
```

UNIX

Form:

```
% ps [option(s)]
```

Example:

```
% ps
PID     TT     STAT   TIME     COMMAND
6682    p1     S      0:01     -csh[system] (csh)
7415    p1     R      0:00     ps
```

Example:

```
% ps -l
F    S UID     PID     PPID   C   PRI  NI  P   SZ:RSS   WCHAN    TTY
TIME    CMD
b0   R 29288 16974 16946 12   66   20  0    398:166   -
ttyq3   0:00    ps
b0   S 29288 16946 16945  0   39   20  *    113:96    881f4410 ttyq3
0:01    csh
```

In the first example, ps without options (compare with the OpenVMS command SHOW PROCESS) provides a brief summary of your own processes. In this example, the user is running only two processes: one child running the ps command and the C shell parent process that forked the child process (see Section 2.1.1 for a discussion of parent and child processes). The user initiated each process from the terminal ttyp1, a pseudoterminal used in a network connection (see Section 3.1). The csh process has been stopped (S) for a short period, and ps is running (R). The csh process has consumed one minute of CPU time.

In the second example, ps -l (compare with the OpenVMS command SHOW PROCESS /FULL) provides additional information on the user's processes as follows:

UID	Numerical process identifier (compare with the OpenVMS PID)
PPID	Numerical process identifier of parent process
CP	Short-term CPU utilization factor
PRI	Process priority (compare with the OpenVMS priority)
NI	Process scheduling increment
SZ	Virtual memory size of the process in kilobytes (compare with the OpenVMS peak virtual size)
RSS	Real memory size of the process in kilobytes (compare with the OpenVMS peak working set size)
WCHAN	Event address for which process is waiting

The average user will likely never need some of the information given by ps -l. Therefore, we discuss only the commonly used fields.

PPID displays the identification number of the parent process that forked the process under examination. This information is useful if you need to trace the parent process. In this example, the PPID of 18228 for the process running the ps command is the PID of the parent shell process. The priority (PRI) determines the amount of the available CPU resources that the system will devote to the process. Unlike OpenVMS, where base priorities range from 1 to 15, UNIX priorities use zero as the baseline, with positive numbers indicating lower priority and negative numbers higher. Section 12.3.3 describes how you may lower the priority of a running process or a process about to run a command. SZ and RSS indicate the relationship between how much physical memory a process may theoretically use and how much it has access to. Processes where SZ vastly exceeds RSS may be running inefficiently. RSS corresponds to the peak working set size of an OpenVMS process, the former expressed in kilobytes and the latter in 512-byte pages.

The examples of ps given thus far display features of your own processes. You may also display the characteristics of other types of processes (compare with the OpenVMS commands SHOW SYSTEM, SHOW PROCESS / IDENTIFICATION, and MONITOR PROCESS). Other UNIX processes fall into two classes: user processes (both your own and others') and processes not attached to a terminal and owned by root. The latter processes, called *daemons*, usually start when the system is booted and are part of the operating system. You may display these two process classes with the -a and -x options, respectively.

UNIX

Example:

```
% ps -aux | head
USER     PID     %CPU %MEM SZ    RSS   TT    STAT  TIME    COMMAND
fred     24790   31.0 2.6  240   178   p0    R     0:00    ps -aux
george   24881   22.0 1.8  131   119   p3    R     0:1     /usr/george/myprog
fred     24791   4.0  0.3  36    14    p0    S     0:00    head
root     24520   2.3  1.1  85    74    p0    S     0:19    dlogin
fred     24521   0.5  1.1  130   72    p0    S     0:07    -csh (csh)
root     3624    0.2  1.8  131   119   ?     S     324:23  /etc/rwhod
root     3611    0.1  0.2  5     3     ?     S     65:36   /etc/update
root     3614    0.0  0.3  31    11    ?     I     15:54   /etc/cron
root     1       0.0  3.6  270   251   ?     I     3:08    init
root     3580    0.0  1.1  9     74    co    S     0:55    swapin
```

The command ps -aux | head pipes the output of the ps command to head (see Section 8.2.3), which displays the first 10 lines of the output, in this case the 10 processes consuming the largest percentage of CPU resources. Unlike ps -u, this command includes processes owned by other users (–a) and processes not attached to a terminal or the system console (–x). Note that these ps command options use the BSD syntax—the ps command also accepts UNIX98 on many other versions of UNIX and GNU-style options on distributions of Linux. Since the processes owned by the operating system are not associated with a terminal, the TT field displays a question mark. Examples of such daemons include /etc/rwhod, a program that acts as both a collector and broadcaster of network information. Current users are broadcast over the network, while information on remote users is collected for use by the local rwho command; /etc/update, which periodically updates the file-system pointer file to assure file integrity in the event of a system crash; /etc/cron, which executes commands at preset intervals, such as a timestamp used for accounting purposes (compare with the OpenVMS process OPCOM); init, which initiates a terminal session (see Section 3.1); and swapin (compare with the OpenVMS process SWAPPER), which controls the swapping of data from physical memory to a secondary cache.

12.1.4　Monitoring Disk Usage: du

The command du (disk utilization) provides information on how much disk space the system's users are utilizing (compare with the OpenVMS command DIRECTORY /SIZE /TOTAL). You can use du to examine your own files or any user's files that are world-readable.

OpenVMS

Form:

```
$ DIR/SIZE file-spec[, ...]
```

Example:

```
$ DIR/SIZE/TOTAL DUA1:[FRED...]*.*;*
Directory DUA1:[FRED]
Total of 10 files 1000 blocks
Directory DUA1:[FRED.SCRATCH]
Total of 1 file 500 blocks
Grand total of 2 directories, 11 files,
1500 blocks
```

UNIX

```
% du [option(s)] directory
```

```
% du ~fred
512 /usr/fred
256 /usr/fred/scratch
```

Example:

```
% du -s ~fred
768 /usr/fred
% du -a
[not shown]
```

The command du reports the total size of all files in each directory in 512-byte blocks, starting with the directory specified or the current directory if no directory is specified, and moving down the directory tree. In the first example, `du ~fred` without options reports the disk usage of all directories belonging to user `fred`. In the second example, `du -s ~fred` (summary) gives only the total size of all files owned by user `fred`. In the last example, `du -a` lists the size of all files in the directory hierarchy, starting at the present working directory (not shown).

12.1.5 Monitoring Process Resource Limits: `limit` and `ulimit`

The commands `limit` (a built-in of the C shell) and `ulimit` (a Korn shell and bash built-in) list the system resources available to a given user process. As we shall see in Section 12.3.4, you can also use them to change the value assigned to a particular resource.

OpenVMS

Example:
```
$ SHOW PROCESS/FULL
[not shown]
```

UNIX (c shell)
Form:
```
% limit resource value
% limit
cputime          unlimited
filesize         unlimited
datasize         unlimited
stacksize        8192 kbytes
coredumpsize     0 kbytes
memoryuse        unlimited
descriptors      1024
memorylocked     unlimited
maxproc          7168
openfiles        1024
```

UNIX (Tru64 Korn Shell)
```
$ ulimit -a
time(seconds)         unlimited
file(blocks)
unlimited
data(kbytes)
unlimited
stack(kbytes)         8192
memory(kbytes)        504560
```

UNIX (bash)
```
$ ulimit -a
core file size
(blocks, -c) 0
data seg size
(kbytes, -d) unlimited
file size
(blocks, -f) unlimited
max locked memory
```

```
coredump(blocks)        0        (kbytes, -l) unlimited
nofiles(descriptors)    1024     max memory size
vmemory(kbytes)         unlimited (kbytes, -m) unlimited
                                 open files
                                 (-n) 1024
                                 pipe size
                                 (512 bytes, -p) 8
                                 stack size
                                 (kbytes, -s) 8192
                                 cpu time
                                 (seconds, -t) unlimited
                                 max user processes
                                 (-u) 7168
                                 virtual memory
                                 (kbytes, -v) unlimited
```

The values displayed by `limit` that are important to the average user are as follows:

cputime	The maximum amount of CPU time assigned to any one process, usually unlimited
filesize	The maximum size, in kilobytes, of any one file, usually unlimited (i.e., it could be the size of the whole file system)
coredumpsize	The maximum size, in kilobytes, of the core dump file (see Section 12.3.4)
addressspace	The largest virtual address space available to an executable image
descriptors	The maximum number of files in use at one time
memoryuse	The amount of physical memory that one process can consume, usually unlimited (i.e., all physical memory not being used by the operating system is theoretically available to a user's process)

The important values from the Korn and Bourne-Again shells are similar, differing mainly in their wording.

12.2   Monitoring the System

Section 12.1 considered how individual processes consume system resources. This section discusses three commands that review how the sum total of all user processes or all user files affects the available system resources: `vmstat` reviews virtual memory usage and provides other useful statistics; `netstat` analyzes network usage; and `df` reviews the amount of free disk space on each file system.

12.2.1 Virtual Memory Utilization: `vmstat`

You can use `vmstat` (compare with the OpenVMS command SHOW MEMORY /PHYSICAL) either statically or dynamically. In static mode, without a counter or interval option, `vmstat` reports average utilization of certain system resources since boot time. In dynamic mode, `vmstat` reports the current values at intervals until it is terminated or it reaches the count option (the number of times the `vmstat` program is run). An interval of five seconds is useful.

UNIX

Form:

```
% vmstat [interval] [count]
```

Example:

```
% vmstat
Virtual Memory Statistics: (pagesize = 8192)
procs            memory            pages                         intr         cpu
r    w   u   act free  wire fault cow  zero react    pin pout in   sy  cs us  sy  id
3174 202 25  50K 2048  10K  2M    515K 590K 1799 312K 172 131 794  705     2  7   91
```

Example:

```
% vmstat 5 4
Virtual Memory Statistics: (pagesize = 8192)
procs            memory            pages                         intr         cpu
r    w   u   act free  wire fault cow  zero react    pin pout in   sy  cs us  sy  id
3174 202 25  50K 2048  10K  2M    515K 590K 1799 312K 172 131 794  705     2  7   91
3174 202 25  50K 1558  10K  102   0    102  0    0    0   103 89   626     0  5   95
6171 202 25  50K 1553  10K  179   17   128  0    21   0   123 1K   649     6  12  83
3174 202 25  50K 1553  10K  102   0    102  0    0    0   87  45   576     0  4   95
4173 202 25  50K 1552  10K  103   0    103  0    0    0   108 235  640     1  5   94
```

In the first example, taken from Tru64 UNIX, `vmstat` without arguments reports average statistics since boot time. The most important fields are as follows:

`procs`	*Process statistics*: running (`r`), awaiting resources (`b`), and swapped (`w`)
`memory`	*Memory utilization*: virtual pages of 1,024 bytes in use (`avm`) or free (`fre`)

page	*Paging activity*: reclaims (re), pages in (pi), pages out (po), and anticipated short-term memory shortfall [i.e., how much paging is likely to occur (de)]
faults	*Faulting*: device interrupts per second (in), system calls per second (sy), indicating the demand being placed on the kernel, averaged over the last five seconds (The fields cs and vs show features found only on a vector processor and represent a vendor-specific enhancement to UNIX. These fields are not discussed further.)
cpu	*CPU utilization*: user (us), system (sy), and idle (id), in seconds

The second example, vmstat 5 4, reports statistics every five seconds for four counts.

12.2.2 Network Utilization: netstat

The command netstat is used principally by the system administrator. Therefore, this section discusses netstat only briefly for the benefit of those users for whom network utilization may be an issue. If you are unfamiliar with the nomenclature introduced here, you may wish to return to this section after reading Chapter 13.

Like vmstat, netstat operates in both a static and a dynamic mode, as illustrated in the examples below.

UNIX

Form:

```
% netstat [options] [interval] [system] [core]
```

Example:

```
% netstat -i
Name  Mtu  NetworkAddress              Ipkts      Ierrs  Opkts      Oerrs  Coll
ln0   1500 DLI none                    15801688   0      7091305    1471   390544
ln0   1500 <Link> 08:00:2b:35:b3:94    15801688   0      7091305    1471   390544
fta0  4352 DLI none                    83525851   0      97596376   0      0
fta0  4352 <Link> 08:00:2b:a2:1e:9e    83525851   0      97596376   0      0
fta0  4352 fddi-ringpauline.sdsc.edu   83525851   0      97596376   0      0
```

Example:

```
% netstat -i 5
input          (ee0)      output          input       (Total) output
packets  errs  packets  errs colls  packets     errs    packets     errs   colls
83345572 177   9629257    0    0     1840810813  1939    1150908994  34850  0
327      0     2          0    0     3780        0       635         0      0
282      0     1          0    0     6406        0       3621        0      0
327      0     2          0    0     3780        0       635         0      0
282      0     1          0    0     6406        0       3621        0      0
```

Linux

Form:

```
% netstat [options]
```

Example:

```
% netstat
Active Internet connections (w/o servers)
Proto Recv-Q Send-Q Local Address          Foreign Address         State
tcp       0      0  www.unh.edu:http       as3-4-109.NIN.Kerk:3247  SYN_RECV
tcp       0      0  www.unh.edu:http       h411s142b277n134.u:4391  SYN_RECV
tcp       0      0  www.tnh.unh.edu:http   d-207-5-169-61.s-:64470  SYN_RECV
tcp       0      0  www.unh.edu:wnd        h00045ad7f579.ne.c:4179  SYN_RECV
tcp       0      0  www.unh.edu:http       student9a-261.unh.:1141  ESTABLISHED
tcp       0      0  unhinfo.unh.edu:http   gliglnukay.ne.cli:21035  ESTABLISHED
tcp       0      0  unhinfo.unh.edu:ftp    hgd095b0e7fff.ne.:33477  ESTABLISHED
tcp       0      0  www.unh.edu:http       cache-mtc-am02.pr:54525  TIME_WAIT
```

Example:

```
netstat -I
Kernel Interface table
Iface  MTU Met   RX-OK RX-ERR RX-DRP RX-OVR   TX-OK TX-ERR TX-DRP TX-OVR Flg
eth0   1500 0113869908    0      0 0130439640    0      0      0 BMRU
eth0:  1500  0   - no statistics available -    BMRU
eth0:  1500  0   - no statistics available -    BMRU
eth0:  1500  0   - no statistics available -    BMRU
eth0:  1500  0   - no statistics available -    BMRU
eth0:  1500  0   - no statistics available -    BMRU
eth0:  1500  0   - no statistics available -    BMRU
...
```

Example:

```
% netstat -i
Kernel Interface table
Iface  MTU Met   RX-OK RX-ERR RX-DRP RX-OVR   TX-OK TX-ERR TX-DRP TX-OVR Flg
eth0   1500 0113869908    0      0 0130439640    0      0      0 BMRU
eth0:  1500  0   - no statistics available -    BMRU
eth0:  1500  0   - no statistics available -    BMRU
eth0:  1500  0   - no statistics available -    BMRU
eth0:  1500  0   - no statistics available -    BMRU
eth0:  1500  0   - no statistics available -    BMRU
eth0:  1500  0   - no statistics available -    BMRU
...
```

Example:

```
% netstat
Active Internet connections (w/o servers)
Proto Recv-Q Send-Q Local Address          Foreign Address         State
tcp       0      0  www.unh.edu:http       as3-4-109.HIP.Berk:3247  SYN_RECV
tcp       0      0  www.unh.edu:http       as3-4-109.HIP.Berk:3243  SYN_RECV
tcp       0      0  www.unh.edu:http       h114s144a177n134:4391    SYN_RECV
tcp       0      0  www.tnh.unh.edu:http   d-207-5-169-61.s-:64570  SYN_RECV
tcp       0      0  www.unh.edu:http       h00045ad7e179.ne.c:4180  SYN_RECV
tcp       0      0  www.unh.edu:wnd        h00045ad7e179.ne.c:4179  SYN_RECV
tcp       0      0  www.unh.edu:http       student3a-621.unh.:1141  ESTABLISHED
tcp       0      0  unhinfo.unh.edu:http   russellkay.ne.cli:21035  ESTABLISHED
tcp       0      0  unhinfo.unh.edu:ftp    h00095b0e7fff.ne.:33477  ESTABLISHED
tcp       0      0  www.unh.edu:http       cache-mtc-am02.pr:54525  TIME_WAIT
tcp       0      0  unhinfo.unh.edu:ftp    h00095b0e7fff.ne.:33541  ESTABLISHED
tcp       0      0  unhinfo.unh.edu:ftp    h00095b0e7fff.ne.:33223  ESTABLISHED
tcp       0      0  www.unh.edu:http       h0040f40a4dcc.ne.c:2095  TIME_WAIT
tcp       0      0  unhinfo.unh.edu:ftp    pool-64-223-148-79:3030  ESTABLISHED
Active Internet connections (w/o servers)
Proto Recv-Q Send-Q Local Address          Foreign Address         State
tcp       0      0  www.unh.edu:http       as3-4-109.HIP.Berk:3247  SYN_RECV
```

```
tcp          0          0 www.unh.edu:http          as3-4-109.HIP.Berk:3243      SYN_RECV
tcp          0          0 www.unh.edu:http          h114s144a177n134.u:4491      SYN_RECV
tcp          0          0 www.tnh.unh.edu:http      d-207-5-169-61.s-:64570      SYN_RECV
tcp          0          0 www.unh.edu:http          h00045ad7e179.ne.c:4180      SYN_RECV
tcp          0          0 www.unh.edu:wnd           h00045ad7e179.ne.c:4179      SYN_RECV
tcp          0          0 www.unh.edu:http          student3a-621.unh.:1141      ESTABLISHED
tcp          0          0 unhinfo.unh.edu:http
russellkay.ne.cli:21035             ESTABLISHED
tcp          0          0 unhinfo.unh.edu:ftp       h00095b0e7fff.ne.:33477      ESTABLISHED
tcp          0          0 www.unh.edu:http          cache-mtc-am02.pr:54525      TIME_WAIT
tcp          0          0 unhinfo.unh.edu:ftp       h00095b0e7fff.ne.:33541       ESTABLISHED
tcp          0          0 unhinfo.unh.edu:ftp       h00095b0e7fff.ne.:33223       ESTABLISHED
tcp          0          0 www.unh.edu:http          h0040f40a4dcc.ne.c:2095      TIME_WAIT
tcp          0          0 unhinfo.unh.edu:ftp       pool-64-223-148-79:3030      ESTABLISHED
```

The command `netstat -i` provides information on each available interface. In the Tru64 UNIX example, `fta0` is the Ethernet interface, and `ln0` is a serial line. `Mtu` expresses the maximum size of a packet. `Network` gives the Internet address, and `Address` gives the Internet host name. The remaining fields describe network activity since the computer was last booted: input packets (`Ipkts`), output packets (`Opkts`), input errors (`Ierrs`), output errors (`Oerrs`), and collisions (`Collis`). The number of collisions provides a clue as to how heavily the network is being utilized: Two host computers must attempt to send data at exactly the same time to produce a collision. This situation is known as *network contention*. Given the high speed of transmission, network utilization must be heavy before `netstat` registers a significant number of collisions. The command `netstat -i 5`, also from Tru64 UNIX, updates this information every five seconds. The first entry provides the statistics accumulated since the computer was booted, and the following entries provide statistics at five-second intervals.

This unadorned `netstat` command, the third example, comes from a Red Hat Linux system. Without options it provides information on the status of each Internet connection. `Recv-Q` and `Send-Q` indicate the number of packets waiting to be received and sent, respectively, to a particular host.

12.2.3   **File-System Utilization:** `df`

The command `df` (disk free) determines the amount of free disk space on all mounted file systems, including the file system containing a user's files (compare with the OpenVMS command `SHOW DEVICES /FULL`). The `df /dir` command reports disk space utilization for the file system `/dir` only. If `df` reports that the file system is full, you will be unable to create a new file or save the editing session of an existing file. In OpenVMS, if you wish to save the editing session of an important file to a disk device that is full, you must either ask the system administrator to make space available or spawn another process to delete some of your files from the disk that is full. In UNIX, you can stop the current process, fork a new copy of the shell, delete unwanted files, return to the editing session, and save the file.

OpenVMS

Form:

```
$ SHOW DEVICES [device-name[:]]
```

Example:

```
$ SHOW DEV/FULL DAD21:
Disk DAD21: (SOLAR), device type RRD42, is online, mounted, software write-locked, file-oriented
device, shareable, error logging is enabled.
Error count          0              Operations completed          30265
Owner process        " "            Owner UIC                     [SYSTEM]
Owner process ID     00000000       Dev Prot                      S:RWPL,O:RWPL,G:R,W
Reference count      1              Default buffer size           512
Total blocks         1250600        Sectors per track             4
Total cylinders      52109          Tracks per cylinder           6
Allocation class     1
Volume label         "AXPBINDEC976" Relative volume number        0
Cluster size         3
Transaction count    1
Free blocks          113872         Maximum files allowed         69444
Extend quantity      64             Mount count                   1
Mount status System                 Cache name                    "_$1$DUA31:XQPCACHE"
Extent cache size    64             Maximum blocks in extent cache 11387
File ID cache size   64             Blocks currently in extent cache 0
Quota cache size     0              Maximum buffers in FCP cache   2409
Volume owner UIC                    [SYSTEM]                       Vol Prot S:RWCD,O:RWCD,
                                                                     G:RWCD,W:RWCD

Volume status: write-back caching enabled.
```

UNIX

Form:

```
% df [option(s)] [filesystem]
```

Example:

```
% df
Filesystem   total    kbytes   kbytes   percent
node         kbytes   used     free     used     Mounted on
/dev/ra0a    7415     6354     320      95%      /
/dev/ra0g    41847    33635    4028     89%      /usr
```

The command df without options or arguments reports on all mounted file systems; in this example, there are two. The fields provide information on two file systems, / and /usr, mounted in the a and g partitions of the physical device ra0. The fields are self-explanatory. The UNIX command df reports only file-system utilization, whereas the OpenVMS command SHOW DEVICES /FULL also reports the physical characteristics of the device. Section 2.3 describes how to determine the physical characteristics of a file system. The command df -i (not shown) reports the file-system block and fragment size.

12.3   **Modifying Processes**

UNIX provides five commonly used commands to modify user processes: `kill`, to terminate a process completely; `at`, to start a process at a later time; `nice`, to lower the priority of a process to be executed; `renice`, to lower the priority of a process already running; and `limit`, to reduce the resource limits of a process. Only the system administrator can increase the priority of a process or kill other users' processes.

Some OpenVMS users can modify features of their own processes other than the priority using the SET PROCESS command. The ability to make these modifications depends on the privileges assigned by the OpenVMS system administrator. UNIX does not provide the same flexibility, since the system administrator cannot assign a subset of privileges to individual users.

12.3.1   **Deleting a Process:** `kill`

The command `kill` (compare with the OpenVMS command STOP/IDEN-TIFICATION) deletes processes. It is a built-in feature of the C and Korn shells, but is a separate command in bash and the Bourne shells. To use `kill`, you must specify a process identification number, which you can determine with the `ps` command. The effect of `kill` may vary in different shells. The feature of `kill` described here relates to all shells.

OpenVMS	UNIX
Form:	
`% kill -[option(s)] processid`	`$ STOP/ID = pid`
Example:	
`% kill -9 2019`	`$ STOP/ID = AA2019`

In this example, `kill -9 2019` deletes the process with the process identification number `2019`. The man page for `kill` indicates that the `-9` option is a "sure kill" and will therefore remove a process under all circumstances. Most users will not need to use more than this version of the `kill` command. See Section 10.9.1 for further discussion of `kill`.

12.3.2   **Delaying Execution:** `at`

The command `at` instructs the shell to begin processing commands at a later time. The commands may reside in a UNIX file known as a *shell script*, which corresponds to an OpenVMS command procedure, or commands may be entered at the terminal. In either instance, you do not need to be logged in when the system executes the commands. You must redirect output from the commands to a file or else you will lose it. You may specify various formats for the time of execution, as shown in the following examples. Note that at is available on Linux, but the output looks a little different than the UNIX examples provided here.

OpenVMS	**UNIX**
Form:	
`$ SUBMIT/AFTER = `*`time file`*	`% at `*`time`*` [`*`day`*`] [`*`file`*`]`
`$ RUN PROCESS /DELAY = `*`delta-`*	
`time file`	
Example:	
`$ SUBMIT/AFTER = 23:00`	`% at 2300`
`TEST.COM`	`test > test.out`
	`<CTRL>-D`
Example:	
`$ SUBMIT/AFTER = -`	`% at 8am jan 24`
`24-JAN-1988:08:00 TEST.COM`	`test > test.out`
	`<CTRL>-D`
	`% at 1530 fr`
	`test > test.out`
	`<CTRL>-D`
	`% at 1530 fr week`
	`test > test.out`
	`<CTRL>-D`

The command at 2300 processes the commands contained in the file test, starting at 23:00 hours (11 P.M.) on the day the at command was issued. If the command was issued at 11:30 P.M., then the system will execute the commands at 11:00 P.M. the following day.

You must type the script filename and any redirection on the following lines. The system will not execute a shell script if it is entered on the same line as the at command. Rather than the name of a shell script file, you may enter any sequence of commands on the following lines. In either instance, input to the at command is terminated by entering <CTRL>-D.

The command at 8am jan 24 begins processing at 8:00 A.M. on January 24 of the current year if issued before January 24 or of the next year if issued after. The command `at 1530 fr` begins processing on Friday at 3:30 P.M. The command `at 1530 fr week` begins processing at 3:30 P.M. a week from the coming Friday. In all of these examples, the output is directed to the file `test.out`. Error messages will be lost (but could have been saved with a `>&` redirection).

The daemon `cron` will start the `at` program at intervals. The program `cron` looks in the file `/usr/lib/crontab` to determine how often to process `at` requests. A typical interval is 15 minutes, and so a job scheduled to start at 15:31 may not actually start until 15:45.

One basic difference between OpenVMS and UNIX that affects `at` is that UNIX can "remember" the directory from which a command was issued. For example, an OpenVMS user submitting a command file to a batch queue must include commands to set the default directory if commands address files not found in the login directory. UNIX assumes that the default directory is the one from which the command was issued and not the home directory.

12.3.3   Lowering the Priority: `nice` and `renice`

The command `nice` lowers the priority of a command or a file containing a group of commands (a shell script) prior to execution. The C shell includes `nice`, but it is a separate program for bash users. Recall that the higher the number associated with the priority, the lower the priority.

OpenVMS	UNIX
Form:	
`$ SET PROCESS/PRIORITY = n`	`% nice +[number] command [arguments]`
Example:	
`$ SET PROCESS/PRIORITY = 1`	`% nice +10`
Example:	
`$ SET PROCESS/PRIORITY = 1`	`% nice +10 f77 myprog.f`

The command `nice +10` adds 10 to the priority of the current shell; that is, it reduces its priority. Similarly, `nice +10 f77 myprog.f` adds 10 to the priority of the FORTRAN compilation of the source file `myprog.f`.

The command `renice` reduces the priority of processes that are already running. The operating system reduces priority automatically, but you can do so manually. You can reduce a single process, all of a user's processes, or all processes owned by members of the same group. Once you reduce them, you cannot raise the priority of these processes. Only the system administrator can increase the priority of any process running on the system.

OpenVMS	UNIX
Form:	
`$ SET PROCESS/PRIORITY = 1/ID = ` *nn*	`% renice ` *priority* ` -[p ` *pid*`] \`
	`-[g ` *group*`] [` *user*`]`
Example:	
`$ SET PROCESS/PRIORITY= 1/ID = 37`	`% renice 10 -p 71823`
	`% renice 10 -g admin`
	`% renice 10 -u fred`

In the examples below, the command `renice 10 -p 71823` decreases by 10 the priority of the running process with the identification number `71823`. The command `renice 10 -g admin` lowers the priority of all processes owned by members of the group `admin`, provided the command is issued either by a member of the group `admin` or by the user `root`. Finally, `renice 10 -u fred` lowers the priority of all processes owned by user `fred`, provided `fred` (or `root`) makes the request.

12.3.4 Lowering System-Resource Utilization: `limit` Revisited

You have already used `limit` to display the system resources available to a process. You may also use `limit` to reduce them.

OpenVMS	UNIX
Form:	
`$ SET PROCESS[/`*qualifier(s)*`]`	`% limit ` *resource value*
process name	
	Example:
	`% limit coredumpsize 0`

The command `limit coredumpsize 0` prevents the creation of a core dump file in the event of program failure. Users who do not intend to analyze a memory dump might do well to set this value to 0, thereby preventing large unwanted files from occupying disk space.

The bash and Korn shell built-in `ulimit` commands are similarly capable of changing your resource limits. All varieties operate within what are called "soft" and "hard" limits. The soft limits are your current process limits, while the hard limits are systemwide values set by the system administrator.

12.3.5 Running Commands When the System Load Level Permits: `batch`

The `batch` command is very similar to the `at` command described in Section 12.3.2. The two differ in that the `at` command is oriented towards running commands at a specified time, whereas the `batch` command is oriented toward running commands when the system load level reaches a predetermined value.

12.4 Summary

The following scenario uses some of the commands introduced in this chapter. Fred wishes to compile and then run a large C program.

UNIX

Example;

```
% w
   8:48am up 46 days, 11 hrs, 5 users, load average: 0.00, 0.00, 0.00
User      tty    from                 login@    idle     JCPU   PCPU   what
julia     q0     132.239.70.215       17Nov97   40days   1:06   2      -csh
julia     q1     132.239.70.215       19Nov97   38days   3      1      -csh
julia     q2     132.239.70.215       19Nov97   38days   1      1      -csh
sarah     q3     hercules.sdsc.edu    8:36am             2      2      w
julia     q5     132.239.70.215       21Nov97   36days   5      1      -csh
% cc -o myprog.exe myprog.c >& myprog.out &
[1] 16335
% ps -aux | head
USER      PID    %CPU   %MEM   SZ    RSS   TT   STAT   TIME    COMMAND
fred      14516  39.8   11.0   536   244   p7   R      0:01    cc myprog.c >& myprog.out
joyce     4857   24.8   16.0   236   224   14   R      47:52   f77 /usr/joyce/list.f
jack      14064  19.8   10.3   104   44    15   R      0:00    /usr/public/xplor
jill      14093  16.8   20.2   28    16    27   R      61:39   /usr/public/fft
fred      14517  0.6    0.2    56    28    p7   S      0:00    head
root      81     0.4    0.5    160   100   ?    I      45:17   /etc/routed
root      14468  0.4    0.3    104   44    p0   I      0:12    rlogind 803b6202.1022
root      87     0.3    0.4    128   80    ?    S      19:31   /etc/rwhod
fred      14065  0.2    0.4    260   64    p7   S      0:00    -csh[system] (csh)
% df /usr
Filesystem   total         kbytes     kbytes     percent
node         kbytes        used       free       used       Mounted on
```

```
/dev/ra0g      41847      35060     2603      93%          /usr
% at 2300
myprog.exe > output
<CTRL>-D
```

Fred first issues the command w to determine the number of users and the load on the system. The system is being heavily utilized, having sustained a workload of greater than 5 over the past 15 minutes (that is, five similar computers are necessary to process the workload efficiently). Fred decides to compile and link his program now and, provided no errors occur, run the application later in the evening when the system load will likely be less. The command cc --o myprog.exe myoprog.c >& myprog.out & performs the compilation in the background and directs terminal output and error messages to the file myprog.out and the executable image to myprog.exe. See Section 7.4 for a discussion of background processing. For now it is sufficient to understand that multiple processes may be running simultaneously. Hence, while the system performs the compilation, Fred determines the percentage of system resources utilized by the compilation with the command ps -aux | head, which forks a new process and displays the 10 processes currently consuming the most CPU time. Seeing that he is utilizing 39.8% of the available CPU resources, Fred waits for the compilation to finish. Then Fred issues the command df /usr, which shows 2.6 MB of disk space available on the file system on which he wants to run his application. The disk space is sufficient for the output of myprog.c, assuming that the amount of free disk space is not going to change significantly between now and the time that myprog.c writes output to the file system. The command at 2300 will start the application at 11:00 P.M. this evening, regardless of whether or not Fred is logged in. The command myprog.exe > output will run the program, directing output to the file output; no error messages will be saved. Fred terminates input to the at command with <CTRL>-D. Fred then goes home, having performed his good deed for the day.

13

Networking

13

Networking

The new electronic independence recreates the world
in the image of a global village.

—*Marshall McLuhan*

Networking is as ubiquitous today as computers themselves. Few computers operate in isolation, but are part of networks of computers within an organization (intranet) or throughout the world (Internet). (We will use the terms *network connection* and *Internet* interchangeably throughout this chapter.) Underneath the hood are many types of processors, running a variety of operating systems.

The UNIX user, often even more than the OpenVMS user, performs a variety of network-related tasks. This chapter identifies those tasks and describes the commands required to perform them. Unfortunately, this entails more than the relatively simple matter of defining a single command for each task: The commands vary according to the type of connection existing between the UNIX computers, the type of access permitted by the system administrator of each computer, and the type of access permitted by the owner of each remote account you might want to access. For the purposes of this discussion, we consider two types of connection:

- *Network:* a fast, continuous connection using dedicated communication

- *Modem:* a slow, intermittent connection using telephone lines, in which tasks are often queued for transmission by means of the UNIX to UNIX CoPy (UUCP) utility

To further complicate the situation, the commands used in network communications are subdivided according to whether the connection is to a UNIX *trusted host* or *nontrusted host*. The OpenVMS analog to a UNIX trusted host is a proxy login. To perform a task on another OpenVMS computer, OpenVMS users issue a given command whether they have a proxy login or not. The OpenVMS user provides username and password information for the other computer only if a proxy login is not available. For example, to copy an OpenVMS file to another OpenVMS computer, the user invokes the COPY command and provides username and password information in the instance of a nonproxy login, but no username and password information in the case of a proxy login. UNIX users issue completely different commands depending on whether file copying occurs between trusted or nontrusted hosts: rcp between trusted hosts, and ftp between nontrusted hosts. The syntax used by these two commands is different. The rcp command resembles the cp command for local file copying (see Sections 4.10 and 8.3.1), whereas ftp uses a syntax different from anything we have encountered before. Hence, copying to a trusted host simplifies file transfer because there is no new syntax to remember. The disadvantage of communicating with trusted hosts is that the security of a user's files may be more easily compromised than when communicating with nontrusted hosts. As we shall see, if an intruder gains access to a user's files on one computer, it is a simple matter to gain access to that same user's files on any trusted host computer.

This chapter is organized into two major divisions based on the type of connection between the host computers: Section 13.2 covers network connections and Section 13.3 covers modem connections. Each of these two divisions is further subdivided based on task. Table 13.1 summarizes these tasks and indicates the section of the chapter where you can find additional information.

Note in Table 13.1 that NFS is not a command, but a protocol that permits access to remote file systems with standard UNIX commands.

The tasks of remote login, file transfer, and sending mail require no further clarification. Remote command execution involves issuing a command on one computer for execution on another computer. Remote file access involves transparently accessing files located on a remote computer as if those files were located on the local computer. Experienced DECnet users should note that task-to-task communication, whereby a program on one node interacts directly with a program on another node, is beyond the scope of this book.

Table 13.1   *Commands Used for Communication Between UNIX Hosts*

Task	Network Trusted Host	Nontrusted Host	Modem
Remote login	`rlogin` `(13.2.4.1)`	`telnet` `(13.2.4.2)`	`tip/cu` `(13.3.3)`
File transfer	`rcp` `(13.2.6.1)`	`ftp` `(13.2.6.2)`	`uucp/uusend` `(13.3.5)`
Sending mail	`mail` `(13.2.5)`	`mail` `(13.2.5)`	`mail` `(13.2.5)`
Remote command execution	`rsh` `(13.2.7)`		`uux` `(13.3.6)`
Remote file access	`NFS` `(13.2.8)`	`NFS` `(13.2.8)`	

Several features of networking, not necessarily obvious from Table 13.1, need to be understood from the outset:

- The commands uucp, uusend, and uux are part of the UUCP utility for performing tasks between local and remote hosts. The commands tip and cu are separate programs that may use the same modems (or any serial connection) as UUCP to dial remote hosts on which they can conduct terminal sessions.

- Tasks based on network connections use r, or *remote*, commands—rcp, rlogin, and rsh—for trusted hosts, and telnet and ftp for nontrusted hosts.

- Sending mail to users on other computers employs the mail utility (see Chapter 6) regardless of the type of connection between the computers. The format of the mail address, however, differs from computer to computer.

- Remote file access via NFS is available only using network connections.

The use of NFS requires further discussion. You can think of NFS as a procedure whereby a file system mounted on one computer may also be mounted on a remote computer. This means that you can access a file with the file-management commands discussed in Chapters 4 and 8, whether the file resides on a local or remote computer. The OpenVMS analog to UNIX NFS is the OpenVMS cluster, although a cluster file system gives a much more thorough impression of local file access.

This chapter concludes with a brief discussion of two topics that, although not concerned with commands, can be important to the UNIX user faced with a distributed computing environment. The first introduces Usenet, a UNIX bulletin board for the dissemination of electronic information. The second explains network communications between UNIX and OpenVMS computers.

Before examining how you may perform tasks on a number of computers, you should have a basic understanding of how communication occurs between computers: both between UNIX processors and between UNIX and non-UNIX processors. We start with a simple discussion of how computers communicate, introducing nomenclature used throughout the remainder of the chapter. Included in this discussion are examples of several UNIX commands with which you can inquire into the characteristics and status of UNIX computers communicating via network or modem.

13.1 Communication Overview

Once two UNIX computers are connected by a physical link, the potential exists for communication between them. Each computer is called a *host* (compare with the OpenVMS DECnet term *node*). Hosts are characterized by a *host name* (in OpenVMS, a *node name*). The computer to which a user's terminal is connected is called the *local host* (in OpenVMS DECnet, *local node*), and all other computers are called *remote hosts* (in OpenVMS DECnet, *remote nodes*).

The speed with which communication takes place varies greatly and is a function of the physical link. Modem connections are simple. The host receiving data via a modem treats it no differently from input from any terminal. If a UNIX host has a modem that can both originate and answer calls, the UUCP software (part of nearly all versions of the UNIX operating system) enables the host to join a large conglomeration of UNIX processors for file, mail, and news exchange. To reduce telephone costs, exchange usually occurs via a number of intermediate hosts on a *store-and-forward* network. Each intermediate host receives a complete copy of the file being transferred before it passes it along to the next host. The system administrator maintains data for remote hosts (e.g., telephone numbers) and the types of connection they afford in the files `/usr/lib/uucp/L.*`. Typically, at some predetermined time each day, one UNIX host will automatically dial another and exchange files, mail, or news. The time delay from queuing the information precludes any interactive access. As you can imagine, UUCP connections are disappearing in favor of network connections as the Internet continues to expand.

To establish a network-based connection between hosts is not as simple as establishing a modem-based connection using an RS-232 (terminal) interface. High-speed data transmission and the ability to perform task-to-task communication require specialized hardware and software. If computers from different manufacturers running different operating systems wish to communicate, they must adopt a standard interface.

One such interface, Ethernet, is used by OpenVMS and most UNIX-based processors. Ethernet defines not only the wiring and type of plugs that connect computers, but also the format of the data sent. Data is broken into discrete entities called *packets*. Each packet contains a part of the data being sent, the local host name, the remote host name, and a sequence number. The receiving host uses the sequence number to reassemble packets in the correct order, which is particularly important if packets must be resent because an error occurred during transmission.

Modem-based data transfers may simply be a stream of data, started and stopped in the same way data from a terminal is started and stopped. However, some software supporting modem-based data transfers, such as Kermit, also transfer data in packets.

Depending on the networking protocol that is being used, OpenVMS and UNIX may use different methods to format data in that part of the packet devoted to user data. At one time, DECnet was the only networking protocol available for OpenVMS. DECnet systems and UNIX format data differently from TCP/IP. TCP/IP networking is bundled with recent releases of OpenVMS, although several functions require an additional license.

You can use DECnet and TCP/IP on the same Ethernet network, but only a host that understands the format you use can interpret it; a format that the host cannot interpret is ignored. Different versions of UNIX use the TCP/IP definition in different ways. BSD uses a *socket* and System V uses a *stream*. Discussion of sockets and streams is beyond the scope of this book; they do not affect how the average user performs networking tasks. In BSD, however, you may encounter a file type that indicates a socket (see Sections 2.3.2).

Modem-based communications first require that you establish a physical connection, accomplished by one host dialing another on the telephone exchange in the same way voice connections are established. Hosts on a network are always connected; during transmissions over the network each host looks at each packet to determine whether it is destined to receive it. If so, it responds immediately, thus making interactive communications possible. Computers on a network supporting the TCP/IP protocol, or linked to a gateway which supports TCP/IP, are said to be part of the Internet network.

13.1.1 Addressing Communications

Network and modem communications to a user on a remote host require an address akin to a postal address. Each user's address is defined uniquely using a combination of the login name and the name of the local host. The format of the address differs for network and modem communications, and both of these differs from the OpenVMS DECnet network address. Table 13.2 summarizes each format.

Table 13.2 *OpenVMS DECnet and UNIX Mail Address Formats*

	DECnet	Network (Internet)	Modem (UUCP)
Form:	*NODE*::*USER*	*user@host*	*site1*!*site2*!*user*
Example:	BOSTON::FRED	fred@boston.chem .mit.edu	newyork!boston!fred

The UUCP (modem-based) host name need not be the same as the network host name if the host supports both types of communication. However, to avoid confusion, the system administrator usually makes them identical. Network and UUCP addresses are discussed further below.

13.2 Network Communications

This section is devoted to a discussion of communications among UNIX processors connected via a network.

13.2.1 Network Addresses

A user may determine the name of the local host in a network environment with the command `hostname` (compare with the OpenVMS command `SHOW LOGICAL SYS$NODE` for systems running DECnet). Usually this is unnecessary, as the host name is displayed as part of the banner message prior to the login prompt.

OpenVMS	UNIX
Example:	
`$ SHOW LOGICAL SYS$NODE`	`$ hostname`
`CUHHCA::`	`cuhhca`

Example:
```
$ grep cuhhca /etc/hosts
128.59.98.1 cuhhca.hhmi.columbia.edu cuhhca
            babbage.columbia.edu
            babbage.hhmi
            babbage.hhmi.columbia.edu babbage
            cuhhca.columbia.edu cuhhca.hhmi
```

The file `/etc/hosts` stores definitions of local and remote hosts potentially reachable on the Internet. In the above example, `grep cuhhca /etc/hosts` searches this file for the host `cuhhca`. Associated with the host name is an Internet address (`128.59.98.1`) and one or more other names. The first name (`cuhhca.hhmi.columbia.edu`) is the official Internet host name; any others (e.g., `cuhhca`) are aliases. A user wishing to access a remote host can use the Internet address, the official name, or any of the aliases. It is often easiest to use an alias.

An alias will not work in those cases where the address must be resolved; that is, it is not in the `/etc/hosts` file and must be resolved by a name server (see Section 11.7.4). In those cases, the official IP address must be given.

13.2.2 Network Status

Section 12.2.2 introduced the command `netstat` for monitoring the utilization of a network. Network utilization statistics are of little concern to many users. The status of a remote host, however, is of concern. Just because a network host exists does not necessarily mean it is available; it may be down for preventive maintenance or because of hardware failure. The command `ruptime` (compare with the OpenVMS command SHOW NETWORK for nonend nodes) displays which network hosts are available in the immediate vicinity. Information will not be given for remote hosts beyond the network gateway.

OpenVMS

Example:

```
$ SHOW NETWORK
The following network service is available at this time:
Product: DECNET Manufacturer: Digital Equipment Corporation
Node: CUTRA Address(es): 19.215
Network Type: DNA IV Interface(s): net 0
Node Volatile Characteristics as of 22-NOV-1997 10:36:09
Executor node = 19.215 (CUTRA)
Identification = DECnet for OpenVMS Alpha V6.2
...
Link    Node    PID         Process    Remote link    Remote user
8201    19.117  20200094    REMACP     25330          JONES
8200    19.129  20200094    REMACP     24711          SMITH
Node Counters as of 21-NOV-1997 10:36:10
Executor node = 19.215 (CUTRA) ...
```

UNIX

Example:

```
$ ruptime
apne292b   up     48 + 03:00  1 user. load   0.01, 0.00, 0.00
columbia   down ??:??
cocca          up     18 + 04:00  4 users. load   0.09, 0.11 0.14
cuhhca         up      6 + 21:15  8 users. load   6.72, 6.38, 5.93
cuhhmd         up     18 + 05:04  5 users. load   0.77, 0.46, 0.27
```

The fields displayed by ruptime (taking cuhhca as an example) are as follows:

cuhhca	Remote host name
up 6 + 21:15	System has been up for 6 days, 21 hours, and 15 minutes
8 users	8 users are currently logged into the system
load 6.72 6.38 5.93	5 minutes ago the system load was 6.72, 10 minutes ago it was 6.38, and 15 minutes ago it was 5.93

To detect the network status of UNIX hosts beyond the immediate vicinity, use the ping command. The ping command detects whether a host is reachable.

In the first example, ping -q escher checks whether host escher is reachable. The result is typical of Linux; other implementations of UNIX return slightly different results. In the second example, the -c option reports on the status of packets sent and the roundtrip time for the ICMP echo used by ping.

UNIX

Form:

```
ping [options]
```

Example:

```
$ ping -q escher
PING escher (123.123.123.123) from 123.123.137.12 : 56(84) bytes of data.
<CTRL>-C
```

Example:

```
$ ping -c 3 escher
PING escher (123.123.123.123) from 123.123.137.12 : 56(84) bytes of data.
64 bytes from foo.bar (123.123.123.123): icmp_seq=1 ttl=64 time=0.187 ms
64 bytes from foo.bar (123.123.123.123): icmp_seq=2 ttl=64 time=0.184 ms
64 bytes from foo.bar (123.123.123.123): icmp_seq=3 ttl=64 time=0.161 ms
--- foo.bar ping statistics ---
3 packets transmitted, 3 received, 0% loss, time 2016ms
rtt min/avg/max/mdev = 0.161/0.177/0.187/0.015 ms
```

13.2.3 What Is a Trusted Host?

Before we examine specific commands used in network communication, we must elaborate on the concept of a *trusted host*. As stated in Section 13.1, the commands used to communicate with a trusted host may differ from those used to communicate with a nontrusted host. Trusted host commands simplify access by bypassing the password security check otherwise required. The system administrator of each host defines which remote hosts and which users on those hosts are trusted. Let us follow the sequence of events when user Fred, login name `fred`, on local host a attempts to communicate with remote host b using a trusted host r command. To simplify the initial discussion, we assume that Fred has identical login names on both hosts a and b, although, as we shall see, this is not a requirement.

To communicate, `fred` on host a must have access to an account on host b. When `fred` makes a communication request from host a to host b, for example, for a remote login or a file copy, host b first checks the file /etc/ hosts.equiv to see if host a is defined. The file /etc/hosts.equiv contains official Internet host names for trusted hosts. If it finds an entry for host a, host b checks its /etc/passwd file for the login name `fred`. If it is found, access is given to account `fred` on host b without checking password information; that is, if an entry for host a exists in host b's /etc/hosts.equiv file, any user who has the same login name on host a and b has trusted host access.

If an entry for host a is not found in host b's /etc/hosts.equiv file, then the hidden file ~*user*/.rhosts (~fred/.rhosts in this example) is searched for personalized trusted host access. This file, if it exists, contains a list of Internet hosts, one per line. Each host name listed may be followed by one or more login names separated by spaces, defining which users from that host may make r command requests. If an entry for host a is found in this file, assuming that no login name(s) follow the entry for host a, then the /etc/passwd file is checked for the login name fred (i.e., the login names on the local and remote hosts are assumed to be the same). If login name fred is found, access is given to the system. Once again, the password is not checked.

What if the user's login names are not the same on host a and b? By default, ~*user*/.rhosts on host b is the file .rhosts in the directory ~*user*, where ~*user* is the name of the user making the request from host a. The user's communication request from host a can specify the search of an alternative ~*user*/.rhosts file. If this alternative file is searched, access is given to host b only if the ~*user*/.rhosts file specified contains an entry for host a followed by the login name of the person on host a making the request.

For example, let us again consider login name fred on host a, this time making a communication request to login name george on host b. First, the login name george must exist on host b. Second, ~george/.rhosts must contain an entry for host a followed by the login name fred. As you can see, access of this type is useful if a user has different login names on two hosts and wants the convenience of trusted host access. Some system administrators may regard the creation of a ~*user*/.rhosts by the user as too great a security risk. One alternative, available on some UNIX systems, is to have the user root own the ~*user*/.rhosts file.

The following example emphasizes the concept of trusted host access. User fred on network host cuhhca displays the file /etc/hosts.equiv, which indicates definitions of two trusted hosts. Any remote user on cuhhmd.hhmi.columbia.edu or cubsun.biol.columbia.edu who has an identical login name on cuhhca can access cuhhca with trusted host r commands.

Further, ~fred/.rhosts indicates that user george from host cuchmc.hhmi.columbia.edu can access account fred on cuchca. Note that this does not imply that fred on cuhhca can access account george on cuchmc.hhmi.columbia.edu.

With these concepts in mind, we now turn to the specific commands that perform tasks on both trusted and nontrusted remote UNIX hosts.

OpenVMS	UNIX
Example:	
`$ SHOW LOGICAL SYS$NODE`	`$ hostname ; whoami`
`CUHHCA::`	`cuhhca`
	`fred`
Example:	
`$ SHOW NETWORK`	`$ cat /etc/hosts.equiv`
`[not shown]`	`cuhhmd.hhmi.columbia.edu`
	`cubsun.biol.columbia.edu`
	`$ cat ~fred/.rhosts`
	`cuchmc.hhmi.columbia.edu`
	`george`

13.2.4 Remote Login

Two UNIX commands perform remote network logins: `rlogin` for trusted hosts and `telnet` for all other Internet hosts. Table 13.3 compares remote login facilities between TCP/IP systems and OpenVMS systems using traditional DECnet.

Table 13.3 *Comparison of Remote Login Commands*

OpenVMS DCL Command	TCP/IP Command
`SET HOST` or `SET HOST/TELNET`	`telnet`
`SET HOST` or `SET HOST/RLOGIN`	`rlogin`

The methods for establishing a network connection on OpenVMS depend on the network protocol that is being used: DECnet or TCP/IP.

To connect from a DECnet node to a DECnet-only node, use the following format:

```
$ SET HOST DECnet-node
```

To connect from a DECnet-Plus node to another DECnet-Plus node, use the following format:

```
$ SET HOST DECnet-node.computer-name.company.com
```

To connect from a DECnet node to a TCP/IP system, use either of the following formats:

```
$ SET HOST/TELNET host-name.computer-name.company.com
$ SET HOST/RLOGIN host-name.computer-name.company.com
```

13.2.4.1 Trusted Host: `rlogin`

The `rlogin` command is an example of an `r` command for trusted host access. In the following example, the network protocol for OpenVMS is DECnet.

OpenVMS   **UNIX**

Form:

```
$ SET HOST [QUALIFIER(S)] -
NODE_NAME
```

```
$ rlogin host_name [-option(s)]
```

Example:

```
$ SHOW LOGICAL SYS$NODE:
CUHHMC::
```

```
$ hostname
cuchmc
$ whoami
fred
```

```
$ SHOW PROCESS
Pid: 00000A31 Proc. Name: FRED
UIC: [FRED.GRP] Priority: 4
Default file spec: DUA1:[FRED]
```

```
$ SET HOST CUHHMD
Welcome to CUHHMD
Last login: Fri May 29-1998 15:44:01
Last non-interactive login on
Friday, May 29-1998 01:01
$
```

```
$ rlogin cuhhmd
Last login: Fri May 29 15:44:01 from
1.81
$
```

```
$ rlogin cuhhca -lgeorge
...
$ hostname
cuhhca
$ <CTRL>-Z
$ hostname
cuhhmc
$ fg
rlogin cuhhca -lgeorge
$ hostname
cuhhca
$
```

In the first example, `rlogin cuhhmd` logs `fred` on the local host `cuchmc` into the account `fred` on remote host `cuhhmd`. In the second example, `rlogin cuhhca -l george` requests a remote login to the trusted host cuhhca. Note that rather than requesting a login to the default account fred, this command requests a login to the account george with the -1 option. If the directory ~george on the trusted host cuhhca contains an .rhosts entry that permits access from fred on host cuchmc, then the connection is successful. If the user's rlogin attempt is invalid, the remote host requests password information rather than rejecting the request (compare with telnet below).

A useful feature of rlogin, also offered by telnet, is the ability to toggle between the local and the remote host, as illustrated in the latter part of the second example. <CTRL>-Z suspends the local rlogin process and returns control to the shell there. The fg (foreground) command restarts the suspended process and reconnects the user to the remote host. Hence, once you make a connection to a remote host, you can use both the local and the remote host without having to reestablish the connection with rlogin.

13.2.4.2 Nontrusted Host: `telnet`

The command telnet establishes a login session on a remote host, trusted or nontrusted. In either instance, the remote host requests login name and password information. In the following example, the network protocol on OpenVMS is DECnet.

OpenVMS	UNIX
Form:	
`$ telnet host`	`$ SET HOST node`
Example:	
`$ telnet cuhhia`	`$ SET HOST CUHHIA`
`Trying ...`	`CUHHIA:: OpenVMS NODE`
`Connected to`	`Username: SYSTEM`
`cuhhia.hhmi.columbia.edu.`	`Password:`
`Escape character is '<CTRL>]'`	`Welcome to OpenVMS 7.0`
`IRIS UNIX (cuhhia)`	
`login: system`	
`Password:`	
`IRIS Workstation`	
`$ <CTRL>-]`	
`telnet>z`	
`Stopped`	
`$ hostname`	
`cuhhca`	

```
$ fg
telnet cuhhia
$ hostname
cuhhia
```

In this example, `telnet cuhhia` makes a connection to the Internet remote host `cuhhia`, which then prompts for a login name and password (compare `rlogin`). Like `rlogin`, a useful feature of `telnet` is the ability to toggle between the local and the remote host, issuing commands in either environment. `<CTRL>-]` (close square bracket) escapes to the `telnet>` prompt; the `telnet` command `z` generates a new copy of the shell on the local host that can accept commands, in this example, `hostname`; `fg` returns the `telnet` shell to foreground as described in Section 7.3; and the terminal session resumes on the remote host as shown by the display of the remote host's name in response to the `hostname` command. Additional commands that you may issue at the `telnet` prompt appear in Table 13.4.

Table 13.4   `telnet` *Commands*

Command	Function
open host	Open a connection to the named host
close	Terminate a session and return to `telnet` prompt
quit	Terminate a session and return to local shell
z	Suspend `telnet` and invoke copy of local shell (C shell only)
escape char	Set the escape character (default `<CTRL>-]`)
status	Report current `telnet` status
options	Toggle options indicated by `status`
crmod	Toggle carriage-return mode
?	Get help on the above

13.2.5 Sending Mail

Chapter 6 discussed the `mail` utility extensively. We now discuss the elements unique to sending mail to remote users on other network hosts. Users need only an understanding of the format of the mail address. Depending on the networking protocol that is installed, OpenVMS supports either a DECnet mail address of the form *NODE*::*USERNAME*, or the Internet mail form *user@host*. UNIX supports two forms of mail address; for Internet mail there is *user@host*, and for UUCP mail there is *host*!*user*. Since each is discussed online in the man page `mail-addr`, only a synopsis is given here.

The Internet host name is a hierarchical arrangement. For example, the address `cuhhca.hhmi.columbia.edu`, which we have seen on several occasions, implies that the address will be interpreted by the `edu` routing tables, which sends the message to the `columbia` gateway, then to the subdomain `hhmi`, and lastly to the host `cuhhca`. For the average user, the terms *routing table, gateway,* and *subdomain* are not important. You only need to know that `edu` is the name of all computers in educational institutions, `columbia` is a gateway to all Internet hosts at Columbia University, `hhmi` covers all computers in the Howard Hughes Medical Institute at Columbia University, and `cuhhca` is the specific computer. You do not need to remember such routing if the system administrator defines a simple alias in the `/etc/hosts` file.

The following examples compare with the OpenVMS and UNIX methods for sending mail.

OpenVMS	**UNIX**
`To:` *NODE*::*USER*	`$ mail` *user@host*
	`$ mail`
`To:` `SMTP%"`*user@host*`"`	`fred@cuhhmc.chem.columbia.edu`
`To:` `SMTP%"joe@topdoc.net"`	
`To:` *user@host*	
`To:` `joe@topdoc.net`	

The first OpenVMS example above shows the form for sending mail between DECnet systems. The second example shows the form for sending mail from OpenVMS to a TCP/IP host, using Simple Network Transfer Protocol (SMTP). The third example shows how to send mail from an OpenVMS system running TCP/IP to another TCP/IP system.

13.2.6 File Transfer

How you perform file transfer between a local and a remote UNIX host depends on whether trusted host access is available. If trusted host access is available, you can use the command `rcp` (remote copy). The `rcp` command uses the same syntax as cp (copy; see Section 4.10), along with a host name followed by a colon. Compare rcp to OpenVMS proxy login access, which extends the features of the COPY command to include a node name followed by :: (double colon). COPY is similar to rcp in that username and password information are not required.

If trusted host access is not available, you can use the ftp utility. The ftp utility first requires that you establish a connection to the remote host and then use a command syntax different from both cp and rcp to transfer files.

TCP/IP networking differs from DECnet for both types of file access in that the user must have an account on the remote machine to enable file transfer even when the remote file is readable by all users. DECnet users may copy a world-readable file from a remote host whether they have a username on that node or not. The inability of UNIX to let remote hosts read world-readable files becomes a problem when you have files you wish to make available for export. A method commonly used to circumvent this problem is to set up anonymous ftp, that is, to establish a guest account (often called anonymous with a password of guest or your e-mail address on the local computer), which permits ftp connections to specific directories where these files reside.

Table 13.5 compares TCP/IP and OpenVMS DCL file transfer commands.

Table 13.5   *Comparison of the File Transfer Commands*

TCP/IP	OpenVMS DCL Command
ftp>get	COPY/FTP
ftp>put	COPY/FTP
ftp>Is	DIRECTORY/FTP

13.2.6.1 Trusted Host: rcp

The following examples show various uses of rcp and compares them to their OpenVMS DECnet proxy login counterparts.

In the first example, rcp cuhhmd:/usr/user1/junk myfile copies the file /usr/user1/junk from the trusted remote host cuhhmd to myfile in the present working directory on the local host. In the second example, rcp myfile cuhhmd:/usr/user1/junk copies myfile in the present working directory on the local host to the file junk in the directory /usr/user1 on the remote trusted host cuhhmd. For file transfer to occur, the same login

OpenVMS	UNIX

OpenVMS

Form:
```
$ COPY[/QUALIFIER(S)] -
NODE::source_file target_file
```
Example:
```
$ COPY CUHHMD::DUA0: [USER1] -
JUNK.DAT MYFILE.DAT
```
Form:
```
$ COPY[/QUALIFIER(S)] -
source_file NODE::target_file
```
Example:
```
$ COPY MYFILE.DAT-
CUHHMD::DUA0:[USER1]JUNK.DAT
```

UNIX

```
$ rcp hostname:source_file target_file
```

```
$ rcp cuhhmd:/usr/user1/junk myfile
```

```
$ rcp source_file hostname:target_file
```

```
$ rcp myfile cuhhmd:/usr/user1 junk
```

Form:
```
$ rcp -r source_directory \
hostname:target_directory
```
Example:
```
$ rcp -r ~fred/programs cuhhmd:\
/usr/fred/programs
```

Example:
```
$ COPY MYFILE CUHHMD::DUA2: -
[.PROGRAMS]JUNK
```
Example:
```
$ COPY MYFILE -
CUHHMD::DUA2:[.PROGRAMS]
```

```
$ rcp myfile cuhhmd:programs /junk
```

```
$ rcp myfile cuhhmd:programs
```

name must own the remote directory /usr/user1 on cuhhmd, as well as the files on the local host, unless modified by a cuhhmd:~*user*/.rhosts entry. Moreover, the directory /usr/user1 must already exist on cuhhmd; the command will not create it.

The third example, rcp -r ~fred/programs cuhhmd:/usr/ fred/ programs, illustrates copying a directory structure (-r option for recursive copying) across the network. In the UNIX example given here, the local directory programs, any subdirectories of programs, and all files therein are recreated on the remote host cuhhmd in the directory /usr/fred/programs in the same way as the cp command copies directory structures on a single host (see Section 8.3.1).

In the fourth example, rcp myfile cuhhmd:programs/junk illustrates the use of a relative pathname to specify a file on the remote host. The command copies `myfile` to *~user*/programs/junk on the remote host. Relative pathnames on a local host start from the present working directory; relative pathnames on a remote host start from the parent directory of the user. Note that if the directory *~user*/programs on the remote host did not exist, it would not have been created. Rather, an error would have occurred.

The last example extends the concept of using a relative pathname. Because `rcp myfile cuhhmd:programs` does not include an output filename (`programs` is a directory), the file is copied with the same name to *~user*/programs/myfile.

13.2.6.2 Nontrusted Host: `ftp`

Section 13.2.6.1 showed that file transfer between trusted hosts is no more cumbersome than transfers between OpenVMS nodes using DECnet, and it offers the additional feature of simple directory structure copying. Copying between nontrusted hosts is not so straightforward.

The `ftp`, or file transfer program, a utility for file transfer between nontrusted network hosts, establishes a connection to a remote host for which a login name and password are required. The `ftp` utility is also available for OpenVMS. Once an `ftp` connection is established, you can issue a variety of commands on either the local or the remote host, including `?`, which provides help on available `ftp` commands. A subset of commonly used `ftp` commands appears in Table 13.6. As a pleasing departure from standard UNIX practice, you may abbreviate these commands.

Table 13.6   *Subset of* `ftp` *Commands*

Command	Function
`!`	Issue shell command on local host
`ascii`	Set file transfer type to ASCII (default)
`binary`	Set file transfer type to binary
`bye (or quit)`	Terminate connection to remote host and exit `ftp`
`cd`	Change present working directory on remote host
`close`	Terminate connection to remote host; do not exit `ftp`
`delete`	Delete a file on remote host
`get (or recv)`	Copy file from remote to local host
`help (or ?)`	Get help on available commands

Table 13.6 *Subset of* ftp *Commands (continued)*

Command	Function
lcd	Change directory on local host
ls	Get directory listing on remote host
mdelete	Delete multiple files on remote host
mget	Retrieve multiple files from remote host
mkdir	Create a directory on remote host
mput	Copy multiple files from local to remote host
open	Establish a connection to remote host
prompt	Toggle interactive prompting
put (or send)	Copy single file from local to remote host
pwd	Display current working directory on remote host
rename	Rename a file on remote host
rmdir	Remove a directory on remote host
status	Display the status of ftp

You can avoid entering your login name and password each time you make a connection with ftp by using the hidden file *~user*/.netrc, which resides in the parent directory of the local host (compare with *~user*/.rhosts, which resides on the remote host).

UNIX

Form:

% machine *host* login *username* password *password*

Example:

% cat ~fred/.netrc
machine cuhhmd.hhmi.columbia.edu login fred password mypassword

In this example, the user can make an ftp connection to the remote host cuhhmd.hhmi.columbia.edu using the login name fred and the password mypassword. The host name must be the official Internet host name, that is, the first entry for the host in the /etc/hosts file and not an alias. As the ~*user*/.netrc file contains a user's password on a remote host, the file should not be readable by anyone except the user (and root). In fact, ~*user*/.netrc will not function if the world or group has access to the file. (Not all versions of UNIX include this security feature. Implementations that do function despite world or group access to ~*user*/.netrc open a significant security risk.) The following examples show ftp connections to a remote host, both with and without a ~*user*/.netrc file.

UNIX

Form:

```
$ ftp [option(s)] host
```

Example:

```
$ ftp cuhhmd
Connected to cuhhmd.hhmi.columbia.edu.
220 cuhhmd FTP server (Version 4.1 Tue Mar 31 21:45:47 EST 1997)
ready.
Name (cuhhmd.hhmi.columbia.edu:): fred
Password (cuhhmd.hhmi.columbia.edu:fred): [password not echoed]
331 Password required for fred.
230 User fred logged in.
ftp>pwd
251 "/usr/users/fred" is current directory.
ftp>bye
221 Goodbye.
$
```

Example:

```
$ cat .netrc
machine cuhhmd.hhmi.columbia.edu username fred password mypassword
$ ftp cuhhmd
Connected to cuhhmd.hhmi.columbia.edu.
220 cuhhmd FTP server (Version 4.1 Tue Mar 31 21:45:47 EST 1997)
ready. 331 Password required for fred.
230 User fred logged in.
ftp>pwd
251 " /usr/users/fred" is current directory.
ftp>bye
221 Goodbye
$
```

Only the second example uses a ~*user*/.netrc file. In both examples, the ftp command pwd is issued on the remote host to determine the current working directory on that host. In both examples, ftp is terminated with the command bye, which logs the user off the remote host and returns the local shell prompt.

The ~*user*/ .netrc file may also be used to enable `anonymous` `ftp`; see the man page for details.

We now turn to `ftp` commands that may be used once a connection has been made.

UNIX

Example:

```
ftp>!ls bob.txt
bob.txt
```

Example:

```
ftp>put
(local-file) bob.txt
(remote-file) old.txt
```

Example:

```
ftp>put bob.txt
```

Example:

```
ftp>ls bob.txt
200 PORT command okay. 150 Opening data connection for /bin/ls
(128.59.93.1,1651) (0 bytes). bob.txt
226 Transfer complete.
211 bytes received in 0.39 seconds (0.54 Kbytes/s)
```

Example:

```
ftp>mget
(remote-files) batch.out.*
mget batch.out.223? y
mget batch.out.234? y
mget batch.out.235? y
```

Example:

```
ftp>status
Connected to cuhhmd.hhmi.columbia.edu
Mode: stream; Type: ascii; form: non-print; Structure: file
Verbose: on; Bell: off; Prompting: on; Globbing: on
Hash mark printing: off; Use of PORT cmds: on
```

Example:

```
ftp>prompt
Interactive mode off
```

Example:

```
ftp>mput batch.out.*
ftp>
```

In the first example, `!ls bob.txt` determines that the file `bob.txt` exists in the current directory of the local host. Any command that begins with an exclamation point (`!`—referred to as "bang" in UNIX parlance) instructs `ftp` to pass the command to the shell on the local host for execution; that is, `ftp` forks a new shell to execute the local command. In the second example, `put` without arguments prompts `ftp` to request, first, the name of the existing file to be copied from the local host and, second, the name it is to receive on the remote host. Then `bob.txt` on the local host is copied (`put`) to `old.txt` on the remote host. The third example, `put bob.txt`, illustrates a situation in which the local, but not the remote, file name is given: The file is copied (`put`) to the remote host with the same name that it had on the local host. In the fourth example, `ls bob.txt` verifies that the copy was successful by checking for the existence of `bob.txt` on the remote host.

In the fifth example, `mget` copies (gets) multiple files from the remote host. By default, the user is prompted to copy each file (compare with the OpenVMS command `COPY/CONFIRM`). You may turn off interactive prompting in one of two ways. First, the `ftp` command `prompt` will toggle the value of interactive prompting; you can determine the current value (on or off) with the `ftp status` command. Second, you can invoke `ftp` with the `-i` option (not shown), which suppresses interactive prompting. The last example, `mput batch.out.*`, illustrates multiple copying from the local to the remote host with interactive mode off: All files are copied without comment.

In the fourth example, `ftp` displays diagnostic messages indicating the total number of bytes transferred and the rate of transfer. These diagnostics are displayed during all `ftp` transfers, but have been omitted from all but the fourth example for the sake of brevity.

13.2.7   Remote Command Execution: `rsh`

You may not issue commands on a remote host from a local host unless the local host is trusted by the remote host. For nontrusted hosts, the local user must first login to the remote host and then issue commands either through `telnet` or `ftp`.

The utility `rsh` (remote shell) executes a command or a shell script on a remote trusted host by invoking a shell on the remote host, which then executes the command. Any command that can be interpreted by the shell on a remote host is valid. OpenVMS commands are always interpreted by the local node. This fact does not present a problem when accessing files, as OpenVMS file specifications may include a remote node. For example, the OpenVMS user wishing to display the contents of a directory on node BOSTON might enter the command `DIRECTORY BOSTON::DUA2:[FRED]`. The UNIX user accomplishes the same task with the command `rsh boston "ls ~fred"`. Both the OpenVMS and the UNIX commands are straightforward. However, what if the local user wishes to review the list of interactive users on node BOSTON?

OpenVMS	**UNIX**
Example:	
| ```
$ TYPE BOSTON::DUA2:[FRED] -
CMD.COM
$ DEFINE/USER SYS$OUTPUT
SYS$NET
$ 'P1'
$ TYPE BOSTON::DUA2:[FRED] -
CMD.COM
"TASK=CMD SHOW USERS"
``` | ```
$ rsh boston "who"
``` |

UNIX accomplishes the task by invoking a remote shell to execute the who command. OpenVMS requires invoking a command procedure created on the remote node.

The following examples illustrate the functionality of rsh when combined with piping and input/output redirection.

OpenVMS	**UNIX**
Form:	
| ```
$ COMMAND[/QUALIFIER(S)] -
NODE::DEVICE:[DIRECTORY]FILE
``` | ```
$ rsh host [option(s)] command(s)
``` |
| **Example:** | |
| ```
$ PRINT/REMOTE CUHHMD::DUA1:-
[FRED] CUHHMD::DUA1:[FRED]
MYFILE.DAT
``` | ```
$ rsh cuhhmd cat "usr/fred/myfile"|\
lpr
``` |
| **Example:** | |
| ```
$ COPY CUHHMD::DUA1:[FRED]A.DAT -
CUHHMD"FRED

MYPWD"::DUA1:[FRED]B.DAT
``` | ```
$ rsh cuhhmd "cat /usr/fred/a > \
/usr/fred/b"
``` |
| **Example:** | |
| ```
$ COPY MYFILE.DAT CUHHMD::SYS$PRINT
$ TYPE CUHHMD::DUA2: [GEORGE]MYFILE
``` | ```
$ cat myfile | rsh cuhhmd "lpr -"
$ rsh cuhhmd -lgeorge "cat myfile"
``` |

The first example, rsh cuhhmd "cat /usr/fred/myfile" | lpr, illustrates local printing of a file resident on the remote host cuhhmd. Rather than displaying the remote file /usr/fred/myfile, the output is piped to the default line printer (see Section 7.1). Note that the pipe is interpreted by the local shell because it is not contained in double quotes. In the second example, rsh cuhhmd "cat /usr/fred/a > /usr/fred/b" redirects the output of the cat command to the file /usr/fred/b; since double quotes surround the output redirection, the remote host performs the operation. Note that the result would be the same using the command rsh cuhhmd "cp /usr/fred/a /usr/fred/b". In the third example, cat myfile | rsh cuhhmd "lpr -", rather than displaying the contents of myfile, the output is piped to the rsh command, which prints it on the default line printer attached to the remote host cuhhmd. The last example, rsh cuhhmd -lgeorge "cat myfile", illustrates further the use of the -l option (compare rlogin). The local user invokes the remote shell through the account george on the remote host cuhhmd, assuming the file ~george/.rhosts is present to permit remote access by the local user initiating the request. The file myfile in the parent directory of user george will be displayed.

13.2.8   Transparent File Access: NFS

NFS software permits a user to access files physically located on devices attached to remote hosts as if they were attached to the local host. NFS software must reside on both the local and the remote host. OpenVMS users familiar with the OpenVMS cluster should note that the features of NFS and OpenVMS clusters appear similar when it comes to file access. An OpenVMS cluster user requests access to a file using an ordinary file specification; the NFS user specifies a file system. In both cases, the physical location of the file is irrelevant. For example, the user who lacks access to NFS and wishes to display a file on a remote trusted host would use the rsh (remote shell) command, which includes the remote host name. If the file system on which the file resides is available via NFS, however, the user can issue the cat command.

NFS originated with Sun Microsystems and runs on all computers that support a version of the UNIX operating system, as well as on OpenVMS (with proper licensing) and other operating systems. Therefore, you can directly access files on a variety of hardware types. You can determine whether NFS is running on your UNIX system by looking for the NFS daemon. A daemon is a process owned by the superuser (root); it is usually started at boot time and performs some background function. In this example, ps -aux | grep nfsd searches the list of all processes running on the system for nfsd, the NFS daemon. Note that these ps command options work with BSD UNIX. The command options vary on other versions of UNIX.

UNIX

Example:

```
$ ps -aux | grep nfsd
system  12384   0.4   0.2   72   36 p3    S 0:00   grep nfsd
root     3989   0.0   0.1   68    0 ? I    1:19    nfsd 4
root     3990   0.0   0.1   68    0 ? I    1:13    nfsd 4
root     3988   0.0   0.1   68    0 ? I    1:16    nfsd 4
root     3987   0.0   0.1   68    0 ? I    1:06    nfsd 4
```

If one or more NFS daemons is running, you can list remote file systems available locally with the df command.

UNIX

Example:

```
$ df
Filesystem     kbytes     used    avail   capacity   Mounted on
/dev/da0a      18067      13708   2552    84%        /
/dev/da0h      108645     96273   1507    98%        /usr
cuhhia:/usr1   56144      26315   26318   50%        /cuhhiausr1
```

Remote file systems accessible via NFS are displayed in the form *host-name*:*filesystem*, where *hostname* is the first part of the Internet host name and *filesystem* is the name of the file system on the remote host. The above example displays three file systems, two local and one remote. The remote file system cuhhia:/usr1 is accessed as /cuhhiausr1 on the local host.

UNIX

Example:

```
$ ls /cuhhiausr1
aronson horton mms purnick weiss
$ rlogin cuhhia
IRIS Workstation
$ ls /usr1
aronson horton mms purnick weiss
```

The command ls /cuhhiausr1 provides a directory listing of the remotely mounted file system cuhhia:/usr1. This directory listing is verified by an `rlogin` to the remote host `cuhhia`, which has the identical file system known locally as `/usr1`.

You can list the local file systems available for mounting on remote hosts by displaying the file `/etc/exports`.

UNIX
Example:
```
$ hostname ; cat /etc/exports
cuhhca
# nfs exports file 4/5/98
#
/data1
/usr
```

The command `hostname ; cat/etc/exports` indicates that the local host `cuhhca` has two file systems, `/data1` and `/usr`, available for remote mounting.

13.2.9 Secure Shell

While not strictly related to the topic of teaching UNIX to OpenVMS users, another approach worth mentioning is to create a remote terminal session, the Secure Shell, or `ssh`.

The Secure Shell was an attempt to plug a number of security holes inherent in the r commands (`rlogin`, `rsh`, `rcp`) and in the X Windows system. With `ssh` you can log into a remote computer, execute commands remotely, and move files across a network. It uses encryption to provide strong authentication and secure communications over unsecure channels.

Use of `ssh` is similar to the r commands discussed previously—there are corresponding `slogin`, `ssh` and `scp` commands—the main difference appearing to be the need to enter a pass phrase to establish a secure session.

It's worth noting that the protocols used by `ssh` are in the public domain and that other commands are available to perform a subset of secure tasks.

13.3 Modem Communications

We now turn to communications via standard telephone lines using modems attached to the local and the remote computer.

13.3.1 UUCP Addresses

The format of a UUCP address (see Table 13.2) requires further explanation. First, while the examples in this chapter all assume use of the Korn shell, use of the C shell would require a backslash character (\) to prevent interpretation of the exclamation point (!) C shell and bash metacharacter as a history substitution (see Section 3.4). Second, the address may also be a path indicating that the message must pass through an intermediate *site1* to reach the final destination *site2*.

The UUCP user may determine the UUCP host names of the local and reachable remote hosts using the commands uuname -1 and uuname, respectively.

> **UNIX**
> **Form:**
> ```
> $ uuname [-l]
> ```
> **Example:**
> ```
> $ uuname
> clapple
> cucard
> ```
> **Example:**
> ```
> $ uuname -l
> cuhhca
> ```

These examples show two systems, clapple and cucard, which can be reached directly by UUCP; they also show that the UUCP name of the local host is cuhhca.

13.3.2 UUCP Status

UUCP offers no mechanism to determine whether a remote host is currently reachable. If a remote host is not available when UUCP attempts to make a connection, UUCP will continue making attempts at regular intervals defined by the system administrator until a connection is made.

13.3.3 Remote Login: tip and cu

UUCP provides only batch processing (spools requests) and, therefore, precludes any type of interactive communication, including remote login.

However, if serial line communications (e.g., dial-out and dial-in modems) are available, you can use the commands tip and cu (compare with the OpenVMS command SET HOST/DTE) to conduct a terminal session on a remote host. Both tip and cu require that you physically initiate a session; UUCP automatically establishes a connection at some predefined time. The commands tip, cu, and those of UUCP may share the same serial line.

Only the use of tip is considered here. The system administrator of the local host maintains a file /etc/remote, which contains characteristics of the remote hosts reachable via tip. This simplifies access to remote hosts, since you do not need to specify explicitly the characteristics required to make a connection each time you attempt communication.

UNIX

Example:

```
$ cat /etc/remote
# sample entry from an /etc/remote file
#
cuccfa/9600 Baud Able Quadracall attributes:\
:dv = /dev/cua0:br#9600:cu = /dev/cua0:at = vadic:du


$ tip [-v] [-speed] system-name or phone #


$ tip -56000 cuccfa
```

The first example cat /etc/remote, illustrates the format of the file for defining the characteristics of remote hosts. Since this file is established by the system administrator, we will not discuss it further. The command tip -56000 cuccfa establishes a connection to the remote host defined in the /etc/remote file. Rather than the default baud rate of 9,600 (br#9600), 56,000 is specified. Alternative phone numbers can be maintained in a file that defaults to /etc/phones, but may be a user's private telephone directory, which is pointed to by the environment variable defined by the command setenv PHONES path.

Once a connection has been made, you can issue a variety of commands to the tip program to initiate some action on the local or remote host. Table 13.7 summarizes these commands, including commands to transfer files, issue commands on the local or remote host, and set a variable.

Table 13.7 *Subset of* tip *Commands*

Command	Function
~<CTRL>-D or ~.	Log out of remote machine and exit tip
~c [*name*]	Change directory on the local host to *name*
~!	Begin subshell on local host
~>	Prompt for local file; copy to remote host
~<	Prompt for remote command to copy to local host
~p *from* [*to*]	Like ~>, but file specified as part of command
~t *from* [*to*]	Like ~<, but command specified as cat
~|	Pipe output from remote command to local process
~s	Set or query a variable
~?	Help with these commands

13.3.4 Sending Mail

Sending UUCP mail uses the mail utility discussed in Chapter 6. UUCP mail messages that need explicit routing to reach a distant site by passing through other sites take the form *site1*!*site2*!*site3*!*user* (assuming Korn shell syntax); that is, the message passes first to *site1*, then to *site2*, and then to *user* at *site3*. Users should consult the system administrator for information on the explicit routing required to reach remote hosts.

OpenVMS

UNIX

Form:

```
$ mail host!user
```

Example:

```
$ MAIL
MAIL> SEND
To: CUHHMD::FRED
```

```
$ mail c1apple!bobs
```

13.3.5 File Transfer: uucp and uusend

The commands uucp and uusend are part of the UUCP group of programs. The uucp command copies only to an immediate neighbor, that is, a remote host dialed into directly, whereas uusend can pass files to remote hosts through a number of intermediate host connections. You should use these commands only when no network connection is available, since they are spooled for processing via slow modem connections rather than processed interactively using a fast network.

Note the distinction between uucp (lowercase) and UUCP (uppercase). UUCP refers to a collection of programs used for modem communications that includes uucp and uusend. These commands, like their UUCP counterpart uux, use a similar syntax. You can use uucp to copy in both directions, both from and to a remote host, whereas uusend will copy only from a local to a remote host.

For uucp and uusend to function, local, remote, and (in the case of uusend) intermediate hosts must be running UUCP. An account uucp handles the request spooled by the local host. Like any user account, uucp has a parent directory ~uucp, usually designated /usr/spool/uucp. Unlike a normal user account, the parent directory has world read, write, and execute access, for it must be able to receive UUCP files from remote hosts. Alternatively, you may have a subdirectory with world read, write, and execute access to receive UUCP files from a user on a remote host. If so, the user sending a file to this directory via UUCP must know of its existence.

We will look at some examples of using uucp before turning to uusend.

UNIX
Form:
```
$ uucp [option(s)] local_file remote_file
```
Example:
```
$ uucp myfile cuhhmd!~uucp
```
Example:
```
$ uucp -m myfile1 myfile2 myfile3 cuhhmd!~fred/scratch
```
Example:
```
$ uucp [option(s)] remote_file local_file
```
Example:
```
$ uucp cuhhmd!~fred/book/chap\[0!9\]~george/book
```
Example:
```
$ uucp myfile cuhhmd!~uucp/fred/yourfile
```

In the first example, uucp myfile cuhhmd!~uucp spools the local file myfile for copying to the public directory uucp on the remote host cuhhmd; by default, the remote file will be given the name myfile. (Recall the *host*!*user* address syntax of UUCP from Section 13.3.1). The local user may inform the remote user destined to receive the file of its impending arrival by mail. You notify the recipient with the option *nuser*: for example, `nfred` will cause UUCP on the remote host to automatically send a mail message to remote user `fred` informing him of the arrival of the file.

The second example, `uucp -m myfile1 myfile2 myfile3 cuhhmd !~fred/ scratch`, illustrates the copying of multiple files to the subdirectory `scratch` of user `fred` on the remote host `cuhhmd`. The `-m` option directs UUCP to send mail to the local sender when successful file transfer has occurred. Without this option, the local user sending the file has no way of knowing when the file transfer occurred.

The third example, `uucp cuhhmd!~fred/book/chap\[0-9\] ~george/book`, illustrates copying from a remote to a local host. Any file from `chap0` through `chap9` in the subdirectory `book` of remote user `fred` is copied to local user `george`'s subdirectory `book`. Note that the remote directory `~fred/book` and the files `chap0` through `chap9` must be world readable and that the local directory `~george/book` must be world writable. The characters `[` (open square bracket) and `]` (close square bracket) are shell metacharacters and, therefore, must be preceded by `\` to prevent immediate interpretation by the shell on the local host.

The last example, `uucp myfile cuhhmd!~uucp/fred/your-file`, illustrates directory creation with `uucp`. The file `myfile` on the local host is copied to a subdirectory `fred` of `~uucp`. If that subdirectory did not exist on the remote host, it would have been created.

We now turn to `uusend`. As noted above, `uusend` sends, but does not receive, files through intermediate hosts to a final destination. Each host must have `uusend`. UUCP does not necessarily imply `uusend`, as some versions of UNIX UUCP support `uucp`, but not `uusend`. One disadvantage of `uusend` as compared to `uucp` is its lack of a *mechanism* to determine whether a file has arrived at a remote host. One advantage of `uusend` over `uucp` is that you may set file protections when the file reaches a remote host; with `uucp` the remote file is always world readable and, therefore, not secure.

UNIX
Form:
```
$ uusend local_file site1!site2...!sitex!remote_file
```
Example:
```
$ uusend myfile cuhhca!cuchmc!c1apple!~uucp
$ uusend - cuhhca!cuhhmc!c1apple!~uucp/outfile
[text entered here]
<CTRL>-D
$ myprog | uusend - cuhhca!cuhhmc!c1apple!~uucp/outfile
```

```
$ uusend -m 700 myfile cuhhca!cuchmc!clapple!/usr/fred/scratch \/
outfile
```

In the first example, `uusend myfile cuhhca!cuchmc !clapple !~uucp` copies the local file `myfile` to the final destination `~uucp/myfile` on remote host `clapple`. Note that the name of the remote file defaults to `myfile`. To get to the final destination, the file passed through the intermediate hosts `cuhhca` and `cuchmc`. In the second example, `uusend - cuhhca!cuhhmc!clapple !~ uucp/outfile` follows the same route as the first example. However, the - (dash) metacharacter indicates that input is `stdin` and not a file. All text entered at the terminal will be sent to the remote file `~uucp/outfile` on `clapple` until you issue a `<CTRL>-D`. The third example, `myprog | uusend - cuhhca!cuhhmc!clapple !~uucp/outfile`, expands on this concept. Rather than send the output of the program `myprog` to the terminal, it is piped to the `uusend` command, which copies it to `~uucp/outfile` on the remote node `clapple`.

The last example, `uusend -m 700 myfile cuhhca!cuchmc!clapple!/usr/fred/scratch/outfile`, illustrates the use of the `-m` option to set the protection of the file copied to the remote host. The file `myfile` is copied to the final destination of `/usr/fred/scratch/outfile`. Although the directory `/usr/fred/scratch` must allow world write access in order to accept the file, the protection of the file is set to `700`, which indicates full access by the owner and no access by other classes of users.

13.3.6 Remote Command Execution: uux

The `uux` command is a UUCP program for executing a small subset of commands on a remote host. Like other UUCP modem-based requests, requests generated by `uux` are spooled for processing. Its response, therefore, is not fast enough to be interactive. The system administrator of the remote host defines the commands that you can run on that host. The commands reside in the file `/usr/lib/uucp/L.cmds`.

In the `L.cmds` file shown above, `PATH=/bin:/usr/bin:/usr/ucb` indicates the directories that will be searched to locate the allowable commands. The allowable commands follow, one per line. Some versions of UNIX extend the functionality of this file, for example, by stating explicitly which commands can be executed by which remote hosts. The features described here are common to all versions.

UNIX

Example:

```
$ cat/usr/lib/uucp/L.cmds
PATH = /bin:/usr/bin:/usr/ucb
rmail
rnews
lpr
uusend
bnproc
unbatchnews
uux
```

If a remote command request is unsuccessful, the local user is notified by mail on the local machine. The following examples illustrate various uses of uux, using either local or remote files for both input and output.

UNIX

Form:

```
$ uux host!command "input-output control"
```

Example:

```
$ uux cuhhmd!who "> ~fred/scratch/who.out"
```

Example:

```
$ uux cuhhmd!who "> cuhhmd!~uucp/scratch/who.out"
```

Example:

```
$ uux !lpr "< cuhhmd!~uucp/scratch/who.out"
```

Example:

```
$ uux !diff cuhhmd!/tmp/file1 cuhhca!/tmp/file2"> !diff.out"
```

Example:

```
$ uux -m cuhhmd!lpr < printfile.txt
```

In the first example, uux cuhhmd!who "> ~fred/scratch/who.out" executes the who command on the remote host cuhhmd. The result of the uux command is output to the file who.out on the local host. The uux output must always be output to a local file, since stdout has no meaning to the who command executed remotely. Note also the use of double quotes: Without them, the shell directs the output of the local uux command to the file who.out; with them, output from the remote execution of who is placed in the local file who.out. As who.out is to be written by the UUCP utility and not the user issuing the uux command, the directory to which it writes the output must be world writable, and an absolute pathname must be given unless the file is to be written to a directory owned by the `uucp` account.

In the second example,

```
uux cuhhmd!who "> cuhhmd !~ uucp /scratch/who.out"
```

copies the result of the remote `who` command to the file `~uucp/scratch/who.out` on the remote host `cuhhmd`, rather than to the local host. The third example, `uux !lpr "cuhhmd!~uucp /scratch/who.out"`, illustrates the execution of a command on the local host using a file from the remote host `cuhhmd`. The command `!lpr` without a preceding host name indicates a file to be printed on the default line printer on the local host. The fourth example also illustrates local command execution, but introduces the use of files from two remote hosts as input to the command. The command `uux !diff cuhhmd!/tmp/file1 cuhhca!/tmp/file2 ">! diff.out"` executes the `diff` command locally using two remote files located on hosts `cuhhmd` and `cuhhca`. The output is placed in the local file `diff.out`.

The fifth example, `uux -m cuhhmd!lpr < printfile.txt`, illustrates how to print a local file on a remote line printer connected to `cuhhmd`. The `-m` option notifies the user on the local host by mail when the command has been executed—in this instance, when the file is spooled for printing.

13.4   Usenet: Electronic Bulletin Board

Usenet grew out of the expanding UUCP network to disseminate information of interest to UNIX users. Usenet is like a newsstand where each magazine on that newsstand is a newsgroup covering a particular topic. Examples of newsgroups include the following:

- Public-domain software
- Hardware/software technological reviews
- Employment opportunities
- Games
- Bug fixes
- Field topics such as biology, medicine, and chemistry

Usenet differs from a newsstand in that users can reply to news (like a letter to the editor) and can post news. The programs that permit these activities and that the system administrator uses to manage news are known as *Netnews*. Netnews was developed at Duke University in the late 1970s. There are may free newsreader programs, and many Web browsers allow you to read newsgroups directly from the browser. There are also a number of Web sites that allow you to access newsgroups.

If you are a user of a UNIX system and want to find out whether news is available, try commands like `newsgroups` (list of newsgroups) or `rn` (read news). It is beyond the scope of this book to teach you how to set up a news spooler or to use news.

13.5 Communications Between OpenVMS and UNIX

There is a number of vendor-dependent solutions that permit communications between OpenVMS nodes and UNIX hosts. It is beyond the scope of this book to discuss each of these. The TCP/IP protocol is the "language of the Internet," that is, the underlying protocol; therefore, it makes the most sense to use this protocol to communicate between OpenVMS and UNIX computers.

13.6 Summary

Once again, a scenario from daily use will summarize the networking features described in this chapter. UNIX user Janet Smith has just relocated and must develop applications on two UNIX hosts. On the host `apple`, to which her terminal is connected, her login name is `smithj`. On the other host, `orange`, her login name is `janet`.

UNIX

Example;

```
$ whoami ; hostname
smithj
apple
```

Example;

```
$ grep orange /etc/hosts
126.21.36.1 orange.dept.company.edu orange
$ telnet orange
Trying ...
Connected to orange.dept.company.edu
Escape character is '<CTRL>]'.
UNIX. RELEASE BSD 4.3 (orange)
```

```
login: janet
Password:
Never logged in

$ set prompt="orange> "


orange> cat /etc/hosts.equiv
grape.dept.company.edu
pear.dept.company.edu
peach.dept.company.edu

orange> ls -l .rhosts
-rw-rw-r— 1 root 30 Jun 11 09:25 .rhosts
orange> cat .rhosts
apple.dept.company.edu smithj
orange> exit
Connection closed

$ rlogin orange -ljanet
Last login: Thu Jun 16 10:58 from apple
orange> exit
Connection closed


$ uuname
amsterdam
london
purdue

$ uucp -m purdue!~janet\*.\* ~uucp/smithj
[some time later]

$ cp ~uucp/smithj/*.* ~smithj

$ rsh orange -ljanet "rcp apple:~smithj/*.* ~janet/*.*"
$ mail purdue!root
Subject: Thanks
Thank you for your help over the years
.
Cc:
```

Janet Smith logs in and issues the command whoami ; hostname, which displays her login name and the name of the local host. Knowing that the remote UNIX host she is going to use is on the same network, she searches the /etc/hosts file to see if it is defined. The command grep orange /etc/hosts reveals that the host she seeks is defined, with the official name orange.dept.company.edu and the alias orange. She uses the command telnet orange to log into this remote host using the login name janet. To avoid any confusion that may arise by not knowing what host she is using at any given time, Janet uses the command `PS1="orange> "` to change the prompt of the remote host from the default $ for the Korn shell to the name of the remote host. Note that the prompt is contained in quotes to prevent the shell from misinterpreting > as a shell redirection metacharacter. Janet also includes this set command in the file `.profile` so that the prompt is set to `orange>` the next time she logs in (not shown).

The command `cat /etc/hosts.equiv` establishes that the system administrator of the remote host `orange` does not consider `apple` a trusted host. However, the commands `ls -l .rhosts` and `cat .rhosts` reveal that the system administrator has established a user-specific trusted host definition indicating that `smithj` from host `apple.dept.company.edu` may access this account without supplying password information. She tests her access by logging out of the remote host and issuing the command `rlogin orange -ljanet`, which indeed gives her trusted host access to the remote host.

Next, Janet checks the remote hosts available from host `apple` using UUCP with the command `uuname`. Since she can reach `purdue`, the computer she used at her previous location, Janet issues the command `uucp -m purdue!~janet\*.\* ~uucp/smithj` to copy files from her home directory at the old location to the subdirectory `smithj` of `uucp`. The -m option informs her by mail when the copy operation has taken place. Some time later, Janet issues the command `cp ~uucp/smithj/*.* ~smithj` to copy the files to her parent directory on the local host `apple`; then, `rsh orange -ljanet "rcp apple:~smithj/*.* ~janet/*.*"` copies these files to the remote host `orange`. Note that Janet must use `rsh` even though `rcp` is simpler, because `rcp` does not support the -l option, which Janet needs as her local and remote login names differ. The option -ljanet indicates that the remote login is to the account `janet` rather than the default `smithj`.

Finally, Janet sends UUCP mail to the address `purdue\!root` to thank the system administrator of host `purdue` for her help over the years (system administrators need this kind of encouragement!).

Command Summaries

Table A.1 *OpenVMS Commands with UNIX Equivalents*

OpenVMS DCL Command	UNIX Equivalent	Section	UNIX Function
:= =	alias	3.2.2	Define an alias for a command
:=	set[†]	3.2.2	Set shell variable
=	=[‡]	10.7, 3.2.3	Set shell variable
:== ==	setenv[†] export[‡]	3.2.1	Define an environment variable (meanings differ between shells)
@	*source file*[†] . *file*[‡]	10.9.4, 3.2.2	Have parent process invoke a script
ANALYZE /CRASH_DUMP /COPY	savecore		Copy crash dump out of a dump file
ANALYZE /DISK_STRUCTURE	bcheckrc, fsck		Consistency check file system
ANALYZE /IMAGE	odump -Dlh *file*		List the virtual address sections, file offsets, and references to shared libraries in an executable file
APPEND	cat	4.8	Concatenate files
ASSIGN	ln -s	8.4.10	Create a pointer to a file

Table A.1   *OpenVMS Commands with UNIX Equivalents (continued)*

OpenVMS DCL Command	UNIX Equivalent	Section	UNIX Function
ATTACH	fg	7.3.3	Bring a job to the foreground
ATTACH	bg	7.3.3	Move a process to the background
BACKUP	dump, vdump	11.5.1	Back up files
BACKUP	tar	7.2.1	Back up files to a *tar* file
BACKUP	tar -x		Restore files from a *tar* file
BACKUP /INITIALIZE	tar -c		Create new a save-set at beginning of tape
BACKUP /LIST	tar -t		List contents
BACKUP /LOG	tar -v		Report progress
BACKUP /NOREWIND	tar -r		Write at end of existing *tar* files
	tar -u		Write only files not already on tape
	tar -f		Use alternative file or device
BACKUP /RECORD	tar -m		Update file's modification date upon restore
BACKUP	restore, vrestore	11.5.2	Restore files
CALL	. *file*† source *file*†	3.2.2, 10.9.4	Invoke a script in context of parent process
CC	cc	9.1	Compile a C program
CLOSE *logical*	n<&-		End reading from, or writing to, a file on unit *n*
COPY	cp	4.10, 8.3.1	Copy a file

Table A.1   *OpenVMS Commands with UNIX Equivalents (continued)*

OpenVMS DCL Command	UNIX Equivalent	Section	UNIX Function
COPY /CONFIRM	cp -i	4.10	Confirm before copying
COPY /FTP	ftp	13.2.6.2	Copy to/from non-trusted remote host
COPY (with proxy login)	rcp	13.2.6.1	Copy to/from trusted remote host
	rcp -r		Recursively copy subdirectories
CREATE *file*	touch *file*	8.4.7	Create or update *file*
	cat <<*word* *file*		Create a file, accepting terminal input until a line consisting exactly of *word*
	touch -c		Affect existing files only
CREATE /DIRECTORY	mkdir	4.5	Create a directory
DEBUG	dbx		Invoke interactive debugger
DEFINE	ln -s	8.4.10	Create a pointer to a file
DELETE	rm	4.12	Delete a file
DELETE /LOG	rm -e		Print a message after deleting file
DELETE /CONFIRM	rm -i		Confirm deletion
	rm -r	4.6	Delete a directory and all subdirectories
DELETE	rmdir	4.6	Delete an empty directory
DELETE /ENTRY	lprm	7.1.3	Remove queued line printer job
	lprm -*user*		Remove all jobs owned by a *user*

Table A.1 *OpenVMS Commands with UNIX Equivalents (continued)*

OpenVMS DCL Command	UNIX Equivalent	Section	UNIX Function
	lprm -P*queue*		Remove all jobs from specified *queue*
DELETE /SYMBOL	unset‡ unset†		Remove a shell variable
DIFFERENCES	diff	8.4.3	Display all differences in files or directories
DIFFERENCES /IGNORE=CASE	diff -i		Ignore case differences
DIFFERENCES /IGNORE=SPACING	diff -b or diff -w		Ignore spaces and tabs
DIFFERENCES /SLP	diff -e	8.4.3	Generate editing changes for *ed*
	diff -r		Compare directories
DIFFERENCES /MAXIMUM=1 / MATCH=1	cmp	8.4.3	Display first difference in two files
DIFFERENCS /PARALLEL	diff -y	8.4.3	Display differing files side-by-side (GNU Linux)
DIFFERENCES /NUMBER *file* NL:	cat -n or pr -n	4.8 8.2.3	Display a file with line numbers
DIRECTORY	ls	4.1, 8.1.1	List files
DIRECTORY	ls -x		List files across the page (rather than down a column)
DIRECTORY [...]	ls -R		Recursively list subdirectories
DIRECTORY [...] *file*	find *path -* *name string* -print	4.7, 8.4.4	Find all specified instances of a file down a directory tree
DIRECTORY [...]*.DIR	ls -l	grep "^d"	4.2, 8.4.5	List directory files themselves, not their contents

Table A.1   *OpenVMS Commands with UNIX Equivalents (continued)*

OpenVMS DCL Command	UNIX Equivalent	Section	UNIX Function
DIRECTORY [...]*.DIR	ls -d `find . -type d`	4.2, 8.4.5	Recursively list directory files themselves, not their contents
DIRECTORY /BY_OWNER=*uic*	ls -l path | grep *owner*	4.1, 8.4.5	List only those files owned by *owner*
DIRECTORY /COLUMN=1	ls -1	8.1.1	List one file per line
	ls -a or ls -A	4.1	Include hidden files in directory listing
DIRECTORY /DATE /MODIFIED	ls -c -l	4.1	List by creation/modification time
	ls -F	2.3	Append character to designate file type
DIRECTORY /DATE /SIZE /OWNER /PROTECTION	ls -l	4.1	List directory files; long listing
	ls -r	8.1	List in reverse order
DIRECTORY /OWNER	ls -g	8.4.2	Include group (used with -l)
DIRECTORY /SIZE	ls -s		Display file sizes in 1,024-byte units, rather then bytes
	ls -u		List according to access time
	ls -C	8.1.1	Override one file per line
	ls -t	8.1.1	Sort by date last modified
DIRECTORY /SIZE /TOTAL	du	12.1.4	Summarize disk usage by directory
	du -a		Summarize disk usage for all files
DIRECTORY /SIZE /NOTRAILING	du -a *file*		Display file size in 512-byte blocks

Table A.1 *OpenVMS Commands with UNIX Equivalents (continued)*

OpenVMS DCL Command	UNIX Equivalent	Section	UNIX Function
	du -s *path*		Summarize disk usage giving total size only
DIRECTORY /NOHEAD /NOTRAILING[...]	find	4.7, 8.4.4	Find a file
	find -print		Find files and print the path to each file found
DIRECTORY [...] /BEFORE=*time* /MODIFIED	find -ctime+*n*		Find files modified more (+) than n days ago
DIRECTORY [...] /SINCE=*time* /MODIFIED	find -ctime-*n*		Find files modified fewer (-) than n days ago
DIRECTORY [...] /SINCE=*delta* /BEFORE=*time*	find -ctime *n*		Find files modified exactly n days ago
	find -newer *file*		Find files modified more recently than *file*
DIRECTORY /BY_OWNER=*uic*	find -group		Find files in specified group
DIRECTORY	find -name		Find files by name
	find -perm		Find files by file protection
	find -type		Find files by file type
DIRECTORY /BY_OWNER=*uic*	find -user		Find files by ownership
	find -exec *cmd* {} \;		Find files and issue command on files found
	find -ok *cmd* {} \;		As -exec, but request confirmation of action
DIRECTORY /FULL	stat	4.2	Display long listing of directory

Table A.1 *OpenVMS Commands with UNIX Equivalents (continued)*

OpenVMS DCL Command	UNIX Equivalent	Section	UNIX Function
DIRECTORY /FTP	ftp	13.2.6.2	Display directory of a remote node
DISMOUNT *disk*	umount *path*		Take a file system offline
DISMOUNT /UNLOAD	mt rewoffl mt offline	7.2.3	Rewind and unload tape
DUMP	od	8.2.2	Dump a file in various formats
DUMP /ASCII	od -a		Dump a file in ASCII
DUMP /HEXADECIMAL	od -h		Dump a file in hexadecimal
DUMP /OCTAL	od -o		Dump a file in octal
EDIT /TPU EDIT /EDT	vi or emacs	5.2	Call screen editor
EDIT /RECOVER	vi -r		Recover screen editing session
EDIT /EDT	ex	5.1	Call line editor
EDIT /RECOVER	ex -r		Recover line editing session
	ed	5.1	Call primitive line editor
EXCHANGE	dd	7.2.2, 7.2.4	Backup/restore non-standard files
EXIT	exit	10.1	Terminate a script or interactive session
FORTRAN	f77	9.1	Compile and link FORTRAN program
	f77 -c		Suppress linking
	f77 -g		Create symbol table for profiling

Table A.1 *OpenVMS Commands with UNIX Equivalents (continued)*

OpenVMS DCL Command	UNIX Equivalent	Section	UNIX Function
	f77 -gp		Create object file for profiling
	f77 -S		Save assembler code
FORTRAN /OUTPUT=*file*	f77 -o *file*		Place executable in *file*
	f77 -l lib		Include library in load step
FORTRAN /LIST	error	9.3	Place syntax errors in code
GOTO	goto†	10.8.10	Jump to specified label in script
HELP *command*	man *command*	3.6	Online help
HELP INSTRUCTIONS	man *man*		Instructions on how to get help
HELP HINTS	man -k *topic*		Summarize help by topic
	man -f *command*		Summarize help by command
INITIALIZE *disk*	disklabel - rw disk type ; newfs partition		Set up a disk file system (Tru64 only)
INQUIRE *var* /NOPUNCTUATION *prompt*	read *var*?prompt‡ set *var* = $<†	10.2.2	Prompt and accept interactive input as the value of *var*
INSTALL ADD / PRIVILEGED=(CMKRNL) *image*	chmod +s *file*	11.6.4	Give user special privileges when executing a command
LIBRARY	ar	9.5	Call Library maintainer
LIBRARY /CREATE	ar -cr		Create library
LIBRARY /EXTRACT	ar -x		Extract module(s)
LIBRARY /INSERT	ar -q		Insert module(s)

Table A.1 *OpenVMS Commands with UNIX Equivalents (continued)*

OpenVMS DCL Command	UNIX Equivalent	Section	UNIX Function
`LIBRARY /LIST`	`ar -t`		List module(s)
`LIBRARY /REPLACE`	`ar -r`		Replace module(s)
	`ar -m`		Move module(s)
	`ranlib`	9.5	Randomize library
`LICENSE`	`lmf`		Examine or manipulate software licenses (Tru64)
`LINK`	`ld`	9.1	See `CC`
`LOGIN procedure /CLI`	`/usr/bin/sh,` `/usr/bin/` `csh,` `/usr/bin/` `bash,` `/usr/bin/` `ksh, etc.`	3.1	Specify shell used to interpret commands
`LOGIN.COM`	`.login†,` `.profile‡,` `(per login session)` `.chsrc†,` `$ENV‡ (per window or script)`	3.2	Automatically execute scripts when logging in, creating new windows, or executing a script
`LOGOUT`	`logout†` `exit‡`	3.3, 10.1	Terminate a terminal session
`MAIL`	`Mail, mail,` `mailx,` `binmail,` `dxmail, etc.`	6.1	Send or receive e-mail
`MERGE`	`sort -m`	8.4.6	Merge sorted files
`MOUNT`	`mount`		Make a file system available for use
`ON CONTROL_Y`	`onintr†` `trap‡`	10.9.1	Change execution flow based on some event
`OPEN logical file`	`exec n<file‡`	10.9.5	Assign unit *n* to file for input or output

Table A.1   *OpenVMS Commands with UNIX Equivalents (continued)*

OpenVMS DCL Command	UNIX Equivalent	Section	UNIX Function
PHONE	talk [*ttyname*]	6.3	Communicate interactively with another user
PIPE	| (pipe character)	2.1.2	Execute one or more command strings from the same command line
PRINT	lpr	7.1.1	Print a file on the default line printer
PRINT /COPIES=*n*	lpr -#*n*		Print *n* copies of a file
	lpr -f		Print a file and format using FOR-TRAN carriage control
PRINT /DELETE	lpr -r		Print a file and remove file after printing
PRINT /FLAG	lpr -h		Print a file without header page
PRINT /FORM	lpr -l*n*		Print a file and make page *n* lines (default = 66)
PRINT /NAME	lpr -J*jobn*		Print a file and include *jobn* on first page
PRINT /NOTIFY	lpr -m		Print a file and send mail upon completion
PRINT /NUMBER_UP=*n*	lpr -N*n*		Print a file and print *n* pages per side of paper
	lpr -p		Print a file and preformat with pr
PRINT /QUEUE	lpr -P*queue*		Print a file on specified *queue*

Table A.1 *OpenVMS Commands with UNIX Equivalents (continued)*

OpenVMS DCL Command	UNIX Equivalent	Section	UNIX Function
	`lpr -s`		Print a file from user directory, not spool directory
	`pr`	8.2.3	Preformat file before printing
	`pr -f`		Preformat file before printing; use form feeds, not blank lines
`PRINT /HEADER`	`pr -h string`		Preformat file before printing; replace header with *string*
	`pr -l n`		Preformat file before printing; make page *n* lines (default = 66)
	`pr -m`		Preformat file before printing; merge files and print side by side
`PRINT /PAGES=(n,"")`	`pr +n`		Preformat file before printing; begin at page *n*
	`pr -n`		Preformat file before printing; use *n* column output
	`pr -t`		Preformat file before printing; omit default page header and trailer
	`pr -w n`		Preformat file before printing; set line width to *n* (default = 72)
`READ`	`read`[‡]	10.2.2, 10.9.5	Read input from a file
`RECALL`	`!`[†] `r`[‡]	3.5	Recall previous command

Table A.1   *OpenVMS Commands with UNIX Equivalents (continued)*

OpenVMS DCL Command	UNIX Equivalent	Section	UNIX Function
RECALL /ALL	history[†] ![†]	3.5	Recall command lines
RENAME	mv	4.11	Rename a file
RENAME /CONFIRM	mv -i		Confirm that file is renamed
	mv -f		Override unwilling permissions
REPLY /USER	write	6.3	Send message to a logged-in user
RUN /DEBUG	dbx	9.3	Debug a program
RUN /DETACHED	*command*&		Run command in separate process
RUNOFF	nroff and troff		Format text
RUNOFF /PAGE	-o		Format text; selected pages only
	-m*macro*		Format text; use definitions in *macro*
SEARCH /EXACT *file pattern*	grep *pattern file*	8.4.5	Search file(s) for *pattern*; match case exactly
SEARCH	grep -i		Search file(s); ignore case distinctions
SEARCH /NUMBERS	grep -n		Search file(s); precede each match with line number
SEARCH /MATCH=NOR	grep -v		Search file(s); list only lines that do not match
SEARCH /WINDOW=0	fgrep -l		Search file(s); return only name of file that contains match

Table A.1 *OpenVMS Commands with UNIX Equivalents (continued)*

OpenVMS DCL Command	UNIX Equivalent	Section	UNIX Function
SEARCH /STATISTICS	fgrep -c		Search file(s); list only count of lines that match
SEARCH /WINDOW=(0,5)	more -5 +/ *pattern file*	8.2.1	Find a line in a file matching *pattern*; print it and the four lines following
SET BROADCAST= NOMAIL	biff n	3.2.1	Turn off incoming mail notification
SET BROADCAST	mesg y	6.3	Control message receipt from talk and write commands
SET CPU *state*	psradm pset_create		Manipulate CPUs and processor sets on an SMP system (Tru64)
SET DEFAULT	cd	4.4, 8.3.2	Change directory
SET DISPLAY /CREATE *host*	DISPLAY=*host*† set DISPLAY *host*†		Have newly created windows appear on the screen of another host system
SET FILE /ENTER	ln	8.4.10	Create a hard link to a file (one file, two names)
	ln -s		Assign one file to another across file systems
SET FILE /OWNER	chgrp, chown	8.4.2	Change group ownership of a file
SET HOST	rlogin	13.2.4.1	Perform network login to trusted host
SET HOST /RLOGIN	rlogin -l*user*		Perform network login to trusted host with different login name

Table A.1 *OpenVMS Commands with UNIX Equivalents (continued)*

OpenVMS DCL Command	UNIX Equivalent	Section	UNIX Function
`SET HOST /TELNET`	`telnet`	13.2.4.2	Perform network login to nontrusted host
`SET HOST 0`	`rlogin localhost`		Perform network login to current host
`SET HOST 0 /LOG[=file]`	`script [file]`		Make a transcript of a terminal session (default file transcript)
`SET HOST /DTE`	`tip`	13.3.3	Dial remote host
`SET LOGINS /INTERACTIVE=0`	`touch /etc/ nologin`	11.3.1	Disable interactive logins
`SET MAGTAPE`	`mt`	7.2.3	Manipulate magnetic tape
`SET MAGTAPE /SKIP=RECORDS=n`	`mt fsr n`		Manipulate magnetic tape; skip forward n records
`SET MAGTAPE /SKIP=RECORDS=-n`	`mt bsr n`		Manipulate magnetic tape; skip backward n records
`SET MAGTAPE /SKIP=FILES=n`	`mt fsf n`		Manipulate magnetic tape; skip forward n files
`SET MAGTAPE /SKIP=FILES=-n`	`mt bsf n`		Manipulate magnetic tape; skip backward n files
`SET MAGTAPE /SKIP=END_OF_TAPE`	`mt seod`		Manipulate magnetic tape; skip to end of recorded data
`SET MAGTAPE /END_OF_FILE`	`mt eof`		Manipulate magnetic tape; write an EOF mark
`SET MAGTAPE /REWIND`	`mt rewind`		Manipulate magnetic tape; rewind a tape to its beginning

Table A.1   *OpenVMS Commands with UNIX Equivalents (continued)*

OpenVMS DCL Command	UNIX Equivalent	Section	UNIX Function
SET ON	set -e[‡]	10.9.1	Automatically check for errors in a script
SET PASSWORD	passwd, yppasswd	3.2.4	Change the password locally (passwd) and in an NIS environment (yppasswd).
SET PREFIX *fao-string*	PS4=*string*[‡]	3.2.3, 10.10	Set debug prefix to *string*
SET PROCESS /PRIORITY	nice, renice	12.3.3	Change the run priority of a process
SET PROMPT=*string*	set prompt *string*[†] PS1=*string*[‡]	3.2.3	Change the shell's prompt string for a new command
SET PROTECTION	chmod	8.4.1, 11.6.4	Change file protection
SET PROTECTION [...]	chmod -R		Change file protection; recursively descend directories
SET PROTECTION /DEFAULT	umask	3.2.1, 8.4.1	Change the default protection
SET TERMINAL	tset and stty	3.1	Set the terminal characteristics
SET TERMINAL /PAGE=*n*	stty rows *n*		Set the number of lines that make up a terminal page (often accomplished by resizing a window)
SET TERMINAL /WIDTH=*n*	stty columns *n*		Set the number of characters typed across a screen (often accomplished by resizing a window)
SET TERMINAL /BROADCAST	mesg y	6.3	Permit broadcast interruptions

Table A.1 *OpenVMS Commands with UNIX Equivalents (continued)*

OpenVMS DCL Command	UNIX Equivalent	Section	UNIX Function
SET UIC	su	11.6.2	Temporarily substitute the superuser ID
SET VERIFY	csh[†] or ksh[‡]	10.10	Verify command/script execution
	csh -x		Echo command after variable substitution
	csh -v		Echo command line prior to execution
	csh -X or ksh -x		As –x, but include .cshrc (C shell) or $ENV (Korn shell)
	csh -V or ksh -v		As –v, but include .cshrc (C shell) or $ENV (Korn shell)
SET WORKING_SET	ulimit -v[‡] and ulimit -m[‡]		Control virtual memory used by a process
SHOW BROADCAST	mesg	6.3	Show which types of messages other users can write to your terminal
SHOW CPU	sizer -p		Show number of available CPUs
SHOW CPU	psrinfo		Show CPU info about an SMP system
SHOW DEFAULT	pwd	4.3	Display current directory
SHOW DEVICES TT:	tty	3.1	Display device to which a terminal or window is connected

Table A.1   *OpenVMS Commands with UNIX Equivalents (continued)*

OpenVMS DCL Command	UNIX Equivalent	Section	UNIX Function
SHOW DEVICES /FILES	fuser		Show PID of those accessing file or file system
SHOW DEVICES /FULL	df [*filesystem*]	12.2.3	Display information on a file system
	df -i		Give block and fragment size
SHOW LOGICAL	printenv or env or find -lname '*' -print	3.2	Display environment characteristics
SHOW LOGICAL SYS$NODE	hostname	13.2.1	Display local host name
SHOW MAGTAPE	mt status	7.2.3	Display status of tape unit
SHOW MEMORY /FILES	swapon -s		Display swapping capacity and usage
SHOW MEMORY /PHYSICAL	vmstat	12.2.1	Display memory utilization
SHOW NETWORK	netstat	12.2.2	Display network utilization
	ruptime	13.2.2	Display uptime of remote hosts
SHOW PROCESS	who am i or whoami	12.1.1	Display process information
SHOW PROCESS	ps	12.1.3	Display information on processes
SHOW PROCESS /ALL	ps -l		Display information on processes; long listing
SHOW PROCESS /RIGHTS	groups	3.1	Display group membership
SHOW PROCESS /SUBPROCESS	jobs	7.3.2	Display background job queue

Table A.1 *OpenVMS Commands with UNIX Equivalents (continued)*

OpenVMS DCL Command	UNIX Equivalent	Section	UNIX Function
SHOW PROCESS /QUOTAS	limit[†] ulimit[‡]	12.3.4, 12.1.5	Display the values of a process's resource limits
SHOW PROTECTION	umask -s		Show default file permissions
SHOW QUOTA	quota		Show process quotas and limits
SHOW QUEUE SYS$PRINT	lpq	7.1.2	Display default print queue status
SHOW QUEUE *queue*	lpq -P*queue*		Display print queue status for *queue*
SHOW STATUS	time	10.9.3	Display resources used by a process
SHOW SYMBOL *name*	alias *name*	3.2.2	Show command string associated with *name*
SHOW SYSTEM	ps -aux	12.1.3	Show features of all processes
SHOW TERMINAL	stty flags	3.1	List terminal characteristics
SHOW TIME	date		Display date and time
SHOW USERS	who	12.1.2	Show who is using the system
	w	12.1.2	Show who is using the system; long listing
	rwho	12.1.2	Show who is using remote hosts (in last 30 minutes)
	rwho -a		Show all users
	rwho -h		Show all users in alphabetical order by host

Table A.1   *OpenVMS Commands with UNIX Equivalents (continued)*

OpenVMS DCL Command	UNIX Equivalent	Section	UNIX Function
	`users`	12.1.2	Show who is using the system; short listing
`SORT`	`sort`	8.4.6	Sort and merge
`SORT /KEY`	`sort -n/+n`		Sort and merge before/after field *n*
`SORT /OUTPUT`	`sort -o file`		Sort and merge; direct output to *file*
	`sort -tn`		Sort and merge using alternative field separator *n*
	`sort -n`		Sort and merge in strict ascending numeric order
	`sort -f`		Sort and merge; disregard case of alphanumerics
`SPAWN`	`wait`[†]		Suspend parent process until child completes
`SPAWN /NOWAIT`	`& and <CTRL>-Z`	7.3.1	Fork subprocess and continue parent process execution
`START /CPU`	`online and psradm -n`		Enable a CPU for SMP processing
`STOP /CPU`	`offline and psradm -f`		Disable a CPU from SMP processing
`STOP /ID`	`kill -9 or kill -kill`	12.3.1	Remove a process
`SUBMIT`	`batch`		Start a process in batch mode
`SUBMIT /AFTER`	`at`	12.3.2	Start a process at a later time

Table A.1 *OpenVMS Commands with UNIX Equivalents (continued)*

OpenVMS DCL Command	UNIX Equivalent	Section	UNIX Function
SYSGEN INSTALL *pagefile*	swapon pagefile		Make a file available for paging or swapping
TYPE	cat	4.8	Display a file
	cat -n pr -n	8.2.3	Display a file with line numbers
	cat -s		Display a file; suppress multiple blank lines
TYPE	less	4.9	Display a file
TYPE /PAGE NL:	clear		Clear a terminal screen
TYPE /PAGE	more, page, less	4.8 4.9	Pause after each page
	more -c		Refresh screen
	more -f		Truncate rather than wrap long lines
	more -*n*		Display *n* lines (default = 24)
	more +*n*		Begin at line *n*
	more /*string*		Display 2 lines before next *string*
	head	8.2.3	Display the beginning of a file
	head -*n*		Display first *n* lines
TYPE /TAIL	tail	8.2.3	Display the end of a file
	tail -*n*		Display last *n* lines of a file
	tail -r		Display a file in reverse order
WAIT *delta-time*	sleep seconds[‡]		Suspend execution for a specified time

Table A.1 *OpenVMS Commands with UNIX Equivalents (continued)*

OpenVMS DCL Command	UNIX Equivalent	Section	UNIX Function
WRITE *logical string*	echo >> *file*[†] print >> *file*[‡]	2.1.3, 10.2	Append a line(s) to *file*
WRITE SYS$OUTPUT	echo, echo†, print‡	10.2	Write to standard output (exists as both built-in and separate command)
WRITE SYS$OUTPUT F$GETJPI("","USERNAME")	who am i, whoami, id	12.1.1	Display login name

†C shell syntax or built-in command

‡Korn shell syntax or built-in command

Table A.2 lists UNIX commands for which there are no equivalent commands on OpenVMS. Some optional products for OpenVMS do provide some of the functions of these UNIX commands.

Table A.2 *UNIX Commands with No OpenVMS Equivalents*

Command	Section	Function
awk	5.4	Stream (batch) editor
awk -F *sep*		Define field separator as *sep*
awk -f *file*		Use commands contained in *file*
bc and dc		Calculator
cal [*month*] *year*	10.8.2	Create a calendar
dirs†	8.3.2	Display the directory stack
eval	10.9.2	Force evaluation by parent process
exec	10.9.5	Replace interactive shell with commands from script
finger		Display information about a user

Table A.2 *UNIX Commands with No OpenVMS Equivalents (continued)*

`fsplit`	9.2	Split FORTRAN source code file into functional units
`gprof`	9.4	Display extended profile of program execution
`make`	9.2	Maintain dependent files for compilation
`-n`		Echo but not perform commands
`popd`[†]	8.3.2	Make top of directory stack the current directory
`prof`	9.4	Display simple profile of program execution (see `gprof`)
`pushd`[†]	8.3.2	Place a directory on the directory stack p
`+`n		Rotate the directory stack n times
`rsh`	13.2.7	Remote command execution
`sed`	5.3	Stream (noninteractive) editor
`-n`		Display only modified lines
`-e`		Combine editing commands
`set noclobber`[†]	2.1.3	Prevent redirection from overwriting existing file
`set -o noclobber`[‡]	2.1.3	Prevent redirection from overwriting existing file
`tr`	8.4.8	Translate characters in a file
`tr -c` *string*		Translate characters in a file including *string* in each translation
`typeset`[†]	10.2	Define characteristics of a variable
`Uucp ,m`	13.3.5	Send/receive file(s) via UUCP
`uuname`	13.3.1	Display remote host names reachable via UUCP
`-l`		Display local UUCP host name
`uusend`	13.3.5	Send file(s) via UUCP
`uux`	13.3.6	Remote command execution via UUCP

†C shell syntax or available only with the C shell

‡Korn shell syntax or available only with the Korn shell

B

Editor Summaries

General form of commands:

```
EDT   * command linea:lineb
ex    : linea,lineb command options
vi    vi [options] file
Emacs emacs file
```

Table B.1   *OpenVMS EDT Line Mode Versus UNIX ex*

EDT	ex	ex Function
Display Commands		
T*x*	x	Display line *x*
T*x*:*y*	x,y	Display lines *x* through *y*
T.:END (TREST)	.,$	Display current line to end of file
T1..	1,.	Display line 1 to current line
TWHOLE	1,$	Display whole file
T*string*	/string/	Display first line containing string below current line
T-*string*	?string?	Display first line containing string above current line
T*a*:*b*,*x*:*y*	a,b x,y	Display lines *a* through *b* followed by lines *x* through *y*
	x,ynu	Display lines *x* through *y* with line numbers
Manipulation Commands		
L	a	Append after current line

Table B.1 *OpenVMS EDT Line Mode Versus UNIX ex (continued)*

EDT	ex	ex Function
D	d	Delete current line
D*x*:*y*	*x*,*y*d	Delete lines *x* through *y*
S/S1/S2	s/s1/s2/	Substitute string 1 for string 2
S/S1/S2/1:END	s/s1/s2/g	Substitute string 1 for string 2 throughout the file
R.	c	Delete current line and insert
M*x*:*y* TO *z*	*x*,*y*m *z*	Move lines *x* through *y* and paste after *z*
WRITE *file x*:*y*	*x*,*y*a I	Copy lines *x* through *y* to buffer *name*
	y name	Put lines from buffer name after current line
INCLUDE *file*	r *file*	Include file after current line
Miscellaneous Commands		
HELP		Get help
	undo	Reverse last command
QUIT	q!	Quit without saving changes
EXIT	wq	Exit saving changes

Table B.2 *OpenVMS TPU with EDT Keypad Screen Mode Versus UNIX vi*

TPU's EDT* Keypad	vi	vi Function
Entering Text		
	a	Append text after the cursor
(default)	i	Insert text before cursor
[F12] *text* or <CTRL>-H *text*	I	Insert text at beginning of current line
[PF1][0]	o	Open a new line below the cursor
	O	Open a new line above the cursor

Table B.2 *OpenVMS TPU with EDT Keypad Screen Mode Versus UNIX vi (continued)*

TPU's EDT[*] Keypad	vi	vi Function
[F14] or <CTRL>-A	R	Replace characters
	<ESC>	Terminate input mode
Cursor Movement		
arrow keys	Arrow keys or h, j, k, or l	Move the cursor right or left, up or down
[2]	$	Move to the end of the line
[BACKSPACE] or [F12]	^ or 0	Move to the beginning of the line
	H	Move cursor to the top of the screen
	L	Move cursor to the bottom of the screen
	M	Move cursor to the middle of the screen
[4][8]	<CTRL>-F	Scroll file forward one screen
[4] [PF1]# [8]	#<CTRL>-F	Scroll file forward # screens
[5][8]	<CTRL>-B	Scroll file backward one screen
[5] [PF1]# [8]	#<CTRL>-B	Scroll file backward # screens
	<CTRL>-D	Scroll file forward one-half screen
	<CTRL>-U	Scroll file backward one-half screen
[4][1]	w	Move forward one word
[4] [PF1]# [1]	#w	Move forward # words
[5][1]	b	Move backward one word
[5] [PF1]# [1]	#b	Move backward # words
	e	Move to last character of current word
	f*n*	Move forward to next character *n*
	F*n*	Move backward to next character *n*
	;	Repeats f*n*

Table B.2 *OpenVMS TPU with EDT Keypad Screen Mode Versus UNIX vi (continued)*

TPU's EDT[*] Keypad	vi	vi Function
	)	Move forward one sentence
	(	Move backward one sentence
	}	Move forward to beginning of next paragraph
	{	Move backward to beginning of previous paragraph
[4][PF1][PF3] *string* or [4][FIND] *string*	/*string*	Move forward to *string*
[PF3]	N	Repeat pattern search for *string*
[5][PF1][PF3] *string* or [5][FIND] *string*	?*string*	Move backward to *string*
[PF1][7]T*#* or [DO]T*#*	#G	Move to line number #[†]
Changing Text[‡]		
	r	Replace a single character
	R	Replace text to end of line, overwriting characters beneath cursor
[.]	x, <del>	Delete a single character
<del>	<CTRL>-H, X	Delete character before the cursor
[-]	dw	Delete from cursor to beginning of next word
[PF1]#[-]	#dw	Deletes from cursor # words
<CTRL>-J	db	Delete word backwards
	d)	Delete from cursor to end of sentence
	d(	Delete from cursor to beginning of sentence
[PF1][2]	d$ or D	Delete from the cursor to the end of the line

Table B.2 *OpenVMS TPU with EDT Keypad Screen Mode Versus UNIX vi (continued)*

TPU's EDT[*] Keypad	vi	vi Function
[-]	cw	Delete from cursor to beginning of next word and insert
[PF1][2]	c$ or C	Delete from the cursor to the end of the line and insert
[F12] [PF4]	dd	Delete the whole line containing the cursor
[PF1]#[PF4]	#dd	Deletes # lines
[2] <CTRL>-U	cc	As dd, and insert at the beginning of the line
Cut and Paste		
[.]...[6] or REMOVE	y	Yank (copy) text into an alternative buffer
[.][2][6] or REMOVE	yy	Yank (copy) current line into alternative buffer
[PF1][6] or INSERT	p	Paste deleted or yanked text after the cursor
	P	Paste deleted or yanked text before the cursor (EDT and TPU position the cursor after the inserted text, equivalent to P)
[PF1][7] INCLUDE *file*	:r *file*	Include an external file
[PF1][7] WRITE *file* or [DO] WRITE *file*	:w *file*	Write to an external file
Miscellaneous Commands		
[PF1][7]. (EDT only)	<CTRL>-G	Identify line number containing cursor
[PF1] *command*	u	Undo last command
	U	Undo all changes on the current line
[PF1] [7] SPAWN	!	Enter a shell command

Table B.2   *OpenVMS TPU with EDT Keypad Screen Mode Versus UNIX vi (continued)*

TPU's EDT* Keypad	vi	vi Function
[PF1][7] or [DO]	:	Enter an ex command
Leaving the Editor		
[PF1][7] WRITE *file* or [DO] WRITE *file*	:w	Write and save the current file
<CTRL>-Z QUIT	:q	Quit the editor without saving
<CTRL>-Z EXIT or [F10]	:wq (or ZZ)	Write and quit
	:q!	Quit without saving changes
Access to Line-Mode Editors		
[PF1][7] or [DO]	:	Prompt at bottom of screen for an ex command
	Q	Quit vi without saving and begin an ex session

*   EDT keypad keys appear in square brackets.
†   This command works with the old EDT, but not with the EDT keypad under TPU.
‡   Commands that move the cursor can be combined with commands that change text to provide wide-ranging functionality. For example, d) deletes from the cursor to the beginning of the next sentence.

Table B.3   *OpenVMS TPU with EDT Keypad Screen Mode Versus Emacs*

TPU's EDT Keypad*	Emacs	Function
Cursor Movement		
arrow keys	Arrow keys	Move the cursor right or left, up or down
[2] or <CTRL>-E	<CTRL>-E	Move cursor to the end of the line

Table B.3 *OpenVMS TPU with EDT Keypad Screen Mode Versus Emacs (continued)*

TPU's EDT Keypad*	Emacs	Function
`[BACKSPACE]` or `<CTRL>-H` or `[F12]`	`<CTRL>-A`	Move cursor to the beginning of the line
`[DO] TOP`	`<ESC>-<`	Move cursor to the top of the buffer
`[DO] BOTTOM`	`<ESC>->`	Move cursor to the bottom of the buffer
`[4][8]` or `[NEXT]`	`<CTRL>-V`	Scroll file forward one screen
`[5][8]` or `[PREV]`	`<ESC>-V`	Scroll file backward one screen
`[DO] SHIFT RIGHT`	`<CTRL>-x <`	Scroll left
`[DO] SHIFT LEFT`	`<CTRL>-x >`	Scroll right
`[4][1]`	`<ESC>-F`	Move forward one word
`[5][1]`	`<ESC>-B`	Move backward one word
`[4][PF1][PF3]` *string* or `[4][FIND]` *string*	`<CTRL>-S` *string*	Move forward to *string*
`[5][PF1][PF3]` *string* or `[5][FIND]` *string*	`<CTRL>-R` *string*	Move backward to *string*
`[DO] REPLACE`	`<ESC>-%`	Query to replace string with another string
`[DO]WILDCARD FIND`	`<CTRL>-M-S`	Search for a regular expression
`[PF1][7]T#` or `[DO]T#`	`<ESC>-X goto-line`	Move to line number #
Changing Text		
`[.]`	`<CTRL>-D`	Delete a single character
`<del>`	`[BACKSPACE]`	Delete character before the cursor
`[-]`	`<ESC>-D`	Delete word forwards

Table B.3   *OpenVMS TPU with EDT Keypad Screen Mode Versus Emacs (continued)*

TPU's EDT Keypad[*]	Emacs	Function
`<CTRL>-J`	`<ESC>-` `[BACKSPACE]`	Delete word backwards
`[PF1][2]`	`<CTRL>-K`	Delete from the cursor to the end of the line
	`<ESC>-K`	Delete sentence from cursor to ending punctuation
	`<CTRL>-Y`	Restore last deletion
`REMOVE`	`<CTRL>-W`	Delete a marked region
	`<ESC>-SPACE`	Delete all but one space before and after point
	`<CTRL>-T`	Transpose characters
	`<ESC>-T`	Transpose words
	`<CTRL>-X` `<CTRL>-T`	Transpose lines

`[DO]`
`UPPERCASE`
`WORD`
	`<ESC>-u`	Uppercase word

`[DO]`
`LOWERCASE`
`WORD`
	`<ESC>-l`	Lowercase word

`[DO]`
`CAPITALIZE`
`WORD`
	`<ESC>-C`	Capitalize word

`[DO]` `UPPERCASE`	`<CTRL>-X` `<CTRL>-U`	Uppercase selected region
`[DO]` `LOWERCASE`	`<CTRL>-X` `<CTRL>-L`	Lowercase region

`[DO]`
`CAPITALIZE`
	`<ESC>-X`
	`capitalize`
	`region`
		Capitalize region

`[DO] FILL` `PARAGRAPH`	`<ESC>-Q`	Fill paragraph

Cut and Paste

Table B.3 *OpenVMS TPU with EDT Keypad Screen Mode Versus Emacs (continued)*

TPU's EDT Keypad*	Emacs	Function
SELECT	<CTRL>-SPACE or <CTRL>-@	Set mark at cursor position
SELECT <CTRL>-V <CTRL>-L	<CTRL>-X <CTRL>-P	Select entire page as region
[DO] TOP [SELECT] [DO] BOTTOM	<CTRL>-X H	Select entire buffer as region
[PF1][6] or INSERT	<CTRL>-Y	Paste deleted or yanked text after the cursor
[PF1][7] INCLUDE *file*	<CTRL>-X I *file*	Include contents of an existing file
[DO] GET FILE *file* [DO] SET BUFFER READ	<CTRL>-X <CTRL>-R	Open buffer read-only

Leaving the Editor

[PF1][7] WRITE *file* or [DO] WRITE *file*	<CTRL>-X <CTRL>-S	Write and save the current file
[DO] QUIT	<ESC>-X kill-emacs	Quit the editor without saving
[PF1][7] WRITE *file* or [DO] WRITE *file*	<CTRL>-X <CTRL>-W *file*	Write buffer as a new file

Shell Commands

[DO] DCL	<ESC>- !	Enter a shell command
	<ESC> - X shell	Start a shell in a window called shell

Recovery Commands

[DO] RESTORE	<CTRL>-X U or <CTRL>-_	[DO] RESTORE

Table B.3   *OpenVMS TPU with EDT Keypad Screen Mode Versus Emacs (continued)*

TPU's EDT Keypad[*]	Emacs	Function
[DO] RECOVER BUFFER	<ESC>-X recover-*file*	[DO] RECOVER BUFFER

Windows Commands

[DO] TWO WINDOWS	<CTRL>-X 2	Split current window into two vertically
	<CTRL>-X 3	Split current window into two horizontally
[DO] NEXT WINDOW	<CTRL>-x o	Move to other window
[DO] DELETE WINDOW	<CTRL>-x 0	Delete current window
[DO] ONE WINDOW	<CTRL>-x 1	Delete all windows except the current one
[DO] SHOW BUFFERS	<ESC>-X buffer-menu	Display selection list of all open buffers
[DO] SHRINK WINDOW	<ESC>-X shrink-window	Shrink window shorter
[DO] ENLARGE WINDOW	<CTRL>-x ^	Grow window taller
	<CTRL>-x 4 B	Select a buffer in other window
	<CTRL>-x 4 F	Find a file in other window

Help Commands

[HELP]	<CTRL>-H	Display help
	<CTRL>-H T	Display tutorial
[DO] APROPOS *command*	<CTRL>-H A	Show commands matching a string
	<CTRL>-H F	Show the function a key runs

*   EDT keypad keys appear in square brackets.

C

Important UNIX Files

Different implementations of UNIX have historically shown some of their differences by the way they located important files. If a file in this list, particularly a system file, does not appear in the listed directory, try a `find` command to see if it is elsewhere.

Table C.1   *Important Unix Files*

File	Section	Purpose
`/lib`	9.1	Indicates system libraries
`/vmunix`	11.2	Indicates the UNIX system kernel
`/lost+found`	2.2	Indicates the directory containing a file system's lost files
`~user/.bash_profile`		Defines environment for the Bourne-Again shell
`~user/.bashrc`		Defines Bourne-Again shell environment for whole terminal session
`~user/.bash_logout`		Contains Bourne-Again shell commands to be executed upon logout
`~user/.bash_history`		Maintains command history list for Bourne-Again shell
`~user/.cshrc`	3.2.2	Defines environment for the C shell
`~user/.dtprofile`		Defines environment for the CDE desktop
`~user/.emacs`		Defines environment for the emacs editor

Table C.1   *Important Unix Files (continued)*

File	Section	Purpose
~*user*/.exrc		Defines environment for the ex and vi editors
~*user*/.forward	6.1.4	Defines a forwarding mail address
~*user*/.history	3.5	Maintains a command history list for the C shell
~*user*/.hushlogin	3.1	Silences login messages
~*user*/.login	3.2.1	Defines C shell environment for whole terminal session
~*user*/.logout	3.3	Commands to be executed upon logout
~*user*/.mailrc	6.1.8	Defines environment for the mail utility
~*user*/.mwm		Defines Motif window manager menu definitions and keyboard bindings
~*user*/.netrc	13.2.6.2	Defines information for ftp access
~*user*/.profile	3.2.3	Defines environment for the Bourne and Korn shells
~*user*/.rhosts	13.2.3	Defines private remote host access
~*user*/.sh_history	3.5	Maintains a command history list for the Korn shell
~*user*/dead.letter	6.1	Indicates interrupted mail message
~*user*/.dt/dtwmrc		Defines window manager menu definitions and keyboard bindings under CDE
~*user*/mbox	6.1	Contains user's read mail for the binmail mailer
~*user*/.X11Startup		Controls applications that start automatically when an X Windows session is started
~*user*/.Xdefaults		Contains X Windows session manager customizations
/bin/login	3.1	Indicates login program

Table C.1 *Important Unix Files (continued)*

File	Section	Purpose
`/dev/null`	2.2	Indicates null device (bit bucket), used to discard output or to input an immediate EOF
`/dev/tty*`	3.1	Contains special file associated with a terminal connection
`/dev/ptty*`	3.1	Contains special file associated with a pseudoterminal; a network connection
`/dev/Stty*`	3.1	Contains special file associated with a terminal server connection
`/etc/cron`	12.3.2	Contains program to perform tasks at preset intervals
`/etc/disktab`	2.2	Contains description of the characteristics of each physical disk type (e.g., partition size and location)
`/etc/dumpdates`	11.5.1	Contains records of last full and incremental file-system backups; maintained by dump
`/etc/environ`	3.1	Contains program to establish environment variables
`/etc/exports`	13.2.8	Contains file systems that may be exported, that is, mounted by other hosts supporting NFS
`/etc/fstab`	3.2	Contains file-system locations and characteristics
`/etc/getty`	3.1	Contains program to determine terminal characteristics
`/etc/gettytab`	3.1	Contains terminal line descriptions
`/etc/group`	3.1	Contains names of groups and login names of their potential members
`/etc/hosts`	13.2.1	Contains local (static) resolution of network host addresses and their aliases
`/etc/hosts.equiv`	13.2.3	Contains trusted hosts reachable via network
`/etc/init`	3.1	Contains program to initiate tasks during startup and shutdown

Table C.1   *Important Unix Files (continued)*

File	Section	Purpose
/etc/lilo.conf		Indicates LILO configuration file
/etc/magic		Contains list of "magic" numbers used to classify files; sometimes /usr/lib/magic
/etc/man.config		Contains default configuration and path information for the man command
/etc/motd	11.3	Contains message-of-the-day file maintained by the system administrator
/etc/nologin		Contains flag file to prevent further logins
/etc/passwd	3.1	Contains information defining local user accounts on the system
/etc/phones	13.3.3	Contains systemwide remote phone number database of systems commonly accessed via the tip command
/etc/printcap	7.1	Contains description of available printer types
/etc/profile	3.2.3	Contains login initialization for all Korn shell users
/etc/rcn.d	11.3	Contains series of directories with run-level-specific scripts
/etc/rc.local		Contains site-specific startup information
/etc/shells		Contains list of available login shells
/etc/remote	13.3.3	Contains remote systems available to the tip command
/etc/tapecap	7.2	Contains description of available tape drives
/etc/ttys	3.1	Contains terminal initialization data read by /etc/init
/etc/ttytype	3.1	Contains computer port available on the system
/sbin/rcn.d	11.3	See /etc/rc.d

Table C.1   *Important Unix Files (continued)*

File	Section	Purpose
/sbin/update	12.1.3	Maintains file-system integrity
/var/adm/utmp	12.1.2	Records who is currently logged on the system
/var/adm/wtmp	12.1.2	Records all logins and logouts
/usr/lib	9.1	Contains directory of system libraries
/usr/lib/crontab	12.3.2	Contains schedule of programs to be run by /etc/cron at preset intervals
/usr/lib/magic		See /etc/magic
/usr/lib/Mail.rc	6.1.8	Contains systemwide mail environment
/usr/lib/uucp/L.commands	13.3.5	Contains uusend commands accepted from remote hosts
/usr/lib/uucp/L.devices	13.3.1	Contains characteristics of dialout modems used by UUCP
/usr/lib/uucp/L.dialcodes	13.3.1	Contains common dial codes used by the UUCP dialers
/usr/lib/uucp/L.sys	13.3.1	Contains dialing characteristics used by UUCP in reaching remote hosts
/usr/local/lib	9.1	Contains local systemwide libraries
/usr/skel		Contains default user environment files
/usr/spool/mail/user	6.1	Contains incoming mail postbox for user
/usr/spool/uucp	13.3.5	Contains parent directory of UUCP account
/usr/spool/uucp/ERRLOG	13.3.1	Contains error log maintained by the UUCP utility
usr/spool/uucp/LOGFILE	13.3.1	Contains log of UUCP activity
/usr/spool/uucp/SYSLOG	13.3.1	Contains log of UUCP file-transfer activity
/usr/sys/...	9.1	Contains system routines used by the preprocessor

A Procedure for Converting OpenVMS Mail Files to UNIX Mail Files

Ack! Thpft!
—Bill the Cat

If you have been an OpenVMS user for any length of time, you may well have accumulated an e-mail history. If you shift your mail address to a UNIX system, you will probably want to bring that history along with you, without having to switch back and forth between operating systems. We have included an "as is" procedure, part of which runs on OpenVMS and part of which runs on UNIX, to duplicate your OpenVMS MAIL files on the UNIX system. This appendix brings together many of the scripting concepts mentioned in Chapter 10, combining DCL from OpenVMS, Korn shell, and Perl. The authors are grateful to Cliff Straw for providing the example.

D.1   Overview

This document provides a process to convert OpenVMS mail folders to UNIX mail folders in "From" format. UNIX mail folders are used by dtmail, Netscape Communicator, and the mail and mailx commands.

The process converts each folder in an OpenVMS mail file to a UNIX mail folder. The conversion process preserves all of the message header information (Date, From, To, Cc, and Subject).

This is a two-phase process. The first phase executes on an OpenVMS system and extracts all of the folders and mail messages contained in a mail file. The second phase executes on a UNIX system and converts the folders and mail messages to the UNIX mail format.

The following example for an OpenVMS mail environment is used in the instructions below:

The OpenVMS mail directory is HOST::DISK1:[*USER*.MAIL].

The default mail file MAIL.MAI contains the folders CAMPING and SKIING.

Folder CAMPING contains three mail messages and folder SKIING contains one mail message.

The mail file PROJECTS.MAI contains the folder NETSCAPE, which contains two mail messages.

D.2　Conversion Process

Log onto the OpenVMS system containing the mail account.

Create a new directory. Assume this is HOST::DISK1:[*USER*.VMS].

Set default to the directory created in the previous step.

Save the file EXTRACTMAIL.COM in the current directory. (See the example below.)

To extract the default MAIL.MAI file, invoke EXTRACTMAIL.COM with no parameters. To extract a different mail file, pass the full path to the .MAI file as the parameter. A directory is created with the same name as the mail file. A file named FOLDERn.DAT is created for each folder in the mail file where n is a number starting at one (1). A file named FnMm.TXT is created for each message in a folder, where n is the folder number and m is the message number. Thus:

```
$ @EXTRACTMAIL
```

will create the following files:

```
DISK1:[USER.VMS.MAIL]FOLDER1.DAT
DISK1:[USER.VMS.MAIL]FOLDER2.DAT
DISK1:[USER.VMS.MAIL]F1M1.TXT
DISK1:[USER.VMS.MAIL]F1M2.TXT
DISK1:[USER.VMS.MAIL]F1M3.TXT
DISK1:[USER.VMS.MAIL]F2M1.TXT
```

and

```
$ @EXTRACTMAIL DISK1:[USER.MAIL]PROJECTS.MAI
```

will create the following files:

```
DISK1:[USER.VMS.PROJECTS]FOLDER1.DAT
DISK1:[USER.VMS.PROJECTS]F1M1.TXT
DISK1:[USER.VMS.PROJECTS]F1M2.TXT
```

Log onto a UNIX system and create a directory for each of the Open-VMS mail files you extracted in Step 5. Assume these are the following:

```
$HOME/vmsmail/mail
$HOME/vmsmail/projects
```

For each mail file on the OpenVMS system, copy the files to the appropriate directory on the UNIX system. For example, using dcp:

```
# dcp 'host/user/password::disk1:[user.vms.mail]*.*' $HOME
/vmsmail/mail
# dcp 'host/user/password::disk1:[user.vms.projects]*.*'
$HOME/ vmsmail/projects
```

If you choose ftp to copy the files:

```
# ftp -i host
Name: USER
Password:
ftp> lcd vmsmail/mail
ftp> cd [USER.VMS.MAIL]
ftp> mget *.*
ftp> bye
#
```

Change directory to the top of the directory tree you created in Step 6. For example:

```
# cd $HOME/vmsmail
```

Save the files parsemail and parsemail.pl in the current directory and make sure they have *user* execute permission (0700).

Execute the following command:

```
# ./parsemail
```

The converted folders are output to the subdirectory ./UNIXFolders. For the example, the following folders are created:

```
$HOME/vmsmail/mail/UNIXFolders/CAMPING
$HOME/vmsmail/mail/UNIXFolders/SKIING
$HOME/vmsmail/projects/UNIXFolders/NETSCAPE
```

Move the files in the UNIXFolders directories into your UNIX mail hierarchy.

After you verify that the conversion worked properly, you may delete the .dat and .txt files.

```
EXTRACTMAIL.COM
$! A DCL command procedure to perform the OpenVMS work toward converting
$! OpenVMS mail to a format suitable for any UNIX mail handler which
$! accepts "From" format mail files.
$!
$! Originally by Cliff Straw, Digital Equipment Corporation, January 1998
$!
$! Gratefully received and modestly annotated by Richie Holstein, Digital
$! Equipment Corporation, February 1998.
$!
$!
$ on control_y then goto cleanup
$ set broadcast=none
$
$ if ""p1'" .eqs. ""
$ then
$    drawer_name = "MAIL"
$    drawer_file_name = f$parse(drawer_name,"","","NAME","SYNTAX_ONLY")
$ else
$    drawer_file_name = p1
$    drawer_name = f$parse(drawer_file_name,"","","NAME","SYNTAX_ONLY")
$ endif
$
$ datfilename = "sys$disk:[]"drawer_name'_FOLDERS.DAT
$ tmpfilename="sys$scratch:id_folders.tmp"
```

```
$ outfilename="sys$scratch:id_folders.out"
$
$! Generate a .dat file of folders for the drawer.
$
$ open/write tmpfile 'tmpfilename'
$ write tmpfile "$define/nolog/user sys$output "outfilename'"
$ write tmpfile "$mail"
$ write tmpfile "set file "drawer_file_name'"
$ write tmpfile "dir/folder"
$ write tmpfile "$exit"
$ close tmpfile
$ @'tmpfilename'
$ delete/nolog 'tmpfilename';*
$
$! Convert that file so that it has a single folder name per line,
$! and excludes the NEWMAIL and WASTEBASKET folders.
$
$ open/read tmpfile 'outfilename'
$ beg_loop:
$   read tmpfile line
$   if f$extract(0,7,line) .eqs. "Listing" then goto end_beg_loop
$   goto beg_loop
$ end_beg_loop:
$ read tmpfile line
$ open/write outfile 'datfilename'
$
$ folder_loop:
$   read/end=end_folder_loop tmpfile line
$   if f$extract(0,8,line) .eqs. "%MAIL-I-" then goto end_folder_loop
$
$   folder1=f$edit(f$extract(0, 40, line), "TRIM")
$   folder2=f$edit(f$extract(40,40, line), "TRIM")
$
$   if folder1 .nes. "NEWMAIL" .and. folder1 .nes. "" -
       .and. folder1 .nes. "WASTEBASKET"
$   then
$     write outfile ""folder1'"
$   endif
$
$   if folder2 .nes. "NEWMAIL" .and. folder2 .nes. "" -
       .and. folder2 .nes. "WASTEBASKET"
```

```
$    then
$      write outfile ""folder2'"
$    endif
$    goto folder_loop
$ end_folder_loop:
$ close outfile
$ close tmpfile
$ delete/nolog 'outfilename';*
$
$! For each folder, figure out the number of messages in it: Create
$! a file for each folder that will have that folder message count.
$! Extract each message into its own file, with a unique filename based
$! on the folder name (an ordinal) and message number within the folder.
$
$ tmpfilename = "sys$scratch:"drawer_name'_EXTRACT.TMP"
$
$ folder_dir=f$edit("sys$disk:[."drawer_name']", "UPCASE")
$ create/dir 'folder_dir'
$ open datfile 'datfilename'
$
$ foldernum = 0
$ extract_loop:
$    read/end=end_extract_loop datfile folder
$    foldernum = foldernum + 1
$
$    write sys$output "Extracting folder: " + """"folder'""" + -
        " to directory: " + "folder_dir'
$    file=f$edit(""folder_dir'folder"foldernum'.dat", "UPCASE")
$    open/write tmpfile 'tmpfilename'
$    write tmpfile "$ define/nolog/user sys$output "file'"
$    write tmpfile "$ MAIL"
$    write tmpfile "SET FILE "drawer_file_name'"
$    write tmpfile "select """folder'"""
$    write tmpfile "show folder"
$    write tmpfile "$ exit"
$    close tmpfile
$    @'tmpfilename'
$    delete/nolog 'tmpfilename';*
$
$    open/read tmpfile 'file'
$    nummsg_loop:
```

```
$    read tmpfile line
$    if f$extract(0, 17, line) .eqs. "%MAIL-I-SELECTED,"
$    then
$      nummsg = f$element(1, " ", line)
$      goto end_nummsg_loop
$    endif
$    goto nummsg_loop
$  end_nummsg_loop:
$  close tmpfile
$
$  if nummsg .gt. 0
$  then
$    write sys$output "num msg = " + 'nummsg'
$    msgnum = 0
$    open/write tmpfile 'tmpfilename'
$    write tmpfile "$ define/nolog/user sys$output nl:"
$    write tmpfile "$ MAIL"
$    write tmpfile "SET FILE "drawer_file_name'"
$    write tmpfile "SELECT """folder'"""
$    msgnum_loop:
$      msgnum = msgnum + 1
$      msgfile=f$edit("""folder_dir'f"foldernum'm"msgnum'.txt", "UPCASE")
$      write tmpfile ""msgnum'"
$      write tmpfile "EXTRACT "msgfile'"
$
$      if msgnum .lt. nummsg then goto msgnum_loop
$
$    write tmpfile "$ exit"
$    close tmpfile
$    @'tmpfilename'
$    delete/nolog 'tmpfilename';*
$  endif
$
$  goto extract_loop
$ end_extract_loop:
$ close datfile
$
$
$! We have a directory, SYS$DISK:[.<mail-file-name>], which contains
$! a file, FOLDER<f>.DAT, for each folder in the mail file, and one file
$! per message in that folder, F<f>M<m>.TXT. We're ready to proceed on
```

```
$! the UNIX system.
$
$ cleanup:
$ if f$log("datfile") .nes. "" then close datfile
$ if f$log("tmpfile") .nes. "" then close tmpfile
$ if f$log("outfile") .nes. "" then close outfile
$ set broadcast=all
$ exit
parsemail.ksh
```

```
#!/usr/bin/ksh
script_path=`dirname $0`
for FILE in `find . -name "folder*.dat" -print`
do
  foldernum=`basename $FILE .dat`
  foldernum=${foldernum#folder}
  dir=`dirname $FILE`
  outdir=$dir/UNIXFolders
  if [ ! -d $outdir ]
  then
    mkdir $outdir
  fi
  folder= `grep -F "Your current mail folder is" $FILE`
  folder=${folder#Your current mail folder is }
  folder=`echo ${folder%.} | sed 's/[\/*]/_/g'`
  num_msg=`grep -F "%MAIL-I-SELECTED," $FILE | cut -d " -f 2`
  $script_path/parsemail.pl $dir "$outdir/$folder" $foldernum $num_msg
done
parsemail.pl
```

```
#!/usr/local/bin/perl
#
# Cliff Straw
# 22 December 1997
#
require "timelocal.pl";
require "ctime.pl";
$srcdir = $ARGV[0];          # directory containing message files
$outfile = $ARGV[1];         # folder output file
$folder_num = $ARGV[2];      # the folder number
$number_messages = $ARGV[3]; # number of messages in the folder
```

```perl
print "Output file:\t", $outfile, "\n";
#print "Folder number:\t", $folder_num, "\n";
#print "Number msg:\t", $number_messages, "\n";
open(OUTPUT, ">$outfile") || die "$0: could not open [$outfile] for output\n";
$num_output = 0;
for ($i = 1; $i <= $number_messages; $i++) {
  $file = sprintf("%s/f%dm%d.txt", $srcdir, $folder_num, $i);
  # print $file, "\n";
  # print "Processing message ", $i, "\n";
  open(INPUT, $file) || die "$0: could not open [$file] for input\n";
  #
  # parse the message header
  #
  &parse_header;
  if ($valid_header == 1) {
    #
    # output the body of the message
    #
    while (<INPUT>) {
      if (/^From\s.*/) {
        print OUTPUT " ", $_; # workaround for bug
      } else {
        print OUTPUT $_;
      }
    }
    print OUTPUT "\n";
    $num_output++;
  } else {
    print "File ", $file, ": Invalid message header section\n";
  }
  close(INPUT); # close the input file
}
close(OUTPUT); # close the output file
if ($number_messages == 1) {
  print "Wrote ", $num_output, " of 1 message\n\n";
} else {
  print "Wrote ", $num_output, " of ", $number_messages, " messages\n\n";
}
exit;
#
# The first four lines of the input file contain the mail header information.
```

```perl
# Line 1 is the "From" information, line 2 is the "To" field, line 3 is
# the "CC" field, and line 4 is the "Subject" field.
#
sub parse_header
  local($tl);
  local($time, $hours, $minute, $sec, $mday, $wday, $month, $year) = "";
  local(%moy) = ('Jan',0,'Feb',1,'Mar',2,'Apr',3,'May',4,
    'Jun',5,'Jul',6,'Aug',7,'Sep',8,'Oct',9,'Nov',10,'Dec',11);
  local($from, $to, $cc, $subject) = "";
  #
  # Initialize the global valid header flag to false
  #
  $valid_header = 0;
  #
  # read the header lines from the input file
  #
  #
  # Separate the from line into sender, date, and time. The format of the
  # from line is:
  #
  #    From: sender dd-MMM-yyyy hh:mm
  #
  # sender is a string consisting of an e-mail address and personal name
  # dd-MMM-yyyy is the date, month, and year (ex: 22-DEC-1997)
  # hh:mm is the hour and minute (ex: 14:22)
  #
  $_ = <INPUT>;
  if (($from, $mday, $month, $year, $hours, $minute, $sec) =
    $_ =~ /^From:\t(.*) (\d{1,2})-([a-zA-Z]{3,3})-(\d{4,4})
    (\d\d):(\d\d)(.*)/) {
    if ($sec =~ /^:(\d\d).*/) {
      $sec = $1;
    } else {
      $sec = 0;
    }
    $month = "\u\L$month"; # upcase first character, downcase remainder
    #
    # Use timelocal and ctime to get the day of the week for the date
    #
    $tl = &timelocal($sec, $minute, $hours,, $mday, $moy{$month}, $year);
    $time = &ctime($tl);
```

```
  } else {
    return;
  }
  # The "To:" field may be on multiple lines
  $_ = <INPUT>;
  if ($_ =~ /^To:\t(.*)/) {
    $to = $1;
    while (<INPUT>) {
      if (/^CC:/) {
        last;
      } else {
        /\s(.*)/;        # strip leading white space
        $to .= " $1";    # append to $to string
      }
    }
  } else {
    return;
  }
  # The "CC:" field may be on multiple lines
  if ($_ =~ /^CC:\t(.*)/) {
    $cc = $1;
    while (<INPUT>) {
      if (/^Subj:/) {
        last;
      } else {
        /\s(.*)/;        # strip leading white space
        $cc .= " $1";    # append to $cc string
      }
    }
  } else {
     return;
  }
  if ($_ =~ /^Subj:\t(.*)/) {
    $subject = $1;
  } else {
    return;
  }
  #
  # Start the message with the "From - " string. Add the date and
  # time if one was included in the input file
  #
```

```
  if ($time ne "\n") {
    ($wday, $month, $mday, $hours, $year) = split(' ', $time);
    if (substr($hours,1,1) eq ":")
      $hours = "0$hours"; # add a leading 0
    }
    printf OUTPUT "From - %s %s %s %s|
      %s\n",$wday,$month,$mday,$hours,$year;
    printf OUTPUT "Date: %s, %s %s %s
      %s\n",$wday,$mday,$month,$year,$hours;
  } else {
    print OUTPUT "From - \n";
  }
  print OUTPUT "From: ", $from, "\n";
  print OUTPUT "To: ",$to,"\n";
  print OUTPUT "Cc: ", $cc, "\n";
  print OUTPUT "Subject: ", $subject, "\n";
  $valid_header = 1;
  return;
}
```

Where To Look for Further Information

Aside from the official OpenVMS documentation available from HP, there are a handful of books available commercially about OpenVMS; some are published by Digital Press. By comparison, there are hundreds of books available for UNIX and Linux. It is impractical to try to list them here. Check with your local bookstore or use your favorite Web search engine to find a book about a specific UNIX topic.

Likewise, there is plenty of information available on the Web about UNIX and Linux. Virtually all the hardware vendors who support UNIX and Linux provide documentation on their Web sites. We recommend the following Web sites as good places to go for further information.

```
http://www.gnu.org
```

The GNU Project's main site has links to information, documentation, and sources for the various free software tools that run on UNIX and Linux systems, including the bash shell, compilers, programming tools, and applications.

```
http://www.gnu.org/software/emacs/emacs.html
```

This site is the place to start for learning about Emacs.

```
http://www.linux.org
```

From home page for Linux you can download Linux and related applications and find documentation.

```
http://www.unh.edu/cis/docs/vms-to-unix/index.html
```

This is a Web page maintained by the Computing and Information Services Department at the University of New Hampshire; it provides comparisons of OpenVMS with UNIX commands, shells, scripting, and editors.

```
http://www.tru64unix.compaq.com/products/interop/openvms.html
```

This site gives links to third-party vendors that provide emulation products.

Glossary

. (dot) The current directory.

.. (dot-dot) The parent directory of the current directory.

Absolute pathname A pathname that starts at the root directory, that is, with **/**.

Alias The shell mechanism for abbreviating a command line (compare the OpenVMS construct **:=**).

Argument list The list of words from the command line that the shell passes to a command.

ASCII American Standard Code for Information Exchange: a standard character encoding scheme.

Background job A job that is not receiving input from the terminal.

bash Bourne-Again shell. A shell program common on Linux, based on **sh**.

Baud Bits per second; a unit used to describe the transmission speed of data.

Bit bucket Name for the file **/dev/null.** Characters written here are "thrown away"; characters read from here cause an immediate EOF.

Bit map Mapping of the screen such that each pixel is represented in physical memory.

Breakpoint A point set in a source code program that stops the debugger during execution.

BSD Berkeley Software Distribution, the version of UNIX originating at the University of California at Berkeley.

Built-in **command** A command whose code is internal to the shell; the shell does not fork a process to execute the command.

Card image A terminal display representation of a punched card, 80 characters per record.

Child process The process created when the parent process executes the fork system routine.

csh Shorthand for **/bin/csh,** the C shell program.

Current directory The directory to which commands refer by default.

Daemon A system-generated process that performs some system management function in a manner transparent to the user.

Debugging Correcting errors in a program or procedure.

Detached job A job that continues processing after the user has logged out.

Device See *Physical device.*

Directory A UNIX file that contains names of other files or directories.

Directory hierarchy The arrangement of directories in a UNIX file system. The root directory is at the top of the directory hierarchy and contains point-ers to all file systems and hence to all directories on the system.

Directory stack A data structure that stores directories for later recall.

Disk partition Part of a disk onto which a file system is mounted.

Environment The set of characteristics describing a UNIX user's terminal session. The characteristics include the open files, the user and group identification, the process identification, and environment variables.

Environment variable A variable exported automatically to subsequent programs. Environment variables are defined with the **setenv** command.

EOF End-of-file character(s) that denote the end of a file, usually <CTRL>D.

Ethernet Local area network standard providing the two lower levels of the ISO/OSI (International Standards Organization/Open System Interconnect) seven-layer reference model.

Event Past command stored in the history list.

Executable image An executable file located in physical memory.

Extension The part after the . (period) in a pathname. Also called file extension.

Field separator One or more characters used to separate fields in a record; defaults to one or more blanks.

fifo A file intended for continuous use, where the first bytes entered into the file become the first bytes read from it (first in, first out).

File A stream of bytes stored under a unique pathname.

File and device independence Using filenames and device names in commands equivalently; for example, **who** > **out** and **who** > **/dev/lp.**

File descriptor The number UNIX assigns to an open file.

Filename A set of characters used to reference a file. Any character is legal, but it is best to choose from the alphanumeric character set, period, and underscore. BSD filenames may contain up to 255 characters.

Filename expansion Matching filenames in the specified directory according to the following rules: * matches any character sequence including null; ? matches any single character; [] delimits a set of characters; **[n-m]** matches the range of characters **n** through **m** inclusive; **;@** matches the home directory; and {} delimits different parts in a common pathname (see also *globbing*).

File system A hierarchical arrangement of files beginning at the root and mounted in a disk partition.

Filter A program that reads from the standard input, processes it, and writes it to the standard output. Filters are typically used in pipes.

Floating point accelerator Hardware designed specifically to enhance the speed with which mathematical operations are performed on floating point data types.

Foreground job A job that must be completed or interrupted before the shell will accept more commands; a job receiving input from the terminal.

Fork The system routine that creates a new process by duplicating the calling (parent) process.

Globbing Filename expansion using metacharacters.

Group ID A numeric identification designating the group to which a user belongs. The number corresponds to an entry in the **/etc/group** file.

GUI A means of interacting with a user that supplements or replaces the traditional keyboarder and text with a mouse and pictures (Graphical User Interface).

Hard link Associates the same file contents with two or more file names within the same file system.

Header The directory containing the filename.

History list List of previously issued commands.

Home directory The user's default working directory, specified in the **/etc/passwd** file.

Host A computer on a network (compare the OpenVMS node).

Host name The name given to a host (compare the OpenVMS node name).

Inode Pointers used in locating data on a physical device.

Input Data read by a command or user program.

Interrupt A signal, typically generated at the keyboard, which causes the currently executing process to terminate unless special action is taken by the process to handle the signal.

Interrupt handler A set of statements executed upon receipt of an interrupt.

Job A task consisting of one or more processes assigned a job number by the shell and executing in either foreground or background.

Job control Ability of the shell to control multiple jobs.

Job number The number that uniquely identifies a job within a shell session.

Job stack Queue of jobs maintained by the shell.

Job states The current state of a job. (see also *Suspended, Terminated Job,* and *Detached Job.*)

ksh Shorthand for **/bin/ksh,** the Korn shell program.

Link An entry in a directory (that is, a filename) that points to an existing file. Hard links may not span file systems; symbolic links, also called soft links, may.

Link loader Software that combines all the separate modules of a program to create an executable file.

Lock file A file whose existence prevents some function (for example, access to a common database, printing device, or other shared facility).

Login name The name assigned to a user (compare the OpenVMS user-name).

Metacharater A character with a special meaning (for example, > denotes redirection of output).

Modifier See *Variable modifier.*

Multiprocessor Two or more processors sharing common physical memory.

Network contention Two or more packets demanding simultaneous access to the network.

NFS Network File System, a network protocol developed by Sun Microsystems, Inc., to permit access to files on remote computers as if they were located on the local computer (compare the OpenVMS Local Area VMS-cluster).

NIS A distributed name service that allows participating hosts to share access to a common set of administrative and network files (Network Information Service).

Object files Files containing object code produced as the result of a compilation.

Object library A library containing object files.

Option Modifies command execution.

Output Data produced by a command or user program.

Packet A unit of data and other information, for example, local host address, remote host address, sent on a network.

Page The unit of interchange between physical memory and a swapping device; 512 bytes for VAX computers, generally 8192 bytes for Alpha computers.

Parent directory The directory above the current directory; the directory one level closer to the root.

Parent process The originator of the fork call that creates a child process.

Partition Segment of a physical disk onto which a file system is mounted.

Parsing order The order in which the shell evaluates a command line and instigates any special mechanisms (**history**, **alias**, and so on).

Password A special code word known only by the user to permit access to the system. A user's password is stored in encrypted form in the file **/etc/ passwd.**

Pathname The names of all the directories that must be traversed to reach a given destination (file or directory).

Pathname qualifier See *Variable modifer.*

Physical device A piece of hardware attached to the computer; for example, a disk drive, tape drive, printer, or terminal.

Physical device name The name given to a physical device; for example, **/ dev/tty01** (compare the OpenVMS name **TTA1:**), **/dev/da0a** (compare the OpenVMS name **DUA0:**), and **/dev/rmt0h** (compare the OpenVMS name **MUA0:**).

Pipe A connection that allows one program to get its input directly from the output of another program.

Pipelining A hardware architecture that permits different components of an instruction to simultaneously process different data elements.

Pixel A picture element: a point on the screen that is directly addressable by the computer.

Predefined variable A shell variable defined and maintained by the shell.

Prepend To insert at the front.

Preprocessor Software that performs modifications to data so that the data conforms to the input requirements of some other standard software.

Present working directory See *Current directory.*

Priority A number assigned to a process that determines the system resources that the process may receive.

Process A program that is being executed or is waiting to be executed.

Process identification or **process id** An integer that uniquely identifies a process within the system.

Profiling Monitoring how system resources are utilized in a given program.

Protection mask The protection assigned to a file.

Recursion Defined relative to itself; calling a procedure from within a procedure.

Redirection Designating the source or destination of input or output to be a named file or device.

Regular expression Incorporation of metacharacters to define the characteristics of a string.

Relative pathname The names of all directories either above or below the current directory that must be traversed to reach a given destination (file or directory).

RISC Reduced Instruction Set Computer: a hardware architecture that concentrates on performing the most frequently used instructions at an accelerated rate. The less often used instructions are performed by the operating system software.

Root Another name for the superuser.

Root directory Top level of the UNIX directory hierarchy; all directories derive from it.

RS-232 A standard interface used to connect a terminal to a host computer.

Script A shell procedure or program (compare the OpenVMS DCL command procedure).

Search path The ordered list of directories that the shell searches to find commands.

sh Shorthand for the file **/bin/sh,** the Bourne shell program.

Shell The UNIX command interpreter (compare the OpenVMS DCL command language interpreter).

Shell variable An identifier that can hold one or more strings of characters.

Socket Defines an endpoint for a network communication (BSD only).

Soft link Associating the same file contents with two or more file names, either within the same file system or across file systems; also called a symbolic link.

Standard error (stderr) Where error messages are written; the terminal by default (compare the OpenVMS logical name **SYS$ERROR).**

Standard input (stdin) Where input is taken from; the terminal by default (compare the penVMS logical name **SYS$INPUT).**

Standard output (stdout) Where output is written to; the terminal by default (compare the OpenVMS logical name **SYS$OUTPUT).**

Status The state in which a program exists. By convention, 0 indicates a successful exit, non-zero an error.

Store-and-forward A type of network connection in which a complete transmission is passed to one intermediate host before transmission to the next intermediate host begins.

Stream Same function as a socket, used by System V.

Subdirectory A directory that exists within another directory; any directory other than the root directory.

Superuser The login name that has total access to the system; also called **root**.

Suspended job Temporarily stopped foreground or background job.

Symbolic link See *Soft link*.

System load The demand that all processes are placing on the computer. Usually expressed as a number: 1.0 represents 100% utilization; 0.1 represents 10% utilization of system resources.

System routines The set of resident procedures callable by the user.

Tail The last part of a file; or a filename without a directory specification.

Task A defined activity.

TCP/IP Transmission Control Protocol/Internet Protocol: the network protocol used by computers using the UNIX operating system.

Terminal session The interaction that occurs between the user and the computer between login and logout.

Terminated job Permanently stopped job.

Tool A command or utility designed to help get a job done, for example, **make** or **dbx**.

Trusted host A host that permits access without the need to supply password information (compare the OpenVMS proxy login).

Uptime Wall clock time since the system was last booted.

URL The address of an object as it appears to a browser on the World Wide Web, whether that object is on a remote computer, available locally, or a service provided by some computer (Universal Resource Locator).

Usenet Network of computers running UNIX for the exchange of every imaginable type of information.

User identification or **user id** The number associated with each login name. This number is stored in the **/etc/passwd** file.

Utility A command with many options, for example, **mail** or **awk**.

Variable expansion Replacing the variable identifier with its associated string or strings in a shell command line.

Variable modifier Symbol referring to part of a variable, usually under the assumption that its value is a pathname.

Vectorization Hardware that permits a single instruction to act upon multiple data elements.

Word A string separated by blanks, tabs, or the shell special characters >, <, |, &, ;,), and (.

Wordlist A shell variable consisting of more than one word.

Index

Access Control Entries (ACEs), 105
Access Control List (ACL), 103
Administration, 375–410
    file backup/restore, 389–93
    network configuration, 398–409
    network monitoring, 409
    security, 393–98
    software installation, 376–77
    startup procedures, 377–79
    summary, 409–10
    system initialization files, 379–85
    tasks, 375
    user accounts/groups, 385–89
Alias command, 65–66, 72, 74
    defined, 65
    example, 66, 69
Aliases
    definition, 66
    mail, 171
Archiving files, 200–205
Ar command, 98, 257, 275–77
    a option, 277
    b option, 277
    example, 275–76
    m option, 277
    q option, 276
    r option, 277
    t option, 276
    x option, 277
Array elements, referencing, 299

At command, 430–32
    batch command vs., 434
    defined, 430
    example, 431
Authentication, user, 395
Awk editor, 121–22, 151–65
    array use, 160
    defined, 98, 151
    features, 151
    field separators, 152
    flow control, 158–60
    -F option, 152, 154, 155, 163, 164, 250
    functions, 162
    logical/arithmetic operators, 156–57
    mathematical functions, 163
    output formatting, 160–61
    output redirect, 163–64
    patterns and actions, 152–53
    predefined variables, 154–55
    record fields, 152
    scripts, 157–58
    string operators, 161–63
    variable assignment, 155–56
    See also Editors

Background jobs, 209–14
    completed, 212
    defined, 210
    examining, 212–13

manipulating, 213–14
output display, 212
status, 214
See also Jobs
Background processing, 209–14
command execution, 211–12
defined, 209
error messages, 212
output redirect, 212
Backups
examples, 391–92
frequency, 389, 391
full, 391
incremental, 391
process, 390–92
tasks, 389–90
Bash command, 358
Batch
communications, 170–82
jobs, 210
processing, 214–15
Batch command, 434
Berkeley Internet Name Domain (BIND)
service, 406
Berkeley Software Distribution (BSD), 4–5,
253, 258
Bg command, 214
Biff command, 65
Boot sequence, 379, 380–81
Bourne Again shell (bash), 285
case command, 336
comparison operator examples, 308
comparison operators, 306, 307
eval command example, 350
file operators, 311–13
for command example, 328–29
if statement examples, 321–23
mathematical operator example, 316–18
mathematical operators, 316
onintr command example, 348
quoting under, 305–6

select statement example, 337
signed integer arithmetic, 318
string comparisons, 310
until statement example, 325–26
variable assignment, 290
variable distinctions, 290
See also Shells
Bourne shell (sh), 8, 19, 86, 285
directory sequence, 231
regular expression expansion, 46
See also Shells
Break command, 330–32
defined, 330
examples, 331–32
Breaksw statement, 334
Built-in shell commands, 346–58
eval, 349–52
exec, 356–58
onintr, 346, 347–49
source, 355–56
time, 352–55
trap, 346, 347–49
Bye command, 458

Case sensitivity, 27
Case statement, 336
Cat command, 21, 22, 80, 475
defined, 98
examples, 111
more command vs., 110
-n option, 111
Cd command, 107–8
defined, 98, 107
examples, 107
C++ files, 257
Chgrp command, 233–34
defined, 98
OpenVMS correspondence, 233–34
Child processes, 20, 22
Chmod command, 222, 232–33, 395

absolute form, 230
defined, 98
symbolic form, 233
uses, 223
Clear command, 75
Clobbering, 25
Cmp command, 98, 235
Command lines
  editing, 77–82
  recall of, 78
Commands
  abbreviation, 31, 72
  continuation, 32
  defined, 261
  display, 91–92
  format, 31
  history, 79
  manipulation, 92–97
  monitoring, 414
  multiple, 32
  names, 11, 31
  names, redefining, 72
  options, 32
  previewing, 82
  recalling, 78
  running, system load level and, 434
  in scripts, 289
  scrolling through, 80
  structure, 27–32
  substitution, 73
  See also specific UNIX commands
Comments
  defined, 262
  script, 290
Common Open Software Environment
  (COSE), 8
Communications
  addressing, 444
  batch, 170–82
  interactive, 183–84
  modem-based, 443, 464–72

network, 444–64
  between OpenVMS and UNIX, 473
  overview, 442–44
  between UNIX hosts, 441
  with users, 169–87
Comparison operators, 306–10
  bash shell, 306, 307
  bash shell examples, 308
  C shell, 306
  C shell examples, 307–8
  Korn shell, 306
  Korn shell examples, 308
  Perl examples, 308–9
Compilers
  documentation, 257
  specialized, 253
Compiling, 257–60
  simplification, 260–65
  steps, 258
Continue command, 332–34
  defined, 332–33
  examples, 333
Cp command, 60, 112–13
  defined, 98
  examples, 112–13
  -i option, 112
  -r option, 228
Csh command
  -v command, 358, 359
  -x command, 358, 359
.cshrc file, 61
  changes to, 69
  customizing, 65–70
  invoking, 70
  sample, 70
C shell (csh), 8, 19, 86, 285
  command line recall, 79
  comparison operator examples, 307–8
  comparison operators, 306
  continue command example, 333
  .cshrc file, 65–70

filename modifiers, 301–4
file operator example, 314–15
file operators, 311–13
foreach statement example, 327
goto statement example, 339
history substitution, 81
if statement example, 321
.login file, 63–65
mathematical operator example, 316–18
mathematical operators, 316
onintr command example, 347–48
regular expression expansion, 46
script debugging, 358–59
scripts, 286
shift statement example, 340–41
signed integer arithmetic, 318
source command example, 356
string handling capabilities, 286
switch statement example, 334–35
time command example, 352–53
variable assignment, 290
variables, 163
while statement example, 324
See also Shells
<CTRL>, 76
    -C option, 184, 337
    -D option, 187, 337
    -F option, 145
    -G option, 145
    -K option, 142
    -L option, 184
    -_ option, 145–46
    -S option, 140, 146
    -W option, 141, 184
    -X option, 145, 146
    -Y option, 141
    -Z option, 211, 451
Cu command, 465–67

Daemons

defined, 421
    NFS, 462
    TCP/IP, 401
Data Terminal Ready (DTR), 54
Dbx utility, 267–71
    aliases and variables, 268–69
    commands subset, 267–69
    defined, 267
    examples, 270–71
    execution and tracing, 267–68
    printing variables and expressions, 268
    source file access, 268
Dd command, 205–7
    for appending multiple input files, 206
    defined, 198
    input/output default and, 206
    using, 208
Debugging
    programs, 266–71
    shell scripts, 286, 358–60
DECnet
    mail address, 169
    mail address formats, 444
    Phase IV, 399
    software, 398
DEC OSF/1, 6
Dependencies
    defined, 261
    nested, 263
    second-level, 263
Devices
    block, 37
    character, 37
    naming conventions, 38
    null, 37
Df command, 428–29
    defined, 428
    example, 429
    -i option, 429
    without options, 429
Diff command, 235

defined, 98
example, 236–37
-r option, 238
Digital Command Language (DCL)
    interpreter, 18
Digital Network Architecture (DNA), 398
Directories
    adding, to PATH list, 62
    advanced display commands, 222–23
    advanced management commands, 228–31
    changing, 107–8
    content display, 100–102
    copying, 228
    creating, 108
    current, determining, 106–7
    current, listing files in, 102
    deleting, 108–9
    display commands, 91
    grafting, 229
    manipulation commands, 92–93
    naming, 41
    navigation, 228–31
    paths, 62
    run-state, 380–82
    structures, 37–38
Directory files, 42
Directory stack, 221
    building, 107
    defined, 106, 230
    use scenario, 230–31
    working directory in, 230
Dirs command, 106
Disk-to-disk copying, 204–5
Disk usage, monitoring, 422–23
Disk utilization, 422–23
Documentation
    compiler, 257
    printed, 86
    UNIX, 11
Du command, 422–23
    -a option, 423

defined, 422
example, 422
report, 422–23
-s option, 423
Dump command, 198, 201
    for accessing local/remote drives, 390
    record information, 392
    tape header, 201
Dxdiff command, 235, 238

Echo command, 301
    -n option, 299
    return, 305
Ed editor, 119, 120
Edit editor, 119, 120
Editing, 119–66
    command-line, 80
    line-mode, 122–29
Editors
    awk, 121–22, 151–65
    ed, 119, 120
    edit, 119, 120
    Emacs, 77, 119, 136–48
    EVE/TPU, 136, 138, 165
    ex, 119, 120, 122–29
    line, 120
    programmable, 120
    screen, 120
    sed, 121, 148–50
    SLP, 238
    standard, 119
    vi, 77, 119, 129–36
EDT commands, 128
Emacs editor, 77, 119, 136–48, 165
    action commands, 141–42
    automatic file versions, 146–48
    backup copy, 121
    commands, 139
    cursor movement, 139–40
    defined, 120, 136

error recovery, 145–46
favor, 120
files, working with, 143–44
functions, 136
invoking, 136
keyboard macros, recording, 143
modeline information, 138
operating modes, 137
sample session, 37
screen regions, 138
sessions, recovering, 145–46
sessions, starting, 138
shell command execution from, 142
text marking, 140–41
windows, working with, 144–45
See also Editors
ENV file, 70
   customizing, 70–75
   sample, 74
Environment variables, 56
   assignment determination, 61
   ENV, 74
   in .login file, 163
   printing, 293
Error command, 266–67
   defined, 266
   lines, 266
   piping error messages to, 267
Error handling
   flow control and, 342–46
   for Perl statements, 342
Error messages
   background processing, 212
   inserting, 266
   piping, 267
Error(s)
   handling, 11
   redirection, 24–27
   reporting, 32
/etc/group file, 388–89
   defined, 388

example, 388
fields, 388
/etc/hosts file, 405, 445, 448
/etc/networks file, 405–6
/etc/passwd file, 386–88
   access, 387
   defined, 386
   example, 386–87
   world-readable, 388
/etc/printcap file, 194
Eval command, 349–52
   defined, 346, 349
   example, 350, 351
   uses, 349–51
EVE/TPU editor, 136, 138, 165
Exec command, 356–58
   defined, 356–57
   example, 357, 358
Ex editor, 119, 120, 122–29
   a command, 125
   appending with, 125
   c command, 126, 128
   changing with, 126
   co command, 127, 128
   commands, 123
   commands, abbreviating, 122
   copying with, 127–28
   cutting/pasting with, 127–28
   e command, 128
   edit session recovery, 128–29
   external file handling, 128
   features, 120, 122–23
   g command, 127
   i command, 125
   inserting with, 125
   invoking, from vi, 133–34
   line display, 124–25
   m command, 127
   moving with, 127
   p command, 124
   r command, 128

s command, 127
search and replace with, 126–27
syntax, 124
w command, 128
See also Editors
Exit command, 289

F77 command, 21, 22, 27
-c option, 260
examples, 259–60
-o option, 260
-pg option, 272
-s option, 260
Fg command, 21, 22, 214
File definition language (FDL), 246
File extensions, 29–30
File identifiers, 37
File locking, 247
File management, 221–50
advanced commands, 231–49
commands summary, 91–97
commonly-used commands, 98–99
introductory, 91–116
tasks, 97–100
Filenames
case sensitivity, 27
extracting parts of, 304
modifiers, 301–4
recognition, 29
in UNIX compilations, 257
File operators, 310–15
bash shell, 311–13
C shell, 311–13
C shell example, 314–15
defined, 313
Korn shell, 311–13
OpenVMS example, 314
Perl, 311–13
Perl example, 314
Files

absolute definition of, 40
advanced display commands, 223–27
appending, 200
archiving, 200–205
backing up, 390–92
C++, 257
characteristics, 102–6
contents, searching, 240–43
contents comparison, 235
copying, 112–13
creating, 245–46
defining, 33, 40–41
deleting, 114
delimiting, 32
directory, 42
display commands, 91–92
displaying, 110–11
dumping, 226
explicit definition of, 40
finding, 109–10
with fixed record length, 208
header, 258
hidden, 40, 42–43
links, 104
manipulation commands, 93–97
merging, 243–45
multiple references to, 247–49
name display, 222
naming, 27–32
operating on, with Emacs, 143
ordinary, 42
paging, 39, 111–12
permission codes for, 395–96
permissions, 104
permissions, changing, 232–34
as pointers, 223
printing, 194
relative definition of, 40
renaming, 113
residence, 34
restoring, 392–93

script, 289
sorting, 243–45
special, 42
specifications, 33–34
structures, 32–34
swapping, 39
symbolic assembly, 258
system initialization, 379–84
types of, 42
updating, 245–46
writing, to tape, 201–3
See also Directories
File systems
defined, 36
root, 36
in security checklist, 398
utilization, 428–29
File templates, 389
File transfers, 34
command comparison, 454
modem communications, 467–70
network communications, 453–60
nontrusted hosts, 456–60
trusted hosts, 454–56
with uucp command, 467–69
with uusend command, 469–70
Find command, 109–10, 239–40, 250
defined, 98
examples, 110, 239
file types returned by, 239
syntax, 239
using, 109–10
Flags, 262
Flat profiles, 272
Flow control, 320–46
break command, 330–32
breaksw statement, 334
case command, 336
continue command, 332–34
error handling and, 342–46
for command, 327–30

foreach statement, 326–27
goto statement, 338–39
if statement, 320–23
select command, 336–38
shift statement, 339–42
switch statement, 334–36
until statement, 325–26
while statement, 324–25
For command, 327–30
examples, 328–29
list contents and, 328
Foreach statement, 326–27
defined, 326
examples, 327
Foreground jobs, 209, 210
manipulation of, 213–14
output display, 212
See also Jobs
Forking, 20
Forwarding mail, 176
Fragments, 35
From command, 170, 173
Fsplit command, 261
defined, 98
example, 278
Ftp utility, 441, 456–60
after connection, 459
anonymous, 459
commands subset, 456–57
connection, 456, 457
defined, 98, 456
diagnostic message display, 460
status command, 460
termination, 458

Generic queue, 194
Gnu compilers, 17
GNU Linux, 6, 354
GNU Network Object Model Environment
(GNOME), 47

GNU Project, 5
Goto statement, 338–39
  defined, 338
  example, 339
Gprof utility, 256, 271
  children listings, 274
  display, 272
  function entries, 273
  invoking, 271, 381
  obtaining profile data with, 271
  parent listings, 274
  record types, 272
Grep command, 98, 240–43
  -c option, 242
  defined, 240
  examples, 241
  -i option, 242
  -n option, 242
  search string, 240
  syntax, 240
  -v option, 242
Group command, 234
Groups, 388–89
  defined, 388
  multiple, membership, 388
  primary, 389
GUI, 47–48

Hard links, 248
Head command, 110
  defined, 98, 226
  examples, 227
Header files, 258
Hidden files, 40, 42–43
  defined, 42
  list of, 43
  See also Files
History command, 64, 77, 78, 79
History list
  command invocation from, 66

defined, 64
History substitution, 81
Hosts
  communication between, 441
  network-based connection between, 443
  nontrusted, 440, 451–52
  remote, 442
  trusted, 440, 447–49

If statements, 320–23
  bash/Korn shell examples, 321–23
  conditional branches, 320
  C shell example, 321
  examples, 321–23
  nesting, 320
  Perl example, 321–23
If-then-else constructs, 336
Incremental backups, 391
Input redirection, 24–27
Interactive communications, 183–84
Internet
  addressing, 401–2
  mail form, 169
Internet Control Message Protocol (ICMP),
    400
Internet Protocol (IP), 399
Interrupt redirection, 347
INT signal, 349

Jobs
  background, 209–14
  batch, 210
  defined, 209
  foreground, 209, 210, 212
  number, 213
  stack, 213, 214
  status, 213, 214
Jobs command, 76, 212, 214

K Desktop Environment (KDE), 47–48
Kernel, 16
  alternate, 378
  booting, 377–78
  default, 378
  location of, 378
Kill command, 214
  defined, 430
  -l option, 349
  using, 430
Korn shell (ksh), 8, 19, 86
  break command example, 331
  case command, 336
  command number and, 74
  command substitution invocation, 73
  comparison operator examples, 308
  comparison operators, 306
  continue command, 333
  directory sequence, 231
  double-precision floating-point arithmetic, 286
  ENV file, 70–75, 288
  exec command example, 357, 358
  file operators, 311–13
  for command example, 328
  four-layer architecture, 70
  if statement examples, 321–23
  mathematical operator example, 316–18
  mathematical operators, 316
  OLDPWD variable, 231
  onintr command example, 348
  pattern-matching facility, 304
  .profile file, 70–75
  prompting levels, 73
  prompting/reading a response, 299
  quoting under, 305–6
  regular expression expansion, 46
  scripts, 70
  select statement example, 337, 338
  signed integer arithmetic, 318
  string comparisons, 310
  string variables, 290
  syntax, 285
  time command example, 353–54
  until statement example, 325–26
  variable assignment, 71, 290
  variable distinctions, 290
  while statement example, 324–25
  See also Shells
Ksh command, 358

Less command, 111–12, 224–25
  defined, 98
  examples, 112
  functions, 111–12
  options, 225
  -v option, 112
Lexical analyzer, 17
Librarian Utility, 82
Libraries
  maintaining, 275–77
  performance, 275
  randomization, 275
  site-dependent, 277
Limit command, 423–24
  defined, 423
  example, 423–24
  in reducing system resources, 433–34
  values, 424
Line-mode editing, 122–29
Linking, 257–60
Links
  defined, 104, 247
  hard, 248
  symbolic, 248
  use of, 247
Linux, 6
  GNU, 6, 354
  run levels, 379
  third-party mail clients, 170

Ln command, 247–49
    defined, 98
    examples, 249
Loaders, 259
Logging out, 75–76
.login file, 61
    customizing, 63–65
    environment variables in, 163
    from command in, 170
    prompt string, 65
Logout command, 76
Lorder command, 98
Lpq command, 196–97
    defined, 196
    -fred option, 197
    -Plaser option, 197
Lpr command, 194–96, 263
    defined, 194–95
    -f option, 196
    -p option, 195
    -r option, 195
    -s option, 196
Lprm command, 197–98
    defined, 197
    examples, 198
Ls command, 28, 222–23, 463
    -A option, 43, 86, 100
    -a option, 43, 115
    -C option, 223
    defined, 98, 100
    display order, 102
    -F option, 41, 222
    -l option, 66, 102, 106, 222, 223
    -r option, 223
    -R option, 102
    -t option, 223

Macros, 262
Mail
    aliases, 171

commands comparison, 182–83
    deleting, 177–79
    environment, customizing, 180–82
    forwarding, 176
    incoming, 173
    messages, 170
    reading, 173–75
    replying to, 175
    saving, 177–79
    searching, 179–80
    sending, 171–73
    sending (modem communications), 467
    sending (network communications), 452–
        53
    terminating, 180
Mail utility, 169, 170, 441
    -f option, 179
    in forwarding mail, 176
    h command, 187
    interactive responses, 174–75
    message modifiers, 172–73
    message notification, 173
    prompt, 174
    R command, 175–76
    r command, 175–76
    replying with, 175–76
    saving/deleting with, 177–79
    searching with, 179–80
    terminating mail with, 180
    variables, 181
Makefiles, 261
    for compiling programs, 264–65
    for forcing compilation, 265
    modifying, 280
    syntax rules, 262
Make utility, 260–65, 279
    defined, 256
    instructions, 261
    -n option, 263, 279
    uses, 260
Man command, 84

-f option, 86
-k option, 85, 86
Man pages
    defined, 82
    entries, 84
    format, 82–83
    industry standards, 83
    reviewing, 82
    storage, 84
Mathematical operators, 315–20
    bash shell, 316
    C shell, 316
    Korn shell, 316
    list of, 316
    Perl, 316
Menu_script script file, 363–65
Merge command, 99
Messages, 170
    header, 170
    new, notification of, 173
    saving, as files, 178
    See also Mail
Metacharacters
    !, 65
    defined, 43
    examples, 43
    function of, 43
Mkdir command, 28, 108
    defined, 99
    examples, 108
    -p option, 108
Modem communications, 439, 443, 464–72
    file transfer, 467–70
    remote command execution, 470–72
    remote login, 465–67
    sending mail, 467
    UUCP addresses, 465
    UUCP status, 465
Monitoring, 413–29
    disk usage, 422–23
    file-system utilization, 428–29

interactive users, 416–18
network utilization, 426–28
processes, 418–22
process resource limits, 423–24
system, 424–29
UNIX commands for, 414
users, 414–18
virtual memory utilization, 425–26
More command, 110–11, 224, 279
    cat command vs., 110
    -c option, 110
    defined, 99
    examples, 111
    file advance, 224
    responses, 224
    screen advance, 224
Mt command, 198, 207
    defined, 207
    -f option, 207
    options, 207
Multitasking, 21, 191
Mv command, 60, 113
    defined, 99
    examples, 113
    -i option, 113

NCP, 402
Netnews, 473
Netsetup utility, 403–5
Netstat command, 426–28, 445
    defined, 426
    examples, 426–28
    -i option, 428
Network communications, 444–64
    file transfer, 453–60
    network address, 444–45
    network status, 445–47
    remote command execution, 460–62
    remote login, 449–52
    secure shell, 464

sending mail, 452–53
transparent file access, 462–64
trusted host, 447–49
Network File System (NFS), 7, 40, 441, 462–
    64
    daemon, 462
    defined, 462
    origination, 462
    remote file system accessible via, 463
Network Information Services (NIS), 55
Network(s), 439–75
    addresses, 444–45
    configuration, 398–409
    connections, 439
    defined, 398
    monitoring, 409–10
    OpenVMS products, 399
    in security checklist, 397–98
    setting up, 402–6
    status, 445–47
    store-and-forward, 442
    TCP/IP, 399–402
    utilization, 426–28
Nice command, 432
NIS, 406
Nontrusted hosts, 440, 451–52
    file transfer, 456–60
    remote login, 451–52
    See also Hosts
Null devices, 37

Od command, 226
    -a option, 226
    defined, 99
    -h option, 226
    -o option, 226
    uses, 226
Onintr command, 347–49
    defined, 346
    example, 347–48

interrupt redirection, 347
Online help, 82–86
Open Software Foundation (OSF), 7
OpenVMS, 3, 6
    ACEs, 105
    batch jobs, 210
    directory structure, 37–38
    evolutionary pathway, 8
    file-naming scheme, 28
    file specifications, 33–34
    future, 11–12
    genealogy, 9–10
    Librarian Utility, 82
    mail commands comparison, 182–83
    market share, 12
    networking commands comparison, 409
    networking products, 399
    RMS, 42
    spawning, 20
    subprocesses, 20
    tools/utilities, 16, 18–19
    UIC, 106
    UNIX communications, 473
    UNIX vs., 16
Operating systems
    kernel, 16
    topology, 17
    See also OpenVMS; UNIX
Operators
    comparison, 306–10
    file, 310–15
    mathematical, 315–20
Options, 32
Orange Book, 394
"Orderly shutdown," 384
Output redirection, 24–27

Packets, 443
Paging files, 39
Parent processes, 20, 22

Partitions, 34, 35
Passwd command, 75
Passwords, 75
Pattern matching, 151–65
Performance and Coverage Analyzer (PCA),
    271
Perl, 286
    break command example, 332
    comparison operator examples, 308–9
    continue command example, 333
    error handling for, 342
    file operator example, 314
    file operators, 311–13
    file-parsing routine, 304
    for command example, 329
    foreach statement example, 327
    goto statement example, 339
    if statement example, 321–23
    Math::BigFloat math library, 318
    mathematical operators, 316
    onintr command example, 348
    scalar variable type, 291
    scoping mechanisms, 290
    scripts, entering, 293
    shift statement example, 341
    smart-rename script, 367–70
    switch statement example, 335
    UNIX commands via, 287
    until statement example, 326
    variables, 293
    while statement example, 324–25
Permissions, 104
    bits, 395
    codes, 395–96
    file, changing, 232–34
    group ownership, 233–34
    See also Security
Ping command, 446
Pipelines, 23–24
    benefits, 24
    commands forming, 23

defined, 20, 23
Point-to-Point Protocol (PPP), 400
POLYCENTER Software Installation utility,
    376
Pr command, 226–27
    defined, 99, 226–27
    examples, 227
Predefined symbols, 263–64
Predefined variables, 293–95
    list of, 294
    status, 343
    term, 293
    values, 294–95
Prefixes, 262
Preprocessors, 257
    instructions, 257
    tasks, 258
Print command, 194, 195
Printed documentation, 86
Printenv command, 61
Printing files, 194
Print jobs
    display, 197
    removing, 197–98
    submitting, 194–96
Print queues
    default, 196
    examining, 196–97
    using, 192–94
Print spooler, 192
Privileges, 57
    superuser, 57, 395
    user, 57
Processes, 19–23
    in background, 21
    child, 20, 22
    creation, 20
    defined, 19
    deleting, 430
    execution delay, 430–32
    identifiers, 19–20

modifying, 430–34
monitoring, 418–22
multiple, 20
parent, 20, 22
priority, 20
priority, lowering, 432–33
resource limits, 423–24
subprocesses, 20
synchronization, 23
Profiles
  children listings, 274
  flat, 272
  function entries, 273
  parent listings, 274
Profiling, 271–74
  data, obtaining, 271
  defined, 271
.profile file, 61
  customizing, 70–75
  from command in, 170
  sample, 72
Prof utility, 256, 271
  defined, 271
  obtaining profile data with, 271
Programming, 253–81
  shell, 285–371
  UNIX tool summary, 254–56
Programs
  compilation steps, 258
  debugging, 266–71
Ps command, 212, 418–22
  -a option, 421, 422
  defined, 418
  example, 419–20
  -l option, 420
  PPID, 420–21
  -u option, 421
  without options, 420
  -x option, 421, 422
Pushd command, 231
Pwd command, 106–7

Ranlib command, 275–77
  defined, 99, 277
  example, 277
R command, 448
Rcp command, 441, 454–56
  defined, 99, 454
  examples, 455
  -r option, 455
  syntax, 454
Read command, 296
Record management Service (RMS), 42
Redirection, 24–27
  characters for, 26
  interrupt, 347
  overwriting by, 25
Regular expression expansion, 46
Regular expressions, 148, 150
Remote command execution
  mobile communications, 470–72
  network communications, 460–62
Remote hosts, 442
Remote installation services (RIS) software,
    377
Remote login, 449–52
  commands comparison, 449
  modem communications, 465–67
  nontrusted hosts, 451–52
  trusted hosts, 450–51
Renice command, 432–33
Restore command, 198, 392–93
  example, 392, 393
  interactive mode, 393
  -i option, 393
Restoring files, 392–93
Rlogin command, 441, 450–51, 464
  defined, 449, 450
  example, 450
  toggle feature, 451
Rm command, 114

defined, 99
examples, 114
-f option, 114, 280
-r option, 108–9
Rmdir command, 108–9
  defined, 99
  examples, 109
Root file system, 36
Rsh utility, 441, 460–62
  defined, 460
  examples, 461
  functionality, 461
Run levels, 378–79
  defined, 378
  Red Hat Linux, 379
  Tru64, 378
Run_program script file, 360–63
Ruptime command, 445
Rwho command, 416
  -a option, 418
  defined, 416
  display, 418
  -h option, 418
RZ29B, 36

Scripts
  awk, 157–58
  commands in, 289
  comments, 290
  C shell, 286
  debugging, 286, 358–60
  example, 289
  executing, 288–90
  file, 289
  menu_script, 363–65
  passing variables to, 300–301
  Perl, 367–70
  run_program, 360–63
  smart-rename, 367–70
  sourcing, 356

Secure Shell, 464
Security, 11, 393–98
  auditing standards, 394
  authentication, 395
  implementing, 393
  levels, 394
  passwords, 75
  permission codes, 395–96
  violations, monitoring, 396
Security checklists, 397–98
  file systems, 398
  general, 397
  individual users, 398
  networks, 397–98
  user accounts, 397
Sed editor, 121, 148–50
  commands, 149, 150
  defined, 148
  examples, 148
  learning, 148
  operator characters used with, 149–50
  power, 148
  regular expressions, 148, 150
Select statement, 336–38
  defined, 336
  example, 337
Serial Line IP (SLIP), 399
Set command, 60, 65
  cdpath option, 230
  -o option, 72
Sheband notation, 290
Shell programming, 285–371
  built-in commands, 346–58
  comparison operators, 306–10
  debugging scripts, 358–60
  defined, 285
  filename modifiers, 301–4
  file operators, 310–15
  flow control, 320–46
  mathematical operators, 315–20
  overview, 287

script execution, 288–90
variable expansion, 304–6
variables, 290–301
Shells, 17–18
  built-in commands, 346–58
  defined, 8
  initialization files, 288
  variables, 67–69
  See also Bourne Again shell (bash); Bourne
      shell (sh); C shell (csh); Korn shell
      (ksh)
Shell scripts, 27
  DCL command procedures and, 385
  debugging, 358–60
  defined, 430
  executing, on remote trusted host, 460
  input, 27
  passing variables to, 300–301
Shift statement, 339–42
  defined, 339
  example, 340–41
  uses, 340
Shutdown command, 384
Shutdown procedures, 384
Signals, 349
Simple Network Transfer Protocol (SMTP),
      453
Smart-rename script, 367–70
Sockets, 223, 443
Software installation, 376–77
Sort command, 23, 24, 135
  defined, 99, 243
  examples, 243–44
  -n option, 244
  -o option, 244
  sort key, 244
  uniq command with, 244–45
Source command, 70, 355–58
  defined, 346, 355
  example, 356
  -h option, 356

Spawning, 20
Special characters, 43–45
  list of, 44–45
  metacharacters, 43
Special files, 42
Ssh command, 464
Startup procedures, 377–79
  boot sequence, 379, 380–81
  run levels, 378–79
Stat command, 103
Status variable, 343
Store-and-forward networks, 442
Streams, 443
Strings
  comparisons, 310
  delimited, 304
  length, 161
  lowercase, 291
  operators, 161–63
  search, 240
  uppercase, 291
Stty command, 59, 60, 63, 85
Subprocesses, 20
Su command, 395
Suffixes, 262
Superusers, 57, 395
Swapping files, 39
Switch statement, 334–36
  case labels and, 336
  defined, 334
  example, 334–35
Symbolic assembly files, 258
Symbolic links, 248
System initialization files, 379–84
  comparison, 382–83
  directories, 380–82
  shutdown procedures, 384
System mailbox, 170
System monitoring, 424–29
  file-system utilization, 428–29
  network utilization, 426–28

virtual memory utilization, 425–26

Tail command, 110
    defined, 99, 226
    examples, 227
Talk command, 183–84
    defined, 169
    ttyname argument, 184
Tape
    archiving files to, 200–205
    available, determining, 199
    contents, listing, 203
    disk-to-disk copying, 204–5
    extracting files from, 203–4
    manipulation, 207
    OpenVMS-to-UNIX exchange, 208–9
    positioning, 207
    requests, 198
    special formatting, 205–7
    using, 198–209
    writing files to, 201–3
Tape-device files, 199–200
Tar command, 198, 200–205, 390
    absolute/relative file names support, 201
    appending files with, 200
    BACKUP command vs., 200–201
    -c option, 202
    defined, 99
    directory hierarchies and, 200
    file verification and, 200
    -m option, 204
    multiple magnetic tapes and, 200
    -r option, 202
    -t option, 203
    -u option, 202
    -x option, 203–4
Targets, 261
TCP/IP
    basics, 399–402
    defined, 399

Internet addressing, 401–2
    networking files/daemons, 401
    protocols, 399–400
Telnet command, 441, 451–52
    commands, 452
    defined, 451
    example, 451
Terminal
    characteristics, 54–61
    computer port use, 58
    definitions, 58
Third-party mail clients, 170
Time command, 352–55
    argument, 355
    defined, 346, 352
    example, 352–53
    implementations, 352
Tip command, 465–67
    commands subset, 467
    defined, 466
    example, 466
Touch command, 245–46, 261
    defined, 99, 245
    empty file creation with, 245
    examples, 246
Translate characters, 246–47
Transmission Control Protocol (TCP), 399
Transparent file access, 462–64
Trap command, 347–49
    defined, 346
    -l option, 349
Tr command, 246–47
    -c option, 246
    defined, 99, 246
    examples, 246
Trusted hosts, 440, 447–49
    executing shell scripts on, 460
    file transfer, 454–56
    remote login, 450–51
    See also Hosts
Tset command, 59, 60, 63

Tup-edt command, 146
Typeset command, 290

Ulimit command, 423, 434
ULTRIX, 5
Unalias command, 69
Uniq command, 244–45
UNIX
    boot sequence on, 379, 380–81
    BSD, 4–5, 253
    DEC OSF/1, 6
    directory structure, 37–38
    documentation, 11
    evolution, 4–11
    file extensions, 29–30
    file specifications, 33–34
    forking, 20
    future, 11–12
    genealogy, 9–10
    Gnu compiler support, 17
    in high-level language, 6–7
    IBM, 5
    implementation uniformity, 8
    interactive logon sequence, 386
    kernel, 16
    lexical analyzer, 17
    logon to, 385–86
    mail address formats, 444
    mail commands comparison, 182–83
    networking commands comparison, 409
    OpenVMS communications, 473
    OpenVMS vs., 16
    options, 32
    popular versions, 7
    programming tool summary, 254–56
    redirection, 25
    rewrite, 4
    signals, 349
    sorting, 243
    special characters, 44–45

    terminal sessions, 27
    tools/utilities, 16, 18–19
    Tru64, 402, 403
    ULTRIX, 5
    wildcards, 46–47
    Xenix, 5
UNIX Guru Web site, 390
Unmask command, 163–64, 222
Unsend command, 99
Until statement, 325–26
    defined, 325
    examples, 325–26
Usenet, 442, 472–73
    defined, 472
    newsgroups, 472
User Data Protocol (UDP), 399
User environment, 61–75
User Identification Code (UIC), 56, 106
Users
    accounts, 385–89, 397
    authentication, 395
    communicating with, 169–87
    environment, customizing, 389
    groups, 388–89
    monitoring, 414–18
    privileges, 57, 395
    in security checklist, 398
    superuser, 395
/usr/bin/login program, 55, 56
UUCP
    addresses, 444, 465
    automatic connection establishment, 466
    batch processing, 465
    status, 465
Uucp command, 441, 467–69
    defined, 99, 467
    examples, 468
    file transfer with, 467–69
    -m option, 469
Uusend command, 441, 469–70
    disadvantage, 469

example, 469–70
-m option, 470
Uux command, 441, 470–72
  defined, 470
  examples, 470
  -m option, 472

Variable expansion, 304–6
  delimited strings and, 304–5
  result, 304
  types of, 305
Variables, 67–69, 290–301
  assigning, 290
  environment, 56, 61, 74, 163, 293
  name, return, 304
  naming, 291
  passing, to scripts, 300–301
  Perl, 293
  predefined, 293–95
  scalar, 291
  special forms, 295–300
  string, 290
  substitution, 64
  values, in separate elements, 295
Vi editor, 77, 119, 129–36, 165
  action commands, 130–32
  action/movement command combinations,
    133
  cursor movement, 130, 131
  dd command, 132
  defined, 129
  dw command, 133
  ex command invocation from, 129, 133–
    34
  filtering, 135
  keys, programming, 121
  miscellaneous commands, 134–35
  sessions, ending, 135–36
  sessions, recovering, 136
  sessions, starting, 130

u command, 134
zz command, 135–36
  See also Editors
Virtual memory utilization, 425–26
Vmstat command, 425–26
  defined, 425
  example, 425
  fields, 425–26

Wc command, 247
  defined, 99
  examples, 247
W command, 417
Which command, 366–67
While statement, 324–25
  defined, 324
  examples, 324–25
Whoami command, 73, 415
  defined, 415
  example, 415
Who command, 23, 24, 416–17
  defined, 416
  sort command and, 23
Wildcards, 46–47
Word count, 247
Work identifiers, 79–80
  defined, 79
  recalling, 79–80
Write command, 183–84, 187
  defined, 169
  ttyname argument, 184

Xenix, 5